MostUsedWords.com presents

Italian Frequency Dictionary

Master Vocabulary

7501-10000 Most Common Italian Words

Book 4

First Printing, 2017

Jolie Laide LTD
12/F, 67 Percival Street, Hong Kong

www.MostUsedWords.com

Contents

Why This Book?

Hello, dear reader.

Thank you for purchasing this book. We hope it serves you well on your language learning journey.

Not all words are created equal. The purpose of this frequency dictionary is to list the most used words in descending order, to enable you to learn a language as fast and efficiently as possible.

First, we would like to illustrate the value of a frequency dictionary. For the purpose of example, we have combined frequency data from various languages (mainly Romance, Slavic and Germanic languages) and made it into a single chart.

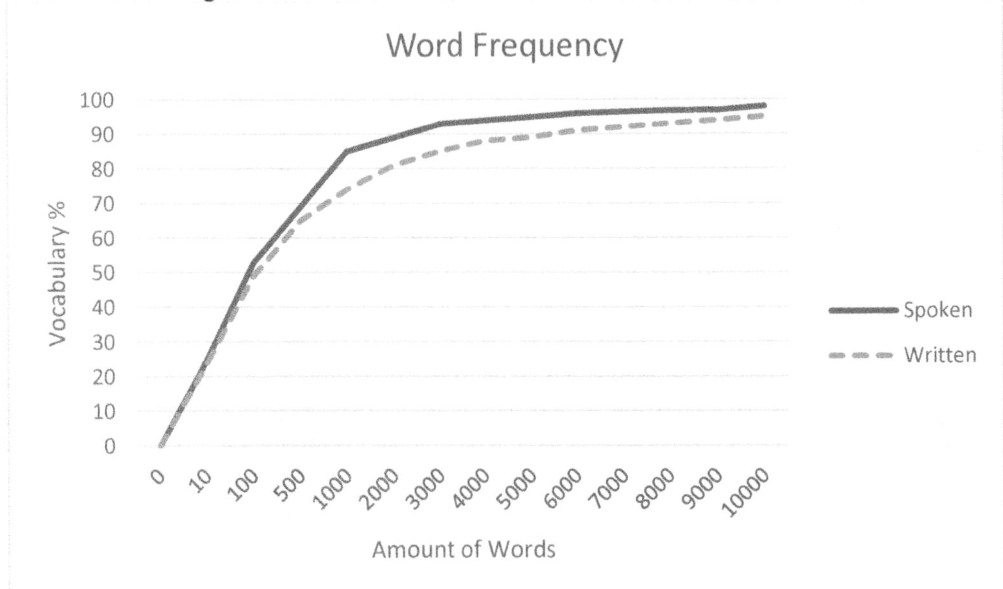

The sweet spots, according to the data seem to be:

Amount of Words	Spoken	Written
• 100	53%	49%
• 1.000	85%	74%
• 2.500	92%	82%
• 5.000	95%	89%
• 7.500	97%	93%
• 10.000	98%	95%

Above data corresponds with Zipfs law and Pareto´s law.

Zipf's law states that given some corpus of natural language utterances, the frequency of any word is inversely proportional to its rank in the frequency table. Thus the most frequent word will occur approximately twice as often as the second most frequent word, three times as often as the third most frequent word, etc.: the rank-frequency distribution is an inverse relation.

For example, in the Brown Corpus of American English text, the word "the" is the most frequently occurring word, and by itself accounts for nearly 7% of all word occurrences (69,971 out of slightly over 1 million). True to Zipf's Law, the second-place word "of" accounts for slightly over 3.5% of words (36,411 occurrences), followed by "and" (28,852). Only 135 vocabulary items are needed to account for half the Brown Corpus.

Pareto's law, also known as the 80/20 rule, states that, for many events, roughly 80% of the effects come from 20% of the causes.

In language learning, this principle seems to be on steroids. It seems that just 20% of the 20% of the most used words in a language account for roughly all vocabulary you need.

To put his further in perspective: The Concise Oxford Paravia Italian Dictionary has over 175.000 words in current use, while you will only need to know 2.9% (5000 words) to achieve 95% and 89% fluency in speaking and writing. Knowing the most common 10.000 words, or 5.6%, will net you 98% fluency in spoken language and 95% fluency in written texts.

Keeping this in mind, the value of a frequency dictionary is immense. At least, that is if you want to speak a language fast. Study the most frequent words, build your vocabulary and progress naturally. Sounds logical, right?

But how many words do you need to know for varying levels of fluency?

While it's important to note that it is impossible to pin down these numbers and statistics with 100% accuracy, these are a global average of multiple sources.

According to research, this is the amount of vocabulary needed for varying levels of fluency.

1. 250 words: the essential core of a language. Without these words, you cannot construct any sentence.
2. 750 words: those that are used every single day by every person who speaks the language.
3. 2500 words: those that should enable you to express everything you could possibly want to say, although some creativity might be required.
4. 5000 words: the active vocabulary of native speakers without higher education.
5. 10,000 words: the active vocabulary of native speakers with higher education.
6. 20,000 words: what you need to recognize passively to read, understand, and enjoy a work of literature such as a novel by a notable author.

Caveats & Limitations.

A frequency list is never "The Definite Frequency List."

Depending on what source material was analyzed, you may get different lists. A corpus on spoken word differs from source texts based on a written language.

That is why we chose subtitles as our source, because, according to science, they cover the best of both worlds: both spoken and written Italian.

The frequency list is based on analysis of roughly 20 gigabytes of Italian subtitles.

Visualize a book with almost 16 million pages, or 80.000 books of 200 pages each, to get an idea of the amount words that have been analyzed for this book. A large base text is vital in order to develop an accurate frequency list.

The raw data included over 1 million entries. The raw data has been lemmatized; words are given in their root form.

Some entries you might find odd, in their respective frequency rankings. We were surprised a couple of time ourselves. But the data does not lie. Keep in mind that this book is compiled from a large amount of subtitle data, and may include words you wouldn't use yourself.

You might find non-Italian loanwords in this dictionary. We decided to include them, because if they're being used in subtitle translation, it is safe to assume the word has been integrated into the Italian general vocabulary.

We tried our best to keep out proper nouns, such as "James, Ryan, Alice as well as "Rome, Washington" or "the Louvre, the Capitol".

Some words have multiple meanings. For the ease of explanation, the examples are given in English.

"Jack" is a very common first name, but also a noun (a jack to lift up a vehicle) and a verb (to steal something). So is the word "can" It is a conjugation of the verb "to be able" as well as a noun (a tin can, or a can of soft drink).

This skews the frequency rankings slightly. With the current technology, it is unfortunately not possible to rightly identify the correct frequency placements of above words. Luckily, these words are very few, and thus negligible in the grand scheme of things.

If you encounter a word you think you won't need in your vocabulary, just skip learning it. The frequency list includes 25 extra words to compensate for any irregularities you might encounter.

The big secret to learning language is this: build your vocabulary, learn basic grammar and go out there and speak. Make mistakes, have a laugh and learn from them.

We hope you enjoy this frequency dictionary, and that it helps you in your quest of speaking Italian.

How To Use This Dictionary

abbreviation	*abr*
adjective	*adj*
adverb	*adv*
article	*art*
auxiliary verb	*av*
conjunction	*con*
interjection	*int*
noun	*gli, i, il, le, la, lo*
numeral	*num*
particle	*part*
phrase	*phr*
prefix	*pfx*
preposition	*prp*
pronoun	*prn*
suffix	*sfx*
verb	*vb*
singular	*sg*
plural	*pl*

Word Order

The most common translations are generally given first. This resets by every new respective part of speech. Different parts of speech are divided by ";".

Translations

We made the decision to give the most common translation(s) of a word, and respectively the most common part(s) of speech. It does, however, not mean that this is the only possible translations or the only part of speech the word can be used for.

Italian English Frequency Dictionary

Rank	Italian Part of Speech [IPA]	English Translation Italian Example Sentence -English Example Sentence
7501	**accertare** vb [attʃertare]	**ascertain** La commissione per il controllo di bilancio non deve mollare la presa e non ho dubbi che l'onorevole Theato si accerterà che venga fatto. -The Committee on Budgetary Control must keep hold of this. I have little doubt that Mrs Theato will see that will happen.
7502	**galleggiante** adj; il [galleddʒante]	**floating; float** Joe ha visto qualche pesce morto galleggiante sul lago. -Joe saw some dead fish floating on the lake.
7503	**mediante** prp [medjante]	**through** La maggior parte degli scienziati crede che questo sia stato provocato dall'uomo, mediante il rilascio di metano, diossido di carbonio e altri gas serra sin dall'industrializzazione. Tuttavia un'altra esigua parte di scienziati ne dubita. -Most scientists believe that this has been caused by man, through the release of methane, of carbon dioxide, and other greenhouse gases since industrialization. A few other scientists doubt this, however.
7504	**filiale** la; adj [filjale]	**branch; filial** Si tratta essenzialmente di società statunitensi provviste di una filiale a Londra. -These are chiefly US companies with a branch in London.
7505	**cattedra** la [kattedra]	**chair** Di come vorremmo finanziare una cattedra a Oxford o a Cambridge. We'd love to endow a chair at Oxford or Cambridge.
7506	**stirare** vb [stirare]	**iron|stretch** Io odio stirare. -I hate ironing.
7507	**coerente** adj [koerente]	**consistent** Per certe cose è molto coerente. -For certain things it's very coherent.
7508	**conquista** la [koŋkwista]	**conquest** L'amore conquista tutto. -Love conquers all.
7509	**negoziato** il [negottsjato]	**negotiation** Dovremo affrontare due difficoltà principali in questo importante negoziato: -We shall have to address two important difficulties in this major negotiation:
7510	**schierare** vb [skjerare]	**deploy|line up** Deve schierare le forze rimanenti intorno alle basi più importanti. -He must deploy his remaining strength around his most valuable Pacific base.
7511	**nume** il [nume]	**numen** –O è un nume tutelare della casa o... -Either he's a domestic goddess, or...
7512	**balzare**	**jump|skip**

	vb	La Scientifica verrà qui domani, e poi potrai di nuovo balzare in sella.
	[baltsare]	-Forensics will be here tomorrow, and you can jump back in then.
7513	**premeditare**	**premeditate**
	vb	Tale decisione equivale a un crimine premeditato contro l'intera nazione.
	[premeditare]	-That decision amounted to a premeditated crime against the entire nation.
7514	**pellegrinaggio**	**pilgrimage**
	il	Aspetterò finché abbiate finito col vostro pellegrinaggio.
	[pellegrinaddʒo]	-I'll wait until you're done with your pilgrimage.
7515	**accessibile**	**accessible|attainable**
	adj	Google non era accessibile ieri.
	[attʃessibile]	-Google was down yesterday.
7516	**residuo**	**residue; residual**
	il; adj	Per l'importo residuo sono stati predisposti una serie di altri progetti destinati alla fase intermedia.
	[rezidwo]	-In the meantime, plans have been worked out for the remaining amount.
7517	**questura**	**police force**
	la	Piuttosto pericoloso aspettarmi in auto fuori dalla questura.
	[kwestura]	-It was pretty risky to wait in the car outside the police station.
7518	**ammalato**	**sick; sick person**
	adj; il	Non hai un aspetto molto buono. Sei ammalato?
	[ammalato]	-You don't look very well. Are you sick?
7519	**orsetto**	**bear cub**
	il	Kary Mullis: "Si si l'avrebbero potuto fare anche per l'orsetto Teddy!"
	[orsetto]	-Kary Mullis: They might have done it for the teddy bear, yeah.
7520	**brama**	**craving|desire**
	la	Sembra che nemmeno questo settore sia esente dalla brama del libero scambio.
	[brama]	-Even in this sector, there would seem to be a craving for free trade.
7521	**vallata**	**valley**
	la	Non avremmo dovuto percorrere la vallata.
	[vallata]	-We shouldn't have driven across the valley.
7522	**ciliegia**	**cherry**
	la	Questa ciliegia è rosso scuro.
	[tʃiljedʒa]	-This cherry is dark red.
7523	**colombiano**	**Columbian**
	adj	Ufficialmente oppone lo Stato colombiano ai narcotrafficanti.
	[kolombjano]	-Officially, it is the Colombian State combating drug traffickers.
7524	**lucente**	**shiny|lucent**
	adj	Sembra però che un oggetto lucente abbia attirato l'attenzione del maschio MacArthur.
	[lutʃente]	-It seems as though a shiny object has captured the male MacArthur's attention.
7525	**ultimatum**	**ultimatum**
	gli	Non mi costringere a farti un ultimatum.
	[ultimatum]	-Don't you harangue me into making an ultimatum...
7526	**relitto**	**wreck|wreckage**
	il	Qualcuno sul nostro relitto doveva tenerci particolarmente.
	[relitto]	-Anyway, it was very important to somebody on our wreck.
7527	**maternità**	**maternity|parenthood**

la[maternit'a] In Asia, il problema della maternità si imbatte in ostacoli religiosi e di casta. -In Asia, the problem of maternity comes up against religious and caste obstacles.

7528 **sciolto** **loose|dissolved**
adj
[ʃolto]
Mi si è appena sciolto il cuore!
-My heart just melted!

7529 **rettile** **reptile**
il
[rettile]
La mortalità è molto alta nei piccoli di rettile che sono lunghi 25 - 30 centimetri.
-There is very high mortality in little baby reptiles who are just 10 to 12 inches long.

7530 **affannoso** **labored|breathless**
adj
[affannozo]
L'emorragia è sotto controllo e non ha febbre, ma il respiro è affannoso, il battito rallentato... e non ha ancora aperto gli occhi.
-Bleeding is under control and no fever, but his breath is labored and his pulse is way down and he hasn't opened his eyes yet.

7531 **sfidante** **challenger; challenging**
il/la; adj
[sfidante]
Primo, dobbiamo essere pronti e disposti a sfidare gli esperti e ad abbandonare l'idea secondo cui essi sono gli apostoli di oggi.
-First, we've got to be ready and willing to take experts on and dispense with this notion of them as modern-day apostles.

7532 **creta** **clay**
la
[kreta]
Sarebbe tipo un'agenzia costruita dalla creta.
-So it would be like a type of agency built from clay..

7533 **ristrutturazione** **renovation**
la
[ristrutturattsjone]
Se richiederà una ristrutturazione totale, sono sicura che saranno soddisfatti con il vecchio sistema.
-If it's going to require a total restructuring, I'm sure they will be satisfied with the old system.

7534 **armeria** **armory**
la
[armerja]
Dashell cambia il codice dell'armeria quasi ogni giorno.
-Dashell changes the key code to the armory on almost a daily basis.

7535 **manipolazione** **handling|falsification**
la
[manipolattsjone]
Ulteriori informazioni sulla somministrazione e la manipolazione di VASOVIST sono riportate al termine del foglio illustrativo.
-Further information regarding the administration and handling of VASOVIST is given at the end of the leaflet.

7536 **mandibola** **jaw|mandible**
la
[mandibola]
Lo ioide è nascosto e protetto dalla mandibola.
-The hyoid is recessed and protected by the jaw.

7537 **napalm** **napalm**
il
[napalm]
Mi piace l'odore del napalm al mattino.
-I love the smell of napalm in the morning.

7538 **petrolifero** **oil well**
lo
[petrolifero]
Non comparabile al primo shock petrolifero del 1973 o al secondo shock petrolifero del 1980.
-Not like the first oil shock of 1973 or the second oil shock of 1980.

7539 **digitare** **type in**
vb
[didʒitare]
Dopo aver digitato la passkey, per concludere l'associazione occorre premere Invio sulla tastiera o sul tastierino numerico.
-After typingthe passkey, you must press Enter on the keyboard or number pad to complete the pairing.

7540 **tecnologico** **technological**
adj
[teknolodʒiko]
Stiamo, inoltre, riflettendo sul sostegno da dare allo sviluppo tecnologico.
-Reflection is ongoing regarding the support for technological development.

7541 **fendere** **cleave|slit**
vb
[fendere]
Un esercito che possa fendere l'Italia, come un coltello fende il burro.
-An army that can cut through Italy like a knife through butter.

7542 **strillo** **scream|squeal**
lo
[strillo]
E ovviamente, non stanno sempre a piangere e strillare. Ma con tre maschi, c'è una buona probabilità che almeno uno di loro non si stia comportando esattamente come dovrebbe.
-And of course, they're not always crying and screaming, but with three boys, there's a decent probability that at least one of them will not be comporting himself exactly as he should.

7543 **frastuono** **uproar**
il
[frastwono]
Una bomba cadde poco lontano dalla mia auto, non troppo vicino, ma con un gran frastuono.
-A bomb fell not far from my car -- well, far enough, but big noise.

7544 **decaffeinare** **decaffeinate**
vb
[dekaffeinare]
Allora vedrò di ordinare il decaffeinato.
-And I will be sure to order decaf.

7545 **colon** **colon**
lo
[kolon]
Ho preso i tre componenti: stomaco, intestino tenue e colon.
-I took the three elements -- stomach, small intestine and colon.

7546 **curiosità** **curiosity**
la
[kurjosita]
Ammetto che sono soggetto alla malattia di curiosità.
-I admit I am subject to the disease of curiosity.

7547 **amarezza** **bitterness**
le
[amarettsa]
Signora Presidente, serpeggia crescente amarezza e rabbia in Polonia.
- Madam President, there is growing bitterness and anger in Poland.

7548 **periscopio** **periscope**
il
[periskopjo]
Userò il periscopio per controllare che la Via sia libera.
-We'll use the periscope to make sure the path is clear.

7549 **impenetrabile** **impenetrable**
adj
[impenetrabile]
Una coltre impenetrabile ricopriva la collina mentre cercava di ricordare...
-An impenetrable blanket lay over the hill as she tried to remember......

7550 **maldestro** **clumsy|maladroit**
adj
[maldestro]
Un tentativo maldestro di rendere George geloso?
-Some misguided attempt to make George jealous?

7551 **contatore** **counter|meter**
il
[kontatore]
Deve azzerare il contatore dei chilometri.
-You have to reset the odometer.

7552 **infamia** **infamy**
le
[infamja]
Signor Presidente, (inizio senza microfono) e voi non avete neppure il monopolio dell'infamia.
-Mr President, (start without microphone) and yourself do not have the monopoly on infamy.

7553 **popolarità** **popularity**

	la	La popolarità non ha niente a che fare con esso.
	[popolarit'a]	-Popularity has nothing to do with it.
7554	**fagotto**	**bassoon**
	il	Lei sta ancora suonando il fagotto?
	[fagotto]	-Are you still playing the bassoon?
7555	**arrossire**	**blush|color**
	vb	Non fatemi arrossire.
	[arrossire]	-Don't make me blush.
7556	**impazienza**	**impatience**
	le	Joe sedeva con impazienza.
	[impattsjentsa]	-Joe sat impatiently.
7557	**infelicità**	**unhappiness**
	le	Io so il perché della tua infelicità qui.
	[infelitʃit'a]	-I know why you aren't happy here.
7558	**considerevole**	**considerable|sizable**
	adj	Joe era molto considerevole.
	[konsiderevole]	-Joe was so considerate.
7559	**specializzare**	**specialize**
	vb	Che succede se si impedisce a un popolo di fare scambi, e di potersi specializzare?
	[spetʃaliddzare]	-What happens when you cut people off from exchange, from the ability to exchange and specialize?
7560	**sbalorditivo**	**amazing**
	adj	Signor Presidente, assistiamo oggi a uno spettacolo sbalorditivo.
	[zbalorditivo]	-Mr President, today we are witnessing something astounding.
7561	**attentato**	**attempt**
	il	Fu un attentato suicida.
	[attentato]	-It was a suicide bombing.
7562	**soma**	**pack|burden**
	la	Tutte le bestie da soma sono animali sacri.
	[soma]	-All beasts of burden are sacred animals.
7563	**irrompere**	**burst**
	vb	Dobbiamo irrompere nel covo dei Giranuvole.
	[irrompere]	-We need to break into the Cloudspinners' lair.
7564	**estetico**	**aesthetic**
	adj	Non ha senso estetico.
	[estetiko]	-She has no sense of beauty.
7565	**bravura**	**cleverness**
	la	The excellent report by our colleague Friedhelm Frischenschlager is a tiny piece of intellectual bravura.
	[bravura]	-L'eccellente relazione dell'onorevole Friedhelm Frishenschlager è un piccolo saggio di bravura intellettuale.
7566	**simbolico**	**symbolic|token**
	adj	Ciò che l'onorevole Ford sta facendo ha un valore simbolico e istituzionale.
	[simboliko]	-There is a symbolic and institutional importance in what Mr Ford is doing.
7567	**fornace**	**furnace**
	la	Hanno trovato molta cenere nella fornace.
	[fornatʃe]	-They found a lot of ashes in the furnace.
7568	**aspirare**	**aspire|suck**

	vb	Spingerle fuori con lo stantuffo ed aspirare la dose corretta.
	[aspirare]	-Push them out with the plunger and withdraw the correct dose.
7569	**pirateria**	**piracy**
	la	La pirateria non sta uccidendo la musica.
	[piraterja]	-Piracy isn't killing music.
7570	**compiacere**	**please|satisfy**
	vb	Lui è molto difficile da compiacere.
	[kompjatʃere]	-He's very hard to please.
7571	**confiscare**	**confiscate|disendow**
	vb	Dovrò confiscare il suo coltello.
	[konfiskare]	-I'll have to confiscate your knife.
7572	**bonificare**	**reclaim**
	vb	Ci dicono di bonificare queste case.
	[bonifikare]	-They tell us to remediate these houses.
7573	**parzialmente**	**partly**
	adv	Loro attraversarono il fiume Delaware parzialmente congelato.
	[partsjalmente]	-They crossed the partly-frozen Delaware River.
7574	**abbonamento**	**subscription**
	il	Ho un abbonamento al Time.
	[abbonamento]	-I have a subscription to Time.
7575	**rimbalzare**	**bounce|bounce back**
	vb	Ora, questo bambino può far rimbalzare un pallone sulla sua testa.
	[rimbaltsare]	-Now this boy can bounce a soccer ball on his head.
7576	**sparpagliare**	**scatter**
	vb	Ma pips, dovevamo sparpagliare gli squadroni, non avevamo scelta!
	[sparpaʎʎare]	-But Pips, we had to disperse our fighter squadrons... we had to!
7577	**candelina**	**taper**
	la	Soffierei sulla candelina ma non riesco a respirare.
	[kandelina]	-I'd blow out my candle, but I can't breathe.
7578	**rimprovero**	**reproach|rebuke**
	il	Quale migliore rimprovero ai difensori del protezionismo di questo spiacevole episodio?
	[rimprovero]	-What better rebuke to the defenders of protectionism than this sorry affair?
7579	**degenerare**	**degenerate**
	vb	Le funzioni uditive sono le ultime, tra le sensoriali, a degenerare.
	[dedʒenerare]	-Auditory functions are the last sensory faculties to degenerate.
7580	**rispettoso**	**respectful**
	adj	Joe è rispettoso.
	[rispettozo]	-Joe is observant.
7581	**predire**	**predict**
	vb	Predire il futuro non è sempre prudente.
	[predire]	-Predicting the future isn't always prudent.
7582	**insicuro**	**insecure**
	adj	Penso che Joe sia insicuro.
	[insikuro]	-I think Joe is insecure.
7583	**superstrada**	**highway|freeway**
	la	Chiunque provenga dalla superstrada dovrà passarci davanti.
	[superstrada]	-Anyone on the freeway will have to drive right in front of it.
7584	**mansione**	**job|duty**

la
[mansjone]
In generale, i lavoratori non sono a conoscenza del modo in cui è stata classificata la mansione loro affidata.
-In general, workers do not know how their job is classified.

7585 **egocentrico** **egocentric; egotist**
adj; il
[egotʃentriko]
Joe è giovane, ricco, viziato ed egocentrico.
-Joe is young, rich, spoiled and egocentric.

7586 **primordiale** **primordial**
adj
[primordjale]
Il documento sottolinea ulteriormente il ruolo primordiale della politica regionale.
-The report further highlights the primordial role of regional policy.

7587 **carie** **caries**
la
[karje]
Aspetto positivo: non ho mai avuto una carie.
-Plus side – I have literally never had a cavity.

7588 **interfono** **intercom**
gli
[interfono]
Prema il bottone dell'interfono quando ha finito.
-Press the button on the intercom when you're finished.

7589 **tibetano** **Tibetan; Tibetan**
adj; il
[tibetano]
Il popolo tibetano e persino i monaci sono pesantemente oppressi.
-In Tibet, there is severe oppression of the Tibetan people, especially of monks.

7590 **attracco** **docking|mooring**
il
[attrakko]
…è stato negato loro il permesso di attraccare in Gran Bretagna.
-..they were refused permission to dock in Britain.

7591 **multinazionale** **multinational**
adj
[multinattsjonale]
L'azienda multinazionale ha diminuito il prezzo di molti prodotti.
-The multinational corporation lowered the price of several products.

7592 **islamico** **Islamic; Islam**
adj; il
[izlamiko]
Si ricordi che la valle Bekaa è la roccaforte del movimento islamico degli Hezbollah.
-However, the Bekaa Valley is a stronghold of the Islamist Hezbollah movement.

7593 **novecento** **nine hundred**
num
[novetʃento]
A livello internazionale, quasi novecento milioni di persone non hanno abbastanza da mangiare.
-Internationally, almost 900 million people don't have enough to eat.

7594 **fascio** **beam|bundle**
il
[faʃʃo]
È un fascio di nervi.
-You're a nervous wreck.

7595 **capitolare** **capitulate; capitular**
vb; adj
[kapitolare]
Anche dopo che vi hanno quasi spazzato via, vi rifiutate di capitolare.
-Even after you were almost wiped out, you refused to capitulate.

7596 **conquistatore** **conqueror**
il
[koŋkwistatore]
Elimina il crimine di invasione e occupazione, assolve, premia e plaude al garante conquistatore.
-It cancels out the crime of invasion and occupation, it acquits, rewards and proclaims the conqueror guarantor.

7597 **sgomberare** **clear**
vb
[zgomberare]
Vicesceriffo, può sgomberare la folla.
-Deputy, you can clear the crowd away.

7598 **iena** **hyena**

	la [jena]	Il miglior riscontro possibile è questo bel diavolo, la iena preistorica gigante. -Best possible match is this handsome devil, the giant prehistoric hyena.
7599	**pentimento** il [pentimento]	**repentance** Cioè il rimorso, la paura, il pentimento, il disagio, la confusione che crea nello Spirito un'azione malvagia: comunque un'azione poco buona. -That is, the remorse, fear, repentance, discomfort, which creates confusion in the Spirit evil action: still a little good.
7600	**colorito** adj; il [kolorito]	**colorful; color** quel punto, il suo capo squadra ha risposto con un linguaggio colorito. -At which point your team leader responded with some colorful language.
7601	**flagello** il [fladʒello]	**scourge|plague** Allora rilasciò loro Barabba e, dopo aver fatto flagellare Gesù, lo consegnò ai soldati perché fosse crocifisso. -Jesus, however, he first had scourged; then he handed him over to be crucified.
7602	**ghiandola** la [gjandola]	**gland** Notevole accumulo di acido nella ghiandola esofagea. -A lot of acid build–up in the esophageal gland.
7603	**preventivo** il; adj [preventivo]	**quote; preventive** Nell'area a te riservata potrai salvare le tue configurazioni, richiedere un preventivo e accedere ai numerosi servizi che Prodir offre ai propri utenti. -On your reserved area, you can save your configurations, request a quotation and access the many services Prodir offers its users.
7604	**imbarcazione** le [imbarkattsjone]	**boat** In questo modo non perderebbero più la nave, poiché la seguirebbero con la loro imbarcazione. -This means that they no longer miss the boat, since they are following in their own little boat.
7605	**toga** la [toga]	**toga|robe** Sai, forse dovresti toglierti la toga... -You know, maybe you should change the toga...
7606	**ricorrente** adj [rikorrente]	**recurrent** Si tratta di un problema ricorrente di cui parlerò alla conferenza dei presidenti. -This is a recurrent problem, and I shall certainly inform the Conference of Presidents.
7607	**diplomazia** la [diplomattsja]	**diplomacy** La diplomazia è una cosa positiva, ma la diplomazia da sola non fornisce tutte le risposte. -Diplomacy is good, but diplomacy of itself will not deliver all the answers.
7608	**inosservato** adj [inosservato]	**unnoticed|unobserved** Se l'omicida non è entrato dalla strada, è possibile che sia passato da qui praticamente inosservato. -If the killer didn't enter via the street, it's possible he could've got in this way virtually undetected.
7609	**dapprima** adv [dapprima]	**at first** Signor Presidente, vorrei dapprima formulare due brevi osservazioni. -Mr President, let me first make two brief observations.

7610 **patologia** la [patolodʒa]
pathology
Le ricerche sembrano indicare che la mortalità non sia dovuta ad una normale patologia.
-It seems on investigation that this bee mortality is not the result of a conventional pathology.

7611 **battezzare** vb [battettsare]
baptize|Christen
Chi crederà e si farà battezzare sarà salvato, ma chi non crederà sarà condannato' ".
-He who believes and is baptized will be saved; but he who does not believe will be condemned."

7612 **nutrice** la [nutritʃe]
nurse
Badate a lui questa sera, nutrice.
-Watch over him this evening, nurse.

7613 **lampadario** il [lampadarjo]
chandelier
Un lampadario a bracci pendeva dal soffitto.
-A chandelier hung from the ceiling.

7614 **faticare** vb [fatikare]
labor|work hard
Senti, tutti i grandi artisti devono faticare un po' nella vita.
-Look, all great artists need a little struggle in their lives.

7615 **tomo** il [tomo]
tome
Da marzo 1999 c'è un nuovo direttore finanziario, che ha scritto un vero e proprio tomo di regole da seguire.
-It is indeed the case that, since March 1999, there has been a new financial director who has written a veritable tome on the rules to be followed.

7616 **nuocere** vb [nwotʃere]
harm
Per prima cosa, non nuocere.
-First, do no harm.

7617 **metamorfosi** la [metamorfozi]
metamorphosis
Quali altre metamorfosi hai avuto? ...
-What are some other metamorphoses that you've had? ... Doesn't have to be fear.

7618 **manichino** il [manikino]
dummy
Dovresti pesare all'incirca come un manichino.
-I think you're, like, just about dummy weight. No.

7619 **congelatore** il [kondʒelatore]
freezer
La campagna presidenziale degli Stati Uniti prenderà sempre più velocità e così il ciclo potrebbe finire nel congelatore per anni.
-The United States presidential campaign will pick up speed and the round might then be put into the deep freeze for years.

7620 **dignitoso** adj [diɲɲitozo]
decent
Molti dei nostri documenti utilizzano le espressioni "lavoro dignitoso" e "lavori dignitosi".
-Many of our documents use the expressions 'decent work' and 'decent jobs'.

7621 **macelleria** la [matʃellerja]
butcher's shop
Mettere su una macelleria.
-To establish oneself as a butcher.

7622 **acquirente** il/la [akkwirente]
buyer|shopper
Queste due distinte denominazioni consentiranno all'acquirente di scegliere un prodotto con cognizione di causa.

-These two different names will enable people buying them to choose a product with full knowledge of the facts.

7623 **laghetto** **pond**
il
[lagetto]
Il ragazzo stava fissando un banco di carpe nel laghetto.
-The boy was gazing at a school of carp in the pond.

7624 **travaglio** **labor|suffering**
il
[travaʎʎo]
Causano la contrazione dei muscoli lisci che simulano il travaglio.
-Causes smooth muscle contractions that mimic labor.

7625 **calamitare** **magnetize**
vb
[kalamitare]
Ho la tendenza a calamitare le persone intorno a me, portandoli ad allinearsi ai miei modi di vedere.
-I have a tendency to magnetize people around me, drawing them into alignment with my own ways.

7626 **carnagione** **complexion**
la
[karnadʒone]
È di carnagione chiara.
-She has a fair complexion.

7627 **riconciliazione** **reconciliation**
la
[rikontʃiljattsjone]
L'intervista era intesa più come una riconciliazione.
— Really? – the interview was intended more as a reconciliation.

7628 **maltrattare** **abuse|mishandle**
vb
[maltrattare]
Ultimamente nelle prigioni turche diverse persone sono state maltrattate a morte.
-In recent times a number of people have died as a result of abuse in Turkish prisons.

7629 **placca** **plate**
la
[plakka]
Pensavo di inserire un innesto fibulare e una placca.
-I thought I'd put in a fibular graft and a plate.

7630 **paragonare** **compare|confront**
vb
[paragonare]
Non ti paragonare a lui.
-Don't compare yourself to him.

7631 **posacenere** **ashtray**
i
[pozatʃenere]
Ho rotto il vostro posacenere.
-I broke your ashtray.

7632 **ostacolare** **hinder|hamper**
vb
[ostakolare]
Siamo pertanto tenuti ad ostacolare la produzione di plutonio.
-For that reason alone we must prevent the production of plutonium.

7633 **denso** **dense|full**
adj
[denso]
La Terra è il pianeta più denso del Sistema Solare.
-Earth is the densest planet of the Solar System.

7634 **motociclista** **motorcyclist**
il/la
[mototʃiklista]
Joe è un grande motociclista.
-Joe is a great motocross rider.

7635 **ascella** **armpit|lath**
le
[aʃʃella]
Linfonodo leggermente ingrossato nell'ascella sinistra.
-Slightly enlarged lymph node in his left armpit.

7636 **esibizionista** **exhibitionist**
il/la
[ezibittsjonista]
Perché 'esibizionista', sono solo...
-Why 'show–off', I am just...

7637 **razziale** **racial**

adj Lui ha lottato contro la discriminazione razziale.
[rattsjale] -He fought against racial discrimination.

7638 **spaccatura** **split**
la
[spakkatura]
Nessuno ha intenzione di creare una vera e propria spaccatura fra gli Stati Uniti e l'Unione europea.
-Nobody is intent on a genuine split between the United States and the European Union.

7639 **seduzione** **seduction|allurement**
la
[seduttsjone]
Per realizzare i suoi fini ricorre alla seduzione, alle minacce, alla violenza.
-In order to achieve his aims, he uses seduction, threats and violence.

7640 **maga** **sorceress**
la
[maga]
Io non sono una maga.
-I'm not a magician.

7641 **occultamento** **concealment|occultation**
il
[okkultamento]
Ci siamo già imbattuti nel problema dell'occultamento nei paesi in cui ci sono state epidemie.
-We have come across the element of concealment already in the countries where this has arisen.

7642 **variazione** **variation|change**
la
[varjattsjone]
..variazione nell'orientamento di politica monetaria dell'Eurosistema. Il nuovo
-...intended as a further change in the monetary policy stance of the Eurosystem.

7643 **adunata** **gathering|muster**
la
[adunata]
Arresti per adunata sediziosa e resistenza, per lo più a sit-in e manifestazioni.
-Arrests for unlawful assembly and resisting arrest, mostly at sit-ins and demonstrations.

7644 **minaccioso** **threatening|ugly**
adj
[minattʃozo]
Tuttavia, le norme per i contenuti di orkut in merito a incitamento all'odio e linguaggio minaccioso sono molto severe.
-Orkut does, however, have a strict policy against hate speech and threatening language.

7645 **brevetto** **patent**
il
[brevetto]
Ho depositato un brevetto.
-I filed a patent.

7646 **statuetta** **statuette**
la
[statwetta]
Ok, quindi probabilmente può notare come la statuetta del Buddha sia un vero affare.
-Okay. So, then, you can probably see that the Buddha statue is the real deal.

7647 **indomani** **next day**
il
[indomani]
Anche questo nostro tempo si colloca «all'indomani della Risurrezione».
-Our time too occurs "on the day after the resurrection".

7648 **trionfale** **triumphal**
adj
[trjonfale]
È trionfale.
-It's triumphal.

7649 **reclusione** **imprisonment**
la
[rekluzjone]
Se volete sapere chi sono i vostri amici, procuratevi una sentenza di reclusione.
-If you want to know who your friends are, get yourself a jail sentence.

7650 **burlare** **make fun of**
vb
[burlare]
Si tratta forse di una burla?
-Is this some kind of hoax?

7651 **approfondire** **deepen**
vb
[approfondire]
Con umiltà dobbiamo approfondire il dialogo fraterno nella fiducia e pazienza.
-We need to deepen fraternal dialogue in confidence and patience with humility.

7652 **pavone** **peacock**
il
[pavone]
È più orgoglioso di un pavone.
-You are prouder than a peacock.

7653 **mandorla** **almond**
la
[mandorla]
Nel caso della mandorla, la differenza di costi si spiega perché la produzione nell'Unione europea avviene in zone estremamente difficili per clima o terreno.
-In the case of almonds, the cost difference is a result of the fact that in the European Union they are produced in very difficult climate and soil conditions.

7654 **ricettatore** **fence**
il
[ritʃettatore]
Vuoi fare di me il ricettatore di beni rubati?
-Are you trying to make me the receiver of stolen goods?

7655 **Macché!** **Not at all!**
int
[makk'e!]
E se ti lavi ti passa? – Macché!
-Does it go if you wash?

7656 **indeciso** **undecided**
adj
[indetʃizo]
Ero indeciso.
-I was indecisive.

7657 **funzionamento** **operation|working**
il
[funtsjonamento]
È importante per il corretto funzionamento della prova.
-This is important for the proper functioning of the test.

7658 **impiccio** **mess|hindrance**
il
[impittʃo]
Vivo... sei soltanto un impiccio, una creatura inutile.
-Alive... you're just a nuisance, a useless creature.

7659 **segheria** **sawmill**
la
[segerja]
Penso che non sia realistico tenere registrazioni continue e fornire prove documentali sul legno dal magazzino alla segheria e poi fino alla fabbrica di mobili.
-I think that it is not realistic here to constantly keep new accounts and provide documentary evidence, from the timber yard and the sawmill right up to the furniture factory.

7660 **ambientare** **set**
vb
[ambjentare]
E' ambientato nel 2055 e tratta dell'unico sopravissuto alla catastrofe climatica.
-It is set in 2055 and focuses on a lone survivor of climate catastrophe.

7661 **bruscamente** **short|brusquely**
adv
[bruskamente]
Si allontanò bruscamente.
-He backed abruptly away.

7662 **lanciatore** **thrower**
il
[lantʃatore]
Quindi il tuo amichetto è un lanciatore.
-So your boyfriend's a pitcher.

7663 **abitato** **inhabited**

adj
[abitato]
Per quanto tempo hanno abitato in Inghilterra?
-How long did they live in England?

7664 **adottivo**
adj
[adottivo]
adopted|foster
Personalmente apprezzo, in qualità di madre adottiva e a nome di tutte le donne che rappresento, la volontà di concedere gli stessi diritti di quelli spettanti alle madri biologiche.
-I personally appreciate, as an adoptive mother and on behalf of all the women I represent, the will to grant the same rights as those of biological mothers.

7665 **antiquato**
adj
[antikwato]
antiquated|outdated
Francamente, il tuo modo di pensare è antiquato.
-Frankly speaking, your way of thinking is out of date.

7666 **strappato**
adj
[strappato]
torn
Joe si è strappato la maglia.
-Joe ripped off his shirt.

7667 **termometro**
il
[termometro]
thermometer
Joe si mise il termometro in bocca.
-Joe put the thermometer in his mouth.

7668 **algebra**
la
[aldʒebra]
algebra
Lei è in conflitto con l'algebra booleana?
-Are you at odds with Boolean algebra?

7669 **bungalow**
i
[buŋgalov]
bungalow
Comprammo questo piccolo bungalow a Santa Monica e, con circa 50,:,000 dollari, ci costruii una casa attorno.
-We bought this tiny little bungalow in Santa Monica and for like 50 grand I built a house around it.

7670 **zarina**
la
[dzarina]
tsarina
L'influenza di Rasputin sulla zarina, e la sua decisione di ritirare le truppe russe dal fronte... devastante per la causa degli alleati.
-Rasputin's influence over tzarina and his call to remove Russian troops from the front devastating to allied cause.

7671 **conversare**
vb
[konversare]
converse
Le persone sorde riescono a conversare nel linguaggio dei segni.
-Deaf people can converse in sign language.

7672 **appassionare**
vb
[appassjonare]
thrill
E' importante che siano sostenuti dall'opinione pubblica, ma non si riuscirà ad appassionare nessuno a un concetto astratto come la biodiversità.
-Public support is important, and nobody gets excited about an abstract idea such as biodiversity.

7673 **innaturale**
adj
[innaturale]
unnatural
Lui morì di morte innaturale.
-He died an unnatural death.

7674 **strepitoso**
adj
[strepitozo]
resounding
Avevamo quattro navicelle, due intorno a Marte, due sulla superficie, un traguardo strepitoso.
-We had four spacecraft, two around Mars, two on the surface -- an amazing accomplishment.

7675 **sventolare**
vb
[zventolare]
wave
Sopra il titolo compare una grande foto di due ragazzi nigeriani che, con un sorriso sdolcinato, sventolano le loro schede elettorali.

-Above the headline, there is a big picture of two coyly smiling Nigerian boys brandishing their ballot papers.

7676 **confessore** il [konfessore]
confessor
Qualora il confessore ritenga doveroso interrogare il penitente, lo faccia con discrezione e rispetto.
-Whenever the confessor considers it necessary to question the penitent, he should do so with discretion and respect.

7677 **sostentamento** il [sostentamento]
sustenance|maintenance
Sono la loro fonte di sostentamento, il loro patrimonio e il futuro dei loro figli.
-It is their livelihood, their heritage and the future of their children.

7678 **napoletano** adj; il [napoletano]
Neapolitan; Neapolitan
L'oratore prosegue in napoletano.
-The speaker continued in Neapolitan.

7679 **moderare** vb [moderare]
moderate
Parallelamente è necessario moderare i toni del linguaggio politico in Irlanda del Nord.
-Equally, there is an urgent need to moderate the language of politics in Northern Ireland.

7680 **fornaio** il [fornajo]
baker
Quindi un fornaio, un buon fornaio, sa come tirare o portare fuori lo zucchero insito e intrappolato nell'amido.
-So a baker, and a good baker, knows how to pull or draw forth the inherent sugar trapped in the starch.

7681 **arduo** adj [ardwo]
arduous|uphill
Questo è arduo.
-This is awkward.

7682 **microbo** il [mikrobo]
microbe
Un solo microbo rovinerà l'intero barile.
-One microbe will destroy this entire barrel.

7683 **inquisizione** la [iŋkwizittsjone]
inquisition
Possiamo chiamarlo maccartismo, oppure caccia alle streghe o inquisizione!!!
-It is McCarthy, the witches of Salem, the Inquisition!

7684 **muratore** il [muratore]
bricklayer
Io sto per lavorare come muratore assieme a mio padre.
-I'm going to work as a builder with my father.

7685 **persico** il [persiko]
perch
Vi voglio sul primo volo per il golfo persico.
-I want you on the first flight to the Persian Gulf.

7686 **espressamente** adv [espressamente]
expressly
La pubblicità non espressamente permessa dovrà pertanto essere vietata in futuro.
-Advertising that is not expressly permitted is then to be banned in the future.

7687 **tirocinio** il [tirotʃinjo]
training
Permettetemi di iniziare con i periodi di tirocinio, o di apprendistato, come talvolta vengono definiti.
-Let me start with traineeships, or internships as they are also sometimes called. I know that the European Parliament regards these as very important, as Ms Turunen's report earlier this year showed.

7688 **bambinaia**
nanny

la | Dobbiamo cessare di agire con questa inclinazione da " bambinaia ".
[bambinaja] | -We must desist from getting into the 'nanny state ' frame of mind.

7689 **virilità** **manhood | virility**
la
[virilit'a]
Non è certo consumando la polvere di corno di rinoceronte che si aumenta la virilità.
-If you are a consumer of powdered rhinoceros horn, your virility is not thereby improved.

7690 **poltiglia** **mush**
la
[poltiʎʎa]
Un uovo sbattuto è una poltiglia, saporita, ma pur sempre una poltiglia.
-A scrambled egg is mush -- tasty mush -- but it's mush.

7691 **bazooka** **bazooka**
la
[baddzooka]
Portarti appresso il bazooka non ha aiutato.
-Carrying your bazooka around has not helped matters.

7692 **filettare** **thread**
vb
[filettare]
macchine tessili per filettare o maschiare i metalli n.c.a.
-machine tools for threading or tapping metal n.e.c.

7693 **assoldare** **engage**
vb
[assoldare]
Gli Stati Uniti hanno annunciato che toglieranno ogni limitazione ai servizi d' intelligence, permettendo loro di assoldare anche criminali.
-The United States has announced that it will lift restrictions on intelligence agencies and give them a free hand to recruit criminals.

7694 **arbitrio** **will**
il
[arbitrjo]
Non può essere lasciato tutto al loro arbitrio.
-Things should not be left to their discretion.

7695 **archiviare** **file**
vb
[arkivjare]
Non credo sia possibile semplicemente archiviare queste 75.000 firme.
-I do not think that we can simply file these 75 000 signatures away.

7696 **svariato** **varied**
adj
[zvarjato]
Ha persone capaci e svariate industrie.
-It has a competent workforce and it has a diverse industry.

7697 **bulldog** **bulldog**
il
[bulldog]
Senza la costruzione di una difesa europea credibile, l'Europa resta un chihuahua che trotterella accanto al bulldog americano.
-Without the development of credible European defence, Europe remains a yapping puppy that is allowed to frolic alongside the American bulldog.

7698 **ortodosso** **orthodox**
adj
[ortodosso]
Dottore, niente in questo processo è molto ortodosso.
-There's nothing very orthodox about this whole trial, Dr. Speer.

7699 **beige** **beige**
il
[beidʒe]
Mi ha indotto a pensare che il suo colore preferito è il beige.
-He tricked me into thinking that his favorite color is beige.

7700 **conversione** **conversion**
la
[konversjone]
A quanto sta il tasso di conversione oggi?
-What is the exchange rate today?

7701 **santino** **holy picture**
il
[santino]
Certo, per la mia collezione di santini.
-Of course, for my holy cards collection.

7702 **gravitare** **gravitate**
vb
[gravitare]
I governi non graviteranno mai verso crimini di questa grandezza spontaneamente o con entusiasmo.

-Governments will never gravitate towards crimes of this magnitude naturally or eagerly.

7703 **jogging** **jogging**
lo
[dʒoddʒiŋg]
Io non voglio andare a fare jogging con lei.
-I don't want to go jogging with you.

7704 **palestinese** **Palestinian; Palestinian**
adj; il/la
[palestineze]
È indubbio che dobbiamo riconoscere le sofferenze della popolazione palestinese.
-There is no doubt that we must recognise the suffering of the Palestinian population.

7705 **prematrimoniale** **premarital|prematrimonial**
adj
[prematrimonjale]
Ha un accordo prematrimoniale?
-Do you have a prenuptial agreement?

√ 7706 **capote** **hood**
la
[kapote]
Forse questa è una capote a rilascio segreto.
-Maybe this is a secret hood release.

7707 **ottimismo** **optimism**
lo
[ottimismo]
Mi piace il tuo ottimismo.
-I like your optimism.

7708 **cosacco** **Cossack**
il
[kozakko]
Tuo nonno era un buon cosacco.
-Your grandfather was a fine Cossack.

7709 **carezza** **caress**
la
[karettsa]
Per una carezza o un complimento daresti tutto.
-In exchange for a caress, a compliment, you'd give it all.

7710 **portacenere** **ashtray**
il
[portatʃenere]
Metti il portacenere dove lo si possa vedere.
-Put the ashtray within eyes reach.

7711 **suscettibile** **susceptible|liable**
adj
[suʃʃettibile]
Joe è suscettibile, vero?
-Joe is touchy, isn't he?

7712 **fedelmente** **faithfully**
adv
[fedelmente]
Si riporta anche fedelmente che alcuni deputati hanno espresso il proprio disaccordo.
-They also faithfully record that a number of Members expressed their discontent.

7713 **indulgente** **indulgent|charitable**
adj
[induldʒente]
Layla era indulgente.
-Layla was forgiving.

√ 7714 **seccare** **dry|bother**
vb
[sekkare]
Mi secca che il Parlamento abbia presentato il suo contributo troppo tardi.
-I am annoyed that Parliament has made its contribution too late.

7715 **collocamento** **placement|placing**
il
[kollokamento]
Un collocamento su base temporanea andato a buon fine fa aumentare le possibilità di un un'assunzione a tempo indeterminato.
-Successful placement on a temporary basis increases the chances of permanent employment.

7716 **avvento** **coming**

il
[avvento]
È importante per l'avvento, infine, di una vera Europa dei cittadini.
-This is important for the advent, at long last, of a genuine citizens ' Europe.

7717 **accompagnatrice** **chaperone**
le
[akkompaɲɲatritʃe]
Io sarò la sua accompagnatrice.
-I'll be your chaperone.

7718 **barricare** **barricade**
vb
[barrikare]
Infatti, invece di costruire barricate sempre più alte, dovremmo chiederci perché le persone vogliono entrare nell'Unione europea.
-We should in fact be addressing the issue of why people want to enter the European Union, instead of building our barricades higher.

7719 **bozza** **draft**
la
[bottsa]
Abbiamo tuttavia ricevuto una prima bozza di proposte.
-We have, however, received an initial outline of the proposals.

7720 **blasfemo** **blasphemous**
adj
[blasfemo]
È blasfemo per un miscredente pronunciare quelle parole.
-It is blasphemous for an unbeliever to speak those words.

7721 **dinamico** **dynamic**
adj
[dinamiko]
Devi essere dinamico.
-You have to be proactive.

7722 **atrocità** **atrocity**
le
[atrotʃit'a]
Per quanto tempo il mondo può aspettare e guardare queste atrocità?
-How long can the world stand by and watch these atrocities?

7723 **escursione** **excursion|hike**
le
[eskursjone]
Fai un'escursione, Joe.
-Take a hike, Joe.

7724 **psicologicamente** **psychologically**
adv
[psikolodʒikamente]
Questo incidente lo ha psicologicamente traumatizzato.
-This accident has psychologically traumatized him.

7725 **ripercussione** **repercussion**
la
[riperkussjone]
Le ripercussioni potrebbero creare una cause célèbre interamente nuova per il terrorismo.
-The backlash could create a whole new cause célèbre for terrorism.

7726 **remare** **row**
vb
[remare]
Pensa a una barca a remi e a un rematore e a come funzionano insieme per raggiungere una destinazione.
-Think of a rowboat and an oar, and the way that they work together to reach a destination.

7727 **incoronazione** **coronation**
le
[iŋkoronattsjone]
È sempre così l'anniversario della sua incoronazione.
-He's always like this at the anniversary of his coronation.

7728 **predicare** **preach**
vb
[predikare]
Predicare è più facile che mettere in pratica.
-To preach is easier than to practice.

7729 **editoriale** **editorial; leader**
adj; lo
[editorjale]
Nel suo editoriale di oggi l'International Herald Tribune scrive una cosa interessante: "La Grecia ha promesso di fare la sua parte e di riequilibrare il bilancio".
-The International Herald Tribune writes something interesting in its leading article today: 'Greece has promised to do its homework and to balance its budget'.

7730 **passivo** **passive; liabilities**
adj; il
[passivo]
Stiamo diventando molto consapevoli dei pericoli del fumo passivo.
-We are becoming very aware of the dangers of secondhand smoke.

7731 **travolgere** **overwhelm**
vb
[travoldʒere]
Di tanto in tanto lasciati anche travolgere.
-Even, on occasion, let it overwhelm you.

7732 **pioniere** **pioneer**
il
[pjonjere]
Un classico ostacolo per un pioniere.
-It's a classic obstacle to a pioneer.

7733 **scampare** **escape**
vb
[skampare]
Signora Presidente, ho qui una lettera di ventotto donne del Darfur, scampate dal teatro di guerra, che è indirizzata all'Unione africana e alla Lega araba.
-Madam President, I have here a letter, written by 28 women from Darfur who managed to escape from the conflict zone, which is addressed to the African Union and the League of Arab States.

7734 **bulldozer** **bulldozer**
i
[bulldoddzer]
Smettete di comportarvi come un bulldozer, smettete di ignorare l'opinione pubblica.
-Stop behaving like a bulldozer, stop sweeping aside public opinion.

7735 **archeologia** **archeology**
le
[arkeolodʒa]
L'archeologia è divertente!
-Archaeology is fun!

7736 **duo** **duo**
il
[dwo]
Eravamo un duo dinamico qui dentro.
-We were... a dynamic duo in here.

7737 **distruttivo** **destructive**
adj
[distruttivo]
La corruzione agisce certamente come un influsso distruttivo sull'Africa.
-Of course corruption acts as a destructive blight on Africa.

7738 **famigerato** **notorious**
adj
[famidʒerato]
Il secondo è l'inclusione nell'elenco dei metodi consentiti del famigerato body scanner.
-The second is the inclusion on the list of possible screening methods of the notorious body scanner.

7739 **missionario** **missionary; missionary**
adj; il
[missjonarjo]
Gregory Pontus, missionario in Thailandia, ha inviato queste foto.
-Brother Gregory Pontus, missionary in Thailand, sent these pictures.

7740 **cicca** **chewing gum**
la
[tʃikka]
Non ho ancora visto un bancomat che regala una cicca Bazooka.
-Now, I haven't yet met an ATM machine that would give me a piece of Bazooka chewing gum,

7741 **idoneo** **suitable**
adj
[idoneo]
Dobbiamo usare il servizio che per sua natura sarà idoneo a soddisfare questo genere di esigenze su un piano pratico.
-We must use the Service as we build it to be able to be your servant in helping you address those issues on the ground.

7742 **sapientone** **wise guy|know-all**
il
[sapjentone]
Dagli un'occhiata, sapientone, e dimmi cosa ne pensi.
-Take a look, wise guy, and let me know what you think.

7743 **ottuso** **obtuse; dolt**

adj; il | Joe non è così ottuso.
[ottuzo] | -Joe isn't that dumb.

7744 **decappottabile** **convertible**
adj
[dekappottabile]
Io guido una decappottabile.
-I drive a convertible.

7745 **raffreddamento** **cooling**
il
[raffreddamento]
Senza raffreddamento si scalda in fretta.
-Without cooling, it gets hot very fast.

7746 **tifone** **typhoon**
il
[tifone]
L'albero cadde durante il tifone.
-The tree fell over in the typhoon.

7747 **incontrollabile** **uncontrollable**
adj
[iŋkontrollabile]
Soltanto la mobilitazione sociale potrà porre fine agli errori di un sistema incontrollabile.
-Social campaigning alone will put a stop to the erring ways of an uncontrollable system.

7748 **burattino** **puppet**
il
[burattino]
Questa società è un burattino politico.
-This corporation is a political puppet.

7749 **virare** **turn**
vb
[virare]
Tenente... devi virare e puntare direttamente sul pianeta.
-Lieutenant... I want you to turn and head directly towards the planet.

7750 **summit** **summit**
il
[summit]
L'imminente summit dovrà determinare se ci sono ancora speranze per resuscitare il Trattato.
-The forthcoming summit will have to determine whether there is any hope of reviving the Treaty.

7751 **corridore** **runner**
il
[korridore]
Sono un corridore.
-I am a runner.

7752 **combustione** **combustion**
la
[kombustjone]
La loro combustione causa un sovrapprezzo di generi e prodotti alimentari nel complesso.
-Their combustion leads to overpricing of feedingstuffs and foodstuffs in general.

7753 **incline** **prone|inclined**
adj
[iŋkline]
Sono incline ad accettare la proposta.
-I lean toward accepting the proposal.

7754 **rena** **sand**
la
[rena]
Mio padre era solo sul fiume col barcone carico di rena.
-My father was alone on the barge laden with sand.

7755 **inondazione** **flood|flooding**
le
[inondattsjone]
La casa è stata portata via dall'inondazione.
-The house was carried away by the flood.

7756 **educativo** **educational**
adj
[edukativo]
Il sistema educativo è in transizione.
-The educational system is in transition.

7757 **involtino** **roulade**
il
[involtino]
Dopo che ha servito quell'involtino di pollo ancora crudo, la scorsa settimana?

-After she served that undercooked chicken roulade to the judges last week?

7758 **autoradio** **car radio**
le
[autoradjo]
In questo modello è inclusa l'autoradio.
-This model includes a car radio as standard.

7759 **negoziatore** **negotiator**
il
[negottsjatore]
Il relatore si è dimostrato un tenace negoziatore nel corso di tutti questi anni.
-The rapporteur has shown himself to be a tough negotiator over all these years.

7760 **confessionale** **confessional; confessional**
adj; il
[konfessjonale]
Status delle chiese e delle organizzazioni non confessionali
-Status of churches and non-confessional organisations

7761 **violentemente** **violently**
adv
[vjolentemente]
Sono violentemente ammalato.
-I'm violently sick.

7762 **seduttore** **seducer**
il
[seduttore]
La parte di seduttore incomincia ad imbarazzarmi.
-This role as seducer is starting to embarrass me a little!

√ 7763 **gestore** **manager**
il
[dʒestore]
È il gestore di un hotel.
-He is the manager of a hotel.

7764 **consulto** **consultation**
il
[konsulto]
Per ulteriori dettagli, consultare Arresto del rinnovo automatico della sottoscrizione.
-For details, see Stop Renewing Your Subscription Automatically.

7765 **mortaio** **mortar**
il
[mortajo]
Una famiglia è stata spazzata via da un mortaio Sky Shadow in Somalia.
-A family was wiped out by a Sky Shadow mortar in Somalia.

7766 **salvagente** **life buoy|life jacket**
il
[salvadʒente]
L'abbiamo gettata in mare aperto senza un salvagente.
-We threw her into the deep end without a life preserver.

√ 7767 **scrigno** **casket** ?
lo
[skriɲɲo]
Sta controllando l'ombra da dentro lo scrigno.
-Somehow he's controlling the shadow from inside the box.

7768 **scontento** **discontent; displeased**
lo; adj
[skontento]
Perché sei scontento della tua vita?
-Why are you dissatisfied with your life?

7769 **idealista** **idealist**
il/la
[idealista]
Qualcuno mi ha definito l'idealista di turno, il sognatore.
-Someone said earlier that I must be the idealist around here, the dream maker.

7770 **eventualità** **eventuality|possibility**
le
[eventwalit'a]
Credo che dobbiate prepararvi a quest'eventualità.
-I think you need to prepare yourselves for that possibility.

7771 **bollente** **boiling**
adj
[bollente]
È bollente?
-Is it boiling?

7772 **coniugale** **conjugal|marital**
adj
[konjugale]
L'amore coniugale si manifesta nell'educazione, come vero amore di genitori.

-In the raising of children conjugal love is expressed as authentic parental love.

7773 **diffuso** adj [diffuzo] **widespread**
Senza questo protagonismo diffuso non ci sarà sostenibilità dello sviluppo.
-Without this widespread committed involvement, development will not be sustainable.

7774 **prole** la [prole] **offspring|children**
Chi si prende cura di loro e della loro prole?
-How are they and their children looked after?

7775 **catechismo** il [katekismo] **catechism**
Non me l'avevano insegnato a catechismo.
-Sorry, that's not what I learned in catechism.

7776 **schiappa** la [skjappa] **duffer**
Gli amici di mia madre pensavano che non ero una schiappa.
-People besides my mother actually thought I didn't suck at it.

7777 **infermità** le [infermit'a] **infirmity**
Questi produttori hanno deciso di vendere le proprie quote perché sono malati, o affetti da infermità o perché sono ormai anziani.
-Their decision to sell the quotas is based on illness, infirmity or old age.

7778 **creditore** il [kreditore] **creditor**
La somma da sequestrare dovrebbe essere calcolata sulla base della rivendicazione del creditore.
-The sum to be attached should be calculated on the basis of the creditor's claim.

7779 **squillare** vb [skwillare] **ring**
E'quanto è avvenuto ad un esile ragazzino, con una squillante vocina infantile, che è stato accusato di molestie sessuali nei confronti della sorellina di cinque anni.
-This is what has happened to a small slip of a boy with a very high-pitched, young child's voice, who has been accused of sexually abusing his five-year-old sister.

7780 **metabolismo** il [metabolismo] **metabolism**
È questione di velocizzare il metabolismo.
-It's all about speeding up your metabolism.

7781 **pareggiare** vb [pareddʒare] **equalize|balance**
Ci occorre anche tale fattore e in questo modo pareggiamo molti nostri svantaggi.
-We need it and it can help us make up for many of our disadvantages.

7782 **chiatta** la [kjatta] **barge**
Devi portare l'astrolabio su quella chiatta.
-You must carry the astrolabe onto that barge.

7783 **vegetazione** la [vedʒetattsjone] **vegetation**
Cerca un appezzamento di vegetazione giallastra.
-Just look for a patch of yellowish vegetation.

7784 **zimbello** lo [tsimbello] **laughing stock**
Signora Presidente, che zimbello deve essere l'UE agli occhi dei suoi concorrenti!
-Madam President, what a laughing stock the EU must be to its competitors!

7785 **fiaba** **fairy tale**

la Joe non sa la differenza tra una fiaba e una favola.
[fjaba] -Joe doesn't know the difference between a fable and a fairytale.

7786 **stesura** **drawing up**
la Vorrei soffermarmi in particolare sulla stesura degli elenchi di terroristi.
[stezura] -I particularly wish to mention the compilation of lists of terrorists.

7787 **zeppelin** **zeppelin**
lo Alcune persone considerano i Led Zeppelin la più grande band mai esistita.
[tseppelin] -Some people consider Led Zeppelin to be the greatest band there has ever been.

7788 **groppa** **back**
la Joe salì in groppa a un cavallo e seguì Jane.
[groppa] -Joe got on a horse and followed Jane.

7789 **fusto** **stem|drum**
il Non è come guidare dalla Pennsylvania al Delaware per comprare un fusto di birra.
[fusto] -It's not like driving from Pennsylvania into Delaware to buy a keg.

7790 **pagnotta** **loaf**
la C'era una volta una ragazza che calpestò una pagnotta per evitare di sporcare le scarpe, e le disgrazie che le successero di conseguenza sono ben note.
[paɲɲotta] -There was once a girl who trod on a loaf to avoid soiling her shoes, and the misfortunes that happened to her in consequence are well known.

7791 **dettagliato** **detailed**
adj È molto dettagliato.
[dettaʎʎato] -It's very detailed.

7792 **attendibile** **reliable**
adj È attendibile questo elenco?
[attendibile] -Is this list reliable?

7793 **inconcepibile** **inconceivable**
adj Sarebbe inconcepibile prolungare ulteriormente il ritardo accumulato dal dicembre 2005.
[iŋkontʃepibile] -It would be inconceivable to add further to the delay which has built up since December 2005.

7794 **docile** **docile|tame**
adj Joe è docile.
[dotʃile] -Joe is meek.

7795 **intestare** **head**
vb Intestare una lettera con il proprio indirizzo.
[intestare] -To head a letter with one's address.

7796 **rendita** **income**
la Con le società attive, c'è una rendita annuale di 200.000 euro.
[rendita] -With assets generating an annual income of 200,000 euros.

7797 **minatore** **miner**
il Io ero un minatore di carbone.
[minatore] -I used to be a coal miner.

7798 **azoto** **nitrogen**
il L'aria è composta principalmente da azoto e ossigeno.
[addzoto] -Air is mainly composed of nitrogen and oxygen.

7799 **opossum** **opossum**

	gli [opossum]	Sia il canguro che l'opossum sono marsupiali. -Both kangaroos and opossums are marsupial animals.
7800	**variabile** adj [varjabile]	**variable** Paghiamo una imposta sul reddito di entità variabile a seconda della dimensione del reddito. -We pay an income tax at varying rates according to the size of income.
7801	**socievole** adj [sotʃevole]	**sociable** Sono socievole. -I'm sociable.
7802	**appendicite** la [appenditʃite]	**appendicitis** "Com'è andata?" "Dicono che sia stata appendicite acuta." -"How did it go?" "They said it was acute appendicitis."
7803	**invadente** adj; il/la [invadente]	**intrusive; intruder** Joe è invadente. -Joe's intrusive.
7804	**oasi** le [oazi]	**oasis** La Terra è la nostra oasi nello spazio. -Earth is our oasis in space.
7805	**trafiggere** vb [trafiddʒere]	**pierce** Quando posso trafiggere uno dei miei amici? -Yes. When can I stab one of my friends?
7806	**trazione** la [trattsjone]	**traction|drive** Metti le mani nell'incisione per maggior trazione. -Put your hand in the incision to get more traction.
7807	**espandere** vb [espandere]	**expand|enlarge** In questo modo, gli studenti dell'Università hanno l'opportunità di espandere i propri orizzonti culturali. -In this way, the students of the University have the opportunity to expand their cultural horizons.
7808	**cronometrare** vb [kronometrare]	**time|minute** Potrebbe avviare il cronometro per il mio intervento sul discarico nell'ambito dei trasporti? -Would you now please start the clock for my speech on discharge with regard to transport?
7809	**riconsiderare** vb [rikonsiderare]	**reconsider** In primo luogo, questa è una crisi economica globale che ci costringe a ripensare e riconsiderare la strategia per l'occupazione. -Firstly, this is a global economic crisis which is forcing us to rethink and re-evaluate the Employment Strategy.
7810	**meditare** vb [meditare]	**meditate|brood** Vado spesso lì a meditare. -I often go there to meditate.
7811	**motivare** vb [motivare]	**motivate** Vado al negozio per motivare mia mamma. -I go to the store to motivate my mom.
7812	**incompetenza** le [iŋkompetentsa]	**incompetence** Solitamente non associo l'incompetenza a te. -Incompetence is not a word I normally associate with you.
7813	**disabile** adj [dizabile]	**disabled** Ho riparato la casa per l'uomo disabile. -I fixed the house for the disabled man.

✓ 7814 **gommone** **rubber dinghy**
il
[gommone]
Usiamo Ling–Ling come un gommone gonfiabile.
-Let's use Ling–Ling as an inflatable raft.

7815 **grafica** **graphics**
la
[grafika]
La grafica del Super Nintendo è sorprendente. È così migliore di quella del Nintendo originale.
-The Super Nintendo's graphics are amazing. They're so much better than those of the original Nintendo.

7816 **ecografia** **echography**
le
[ekografja]
La prima ecografia è sempre difficile da leggere.
-Relax, the first ultrasound's always hard to read.

7817 **analfabeta** **illiterate**
il/la
[analfabeta]
Joe non è analfabeta.
-Joe isn't illiterate.

7818 **ampiamente** **widely**
adv
[ampjamente]
Uno dei meccanismi paneuropei di classificazione ampiamente utilizzati in Europa.
-One of the Pan–European classification schemes that are widely used in Europe.

7819 **patrizio** **patrician; patrician**
adj; il
[patrittsjo]
Lo spero, perché oltretutto non è quello che avrebbe voluto San Patrizio.
-I hope you're right because, apart from anything else, it's not what St Patrick would've wanted.

✓ 7820 **ambulatorio** **surgery; ambulatory**
il; adj
[ambulatorjo]
Domani vado in un ambulatorio gratuito.
-Tomorrow, I'm going to a free clinic.

7821 **sacrilegio** **sacrilege**
il
[sakriledʒo]
So che è un sacrilegio invitare le DG III e XII allo stesso tavolo, ma non mi sembra tanto tragico.
-I know it is sacrilege to invite DG III and DG XII to the same table, but I do not think it is such a bad idea.

7822 **sapienza** **wisdom**
la
[sapjentsa]
Infatti il sapere, posto nell'orizzonte della fede, diventa sapienza e visione di vita.
-Indeed, knowledge set in the context of faith becomes wisdom and life vision.

7823 **bolscevico** **Bolshevik; Bolshevik**
adj; il
[bolʃeviko]
Ha pagato un prezzo molto alto per la pazzia dell'utopia bolscevico-comunista.
-It paid a very high price for the madness of Bolshevik-Communist utopia.

✓ 7824 **prefettura** **prefecture**
la
[prefettura]
Il capo della polizia della prefettura tentò di rendere più stretta la disciplina dei propri agenti.
-The prefectural police chief tried to tighten his police officers' discipline.

✓ 7825 **impeto** **impetus|fit**
il
[impeto]
La musica è un impeto dell'anima.
-Music is an outburst of the soul.

✓ 7826 **domare** **tame**
vb
[domare]
Dovresti domare quella tua piccola giumenta.
-You ought tame that little mare of yours.

7827 **sostituzione** **replacement**
la
[sostituttsjone]
Voce destinata a coprire la sostituzione di attrezzature e macchinari tecnici.
-This item is intended to cover the replacement of technical equipment and installations.

7828 **affrettato** **hurried|hasty**
adj
[affrettato]
Non vediamo alcuna ragione per agire in modo affrettato in questa materia, provocando così più danni che benefici.
-There is no reason to be overhasty in approaching this issue. It would do the cause more harm than good.

7829 **coloniale** **colonial**
adj
[kolonjale]
Si tratta di una situazione post-coloniale e pre-coloniale e non dovremmo più accettarlo.
-This is a post-colonial and pre-colonial situation and we should no longer accept it.

7830 **peseta** **peseta**
la
[pezeta]
Il dollaro avrebbe potuto prendersi gioco della peseta, e con quali conseguenze economiche?
-The US dollar could have played games with the peseta, and what economic effects might that have had?

7831 **bemolle** **flat**
lo
[bemolle]
Canta in si bemolle.
-It's actually in the key of B flat.

7832 **intrigo** **intrigue**
il
[intrigo]
Intrighi e omicidi tra i pittori ottomani di corte del 16° secolo.
-"Intrigue and murder among 16th century Ottoman court painters."

7833 **sopprimere** **abolish**
vb
[sopprimere]
In fondo, se potessero sopprimere il Parlamento europeo, ne sarebbero ben lieti.
-Basically, if they could abolish the European Parliament they would be more than happy.

7834 **mero** **mere**
adj
[mero]
Un mero decadimento produce una vita più ricca.
-Mere decay produces richer life.

7835 **epica** **epic**
le
[epika]
Questa sarà epica!
-This is going to be epic!

7836 **cartellone** **poster|program**
il
[kartellone]
Può prenderlo da qualunque panchina o cartellone.
-You can get my number off of any billboard or park bench.

7837 **ricambiare** **return|reciprocate**
vb
[rikambjare]
E' un peccato che il Parlamento non abbia potuto ricambiare con un livello di partecipazione altrettanto alto.
-It is a pity that Parliament could not reciprocate with an equivalent level of attendance.

7838 **bernoccolo** **bump**
il
[bernokkolo]
Solo un enorme bernoccolo sulla testa.
-Just a gnarly bump on his head.

7839 **visone** **mink**
il
[vizone]
Questo è visone?
-Is this mink?

7840 **malocchio** **evil eye**
il
[malokkjo]
Guarda, sta facendo il malocchio.
-Looks, she is casting the evil eye.

7841 **tendone** **marquee**
il
[tendone]
Perché una fabbrica di birra che sponsorizza eventi sportivi della squadra di adulti non dovrebbe anche mettere a disposizione il proprio tendone per una manifestazione giovanile?
-Why should a brewery which sponsors an adult sports event for a club or association not be allowed to make its marquee available for a youth event too?

7842 **uguaglianza** **equality**
la
[ugwaʎʎantsa]
La parola chiave è uguaglianza.
-The key word is equality.

7843 **alleato** **ally; allied**
il; adj
[alleato]
Il carbone è alleato chimicamente ai diamanti.
-Coal is chemically allied to diamonds.

7844 **sconcertante** **disconcerting**
adj
[skontʃertante]
Era sconcertante.
-It was disconcerting.

7845 **persuasione** **persuasion**
la
[perswazjone]
Ci è voluta un po' di persuasione, ma alla fine sono riuscita a farle mangiare i suoi broccoli.
-It took a little cajoling but I finally got her to eat her broccoli.

7846 **falco** **hawk**
il
[falko]
Il falco ha la vista acuta.
-The falcon has keen eyes.

7847 **bava** **slime**
la
[bava]
Era tutto coperto di sporco, sudore e bava.
-It was all covered in dirt and sweat and drool.

7848 **proibito** **prohibited**
adj
[proibito]
Ballare è proibito.
-Dancing is prohibited.

7849 **perspicace** **perspicacious|discerning**
adj
[perspikatʃe]
Era abbastanza perspicace da capire quello che lui realmente intendeva.
-She had enough sense to understand what he really meant.

7850 **proroga** **extension**
la
[proroga]
Ho chiesto una proroga alla società elettrica.
-I asked for an extension from the power company.

7851 **terapeutico** **therapeutic**
adj
[terapeutiko]
Il secondo aspetto consiste nell'idea del valore aggiunto di un nuovo farmaco sul piano terapeutico.
-The second point is the idea of added therapeutic value for a new medicinal product.

7852 **squaw** **squaw**
le
[skwav]
Say you're ready to make like his squaw.
-Dì che sei praticamente la sua squaw.

7853 **sgabuzzino** **storage room**
lo
[zgabuttsino]
Mio figlio e mia moglie sono stati chiusi in uno sgabuzzino per molti anni, a svilupparlo.
-My son and his wife sat in a closet for many years and developed this.

7854 **preferenza** **preference**

la
[preferentsa]
Loro che rifiutavano la preferenza nazionale rivendicano oggi la preferenza corporativista.
-Those who used to refuse national preference now call for corporatist preference.

7855 **destriero**
steed
il
[destrjero]
Non sei un cavaliere su un bianco destriero.
-You're not some white knight on a steed.

7856 **fiducioso**
confident
adj
[fidutʃozo]
Joe è troppo fiducioso.
-Joe is too trusting.

√7857 **lasso**
period; weary
il; adj
[lasso]
Signor Presidente, onorevoli deputati, dagli interventi ascoltati deduco che l' argomento non può essere esaurito nel breve lasso di tempo riservato al dibattito di questa sera.
-Mr President, ladies and gentlemen, from the speeches I have heard I deduce that this subject cannot be exhausted in the short interval of time set aside for this evening' s debate.

7858 **teiera**
teapot
la
[tejera]
La teiera sta fischiando.
-The teapot is whistling.

7859 **passante**
passing; passer-by
adj; il/la
[passante]
Io sono solamente un passante innocente.
-I'm just an innocent bystander.

7860 **esagerazione**
exaggeration|aggrandizement
le
[ezadʒerattsjone]
Io penso che sia un'esagerazione.
-I think that's an exaggeration.

7861 **distorsione**
distortion
la
[distorsjone]
– Sapevate del rischio di distorsione termica...
-I had announced the risk of thermal distortion which...

7862 **occasionale**
occasional|casual
adj
[okkazjonale]
Ma non è di questa compassione occasionale che stiamo parlando. ~~~ Non rimarrà mai occasionale.
-Then this occasional compassion, we are not talking about -- it will never remain occasional.

√7863 **pedone**
pedestrian|pawn
il
[pedone]
Il sistema elettronico di protezione dei pedoni (EPP) è una soluzione eccellente.
-The Electronic Pedestrian Protection system (EPP) is an excellent solution.

7864 **contorto**
twisted
adj
[kontorto]
Ora immaginate qualcuno contorto come me che cerca di costruire una casa.
-Now imagine someone as twisted as me trying to build a house.

7865 **guantone**
mitt
il
[gwantone]
Avrei dovuto portare quel guantone che hai detto avresti firmato.
-I should have brought that mitt you said you'd sign.

7866 **calciatore**
soccer player
il
[kaltʃatore]
Chi è il vostro calciatore preferito?
-Who's your favorite soccer player?

7867 **megafono**
megaphone

il
[megafono]
La diplomazia del megafono, in questo caso, è del tutto controproducente.
-Megaphone diplomacy, in this case, is totally counterproductive.

7868 **ventuno**
i
[ventuno]
pontoon
Quello che è cominciato ventuno mesi fa nel cuore dell'inverno non può finire in questa notte autunnale. Questa vittoria da sola non è il cambiamento che cerchiamo.
-What began 21 months ago in the depths of winter cannot end on this autumn night. This victory alone is not the change we seek.

7869 **implicazione**
le
[implikattsjone]
implication
Si tratta di questioni che hanno, beninteso, implicazioni e ripercussioni sul processo negoziale.
-Obviously, these issues also have ramifications for this negotiation process.

7870 **lussuoso**
adj
[lusswozo]
luxurious
Un servizio non può essere a basso costo e allo stesso tempo lussuoso.
-A service cannot be cheap and luxurious at the same time.

7871 **corporeo**
adj
[korporeo]
bodily
C'è un uso del linguaggio corporeo.
-There's a use of body language.

7872 **epilessia**
la
[epilessja]
epilepsy
Sono quelle che potrebbero essere iperattive in patologie come l'epilessia.
-And these are some of the cells that might be overactive in disorders such as epilepsy.

7873 **riassunto**
il
[rjassunto]
summary|brief
Ma questo breve estratto è un buon riassunto di ciò che lui disse durante l'intervista.
-But this little excerpt is a very good summary of what he was saying during the interview.

7874 **adolescenza**
le
[adoleʃʃentsa]
adolescence
Jane ha trascorso la sua adolescenza in solitudine.
-Jane spent her girlhood in seclusion.

7875 **carboidrato**
il
[karboidrato]
carbohydrate
Che sembri un grossissimo carboidrato umano.
-You're like one big human carbohydrate.

7876 **natica**
la
[natika]
buttock
Aveva metastasi nella natica destra, e non era in grado di rimanere seduto, neanche con i farmaci.
-He had metastases in his right buttock, and he couldn't sit even with medication.

7877 **tabulato**
il
[tabulato]
printout
Leggi un tabulato, pensi di conoscere una persona.
-Read a printout, figure you know a person.

7878 **ideologia**
la
[ideolodʒa]
ideology
In questo paese c'è solo qualche esempio del fatto che l'ideologia e la religione sono utili nella formazione del carattere delle persone.
-In this country there are only few examples that ideology and religion are helpful in character building for people.

7879 **stilare**
vb
[stilare]
draw up|draft
Per tale motivo è essenziale che il Parlamento continui a stilare la propria relazione.

-That is why it is crucial that Parliament continues to draft its own report.

7880 **ostia** **host**
la
[ostja]
Hai mangiato l'ostia, vicino?
-Have you eaten a Host, neighbor?

7881 **edilizio** **building**
adj
[edilittsjo]
Nel settore edilizio, le direttive hanno effetti disastrosi.
-For the building sector the directives are proving disastrous.

7882 **occulto** **occult|hidden**
adj
[okkulto]
Il carburante per aerei è esente da dazi, il che rappresenta un contributo occulto.
-Aviation fuel is free of duty, a hidden subsidy.

7883 **benevolo** **benevolent|benign**
adj
[benevolo]
Gran parte di ciò che ascoltiamo stamattina si basa sull'idea di uno Stato benevolo.
-Much of what we are hearing this morning is based on the concept of a benevolent state.

7884 **protestante** **Protestant; Protestant**
adj; il/la
[protestante]
Lo sappiamo perché oggi l'etica del lavoro non è più un fenomeno protestante, occidentale.
-We know this because today the work ethic is no longer a Protestant, Western phenomenon.

7885 **profumato** **scented|fragrant**
adj
[profumato]
Voleva tornarvi per esalare in mezzo ai diletti Frati i1 profumo dell'ultimo respiro.
-He wanted to return to exhale among beloved Friars i1 scent of breath.

7886 **muscoloso** **muscular|muscled**
adj
[muskolozo]
Joe è alto e muscoloso.
-Joe is tall and muscular.

7887 **divergenza** **divergence|difference**
la
[diverdʒentsa]
Io non ho alcuna divergenza con voi due.
-I've got no quarrel with you two.

7888 **fumante** **smoking**
adj
[fumante]
Era lì che si doveva andare a fumare, ma era impossibile godersi la sigaretta.
-That was where you had to smoke, but it did not taste good at all.

7889 **manodopera** **labor|manpower**
la
[manodopera]
Abbiamo aumentato la nostra manodopera.
-We've increased our manpower.

7890 **ennesimo** **umpteenth**
adj
[ennezimo]
Si tratta dell'ennesimo dramma di una lunga serie.
-It is the umpteenth drama in a long series.

7891 **sopravvalutare** **overestimate|overvalue**
vb
[sopravvalutare]
Non bisogna sopravvalutare la biotecnologia ma neanche sottovalutarla.
-We should not overestimate biotechnology, but nor should we underestimate it.

7892 **sesamo** **sesame**
il
[sezamo]
Bagel di sesamo tagliato, non tostato.
-Sesame bagel quartered, not toasted.

7893 **vertice** **summit|vertex**

il
[vertitʃe]
Il Vertice di Copenaghen passerà alla storia come un Vertice di totale incoerenza.
-The Copenhagen Summit will go down in history as a summit of total incoherence.

7894 **fronteggiare** **face|cope**
vb
[fronteddʒare]
Oggi siamo quindi meglio attrezzati, molto meglio attrezzati per fronteggiare una crisi.
-So today, we are better, much better placed to cope with a recession.

7895 **gustoso** **tasty|savory**
adj
[gustozo]
Io voglio mangiare qualcosa di gustoso.
-I want to eat something tasty.

7896 **maiuscola** **capital**
la
[majuskola]
Era una parata con la P maiuscola.
-It was a parade with a capital P.

✓ 7897 **disprezzare** **despise|look down on**
vb
[disprettsare]
Non disprezzare un uomo perché è povero.
-Don't despise a man because he is poor.

7898 **ardere** **burn|blaze**
vb
[ardere]
Alle sue parole, i cuori dei due viandanti sconsolati acquistano serenità e cominciano ad ardere di gioia.
-As Jesus speaks, the hearts of the two disconsolate travellers find a new serenity and begin to burn with joy.

7899 **dolente** **sore|sorrowful**
adj
[dolente]
Il fallimento dell'esame era un punto dolente di cui non piaceva parlare.
-Failing the exam was a sore point that he did not like to talk about.

7900 **geometria** **geometry**
la
[dʒometrja]
Dato che π è trascendentale, la quadratura di un cerchio - un problema classico in geometria - è impossibile.
-As π is transcendental, the quadrature of a circle - a classical problem in geometry - is impossible.

✓ 7901 **bivio** **fork**
il
[bivjo]
Dopo il bivio imbocchi l'autostrada.
-After the junction take the motorway.

7902 **biberon** **bottle**
il
[biberon]
È un composto che si trova nel policarbonato, di cui sono fatti i biberon.
-It's a compound that's found in polycarbonate plastic, which is what baby bottles are made out of.

7903 **lozione** **lotion**
la
[lottsjone]
Il miele è più viscoso della lozione per la pelle?
-Is honey more viscous than skin lotion?

7904 **garzone** **boy**
il
[gartsone]
Non stiamo parlando di un garzone che viene licenziato, Lou, è una cosa seria.
-We're not talking about a busboy who got fired, Lou... this is serious business.

7905 **saga** **saga**
la
[saga]
La saga della strana creatura del Manhattan Hospital continua.
-The saga of the strange creature at Manhattan Hospital goes on.

✓ 7906 **azzeccare** **hit|guess**
vb
[attsekkare]
Signor presidente, al termine della Presidenza spagnola molte cose diverse potranno essere dette sul suo operato, e molte ne abbiamo ascoltate stamani, alcune più azzeccate di altre.

-Mr President, at the end of the Spanish Presidency a great deal of things could be said to you about your accomplishments, many of which we have heard this morning, some more positive than others.

7907 **indice** **index|rate**
i
[inditʃe]
In un momento di rabbia ho tirato un pugno al muro e mi sono rotto l'indice.
-In a fit of anger I punched the wall and broke my index finger.

7908 **palombaro** **diver**
il
[palombaro]
No, però potrebbe essere un palombaro.
-No, could be a diver, though.

7909 **sconsiderato** **inconsiderate|thoughtless**
adj
[skonsiderato]
Io penso che Joe sia sconsiderato.
-I think Joe is inconsiderate.

7910 **singhiozzare** **sob**
vb
[siŋgjottsare]
Li sentii singhiozzare.
-I heard them sobbing.

7911 **moribondo** **dying; dying man**
adj; il
[moribondo]
Giunti all'Arcella, non si poté più procedere: il Santo era moribondo.
-All'Arcella arrived, no longer could proceed: the saint was dying.

7912 **patibolo** **scaffold**
il
[patibolo]
Il criminale è stato mandato al patibolo.
-The criminal was sent to the gallows.

7913 **carburatore** **carburetor|carburetter**
il
[karburatore]
Hanno mai scoperto il misterioso carburatore?
-Did they ever find the mysterious carburetor?

7914 **insensato** **senseless**
adj
[insensato]
Quindi la paura non è affatto una reazione insensata.
-So fear is not a crazy response at all.

7915 **scocciare** **bother|be fed up**
vb
[skottʃare]
Puoi scocciare qualcun altro, bello.
-So you can bother someone else, dude.

7916 **belga** **Belgian; Belgian**
adj; il/la
[belga]
Joseph Conrad scrisse "Cuore di tenebra" in parte in base alla sua esperienza personale nel Congo Belga.
-Joseph Conrad wrote "Heart of Darkness" in part based on his personal experience in Belgian Congo.

7917 **ripiegare** **fall back|fold up**
vb
[ripjegare]
Tutte le truppe devono ripiegare e tornare a difendere Tbilisi.
-All troops are to fall back and report to defend Tbilisi.

7918 **acchiappare** **catch**
vb
[akkjappare]
E vedete i due gatti qui, Cina e India, che cercano di acchiappare i topi là sopra.
-And you can see the two cats being here, China and India, wanting to catch the mices over there, you know.

7919 **texano** **Texan**
adj
[teksano]
Soprattutto non con il texano Bush, assassino dei bambini iracheni.
-The American superpower is giving up none of its claims, especially now it has the Texan, Mr Bush, in office, the man who perpetrated genocide on the children of Iraq.

7920 **caparra** **deposit**

la
[kaparra]
A te importa solo riavere indietro la caparra.
-All you care about is getting your deposit back.

7921 **parentela** — **relationship|kinship**
la
[parentela]
Per determinare il suo grado di parentela con il bambino.
-To determine your relationship to the child.

7922 **planetario** — **planetary; planetarium**
adj; il
[planetarjo]
Il sistema di Saturno è un sistema planetario ricco.
-Now, the Saturn system is a rich planetary system.

7923 **docente** — **professor**
il/la
[dotʃente]
Chi sarà il nuovo docente?
-Who will the new teacher be?

7924 **digestione** — **digestion**
la
[didʒestjone]
Le fibre, che hanno noti effetti benefici sulla digestione e gli estratti delle piante fanno parte di tale gruppo di sostanze.
-Fibre, which is known to aid digestion, in the same way as plant extracts, is included.

7925 **mangime** — **fodder**
il
[mandʒime]
Avete ordinato il mangime per i polli?
-Have you ordered the feed for the chickens?

7926 **emiliano** — **emilian**
adj
[emiljano]
Sono venuto per prendere le scarpe di Emiliano.
-I came to get Emiliano's shoes.

7927 **cortigiano** — **courtier**
il
[kortidʒano]
Chi è? Chiese il cortigiano.
-Who is that? the courtier asked.

7928 **aborigeno** — **aboriginal; aborigine**
adj; il
[aboridʒeno]
Ça!" E le donne aborigene africane che venivano a dirmi: "E' proprio così!"
-And then aboriginal women in Africa would come and say, "This is it!"

7929 **coalizione** — **coalition|bloc**
la
[koalittsjone]
Primo: nella mia politica io faccio affidamento sulla coalizione fra consumatori e agricoltori.
-Firstly, in my policy I am building on the alliance between the consumer and the farmer.

7930 **fauna** — **fauna**
la[fauna]
La flora e la fauna selvatiche e gli minacciati sono un bene prezioso e insostituibile. -Endangered wildlife and habitats are a precious and irreplaceable asset.

7931 **stridio** — **screech**
lo
[stridjo]
Lo stridio dei freni fu una bella mossa.
-The squeal of brakes was a nice touch.

7932 **fulminare** — **fulminate**
vb
[fulminare]
Per fulminare qualcuno usi un anello con sigillo.
-You want to electrocute someone, you'll need a signet ring.

7933 **geroglifico** — **hieroglyph; hieroglyphic**
il; adj
[dʒeroʎʎifiko]
Devo dire che grazie al lavoro dei giuristi - in particolare quelli del Parlamento - siamo riusciti a interpretare in modo positivo quel che si è trasformato in un vero e proprio geroglifico.
-I have to say that the lawyers - particularly those from Parliament - have enabled us to interpret the hieroglyphics that this exercise has become in a positive way.

✓ 7934 **distaccato** **detached**
adj Fai il distaccato.
[distakkato] -Play it cool.

✓ 7935 **edile** **building; aedile**
adj; il Lui è un operaio edile.
[edile] -He's a construction worker.

7936 **supremazia** **supremacy**
la In passato, durante la supremazia coloniale, questi paesi erano costretti a farlo.
[supremattsja] -In the past, during colonial supremacy, this was done under duress.

7937 **inarrestabile** **unrestrainable**
adj Cosa succede quando una forza inarrestabile colpisce un oggetto irremovibile?
[inarrestabile] -What happens when an unstoppable force hits an unmovable object?

7938 **prescrivere** **prescribe**
vb Ovviamente, la Commissione non può prescrivere alcun modello aziendale specifico.
[preskrivere] -Obviously, the Commission cannot prescribe specific business models.

7939 **scatolone** **carton**
lo Ci vediamo dopo, vengo a prendere lo scatolone.
[skatolone] -I'll see you after. I have to get my box.

7940 **bombola** **cylinder**
la Di solito finiamo con l'avere una bombola un po' più grande, montata sull'esterno del autorespiratore, così.
[bombola] -And usually we'll have a slightly larger cylinder mounted exterior on the rebreather, like this.

7941 **accelerazione** **acceleration**
la Indirizzateli sui nostri sei, datemi massima accelerazione.
[attʃelerattsjone] -Put 'em on our six, give me maximum acceleration.

7942 **trasportatore** **conveyor|carrier**
il D'altro canto, ritengo che i trasportatori non possano essere ritenuti responsabili per il trasporto di persone che chiedono asilo politico non appena giunte nel territorio di uno Stato membro. -I realise, however, that carriers cannot be held liable for transporting persons who request political asylum immediately upon arrival within the territory of a Member State.
[trasportatore]

7943 **chimera** **chimera**
la La chimera di un accordo resterà sempre solo una chimera, questo va detto forte e chiaro.
[kimera] - A chimera of an agreement will always be just that – this needs to be said loud and clear.

7944 **alfabetico** **alphabetical|abecedarian**
adj Le cartelle cliniche nella maggior parte degli ospedali sono tenuti in ordine alfabetico.
[alfabetiko] -The clinical records in most hospitals are kept in alphabetical order.

7945 **purificazione** **purification|purifying**
la Collé mette le donne contro la purificazione.
[purifikattsjone] -It's Collé who sets the women against purification.

7946 **ciononostante** **nevertheless; in spite of this**
adv; phr Ritengo tuttavia che ciononostante non dobbiamo dimenticare i produttori europei.
[tʃononostante]

-I believe, however, that we should nevertheless remember European producers.

7947 **balsamo** **balm|conditioner**
il
[balsamo]
Non devo nemmeno usare il balsamo.
-I don't even have to use conditioner.

7948 **infuori** **out**
adv
[infwori]
Non accettiamo la violenza all'infuori del dojo.
-We don't condone violence outside of the dojo.

7949 **matricola** **freshman|number**
la
[matrikola]
Joe è soltanto una matricola.
-Joe is only a freshman.

7950 **bestemmia** **blasphemy|curse**
la
[bestemmja]
Le critiche esercitate dalla Svezia contro l'UEM vengono viste alla stregua di una bestemmia proferita in chiesa.
-Swedish criticism of EMU is seen as blasphemy.

7951 **mediatore** **mediator|broker**
il
[medjatore]
Mookie agisce da mediatore tra la comunità nera e la comunità italiana.
-Mookie acts as a mediator between the black community and the Italian community.

7952 **banchina** **quay|wharf**
la
[baŋkina]
Joe è sulla banchina.
-Joe is on the dock.

7953 **addolorare** **grieve|pain**
vb
[addolorare]
Mi addolora sempre vedere l'onorevole Claudia Roth arrabbiarsi in Aula, soprattutto oggi che è il suo compleanno.
-I am always distressed to see Claudia Roth get angry in this House but in particular today because it is her birthday.

7954 **abbattuto** **down|dejected**
adj
[abbattuto]
Abbiamo abbattuto un albero.
-We chopped a tree down.

7955 **siepe** **hedge**
la
[sjepe]
la siepe faceva sì che la casa non si potesse vedere dalla strada
-The hedge formed a screen which hid the house from the road

7956 **documentare** **document**
vb
[dokumentare]
Siamo anche riusciti a documentare tale comportamento irregolare.
-We have also been able to document that irregular conduct.

7957 **disorientare** **disorient|confuse**
vb
[dizorjentare]
Così si disorientano i cittadini, lasciandoli alla mercé delle scelte incontrollabili del grande capitale.
-This disorients people and makes them prey to the unaccountable dictates of big business.

7958 **indietreggiare** **back|retreat**
vb
[indjetreddʒare]
Dite a quella gente di indietreggiare per fare in modo che l'elicottero possa atterrare.
-Tell those people to back off so that the helicopter can land.

7959 **ricatto** **blackmail**
il
[rikatto]
Il Parlamento respinge il ricatto che è alla base di questa impasse di tre anni.
-Parliament rejects the blackmail that is at the root of this three-year deadlock.

7960 **irascibile** **irascible|cantankerous**

adj
[iraʃʃibile]
Tu sei irascibile.
-You're cantankerous.

7961 **gustare** **enjoy|taste**
vb
[gustare]
E invito a gustare la vita e a sognare il futuro.
-It is an invitation to savour life and to dream of the future.

7962 **eloquente** **eloquent|articulate**
adj
[elokwente]
Joe è sicuramente eloquente.
-Joe certainly is eloquent.

7963 **fondale** **backdrop|depth**
il
[fondale]
Fermo sul fondale a cento metri di profondità.
-Resting on a seabed in a hundred meters of water.

7964 **ballata** **ballad**
la
[ballata]
Comporrò una ballata in vostro onore.
-I will compose a ballad in your honor.

7965 **disarmato** **unarmed**
adj
[dizarmato]
Io ero disarmato.
-I was unarmed.

7966 **contrariamente** **contrary to; in spite of**
adv; prp
[kontrarjamente]
Due volte ci è stato rifiutato, contrariamente al regolamento.
-Twice this request has been refused, contrary to the Rules of Procedure.

7967 **competente** **competent**
adj
[kompetente]
Nancy è un'infermiera competente.
-Nancy is a capable nurse.

7968 **goffo** **clumsy; hobbledehoy**
adj; il
[goffo]
Sono goffo.
-I'm clumsy.

7969 **galante** **gallant**
adj
[galante]
Il signor Tanaka è un uomo galante.
-Mr Tanaka is a chivalrous man.

7970 **lastricare** **pave**
vb
[lastrikare]
Fu versato tanto cemento da poter lastricare un'autostrada da New York a San Francisco.
-Enough concrete was poured to pave a highway from New York to San Francisco.

7971 **sintesi** **synthesis**
la
[sintezi]
La relazione Bullmann si sforza di difendere la politica di sintesi e di compromesso.
-The Bullmann report is aimed at retaining a policy of synthesis and compromise.

7972 **persecuzione** **persecution**
la
[persekuttsjone]
Non ha conosciuto la persecuzione religiosa, né la persecuzione classista, né quella delle minoranze religiose.
-There was no religious persecution, no class persecution and no persecution of religious minorities.

7973 **indole** **nature**
il
[indole]
Detto accordo svela la vera indole dei negoziati commerciali internazionali pretestuosamente paritari.
-This agreement discloses the true nature of international trade negotiations on so-called equal terms.

7974 **accumulare** **accumulate|store**

vb
[akkumulare]
Ha provato ad accumulare ricchezza.
-He tried to accumulate wealth.

7975 **accorrere**
vb
[akkorrere]
rush
E non feci in tempo ad aprire bocca, con qualche parola, che mi accorsi che la folla aveva fazzoletti in mano e si asciugava le lacrime.
-And I had only the time to utter a few words that I noticed that the people in the crowd had handkerchiefs in their hands and were wiping their tears.

7976 **grammatica**
la
[grammatika]
grammar
Ho 10 giorni per ripassare tutta la grammatica francese.
-I have 10 days to review the whole French grammar.

7977 **doppiamente**
adv
[doppjamente]
doubly
Mi riferisco in particolare alle donne, che sono doppiamente perseguitate e quindi doppiamente coraggiose.
-I am thinking particularly of the women, doubly targeted and doubly courageous!

7978 **raggiungibile**
adj
[raddʒundʒibile]
attainable
E'altrettanto essenziale arrivare a quelle donne che sono meno informate e raggiungibili.
-It is just as essential to seek out women who are not so well informed and less accessible.

7979 **amazzone**
la[amattsone]
horsewoman
Il mercurio sarà quindi usato nell'estrazione dell'oro nel bacino del Rio delle Amazzoni e distruggerà, contaminandole, enormi aree fluviali. -The mercury will then be used by gold-washers in the Amazon basin and destroy huge river areas by contaminating them with mercury.

7980 **turbante**
il
[turbante]
turban
Che cosa stai nascondendo nel tuo turbante?
-What are you hiding in your turban?

7981 **secchione**
il
[sekkjone]
nerd
Senti, io... capisco questa reazione da secchione vigliacco.
-Look, I... I understand the whole cowardly geek response.

7982 **passe-partout**
il
[passepartout]
skeleton key
Sai, la moralità è un passe–partout.
-You know, morality is a passkey.

7983 **rivoltare**
vb
[rivoltare]
turn over
Quindi, ora dobbiamo farli rivoltare contro Brick.
-So, now we need to get them to turn on Brick.

7984 **ripieno**
il; adj
[ripjeno]
filling; stuffed
Tale carne è destinata a finire nel ripieno dei ravioli o nei dadi per brodo.
-They will end up as the filling for ravioli or in stock cubes.

7985 **celestiale**
adj
[tʃelestjale]
celestial
Ciò che stiamo imparando farà un po' di luce su ciò che gli scrittori romantici e i poeti hanno descritto come "apertura celestiale" della mente dei bambini.
-And what we're learning is going to shed some light on what the romantic writers and poets described as the "celestial openness" of the child's mind.

7986 **guardone**
il
[gwardone]
peeping Tom
Tiri le tende! Il tipo che vive nella casa dall'altro lato della strada è un guardone.

-Close the curtains! The guy living in the house across the street is a Peeping Tom.

7987 **felino** | **feline**
adj
[felino]
Il felino non mangia da due settimane.
-The cat hasn't eaten in two weeks.

7988 **ripetizione** | **repetition|private lesson**
la
[ripetittsjone]
La ripetizione è la madre della memoria.
-Repetition is the mother of memory.

7989 **Mongolia** | **Mongolia**
la
[moŋgolja]
Ulaanbaatar è la capitale della Mongolia.
-Ulaanbaatar is the capital of Mongolia.

7990 **menare** | **lead**
vb
[menare]
Non sai quante suore avrei voluto menare alla scuola cattolica.
-Can't tell you how many nuns I wanted to beat up in catholic school.

7991 **glaciale** | **glacial**
adj
[glatʃale]
Joe è glaciale.
-Joe is cool.

7992 **guaritore** | **healer**
il
[gwaritore]
Siete un guaritore in un villaggio dell'Età della Pietra.
-You are a healer in a Stone Age village.

7993 **epatite** | **hepatitis**
le[epatite]
Una persona con conoscenze da infermiera dovrebbe sapere che l'epatite C complica la gravidanza. -Someone with nurse's training would obviously know that hepatitis c complicates pregnancy.

7994 **combaciare** | **match|join**
vb
[kombatʃare]
Se facessimo combaciare questa forma dalla giusta posizione...
-If we match these shapes up from the right vantage point...

7995 **commodoro** | **commodore**
il
[kommodoro]
Sospetto sia collegato al piano del commodoro.
-I suspect he's connected to the commodore's plans.

7996 **trascrizione** | **transcription**
la
[traskrittsjone]
Ulteriori informazioni su come creare file didascalia e trascrizione.
-Learn more about how to create caption and transcript files.

7997 **estremista** | **extremist**
il/la
[estremista]
I responsabili sono motivati dall'ideologia islamica fondamentalista ed estremista.
-Those responsible are motivated by fundamentalist and extremist Islamist ideology.

7998 **influenza** | **influence|influenza**
la
[inflwentsa]
È la tua influenza!
-It's your influence!

7999 **mammut** | **mammoth**
i
[mammut]
Non ci sono dinosauri o mammut da trovare ora.
-There are no dinosaurs or mammoths to be found now.

8000 **soccorritore** | **rescuer**
il
[sokkorritore]
Sarà felice con il suo soccorritore.
-He'll be quite happy with his rescuer.

8001 **conservatore** | **conservator; Tory**
il; adj
[konservatore]
Churchill è un politico molto conservatore.
-Churchill is a very conservative politician.

8002 **noialtri** **we**
prn
[nojaltri]
Di questo passo, neanche noialtri.
-Nor the rest of us, at this rate.

8003 **vegliare** **watch over**
vb
[veʎʎare]
Toccava a me vegliare e scuoterla prima che la assalissero gli incubi.
-And my job was to stay awake until her nightmares came so I could wake her.

8004 **platea** **audience**
la
[platea]
Ipnotizzi la platea con la tua implacabile precisione.
-And you're hypnotizing the audience with your relentless precision.

8005 **inghiottire** **swallow|gulp**
vb
[iŋgjottire]
Il branco deve essere capace di inghiottire il proprio ego, essere cooperativo e agire in armonia.
-The pack has got to be able to swallow its ego, be cooperative and pull together.

8006 **procione** **raccoon|procyon**
il
[protʃone]
Forse perché indossava un procione in testa.
-Probably because he wore a raccoon on his head.

8007 **narrativo** **narrative**
adj
[narrativo]
Chiaramente non e' affatto interessante dal punto di vista narrativo.
-Obviously this is not interesting at all in the sense of the narrative.

8008 **orchidea** **orchid**
la
[orkidea]
Un'altra cosa che fa è che questa pianta imita un'altra orchidea che solitamente contiene una meravigliosa scorta di cibo per gli insetti.
-The other thing it does is that this plant mimics another orchid that has a wonderful store of food for insects.

8009 **internato** **internee**
il
[internato]
Quindi nel 2004, durante il mio internato in chirurgia, ho avuto la grande fortuna di incontrare il Dott.
-So in 2004, during my surgical residency, I had the great fortune to meet Dr.

8010 **riscrivere** **rewrite**
vb
[riskrivere]
Dovrebbe riscrivere questa frase. Non ha senso.
-You should rewrite this sentence. It does not make sense.

8011 **mercantile** **merchant; merchantman**
adj; il
[merkantile]
Mercantile relations are very important for everybody, and while it is good to denounce the sin, we need to identify the sinners.
-Le relazioni commerciali sono molto importanti e, anche se è bene dire il peccato, è pure necessario dire il peccatore.

8012 **apprezzamento** **appreciation**
lo
[apprettsamento]
Volevo mostrar loro il mio apprezzamento.
-I wanted to show them my appreciation.

8013 **maltempo** **bad weather**
il
[maltempo]
Ho rinunciato all'idea di visitare le attrazioni della città a causa del maltempo.
-I gave up the idea of seeing the sights of the city because of the bad weather.

8014 **icona** **icon**
la
[ikona]
L'orologio del Big Ben è un'icona inglese.
-Big Ben's clock is an English icon.

8015 **macabro** **macabre**

adj | Un commento macabro perché abbiamo perso molti piloti.
[makabro] | -That's a macabre comment because we lost a lot of pilots.

8016 **spunto** | **cue**
lo | Prendo spunto da te.
[spunto] | -I'll take my cue from you.

8017 **ateo** | **atheist; atheistic**
il; adj | "Dio ti benedica." "Io sono ateo."
[ateo] | -"God bless you." "I'm an atheist."

8018 **nostromo** | **boatswain**
il | Né capitano, né ingegnere, né nostromo.
[nostromo] | -Neither captain, nor engineer, nor boatswain.

8019 **sprovvisto** | **devoid**
adj | Un tempo arido e brullo, sprovvisto di qualsiasi compagnia o felicità.
[sprovvisto] | -A bleak and barren time, devoid of any companionship or happiness.

8020 **starnutire** | **sneeze**
vb | Continuo a starnutire.
[starnutire] | -I keep sneezing.

8021 **iato** | **hiatus**
lo | Grazie anche per l'iato nella conversazione.
[jato] | -Thank you as well for the conversational hiatus.

8022 **ingranaggio** | **gear|cog**
il | Nessun diritto, sei un ingranaggio della macchina aziendale.
[iŋgranaddʒo] | -You have no rights as a cog in the corporate machine.

8023 **apostolo** | **apostle**
il | Venne dagli irlandesi con tutti i segni di un apostolo, e quando la gente gli chiese di spiegare la Santissima Trinità, si chinò a terra e prese un trifoglio.
[apostolo] | -He came to the Irish with all the signs of an apostle, and when the people asked him to explain the Blessed Trinity, he reached down to the ground and picked up a shamrock.

8024 **imbattibile** | **unbeatable**
adj | Liu Bei e Zhuge Liang sono una squadra imbattibile.
[imbattibile] | -Liu Bei and Zhuge Liang are an unbeatable team.

8025 **cocca** | **nock**
la | Ci sono due mirini e una doppia cocca.
[kokka] | -There are two sights and a double notch.

8026 **fruscio** | **rustling|swish**
il | Senti un fruscio tra l'erba.
[fruʃʃo] | -And you hear a rustle in the grass.

8027 **sbruffone** | **boaster**
lo | Fa sempre lo sbruffone.
[zbruffone] | -He is always talking big.

8028 **fiaccare** | **sap|weaken**
vb | Occorre altresì fiaccare le resistenze delle imprese costruttrici di automobili, soprattutto per quanto riguarda le norme di sicurezza.
[fjakkare] | -We also need to weaken the resistance of the car manufacturers, particularly with regard to safety standards.

8029 **losco** | **shady|sinister**
adj | Joe non è losco.
[losko] | -Joe isn't creepy.

8030 **telaio** **frame|loom**
il
[telajo]
Abbiamo una cellula di sicurezza in fibra di carbonio che protegge gli occupanti e che pesa un decimo del telaio in metallo tradizionale di un'automobile.
-We have a carbon fiber safety cage that protects the occupants for less than 10 percent of the weight of a traditional steel chassis in a car.

8031 **termite** **termite**
la
[termite]
La termite è un semplice composto di... ossido di ferro e polvere di alluminio.
-Thermite is a simple compound of iron oxide and aluminum powder.

8032 **informale** **informal**
adj
[informale]
Il discorso informale va bene.
-Casual speech is fine.

8033 **svitato** **nutty; screwball**
adj; lo
[zvitato]
Joe ha svitato la lampadina.
-Joe unscrewed the light bulb.

8034 **spessore** **thickness**
lo
[spessore]
Ho trovato la descrizione del libro di poco spessore.
-I found the book's exposition shallow.

8035 **autocontrollo** **restraint**
il
[autokontrollo]
Funzionalità corporea, morfologia ed autocontrollo emotivo.
-Bodily functionality and morphology and affective self-control.

8036 **contrattare** **negotiate**
vb
[kontrattare]
Io amo contrattare.
-I love to bargain.

8037 **deficit** **deficit|deficiency**
il
[defitʃit]
C'è un deficit tariffario, ci sono tariffe regolate che distorcono il mercato.
-There is a tariff deficit, there are regulated tariffs that distort the market.

8038 **olfatto** **smell**
il
[olfatto]
Joe perse il suo senso dell'olfatto.
-Joe lost his sense of smell.

8039 **incrementare** **increase**
vb
[iŋkrementare]
Loro avevano intenzione di incrementare il budget militare.
-They intended to increase the military budget.

8040 **capitalista** **capitalist**
il/la
[kapitalista]
Joe è un capitalista clientelare.
-Joe is a crony capitalist.

8041 **paragonabile** **comparable**
adj
[paragonabile]
Se ne deduce che la crisi attuale è paragonabile al grande crollo del 1929.
-This suggests that the current crisis is comparable to the great crash of 1929.

8042 **avvistamento** **sighting**
il
[avvistamento]
Agiremo per ogni avvistamento di questi uomini.
-We will act on any sighting of these men.

8043 **infortunio** **accident**
il
[infortunjo]
Il lungo viaggio aggravò il suo infortunio.
-The long trip aggravated her injury.

8044 **evoluto** **advanced**
adj
[evoluto]
Joe sembra evoluto.
-Joe seems sophisticated.

8045 **metropoli** le [metropoli]

metropolis

Con il sindaco Ludwig Landmann, Francoforte si trasformò in una metropoli.

-During Ludwig Landmann's time as mayor, Frankfurt developed into a metropolis.

8046 **bobina** la [bobina]

coil|reel

– quella schifosa bobina di compressione.

-Somebody won't replace that compression coil.

8047 **reperto** il [reperto]

find

Intanto, c'è un reperto bloccato da qualche parte tra Francoforte e Glasgow.

-Meanwhile, there's an exhibit stuck somewhere between Frankfurt and Glasgow.

8048 **attributo** gli [attributo]

attribute

L'attributo language="JavaScipt" è un attributo vecchio e obsoleto del tag dello scrip.

-The language="JavaScipt" attribute is an old and deprecated script tag attribute.

8049 **autonomia** la [autonomja]

autonomy

La mancanza di vera autonomia nelle entrate esclude una reale autonomia nelle spese.

-Without real autonomy in income, there will not be real autonomy in expenditure.

8050 **ducato** il [dukato]

duchy|ducat

L'ultima nazione della fila è la Litavia, ovvero il Gran Ducato di Lituania.

-The last in this column of nations is Litavia that is, the Grand Duchy of Lithuania.

8051 **libellula** la [libellula]

dragonfly

Ogni volta che vediamo una libellula sembra di essere più vicini a trovare papà.

-Every time we've seen a dragonfly, it feels like we've been getting closer to finding dad.

8052 **balistico** adj [balistiko]

ballistic

Entrambi con numeri di serie cancellati e nessun riscontro balistico.

-Both had defaced serial numbers and no ballistic matches.

8053 **prestigioso** adj [prestidʒozo]

prestigious

Abbiamo un palazzo prestigioso, ma non disponiamo di una linea ad alta velocità.

-There is a prestigious building here but no high-speed rail service.

8054 **orca** la [orka]

grampus

I'd gone up to photograph Orcas, and we had looked for a week, and we hadn't seen a damn Orca.

-Ero a fotografare le orche, e le cercavamo da una settimana ma non avevamo visto una maledetta orca.

8055 **criceto** il [kritʃeto]

hamster

Joe ricevette un criceto per Natale.

-Joe got a hamster for Christmas.

8056 **eletto** adj [eletto]

elect

Molto è stato fatto del fatto che un afro-americano di nome Barack Hussein Obama potesse essere eletto Presidente. Ma la mia storia personale non è così unica.

-Much has been made of the fact that an African-American with the name Barack Hussein Obama could be elected President. But my personal story is not so unique.

8057 **ascensione** **ascension|mounting**
la
[aʃʃensjone]
Questa ascensione può avvenire anche in presenza di sfide fisiche estreme.
-This upward ascension can happen even in the face of extreme physical challenges.

8058 **strumentale** **instrumental**
adj
[strumentale]
Una previsione cinica, strumentale a giustificare una guerra sbagliata ed illegale.
-A cynical forecast, instrumental in justifying a wrong and illegal war.

8059 **paterno** **paternal**
adj
[paterno]
Il tuo piano creativo e paterno?
-Your creative, fatherly plan?

8060 **memoriale** **memorial**
il
[memorjale]
I have also seen the memorial there and I have talked to the people.
-Ho visitato anche il monumento commemorativo e ho parlato con la popolazione.

8061 **sorellastra** **stepsister**
la
[sorellastra]
Diane è anche la tua sorellastra, George.
-Diane is your half-sister too, George.

8062 **civilizzazione** **civilization**
la
[tʃiviliddzattsjone]
Il Medio Oriente è la culla della civilizzazione.
-The Middle East is the cradle of civilization.

8063 **emanare** **issue|emanate**
vb
[emanare]
Naturalmente non ha senso emanare un regolamento che è rilevante esclusivamente per i passeggeri transfrontalieri.
-It obviously makes no sense to enact a regulation that is only relevant to international passengers.

8064 **scapolare** **scapulary**
lo
[skapolare]
È per lo scapolare, signore.
-It's the scapular, sir.

8065 **contagio** **contagion**
il
[kontadʒo]
Il contagio è avvenuto quell'anno.
-The plague occurred that year.

8066 **comfort** **comfort**
il
[komfort]
Il meccanismo di regolazione dell'altezza incorporato assicura il massimo comfort.
-Built-in height adjustment provides added comfort.

8067 **parodia** **parody|send-up**
la
[parodja]
E' una parodia della democrazia. Una democrazia senza popolo.
-It is a parody of democracy: government by the people, but without the people.

8068 **piedistallo** **pedestal**
il
[pjedistallo]
Mettetela su un piedistallo e veneratela.
-Put it on a pedestal and worship it.

8069 **implacabile** **implacable**
adj
[implakabile]
Voglio rendere omaggio alla sua ricerca implacabile della verità.
-I want to pay tribute to her relentless pursuit of truth.

8070 **calzamaglia** **tights**

	la	Sta indossando una calzamaglia.
	[kaltsamaʎʎa]	-She's wearing tights.
8071	**esiliato**	**exile**
	il	Napoleone fu esiliato sull'Isola d'Elba nel 1814.
	[eziljato]	-Napoleon was exiled to the island of Elba in 1814.
8072	**ippopotamo**	**hippopotamus**
	il	Il problema, ovviamente, é la "generazione ippopotamo".
	[ippopotamo]	-In contrast, of course, we have the Hippo Generation.
8073	**grammofono**	**gramophone**
	il	Vogliamo farci un grammofono, compagno sottotenente.
	[grammofono]	-We want to assemble a gramophone, Comrade Lieutenant.
8074	**trasfusione**	**transfusion**
	la	Controlla la compatibilità del sangue per la trasfusione.
	[trasfuzjone]	-Check the suitability of the blood for transfusion.
8075	**allagare**	**flood**
	vb	Durante la costruzione si è già allagato al pianterreno.
	[allagare]	-It has already flooded on the ground floor during construction.
8076	**lega**	**alloy**
	la	L'ottone è una lega di rame e zinco.
	[lega]	-Brass is an alloy of copper and zinc.
8077	**poligono**	**polygon**
	il	Subito dopo la telefonata sono venuto al poligono.
	[poligono]	-Immediately after the call, I came to the shooting range.
8078	**pasticcino**	**pastry**
	il	Prenda qualche pasticcino danese.
	[pastittʃino]	-Get some Danish pastries.
8079	**consacrare**	**consecrate|devote**
	vb	Tu lo hai respinto e ripudiato, ti sei adirato contro il tuo consacrato.
	[konsakrare]	-"Yet you have rejected and spurned and been enraged at your anointed."
8080	**vantaggioso**	**advantageous|profitable**
	adj	Credo che il multiculturalismo sia vantaggioso per una nazione.
	[vantaddʒozo]	-I believe that multiculturalism is beneficial for a nation.
8081	**manovrare**	**maneuver|handle**
	vb	Manovrare qcs per metterlo in posizione.
	[manovrare]	-To maneuver sth into position.
8082	**contagiare**	**infect**
	vb	Ero finalmente pronto per contagiare chi mi stava attorno con quella repellente piaga sociale che è il razzismo.
	[kontadʒare]	-At last, I was prepared to infect everyone around me with a virulent strain of the social disease that is racism.
8083	**sdraio**	**deckchair**
	le	Sentii il rumore delle onde, uscii e mi sdraiai, con il volto diretto verso la costa, sul prato falciato.
	[zdrajo]	-I heard the murmur of the waves, ran outside and lay down on the freshly mown meadow, my face turned to the sea.
8084	**siccità**	**drought**
	la	È francamente difficile inserire il tema della valutazione della siccità.
	[sittʃit'a]	-The issue of drought assessment is - quite frankly - relatively difficult to incorporate.
8085	**idem**	**idem; ditto; ideally**

prn; il; adv | La risoluzione chiede la totale applicazione del principio ne bis in idem.
[idem] | -The resolution calls for full application of the ne bis in idem principle.

8086 **tagliente** **sharp|cutting**
adj
[taʎʎente]
Chiunque può mettere le mani su un oggetto tagliente.
-Anyone can get their hands on something sharp.

8087 **inesistente** **non-existent**
adj
[inezistente]
La capacità dei governi di far fronte alla crisi è del tutto inesistente.
-The capacity of governments for confronting this crisis is totally non-existent.

8088 **assaporare** **savor**
vb
[assaporare]
Allora lasciaci assaporare la tua essenza.
-Then let us taste what you are made of.

8089 **presentabile** **presentable**
adj
[prezentabile]
Renditi presentabile.
-Make yourself presentable.

8090 **ritaglio** **cut-out|clipping**
il
[ritaʎʎo]
Gli farò ritagliare lettere dal cartoncino per la lavagna."
-I'll have him cut out letters out of construction paper for the board."

8091 **silenziatore** **silencer**
il
[silentsjatore]
Ho fatto quel silenziatore appositamente per Memmo Fierro.
-I made that silencer especially for Memmo Fierro, like, six years ago.

8092 **pulcino** **chick**
il
[pultʃino]
Il pulcino pigola.
-The chick peeps.

8093 **tempia** **temple**
la
[tempja]
Signora Presidente, innanzitutto mi sia permesso, come certo vorreste anche voi, esprimere all'onorevole Simpson il mio dispiacere per la grave ferita alla tempia.
-Madam President, can I first of all, as I am sure you would wish, commiserate with Mr Simpson on his severe temple wound.

8094 **penicillina** **penicillin**
la
[penitʃillina]
Io sono allergico all'aspirina, alla penicillina e ai sulfanilamidi.
-I am allergic to aspirin, penicillin, and sulfa drugs.

8095 **disinfettare** **disinfect**
vb
[dizinfettare]
Il loro rivestimento interno deve essere liscio, facile da lavare, pulire e disinfettare.
-Their internal surfaces must be smooth and easy to wash, clean and disinfect.

8096 **germoglio** **bud|sprout**
il
[dʒermoʎʎo]
In altre parole, i birrai sanno anche come evocare il guasto dai cereali usando germogli e col maltaggio e la torrefazione.
-In other words, the beer-maker knows also how to evoke flavor from the grains by using sprouting and malting and roasting.

8097 **leccapiedi** **toady|flunky**
il/la
[lekkapjedi]
Joe è un bravo leccapiedi.
-Joe is a good kisser.

8098 **sinonimo** **synonymous; synonym**
adj; il
[sinonimo]
C'è un'altra parola per sinonimo?
-Is there another word for synonym?

8099 **remata** **row**

	la [remata]	Ho mandato Mr. e Mrs. Hawkins al mare... per una remata di 48 ore... non torneranno fino a sabato sera. -I've sent Mr. And Mrs. Hawkins away to the seaside... for a 48–hour paddle – they won't be back till Sunday night.
8100	**soprannominare** vb [soprannominare]	**nickname** Qualcuno ha soprannominato questo strumento -eccedendo, credo - scareboard, ma comunque una certa efficacia penso che possa averla. -Somebody nicknamed this device a " scareboard ', overdoing it in my opinion, but I think it has a certain effectiveness.
8101	**negazione** la [negattsjone]	**denial** Né l'esperanto né l'interlingua utilizzano la doppia negazione. -Neither Esperanto nor Interlingua employ double negative.
8102	**virtuoso** adj; il [virtwozo]	**virtuous; virtuoso** Lui è un uomo virtuoso. -He is a man of virtue.
8103	**rimedio** il [rimedjo]	**remedy|help** La legge ha lo scopo di porre rimedio a decenni di discriminazione nei confronti delle minoranze etniche del paese. -The law is meant to redress decades of discrimination against the country's ethnic minorities.
8104	**perseveranza** la [perseverantsa]	**perseverance** L'insegnante disse: "Al di sopra di tutto, ciò che è necessario per il successo è la perseveranza." -The teacher said: "Above all, what is necessary for success is perseverance."
8105	**bruciatura** la [brutʃatura]	**burn|scorch** Avere una bruciatura sulla mano. -To have a burn on one's hand.
8106	**pressa** la [pressa]	**press** Ha comprato una pressa per proiettili, dei bossoli. -He bought a bullet press. Casings.
8107	**emittente** la; adj [emittente]	**issuer; issuing** In linea di principio sosteniamo l'idea di lasciare all'emittente la facoltà di scelta. -We fundamentally support the idea of issuer choice.
8108	**inquietare** vb [iŋkwjetare]	**worry** L'introduzione del concetto di sicurezza nazionale costituisce uno sviluppo inquietante. -The introduction of the concept of national security is a worrying development.
8109	**crasso** adj [krasso]	**crass** Una volta ho lasciato lì la borsa e 60 centimetri di intestino crasso. -You know, I once left a purse and 2 feet of my large intestine there.
8110	**coincidere** vb [kointʃidere]	**coincide** Chiaramente, ricerca e innovazione non coincidono e su questo punto siamo d'accordo. -Research and innovation are clearly not the same thing and we agree with you very clearly.
8111	**deforme** adj [deforme]	**deformed|crooked** First, the emasculation of DG Development will deform not reform external assistance.

-Innanzitutto, l'indebolimento della DG DEV avrà l'effetto di deformare anziché riformare gli aiuti esterni.

8112 **malfunzionamento** **malfunction**
il
[malfuntsjonamento]
L'obiettivo del programma consiste nel far fronte al malfunzionamento dei mercati dei titoli e nel ripristinare adeguatamente il meccanismo di trasmissione della politica monetaria.
-The objective of this programme is to address the malfunctioning of securities markets and to restore an appropriate monetary policy transmission mechanism.

8113 **gotico** **Gothic**
adj
[gotiko]
"Il castello di Otranto" è il primo romanzo gotico in inglese, e ha fissato gli standard di tutto il genere.
-"The Castle of Otranto" is the first gothic novel in English, and it set the standards of the whole genre.

8114 **scolo** **drain**
lo
[skolo]
Tagliare le melanzane a fette di ½ cm circa, salarle leggermente e lasciarle scolare per un'ora circa.
-Cut the aubergines into ½ cm slices, sprinkle with salt and leave to drain for about 1 hour.

8115 **poggiare** **rest|lean**
vb
[poddʒare]
Poggiando su Dio, egli resta proteso, sempre e dovunque, verso ciò che è bello, buono e vero.
-Leaning on God, they continue to reach out, always and everywhere, for all that is beautiful, good and true.

8116 **pesticida** **pesticide**
il
[pestitʃida]
Nel Regno Unito, è usato un pesticida per il mais che contiene circa 15 sostanze attive.
-In the UK a maize pesticide is used that contains around 15 active substances.

8117 **situare** **place|situate**
vb
[sitware]
Ad Hannover c'è uno centro conferenze fra i più moderni, situato direttamente nell'area della fiera, con infrastrutture eccellenti ed impianti per l'interpretazione simultanea.
-Hanover has an extremely modern conference centre which is right there on the exhibition site, and it has excellent infrastructure with full interpreting facilities.

8118 **bandierina** **pennant**
la
[bandjerina]
Avanti, ognuno prenda una bandierina.
-So come on, everybody, take a flag.

8119 **limpido** **clear|limpid**
adj
[limpido]
È limpido.
-It's clear.

8120 **stormo** **flock**
lo
[stormo]
Essere attaccati da uno stormo di storni.
-Being attacked by a flock of starlings.

8121 **larva** **larva**
la
[larva]
I will briefly recall the fact that transgenic maize has been made resistant to the larva of a crop-devastating insect.
-Ricorderò brevemente che il mais transgenico è stato reso resistente alla larva di un insetto devastatore.

8122 **contrabbandiere** **smuggler**

il
[kontrabbandjere]
Un comunicato stampa rilasciato in agosto dall'Ufficio europeo per la lotta antifrode riportava la condanna di un grosso contrabbandiere di sigarette negli Stati Uniti.
-A European Anti-Fraud Office press release in August told of the conviction of a major cigarette smuggler in the US.

8123 **nervosismo** **nervousness|jitters**
il
[nervozismo]
Ricorda, il nervosismo è solo eccitazione rivolta verso te stesso.
-Remember that nervousness is excitement turned inward.

8124 **tovaglia** **cloth**
la
[tovaʎʎa]
La tovaglia è nell'armadio.
-The tablecloth is in the cabinet.

8125 **barricata** **barricade**
la
[barrikata]
Due settimane fa ho disattivato la barricata sul retro.
-Two weeks ago, I came here and I disabled his back barricade.

8126 **globulare** **globular**
adj
[globulare]
E quella è la protezione intorno al grasso globulare.
-And that's the shell around that globular fat.

8127 **strofa** **stanza**
la
[strofa]
Temevo avresti cantato un'altra strofa.
-I was just afraid you'd sing another verse.

8128 **targhetta** **plate**
la
[targetta]
La targhetta e le iscrizioni vengono apposte dal costruttore o dal suo mandatario.
-That plate and those markings must be affixed by the manufacturer or his authorized representative.

8129 **scultore** **sculptor**
lo
[skultore]
Non puoi creare qualcosa dal nulla come uno scultore?"
-Can you make something from nothing as a sculptor?"

8130 **fifa** **funk**
la
[fifa]
Commissario, la FIFA e il CFO si stanno facendo un baffo del diritto comunitario.
-FIFA and the CFO are making a mockery of European Union law.

8131 **flashback** **flashback**
i
[flasbakk]
Inizierò con un flashback che vi riporterà nel 1933.
-I will begin with a flashback to the year 1933.

8132 **derivato** **derivative; offshoot**
adj; il
[derivato]
Ma il valore potenziale ancora maggiore è tutta l'incredibile tecnologia derivata che potrebbe scaturire da questo progetto.
-But potentially more important than this is the tremendous value of the spin-off technology that can come from this project.

8133 **lavorazione** **processing**
la
[lavorattsjone]
La loro massima abilità è stata la lavorazione del legno.
-Their highest skill was woodworking.

8134 **infinità** **infinity**
le
[infinit'a]
E improvvisamente, in questo quadro dell'infinità, Bharat si sentì insignificante.
-And suddenly, in this canvas of infinity, Bharat felt insignificant.

8135 **indiscreto** **indiscreet|prying**
adj
[indiskreto]
Joe è indiscreto.
-Joe is indiscreet.

8136 **acquatico** **aquatic**

adj | Andiamo al parco acquatico.
[akkwatiko] | -Let's go to the waterpark.

8137 **lavata** **wash**
la
[lavata]
Lei non si è ancora lavata le mani, vero?
-You haven't washed your hands yet, have you?

8138 **scarto** **waste**
lo
[skarto]
Sbagliare lo scarto.
-To discard the wrong card.

8139 **cucchiaino** **teaspoon**
il
[kukkjaino]
Lei ha mescolato il tè con un cucchiaino d'oro.
-She stirred her tea with a little gold spoon.

8140 **sudiciume** **dirt|filth**
la
[suditʃume]
La stiamo ripulendo da feccia e sudiciume.
-So we're cleansing the combat zone of scum and filth.

8141 **canzoncina** **ditty**
la
[kantsontʃina]
Quando eri malata ti cantavo quella canzoncina.
-When you were sick, I'd sing you that little song.

8142 **ingorgo** **jam**
il
[iŋgorgo]
L'incidente causò un ingorgo.
-The accident caused a traffic jam.

8143 **nord-est** **northeast**
il
[nordest]
Il pollame arrivava dalla East Anglia e così via, verso la parte nord-est.
-Poultry was coming in from East Anglia and so on, to the northeast.

8144 **tribordo** **starboard**
il
[tribordo]
tutta a tribordo
-hard a-starboard!

8145 **estradizione** **extradition**
le
[estradittsjone]
Hanno presentato richiesta di asilo e la Lituania esige la loro estradizione.
-They are applying for asylum and Lithuania is demanding their extradition.

8146 **sassofono** **saxophone**
il
[sassofono]
Forse posso trasformarlo in un sassofono.
-Maybe I can make it into a saxophone.

8147 **rivestito** **clad**
adj
[rivestito]
Fu solo nel XIV secolo che un pittore italiano vide nel grembo una sorta di tempio greco, rivestito di carne e abiti.
-It was not until the 14th century that an Italian painter recognized the lap as a Grecian temple, upholstered in flesh and cloth.

8148 **catrame** **tar**
il
[katrame]
Dobbiamo incentivare la produzione di tabacco di qualità, con un minor tenore di catrame.
-We must encourage the production of quality tobacco with lower tar levels.

8149 **fava** **bean**
la
[fava]
Prendi due piccioni con una fava.
-Kill two birds with one stone.

8150 **citofono** **intercom**
il
[tʃitofono]
Alex, se puoi sentirmi, usa il citofono della nave.
-Alex, if you can hear me, use the ship's intercom.

8151 **riconquistare** **recapture**

vb | Lei deve impegnarsi a riconquistare la fiducia di questo Parlamento.
[rikoŋkwistare] | -You must show commitment if you are to win back the confidence of Parliament.

8152 **rammollire** **soften**
vb
[rammollire]
Per ottenere il massimo contatto con la pelle, può risultare necessario riscaldare i solidi a 30 oC per sciogliere o rammollire la sostanza di prova o macinarli per ottenere grani o polveri.
-In order to achieve maximum contact with the skin, solids may need to be warmed to 30 oC to melt or soften the test substance, or ground to produce a granular material or powder.

8153 **preferibilmente** **preferably**
adv
[preferibilmente]
Noi vogliamo un assistente, preferibilmente qualcuno con esperienza.
-We want an assistant, preferably someone with experience.

8154 **merlo** **blackbird|merlon**
il
[merlo]
"Povero merlo!", disse Pinocchio al Gatto. "Perché l'hai ucciso?"
-"Poor blackbird!" said Pinocchio to the Cat. "Why did you kill him?"

8155 **radiografia** **radiography|radiograph**
la
[radjografja]
Trattamento dell'ulcera duodenale e gastrica confermata tramite endoscopia o radiografia.
-Treatment of duodenal and gastric ulcer confirmed by endoscopy or radiography.

8156 **sculacciare** **spank**
vb
[skulattʃare]
Chissà, se sei fortunato, te lo lascio sculacciare dopo cena.
-Well, maybe if you're lucky, I'll let you spank it after dinner.

8157 **suonatore** **player**
il
[swonatore]
È il suonatore di flauto dai polsi fortissimi.
-He's the flute player with the strongest wrist.

8158 **lebbroso** **leper; leprous**
il; adj
[lebbrozo]
Non siete un lebbroso, signora.
-You're no leper, Signora.

8159 **unanime** **unanimous**
adj
[unanime]
Per questo motivo il progetto della Tanzania e la costruzione di una fabbrica di armi meritano la nostra attenzione unanime.
-That is why the Tanzanian project and the construction of an arms factory deserve our undivided attention.

8160 **mozzafiato** **breathtaking**
adj
[mottsafjato]
La bellezza artistica del giardino è davvero mozzafiato.
-The artistic beauty of the garden is really breathtaking.

8161 **compassionevole** **compassionate**
adj
[kompassjonevole]
Lei ha dunque inventato la Commissione del capitalismo compassionevole.
-You are therefore inventing the compassionate capitalism Commission.

8162 **bisognoso** **needy**
adj
[bizoɲɲozo]
Lei è bisognoso.
-You're needy.

8163 **euforia** **euphoria**
le
[euforja]
Signor Presidente, si percepisce molta euforia riguardante Galileo.
-Mr President, there is a great deal of euphoria regarding Galileo.

8164 **danneggiato** **damaged**
adj
[danneddʒato]
L'antico manoscritto è stato danneggiato in un incendio.
-The ancient manuscript was damaged in a fire.

8165 **neutrone** il [neutrone]

neutron

La reazione in fondo, quello è litio 6, più un neutrone, darà altro elio, più trizio.
-That reaction at the bottom, that's lithium 6, plus a neutron, will give you more helium, plus tritium.

8166 **tampone** il [tampone]

buffer|pad

Pompate le acque grige al serbatoio anteriore, faranno da tampone.
-Pump the grey water to the forward tank, they'll act as a buffer.

8167 **amianto** il [amjanto]

asbestos

Potrebbe esserci dentro piombo, o amianto.
-That could have lead in it, or asbestos.

8168 **empatia** le [empatja]

empathy

Ho percepito più empatia alla Motorizzazione.
-I've felt more empathy at the DMV.

8169 **diacono** il [djakono]

deacon

Il diacono ha detto di aver visto Montez litigare con Santoya.
-He said the deacon knew of Montez showing up and arguing with Santoya.

8170 **sabotare** vb [sabotare]

sabotage

Tutti i paesi avrebbero infatti potuto sabotare la decisione comune, nessuno però l'ha fatto.
-Every country had the opportunity to torpedo any collective decision - nobody did so, however.

8171 **tetro** adj [tetro]

gloomy|dark

Il loro mondo è tetro, solitario e senza speranza.
-Their world is bleak, lonely and hopeless.

8172 **rallentatore** il [rallentatore]

slow motion

Quanto mi piacerebbe guardarla mangiare una pesca a rallentatore.
-I'd love to watch you eat a peach in slow motion.

8173 **trivella** la [trivella]

auger

E' il foro geologico più profondo mai trivellato.
-So it's the deepest geological bore hole ever drilled.

8174 **ibrido** adj [ibrido]

hybrid

Questo è un ibrido.
-This is a hybrid.

8175 **condizionatore** il [kondittsjonatore]

conditioner

(Risate) "Qualcosa non va col condizionatore -- odore di cinghie bruciate nell'aria."
-(Laughter) "Something's wrong with the air conditioner -- smell of burning V-belts in the air."

8176 **tossina** la [tossina]

toxin

E' pericoloso perché produce una tossina e quella tossina é rilasciata quando il batterio entra nell'intestino.
-It's harmful because it produces a toxin, and that toxin is released when the organism gets into our intestinal tract.

8177 **chemioterapia** la [kemjoterapja]

chemotherapy

Purtroppo la chemioterapia non è sufficiente.
-Unfortunately, chemotherapy isn't going to be enough.

8178 **surrogato** il; adj [surrogato]

surrogate; ersatz

Non va utilizzata come un surrogato di normative auspicabili che non sono state adottate.

-It should not be used as a substitute for desirable but unadopted legislation.

8179 **sfratto** **evicted**
lo
[sfratto]
Abbiamo ricevuto un avviso di sfratto.
-We received an eviction notice.

8180 **molestare** **harass|annoy**
vb
[molestare]
Smettetela di molestare Joe.
-Stop harassing Joe.

8181 **lucidità** **lucidity**
la
[lutʃidit'a]
Non è di meno Europa che abbiamo bisogno; ci serve più Europa, un'Europa che si ispiri alla verità, alla lucidità e al senso di responsabilità.
-It is not less Europe that we need, it is more Europe, but a Europe of truth, clear-headedness and responsibility.

8182 **spargimento** **scatter**
lo
[spardʒimento]
Ma per un po', lo spargimento del mio seme dovrà aspettare.
-But the further spreading of my baby gravy will have to wait.

8183 **perplesso** **puzzled|perplexed**
adj
[perplesso]
Joe rimase perplesso.
-Joe remained puzzled.

8184 **bracciale** **bracelet**
il
[brattʃale]
E parlando di leghe... la vittima indossava questo bracciale di metallo.
-Speaking of alloys, our victim was wearing this metal bracelet.

8185 **evenienza** **eventuality**
la
[evenjentsa]
Samir li userà come scudi umani nell'evenienza di un attacco frontale.
-Samir will want to use them as human shields in the event of a frontal attack.

8186 **samaritano** **Samaritan**
il
[samaritano]
Con amore di samaritano curava i poveri e i senzatetto.
-With the love of the Good Samaritan, he cared for the poor and homeless.

8187 **illudere** **deceive|delude oneself**
vb
[illudere]
Non dobbiamo però illudere noi stessi, né gli altri.
-But we should delude neither ourselves nor others.

8188 **quartetto** **quartet**
il
[kwartetto]
Vorrei menzionare alcuni aspetti fondamentali di questo quarto accordo quadro.
-This is the fourth agreement between the Commission and Parliament.

8189 **elogio** **praise**
Il
[elodʒo]
Joe pronunciò l'elogio.
-Joe delivered the eulogy.

8190 **proiettare** **project|screen**
vb
[projettare]
La campagna elettorale bavarese proietta ombre davvero lunghe.
-The Bavarian election campaign casts a long shadow.

8191 **altruista** **selfless; altruist**
adj; il/la
[altrwista]
Una proiezione che supera l'egoismo e tende all'altro, è altruista, non è estranea, per es., al pensiero di Freud.
-A projection which overcomes selfishness and tends toward the other is altruistic; this is not extraneous, e.g., to Freud's thinking.

8192 **adorazione** **adoration|adorability**

le | Il bambino guarda suo padre con l'adorazione negli occhi.
[adorattsjone] | -The child looks up to his father with worship in his eyes.

8193 **pizzicare** | **pinch|pluck**
vb | Tessa, sentirai un po' pizzicare e bruciare, poi l'anestetico farà effetto.
[piddzikare] | -Tessa, there'll be a slight pinch and burn, then the anesthetic will kick in.

8194 **morbillo** | **measles**
il | Lei ha il morbillo.
[morbillo] | -She has the measles.

8195 **fiorellino** | **floret**
il | Lei è solo un fiorellino.
[fjorellino] | -She is just a wallflower.

8196 **appiccare** | **set**
vb | Pensavo di appiccare davvero un incendio.
[appikkare] | -I was thinking of starting a real fire.

8197 **cero** | **candle**
il | Una fabbrica moderna di aerei usa un processo a cera per metalli, o si potrebbe sciogliere della plastica.
[tʃero] | -A state-of-the-art airplane factory rotating metal wax at fixed metal, or you maybe melt some plastic.

8198 **austriaco** | **Austrian; Austrian**
adj; il | Colui che nasce in Austria è austriaco.
[austrjako] | -Whoever is born in Austria, is an Austrian.

8199 **prosciugare** | **drain**
vb | L'altra condizione è che il fondo non debba prosciugare senza limiti di tempo i fondi comunitari.
[proʃʃugare] | -The other condition is that the fund must not create an open-ended drain on Community funds.

8200 **fotogramma** | **still**
il | Ciascun fotogramma del film contiene informazioni che lo descrivono.
[fotogramma] | -Each frame of the movie has information about itself.

8201 **teologia** | **theology**
la | La teologia istituzionale non è la priorità dei cittadini europei.
[teolodʒa] | -Institutional theology is not the priority of the citizens of Europe.

8202 **casto** | **chaste**
Adj | È ancora Lui che forma e plasma l'animo dei chiamati ad una vita di speciale consacrazione, configurandoli a Cristo casto, povero ed obbediente.
[kasto] | -It is also he who forms and moulds the soul of those who are called to a life of special consecration, configuring them to Christ, chaste, poor and obedient.

8203 **ricadere** | **fall|fall back**
vb | Le sciocchezze tendonoa ricadere dolorosamente su coloro che le dicono.
[rikadere] | -Platitudes tend to rebound painfully on those who mouth them.

8204 **tranello** | **trap|game**
il | Farebbe meglio a dirmi dov'è il tranello.
[tranello] | -You better tell me the catch.

8205 **manto** | **mantle**
il | Possibile che sotto il sacro manto d'amicizia...
[manto] | -Is it possible that, beneath the sacred mantle of friendship...

8206 **compimento** | **fulfillment|completion**

il E portata a compimento quasi sempre.
[kompimento] -And to completion most of the time.

8207 **duetto** **duet**
il Io e Richard Hammond vi suoneremo ora un duetto.
[dwetto] -Richard Hammond and I will now perform a duet.

8208 **allineare** **align|line**
vb Ma è inoltre vero che occorreva allineare questo Atto elettorale alle varie e successive modifiche dei Trattati.
[allineare] -It is also true that it was necessary to adapt this Electoral Act to the various and successive modifications of the Treaties.

8209 **imparziale** **impartial**
adj Sei imparziale.
[impartsjale] -You're unbiased.

8210 **fosco** **dark|gloomy**
adj Tracciare un quadro fosco della situazione.
[fosko] -To paint a gloomy picture of the situation.

8211 **svergognato** **shameless**
adj Lei è svergognato.
[zvergoɲɲato] -You're shameless.

8212 **affliggere** **afflict|plague**
vb La piaga della violenza - spesso organizzata - affligge gli incontri calcistici internazionali da anni.
[affliddʒere] -The scourge of violence - often organised violence - has plagued international football for years.

8213 **manna** **manna**
la Il denaro arrivò come una manna dal cielo.
[manna] -The money came like manna from heaven.

8214 **diagramma** **diagram**
il Questo diagramma renderà chiaro che cosa intendo.
[djagramma] -This diagram will illustrate what I mean.

8215 **rinfrescare** **refresh|cool**
vb Dovrebbe rinfrescare un po' le sue nozioni giuridiche.
[rinfreskare] -He should brush up on his legal knowledge.

8216 **carillon** **carillon**
il Mi hai mentito riguardo al carillon.
[karillon] -You lied to me about the music box.

8217 **ritornello** **refrain**
il Come nel ritornello, quando i due ex capiscono che non dovrebbero tornare insieme.
[ritornello] -Like in the chorus, when the two exes realize that they shouldn't go back to a romantic place.

8218 **lanciafiamme** **flame thrower**
il Mostrammo il mio primo lanciatore di lame rotanti e una sedia lanciafiamme.
[lantʃafjamme] -We had my first saw blade launcher and we had a flamethrower chair.

8219 **marchiare** **mark|stamp**
vb Tuttavia, marchiare un'intera nazione in questo modo è intollerabile.
[markjare] -However, branding a whole nation like this is unacceptable.

8220 **strategico** **strategic**

adj
[stratedʒiko]
Partenariato strategico UE-Brasile - Partenariato strategico UE-Messico (discussione)
-EU-Brazil Strategic Partnership - Mexico Strategic Partnership (debate)

8221 **indennità** **bonus**
le
[indennit'a]
Sembra altresì essere incerta la classificazione dell'indennità.
-There also seems to be uncertainty about the classification of the allowance.

8222 **direttivo** **directive|executive**
adj
[direttivo]
Sono nel direttivo della chiesa, quindi lo posso organizzare in fretta.
-I'm on the church board, so I can arrange to have it happen quickly.

8223 **ubbidire** **obey**
vb
[ubbidire]
Io devo ubbidire.
-I must obey.

8224 **insanguinare** **bathe in blood**
vb
[insaŋgwinare]
C'è questo casino insanguinato e terribile E poi cosa ne viene fuori?
-Where there is this bloody, awful mess happens. ~~~ And then what comes out of it?

8225 **adempiere** **fulfill|perform**
vb
[adempjere]
La politica agricola generale deve quindi adempiere anche una funzione preventiva.
-General agricultural policy therefore also has to fulfil a preventative function.

8226 **organizzatore** **organizer; organizing**
gli; adj
[organiddzatore]
Questa è l'opportunità per essere un organizzatore di comunità.
-This is all the opportunity about being a community organizer.

8227 **brace** **embers**
la
[bratʃe]
Salta dalla padella alla brace.
-Jump out of the frying pan into the fire.

8228 **assunto** **recruit**
il
[assunto]
Io sono assunto?
-Am I hired?

8229 **sfogare** **vent**
vb
[sfogare]
Alti tassi di disoccupazione e bassi salari hanno spinto ancora una volta la gente comune a sfogare il proprio malcontento in manifestazioni di protesta; questa volta è avvenuto in Uzbekistan.
-High levels of unemployment and low wages have once again prompted ordinary people to give vent to their displeasure in protest actions, this time in Uzbekistan.

8230 **miscuglio** **mixture|blend**
il
[miskuʎʎo]
L'aria è un miscuglio di vari gas.
-Air is a mixture of various gases.

8231 **abbronzare** **tan**
vb
[abbrontsare]
Puoi abbronzare la pelle, ma gli organi marciscono.
-You can tan skin, but organs rot.

8232 **orologeria** **watchmaking**
le
[orolodʒerja]
Questi aggeggi sono solo luci e orologeria.
-These things are just lights and clockwork.

8233 **chierichetto** **server**
il
[kjeriketto]
Quand'ero chierichetto, respiravo molto incenso, e ho imparato a dire frasi in Latino, ma ho anche avuto tempo per pensare se la moralità imposta da mia madre si applicava a tutti.

-As an altar boy, I breathed in a lot of incense, and I learned to say phrases in Latin, but I also had time to think about whether my mother's top-down morality applied to everybody.

8234 **altea** la [altea] — **marsh-mallow**
Per la maggior parte bile, ma siamo riusciti a identificare anche altea comune.
-Mostly bile, but we were able to identify althea officinalis.

8235 **tanica** la [tanika] — **tank**
Il costo dell'installazione a posteriori su ciascun veicolo non dovrebbe superare i 100-105 euro, pari al prezzo di una tanica di benzina.
-The cost of retrofitting each vehicle should not exceed 100-150 euros, which is equivalent to one tank of petrol.

8236 **proletariato** il [proletarjato] — **proletariat**
In questo modo, hanno dimostrato quanto avevano torto coloro che sostenevano che il proletariato non avesse patria.
-In so doing they proved those who believed that the proletariat has no fatherland to be mistaken.

8237 **fionda** la [fjonda] — **sling**
Davide uccise Golia con una fionda.
-David killed Goliath with a sling.

8238 **soldatino** il [soldatino] — **toy soldier**
Senti, non sono più il tuo soldatino!
-Listen, I'm not your toy soldier anymore!

8239 **sciacquone** lo [ʃakkwone] — **flushing device**
Joe non dimenticò di tirare lo sciacquone.
-Joe didn't forget to flush the toilet.

8240 **cottura** la [kottura] — **burning**
Mi piacciono le bistecche a media cottura.
-I like my steak medium.

8241 **polmonare** adj [polmonare] — **pulmonary**
La malattia polmonare ostruttiva cronica.
-Chronic obstructive pulmonary disease.

8242 **pestilenza** la [pestilentsa] — **pestilence**
Migliaia di persone morirono durante la pestilenza.
-Thousands of people died during the plague.

8243 **svendita** la [zvendita] — **sale**
Non piace la svendita della sovranità politica e anche monetaria.
-They dislike the selling-off of political and also monetary sovereignty.

8244 **portoricano** adj; il [portorikano] — **Puerto Rican; Puerto Rican**
Jeff, parlami di questo portoricano.
-So, Jeff, tell me about this Puerto Rican.

8245 **lingotto** il [liŋgotto] — **ingot**
20.000, ma non un lingotto di più.
-20,000, but not an ingot more.

8246 **zeta** la [dzeta] — **zed|zeta**
Stasera diventerete confratelli del kappa zeta nu.
-Tonight, you pledges become members of kappa zeta nu.

8247 **psichico** adj [psikiko] — **psychic|mental**
Dovrebbe essere un detective psichico.
-He should be a psychic detective.

8248 **termico** — **thermal**

adj Attivazione scanner termico per verificare se ci sono altre persone.
[termiko] -Activating thermal imaging to confirm other occupants.

8249 **emiro** **emir**
il L'emiro Jaber del Kuwait, la famiglia reale saudita?
[emiro] -Emir Jaber of Kuwait or the Wahhabite family of Saudi Arabia?

8250 **benigno** **benign|genial**
adj Il tumore cha hai nella gamba non è compatibile con un tumore benigno.
[beniɲɲo] -"The tumor in your leg is not consistent with a benign tumor."

8251 **diaframma** **diaphragm|baffle**
il Mi sorprende che non metta il diaframma.
[djaframma] -I'm surprised he doesn't wear the diaphragm.

8252 **dormiglione** **sleepyhead**
il Sono un dormiglione.
[dormiʎʎone] -I'm a late riser.

8253 **supernova** **supernova**
la Tutto quello che serve è che una supernova espolda a pochi anni luce di distanza e saremo tutti morti!
[supernova] -All it takes is for a supernova to go off a few light years away, and we'll all be dead!

8254 **ipermercato** **hypermarket**
il Per ogni posto di lavoro creato all'interno di un ipermercato, se ne perdono da cinque a otto nell'area ad esso circostante.
[ipermerkato] -For every job created in a hypermarket, five to eight are lost in the surrounding area.

8255 **rivoltella** **revolver**
la Appena entrato in Convento mi minacciò con la rivoltella se non tornavo a casa.
[rivoltella] -As soon as I entered the Convent threatened with the revolver if not back home.

8256 **elettrone** **electron**
il Non ha dimensioni per definizione, come un elettrone, stranamente.
[elettrone] -It's by definition dimensionless, like an electron, oddly enough.

8257 **potabile** **drinking|potable**
adj Quanta acqua potabile ci rimane?
[potabile] -How much drinking water do we have left?

8258 **traffico** **traffic**
il Avevo un appuntamento alle 2:30, ma sono rimasto imbottigliato nel traffico e non sono potuto arrivare in tempo.
[traffiko] -I had an appointment at 2:30, but I got caught in traffic and couldn't get there in time.

8259 **sterminare** **exterminate**
vb Ecco perché voleva sterminare i pazzi come te.
[sterminare] -That's why he wanted to exterminate lunatics like you.

8260 **novello** **new|early**
adj Il nuovo governo greco, che quando era all'opposizione disapprovava questi procedimenti penali, se ne sta lavando le mani come un novello Ponzio Pilato.
[novello] -The new Greek Government which, when in opposition, said that it disagreed with these prosecutions, is keeping quiet like a new Pontius Pilate.

8261 **perpetuo** **perpetual**

adj
[perpetwo]
Non esiste il moto perpetuo né in fisica né in economia.
-There is no such thing as perpetual motion either in physics or in economics.

8262 **renna** **reindeer**
la
[renna]
Uso il termine 'sindrome della renna?, che molti colleghi mi hanno già sentito impiegare.
-I use the term 'the reindeer syndrome ', which many colleagues will have heard me say before.

8263 **ciocca** **lock**
la
[tʃokka]
Qualche settimana dopo, diceva, suo figlio stava giocando con una ciocca dei capelli di sua madre, ed ha notato che c'era qualche goccia d'acqua nei capelli.
-A few weeks later, he said that his son was playing with a lock of his mother's hair, and he noticed that there were some drops of water on the hair.

8264 **pesco** **peach**
il
[pesko]
Ho piantato un pesco nel mio giardino.
-I planted a peach tree in my garden.

8265 **indulgenza** **indulgence|pardon**
le
[induldʒentsa]
Ce la fa Lochhead a suscitare la nostra indulgenza?
-Does Lochhead manage to arouse our sympathy?

8266 **strapazzare** **scramble|mistreat**
vb
[strapattsare]
Ho le uova da strapazzare.
-I have to scramble the eggs.

8267 **davanzale** **sill**
il
[davantsale]
La bionda ha davvero un bel davanzale.
-The blonde girl has a really nice cleavage.

8268 **brevemente** **briefly**
adv
[brevemente]
Vorrei soffermarmi molto brevemente sulla reale sostanza dell'odierno dibattito.
-I would like to concentrate very briefly on what this debate is really about.

8269 **affettare** **slice|affect**
vb
[affettare]
Affettare il salmone marinato abbastanza sottile e ricoprire con le fette l’interno di uno stampo a cupola o semisfera.
-Cut the marinated salmon into fairly thin slices and cover the inside of a cupola-shaped or half-round mould with the slices.

8270 **autrice** **authoress**
le
[autritʃe]
L'autrice del libro solleva molte domande sull'appartenenza.
-The author of the book raises lots of questions about the belonging.

8271 **applicato** **applied; resign oneself**
adj; vb
[applikato]
Molte ditte hanno applicato una giornata lavorativa di otto ore.
-Lots of companies have implemented an eight-hour working day.

8272 **rassegnare** **resign oneself**
vb
[rasseɲɲare]
Ci potremmo rassegnare al fatto che di notte tutti i gatti sono bigi.
-We could resign ourselves to the fact that all cats are grey in the dark.

8273 **affumicare** **smoke**
vb
[affumikare]
Sparano a tutto ciò che si muove che sia più grande di un ratto, lo essiccano o lo affumicano.
-They shoot everything, every single thing that moves that's bigger than a small rat; they sun-dry it or smoke it.

8274 **sgarbato** **rude|impolite**

	adj [zgarbato]	Joe è stato molto sgarbato con Jane. -Joe was very rude to Jane.
8275	**birbante** il [birbante]	**rascal** Perché sei silenzioso, piccolo birbante? -Why are you silent, you little rascal?
8276	**bettola** la [bettola]	**tavern** Non è una bettola, signore. -It's not a dive bar, sir.
8277	**distogliere** vb [distoʎʎere]	**divert|distract** Ho fatto tutto ciò che potevo per distogliere la loro attenzione da te. -I've done everything I could to divert their attention away from you.
8278	**mutilare** vb [mutilare]	**mutilate** Non possiamo convivere con le mine antiuomo, perché distruggono e mutilano nel modo più orribile civili innocenti, loro obiettivo. -We cannot live with land mines because they destroy and maim in the most horrible fashion the innocent civilians they target.
8279	**scocciatura** la [skottʃatura]	**nuisance** è stata una vera scocciatura. -It was a real hassle.
8280	**paletta** la [paletta]	**scoop|shovel** Continuavo ad alzare la paletta solo per strapparle un sorriso. -I kept raising my paddle just to get her to smile at me.
8281	**rispedire** vb [rispedire]	**send back** Renderebbe più facile rispedire i profughi in tali Stati. -It would make it easier to send refugees back to such states.
8282	**sedicesimo** num [seditʃezimo]	**sixteenth** La Commissione ha un importante ruolo da svolgere, ma non è il ruolo di un sedicesimo Stato membro. -There is an important role for the Commission, but it is not the role of a sixteenth Member State.
8283	**placare** vb [plakare]	**appease|calm** Dobbiamo placare questi timori, come la Commissione in effetti ha fatto nella comunicazione. -We have to allay these fears and the Commission has indeed done so in its communication.
8284	**aspirazione** le [aspirattsjone]	**suction|aspiration** Potrebbe rischiare una polmonite da aspirazione*. -Because she might get aspiration pneumonia.
8285	**iarda** la [jarda]	**yard** Lei ha comprato una iarda di tessuto. -She bought a yard of cloth.
8286	**lattaio** il [lattajo]	**milkman** È morto il lattaio. -The milkman died.
8287	**indumento** il [indumento]	**garment** Noleggiò l'indumento per la giornata. -He rented the garment for the day.
8288	**ovile** il [ovile]	**fold|pen** Hai almeno tentato di riportarlo all'ovile? -You've made an attempt to return him to the fold?
8289	**baratto**	**barter**

il
[baratto]
Non può essere l'oggetto di un baratto da parte dell'Unione europea, ma un atto spontaneo.
-This should not be the subject of bartering on the part of the European Union; this should be spontaneous.

8290 **tangibile** **tangible**
adj
[tandʒibile]
– Preferisco un'emozione più tangibile.
-I'd rather spend my money on more tangible excitement.

8291 **perlustrare** **search|scour**
vb
[perlustrare]
Mandiamo un elicottero a perlustrare la zona.
-Let's get a chopper in the air and search the area or something.

8292 **vettore** **vector**
il
[vettore]
Solo per inalazione usando un gas vettore idoneo.
-For inhalation use only, using a suitable carrier gas.

8293 **juke-box** **jukebox**
il
[dʒukeboks]
Un vecchio juke–box in un angolo.
-We got an old jukebox in the corner.

8294 **distruttore** **destroyer**
il
[distruttore]
Sono diventato Morte, il distruttore dei mondi.
-I am become death, destroyer of worlds.

8295 **cornicione** **cornice|eaves**
il
[kornitʃone]
Andrò sul cornicione adesso per dirvi...
-I'll go out on a ledge here and say...

8296 **appiccicoso** **sticky**
adj
[appittʃikozo]
Questo riso è appiccicoso.
-This rice is sticky.

8297 **genesi** **genesis**
la
[dʒenezi]
Domani ci interrogheremo sulla strana genesi della moneta unica.
-We will wonder tomorrow about the strange genesis of the single currency.

8298 **piastra** **plate**
la
[pjastra]
Metti il maiale sulla piastra.
-Get that pork on the plate.

8299 **racchetta** **racket**
la
[rakketta]
Quanto costa questa racchetta?
-How much is this racket?

8300 **improvvisazione** **improvisation|ad-lib**
la
[improvvizattsjone]
Invece di spogliarmi, farò improvvisazione teatrale.
-Instead of stripping, I will be doing improv.

8301 **stampato** **printed; printout**
adj; lo
[stampato]
Questo libro verrà stampato l'anno prossimo.
-This book will be printed next year.

8302 **papera** **gosling**
la
[papera]
È simile a una papera.
-It's similar to a duck.

8303 **trasparente** **transparent**
adj
[trasparente]
Sono nominati dalla Commissione secondo una procedura trasparente.
-They shall be appointed by the Commission, in accordance with a transparent procedure.

8304 **soave** **sweet**

adj Ogni mattina e ogni notte nascono alcuni al soave diletto.
[soave] -Every morn' and every night, some are born to sweet delight. la sua voce soaveher dulcet tones

8305 **speculazione** **speculation|flutter**
la È pura speculazione.
[spekulattsjone] -That's pure speculation.

8306 **ingrandire** **enlarge|expand**
vb Consente di ingrandire testo e immagini in una parte qualsiasi dello schermo.
[iŋgrandire] -Lets you enlarge text and images on any section of your screen.

8307 **annegamento** **drowning**
il Il giovane ha salvato la ragazza dall'annegamento.
[annegamento] -The young man saved the girl from drowning.

8308 **colpetto** **tap|flick**
il Sentì un colpetto sulla spalla.
[kolpetto] -He felt a tap on his shoulder.

8309 **baratro** **chasm**
il Possiamo celebrare la nostra fuga dal baratro.
[baratro] -We can celebrate our escape from the abyss.

8310 **convertire** **convert**
vb Ci vuole molto tempo per convertire.
[konvertire] -It takes a long time to convert.

8311 **avaro** **stingy; miser**
adj; il Sono contraria all'impostazione eccessivamente avara del relatore, che propone un periodo massimo durante il quale le regioni possono ricevere finanziamenti nell'ambito dei Fondi strutturali.
[avaro] -I am opposed to the overly penny-pinching approach of the rapporteur, who is proposing a maximum period of time during which regions may receive structural funding.

8312 **unanimità** **unanimity**
la La mozione è stata approvata all'unanimità.
[unanimit'a] -The motion was approved unanimously.

8313 **fobia** **phobia**
la Io ho la fobia dei pagliacci.
[fobja] -I have a fear of clowns.

8314 **designare** **designate|appoint**
vb Dovremo designare una commissione per stabilire i casi in cui si può parlare di istigazione all'omosessualità?
[deziɲɲare] -Appoint a committee to see what is and what is not promotion of homosexuality?

8315 **sotterrare** **bury**
vb Nessuno dovrebbe sotterrare i propri nonni.
[sotterrare] -No person should ever have to bury a grandparent.

8316 **corazzato** **armored**
adj Non provate neanche a spararmi, perché... questo piccoletto... è corazzato.
[korattsato] -Now, don't get any funny ideas about shooting me, 'cause this baby is armored.

8317 **piombare** **fall**
vb Quando Phoenix commetterà un altro MDO... sapremo esattamente dove piombare.
[pjombare]

-When Phoenix performs another MurderDeathKill... ...we'll know exactly where to pounce.

8318 **garbo** il [garbo] **politeness**
Ma noi viviamo qui ad Highbury, dove trattiamo la gente con il rispetto e il garbo che merita.
-But we live here in Highbury, where we treat people with the respect and courtesy they deserve.

8319 **megera** la [medʒera] **shrew|harridan**
Senza di lui, la megera non è così forte.
-Without him, the crone's not so strong.

8320 **inammissibile** adj [inammissibile] **inadmissible**
È inammissibile e non dovremmo permetterlo.
-That is unacceptable, and we should not be accepting it.

8321 **russare** vb [russare] **snore**
Il forte russare di Joe mi ha tenuto sveglio tutta la notte.
-Joe's loud snoring kept me awake all night.

8322 **gioielliere** il [dʒojelljere] **jeweler**
Joe ha assassinato il gioielliere.
-Joe murdered the jeweller.

8323 **sottomissione** la [sottomissjone] **submission|subjection**
Niente sembra più sorprendente a coloro, che considerano le vicende umane con un occhio filosofico, della facilità con cui i molti sono governati dai pochi; e la sottomissione implicita, con la quale gli uomini dimettersi loro sentimenti e passioni di quelle dei loro governanti.
-Nothing appears more surprising to those, who consider human affairs with a philosophical eye, than the easiness with which the many are governed by the few; and the implicit submission, with which men resign their own sentiments and passions to those of their rulers.

8324 **diffamazione** la [diffamattsjone] **defamation|libel**
Dan ha denunciato Linda per diffamazione.
-Dan sued Linda for slander.

8325 **linfa** la [linfa] **sap**
Sono la linfa vitale dell'attività.
-They're really the lifeblood of our industry.

8326 **bossolo** il [bossolo] **box**
A intervalli regolari tolgono un cilindro di ghiaccio, come i guardacaccia esaminano i bossoli dei proiettili, dall'interno del trapano.
-Periodically, they remove a cylinder of ice, like gamekeepers popping a spent shotgun shell from the barrel of a drill.

8327 **stampella** la [stampella] **crutch**
Al fine di raggiungere tale obiettivo, non c'è bisogno, in linea di principio, della moneta unica come stampella.
-In order to achieve that objective, there is no real need for the crutch of the single currency - all that is needed is courage and discipline.

8328 **latitudine** la [latitudine] **latitude**
La latitudine di Annapolis è 38,580 nord.
-The latitude of Annapolis is 38. 58° north.

8329 **impicciare** vb [impittʃare] **meddle**
Dice di non volersi impicciare negli affari di mia mamma.
-He says he doesn't want to stand on my mum's toes.

8330 **destinatario** **recipient|addressee**

il
[destinatarjo]
E il nome del vostro destinatario, per favore?
-And the name of the person you're calling, please?

8331 **birichino** **mischievous; cheeky youngster**
adj; il
[birikino]
Quindi dimmi altro di questo generale birichino.
-So, tell me more about this naughty general.

8332 **risposare** **remarry**
vb
[rispozare]
Non... Non sapevo che si potesse risposare.
-Didn't realize you could remarry.

8333 **scalpore** **sensation**
lo
[skalpore]
Ciò causò un tale scalpore, che dovetti sbarcare al primo scalo.
-It caused such a stir, I was forced to disembark at the next port.

8334 **indebolire** **weaken|impair**
vb
[indebolire]
Non ci possiamo permettere di indebolire le fondamenta dell'integrazione europea.
-We cannot allow ourselves to weaken the foundations of European integration.

8335 **coreografia** **choreography**
la
[koreografja]
Siamo talmente abituati alla coreografia che da origine alla sincronia.
-We're so used to choreography giving rise to synchrony.

8336 **scomodare** **disturb|be inconvenient**
vb
[skomodare]
Mi rendo conto che è un orario un po' scomodo, ma tenere questa discussione a quest'ora ha creato qualche problema anche a me: potrei essere altrove, a consumare una cena a base di asparagi.
-I appreciate that this may have caused inconvenience, but holding this debate at this time presents some inconvenience to me as well: I could be elsewhere consuming asparagus.

8337 **calunnia** **slander|libel**
la
[kalunnja]
Una volta ho dovuto far causa a tua madre per calunnia e diffamazione.
-I once found it necessary to sue your mother... for defamation of character and slander.

8338 **interurbano** **interurban**
adj
[interurbano]
Quest'accessibilità deve essere garantita non solo sugli autobus del trasporto locale, ma anche su quelli del trasporto interurbano.
-We want to have this accessibility not only for local but also for long-distance buses.

8339 **giurisprudenza** **law**
la
[dʒurisprudentsa]
Sta studiando giurisprudenza all'università.
-He is studying law at the university.

8340 **sofà** **sofa**
il
[sof'a]
Questo sofà occupa troppo spazio.
-This sofa takes too much room.

8341 **diadema** **diadem**
il
[djadema]
Se restituisce il diadema, dimenticherò questo triste episodio.
-If you return the tiara, I'm willing to forget this squalid incident.

8342 **marmaglia** **rabble|riffraff**
la
[marmaʎʎa]
La marmaglia del deserto deve ubbidire al nostro giudizio.
-The rabble of the desert must be made to comply with our judgment.

8343 **appropriazione** **appropriation**
le
[approprjattsjone]
Per l'imperialismo non è altro che occupazione, appropriazione e sottomissione.

-For imperialism is no less than occupation, appropriation and subjugation.

8344 **figurina** **figurine**
la
[figurina]
...è una figurina del baseball.
-...it's a baseball card.

8345 **ringhiare** **growl**
vb
[riŋgjare]
Non ringhiare a questo brav'uomo, Bernard.
-Don't growl at the nice man, Bernard.

8346 **generico** **generic**
adj
[dʒeneriko]
Gli alti modernisti hanno detto: "Noi creeremo una specie di spazio singolare generico.
-High modernists said, we will create sort of singular spaces that are generic.

8347 **sfumatura** **shade|nuance**
la
[sfumatura]
La sua faccia dopo il bagno, con una leggera sfumatura di rosso, era bella tanto da confonderla per qualcun altra.
-Her face after the bath, with a slight tinge of red, was beautiful as to mistake her for someone else.

8348 **gocciolare** **drip**
vb
[gottʃolare]
E in cambio offre solo... il fatto di non gocciolare.
-And in return offers only... not to drip.

8349 **insubordinazione** **insubordination**
la
[insubordinattsjone]
Non tollero l'insubordinazione.
-I don't tolerate insubordination.

8350 **telepatia** **telepathy**
la
[telepatja]
Ma la loro principale pratica della telepatia consiste nell'inviarci potenti segnali per farci pensare che non esista.
-But their main exercise of telepathy is to send out powerful signals to the rest of us that it doesn't exist.

8351 **opprimente** **overwhelming|oppressive**
adj
[opprimente]
L'aria è opprimente.
-The air is stifling.

8352 **spremere** **squeeze|squeeze out**
vb
[spremere]
Vediamo cos'altro possiamo spremere dalla biondina.
-Let's see what else we can squeeze out of Blondie.

8353 **ciuffo** **tuft**
il
[tʃuffo]
Il ciuffo di peli sul suo petto.
-The tuft of hair on his chest.

8354 **insetticida** **insecticide**
lo
[insettitʃida]
Nebulizzare i fiori con l'insetticida.
-To spray insecticide onto flowers.

8355 **sceneggiare** **dramatize**
vb
[ʃeneddʒare]
Disse: "Puoi sceneggiare qualcosa per dimostrarlo?"
-He said, "Could you write something down to prove it?"

8356 **scivoloso** **slippery**
adj
[ʃivolozo]
Il pavimento è scivoloso, quindi fate attenzione.
-The floor is slippery, so be careful.

8357 **potenzialità** **potentiality**
le
[potentsjalit'a]
Dalla relazione emerge chiaramente che il turismo presenta enormi potenzialità.
-It clearly follows from this report that tourism has a huge potential.

8358 **smascherare** **unmask**
vb
[smaskerare]
Quindi se volete smascherare uno sguardo di vera felicità, dovrete cercare questa espressione.
-So if you want to unmask a true look of happiness, you will look for this expression.

8359 **fornello** **stove**
il
[fornello]
Avete spento il fornello?
-Did you turn the stove off?

8360 **sudato** **sweaty**
adj
[sudato]
Io sono sudato.
-I am sweaty.

8361 **calamaro** **squid**
il
[kalamaro]
Questo calamaro costa cinque sterline.
-This squid is five quids.

8362 **versante** **side|slopes**
il
[versante]
Sul versante positivo, le misure specifiche proposte dalla Commissione sono accolte con favore.
-On the positive side, the specific measures proposed by the Commission are welcome.

8363 **criterio** **criterion|principle**
il
[kriterjo]
I soldi non sono un criterio di successo.
-Money is not a criterion of success.

8364 **forestale** **forest**
adj
[forestale]
Tali lavori potrebbero essere svolti da "vigili del fuoco forestali privati".
-'Private forester-firefighters' could do this work.

8365 **scià** **shah**
lo
[ʃ'a]
Gli americani consigliarono allo scià di costruire venti centrali nucleari.
-Americans advised the Shah to build twenty nuclear power stations.

8366 **versetto** **verse**
il
[versetto]
Oppure si può sussurrare all'orecchio di un presunto terrorista qualche versetto biblico.
-Or you can whisper in the ear of a supposed terrorist some Biblical verse.

8367 **bravata** **stunt**
la
[bravata]
Mi accusi di essere crudele, e poi orchestri questa bravata.
-You accuse me of being cruel, and you orchestrate this stunt. se fai di nuovo una bravata simileif you pull a stunt like that again

8368 **secondino** **jailer|warder**
il
[sekondino]
Perché, ecco, sto frequentando il secondo anno all'università.
-Because, actually, I'm a sophomore at college right now.

8369 **seggiolino** **seat**
il
[seddʒolino]
Ok, non dimenticarti il seggiolino.
-Okay, don't forget the car seat.

8370 **disastroso** **disastrous|shattering**
adj
[dizastrozo]
Sarebbe disastroso.
-That would be devastating.

8371 **inguine** **groin**
il
[iŋgwine]
Passiamo dalla gamba o dall'inguine.
-We usually go in through the leg or the groin.

8372 **capannone** **shed**

il
[kapannone]
Questo è il mio nuovo, appositamente costruito, capannone per i raggi X.
-This is my new, purpose-built, X-ray shed.

8373 **inimmaginabile**
adj
[inimmadʒinabile]
unimaginable
La vita senza libri è inimmaginabile.
-Life without books is unimaginable.

8374 **crematorio**
il
[krematorjo]
crematory
Ho perso i sensi e mi hanno portata fuori dal crematorio".
-I fainted and was taken out of the crematorium.'

8375 **crema**
la
[krema]
cream
Le dissi di mettersi della crema solare ad alta protezione.
-I told her to wear sunblock.

8376 **poppa**
la
[poppa]
stern
"Piccola", le dirò, "ricorda che tua mamma è un'ansiosa, e che tuo papà è un guerriero, e tu sei la bimba con mani piccole e occhi grandi che non smette mai di chiedere di più".
-Baby, I'll tell her, "remember, your momma is a worrier, and your poppa is a warrior, and you are the girl with small hands and big eyes who never stops asking for more."

8377 **simultaneamente**
adv
[simultaneamente]
concurrently
Solo per farvi un esempio, ogni singolo apice di una radice è in grado di percepire e monitorare simultaneamente e continuamente almeno 15 differenti parametri chimici e fisici.
-Just to give you an example, every single root apex is able to detect and to monitor concurrently and continuously at least 15 different chemical and physical parameters.

8378 **contaminazione**
la
[kontaminattsjone]
contamination
Documenti interni della PG&E sulla contaminazione.
-Internal PG&E documents, all about the contamination.

8379 **strutturale**
adj
[strutturale]
structural
Tuttavia, per un problema strutturale, occorre una risposta strutturale.
-However, for a structural problem we need a structural answer, a structural response.

8380 **dirottamento**
il
[dirottamento]
hijacking|diversion
Si devono condannare anche la pirateria e il terrorismo; mi riferisco al recente dirottamento di due aeroplani e di una nave passeggeri.
-Piracy and terrorism must be condemned too. I refer to the recent hijacking of two aircraft and a passenger vessel.

8381 **manufatto**
il; adj
[manufatto]
artefact; manufactured
Perché una parola è come un manufatto archeologico.
-Because a word is like an archaeological artifact.

8382 **palmare**
adj
[palmare]
palmar
Sarebbe stato bello sapere della videocamera nel mio palmare.
-Would have been nice to know there's a camera in my PDA.

8383 **straziante**
adj
[strattsjante]
heartbreaking|harrowing
È stato straziante.
-It was excruciating.

8384 **irritabile**
adj
[irritabile]
irritable|edgy
Non sono irritabile.
-I'm not cranky.

8385 **proclama**
proclamation

lo [proklama] Il "Proclama per un Mondo Migliore" era diretto alla diocesi di Roma.
-The "Proclamation for a Better World" was addressed to the Diocese of Rome.

8386 **istituire** **establish|charter**
vb [istitwire] Per questo ha senso istituire un dipartimento per il consolidamento della pace.
-For this reason, it makes sense to establish a peacebuilding department.

8387 **contrastare** **counteract**
vb [kontrastare] Contrastare fortemente con...
-To contrast starkly with…

8388 **appieno** **fully**
adv [appjeno] Anche se sono in disaccordo con quello che dite, riconosco appieno il vostro diritto di dirlo.
-Even though I disagree with what you say, I fully acknowledge your right to say it.

8389 **strozzino** **usurer**
lo [strottsino] O forse mostra interesse solo quando i tassi salgono per strozzare i consumatori?
-Or is it only interested in when interest rates will rise again and start throttling consumers?

8390 **celare** **conceal|be hidden**
vb [tʃelare] Vostro padre non si dà troppa pena di celare i suoi piani.
-Your father does not much trouble to conceal his plans.

8391 **intoccabile** **untouchable; untouchable**
adj; il/la [intokkabile] Voi siete un'entità intoccabile, burocratica e senza volto che se ne sta a Bruxelles.
-You are an untouchable, faceless, bureaucratic body in Brussels.

8392 **opprimere** **oppress|bully**
vb [opprimere] Non siamo nel 1900, quando potevano opprimere i lavoratori fino a che non morivano di colera.
-I mean, this isn't the 1900s, where you can just oppress your workers until they get cholera to death.

8393 **assetato** **thirsty**
adj [assetato] Mi svegliai assetato.
-I woke up thirsty.

8394 **invocare** **invoke|call upon**
vb [invokare] Non possiamo invocare vecchi costumi per difendere la persecuzione di omosessuali, bisessuali e transessuali.
-We cannot invoke old customs to defend the persecution of homosexuals, bisexuals and transsexuals.

8395 **oltraggioso** **offensive**
adj [oltraddʒozo] Lei è oltraggioso.
-You're outrageous.

8396 **ardito** **bold**
adj [ardito] Con la politica monetaria e valutaria vogliamo azzardare un passo molto ardito.
-We wish to take a bold step forward with monetary policy.

8397 **pensionamento** **retirement**
il [pensjonamento] Il generale ha vissuto il resto della sua vita pacificamente dopo il suo pensionamento.
-The general lived the rest of his life peacefully after his retirement.

8398 **brocca** **pitcher**

la
[brokka]
Jane ha riempito la brocca fino all'orlo.
-Jane filled the jug to the brim.

8399 **cambiale**
La
[kambjale]
draft|bill
Una volta che la moneta unica esiste, che senso ha che gli Stati restino comunque competenti per regolare, ad esempio, il problema della situazione giuridica della cambiale o dell'assegno?
-Once a single currency has been established, why should states still have the authority to solve, for example, the problem of the legal situation regarding the bill of exchange or the cheque?

8400 **gruzzolo**
il
[gruttsolo]
hoard
Se il suo gruzzolo va in fumo dovrà pur fare una mossa.
-If his nest egg goes up in smoke, he's got to make a move.

8401 **dichiarato**
adj
[dikjarato]
declared|avowed
La corte l'ha dichiarato colpevole.
-The court found him guilty.

8402 **valchiria**
la
[valkirja]
Valkyrie
Sto riscrivendo valchiria perfar si che la maggiorparte delle nostre unità più forti si concentrino solo su berlino.
-I'm rewriting Valkyrie to direct the majority of our strongest units to focus entirely on Berlin.

8403 **scarabocchiare**
vb
[skarabokkjare]
doodle|scribble
Per esempio, non esiste una definizione lusinghiera dello scarabocchiare.
-For example, there's no such thing as a flattering definition of a doodle.

8404 **fervido**
adj
[fervido]
fervent
Sentire un fervido appello per la riforma economica provenire da un Primo Ministro britannico la cui continua indecisione sull'adesione all'euro ha ripercussioni sull'occupazione, sulla crescita e sugli investimenti è non poco irritante.
-To hear a clarion call for economic reform from a British Prime Minister whose continued indecision over joining the euro is hitting jobs, growth and investment, is more than a little galling.

8405 **simulare**
vb
[simulare]
simulate|mimic
Queste sono fatte per simulare la forma reale di un velocista mentre corre.
-These are supposed to simulate the actual form of a sprinter when they run.

8406 **realismo**
il
[realismo]
realism
Quando dico realismo, intendo foto–realismo.
-When I say realism, I mean photo–realism.

8407 **spilorcio**
adj; lo
[spilortʃo]
stingy; miser
Joe sembra spilorcio.
-Joe seems mean.

8408 **masso**
il
[masso]
boulder
Potrebbero spazzare via un grosso masso.
-About enough to take out a big rock.

8409 **crocifissione**
la
[krotʃifissjone]
crucifixion
Uccidere Doyle per non farlo testimoniare è una crocifissione.
-Taking Joey Doyle's life to stop him from testifying is a crucifixion.

8410 **podio**
il
[podjo]
podium|platform
Arnold Raeburn ha appena destituito Malcom Finniston dal podio.
-Arnold Raeburn's just given Malcolm Finniston the heave–ho from the podium.

8411 **smorfia** **grimace**
la
[smorfja]
Ho fatto una smorfia.
-I cringed.

8412 **strofinare** **rub**
vb
[strofinare]
Però bisogna comunque entrarci ben dentro e strofinare per bene.
-You know, but you got to really get in there and scrub it out.

8413 **tacca** **notch|dent**
la
[takka]
Non ogni battaglia vinta è una tacca sul proprio bastone.
-Not every battle you win is a notch on your belt.

8414 **cavallino** **pony; horsy**
il; adj
[kavallino]
Quel cavallino sentirà la mancanza di mio figlio.
-That little horse is going to miss my boy.

8415 **importazione** **import**
le
[importattsjone]
L'importazione di esemplari di specie minacciate di estinzione è subordinata a:
-Importation of specimens of endangered species is subject to:

8416 **duomo** **cathedral**
il
[dwomo]
Alla vigilia di Natale, in tutto l'arcipelago indonesiano sono state fatte esplodere bombe nei pressi di un gran numero di chiese, fra cui il Duomo di Giacarta.
-On Christmas Eve, a large number of coordinated bomb attacks against churches - including the cathedral in the capital, Jakarta - took place at a variety of locations in the Indonesian archipelago.

8417 **fondina** **holster**
la
[fondina]
Starà appendendo la sua fondina ora.
-He's probably hanging up his holster right about now.

8418 **infedeltà** **infidelity|disloyalty**
le
[infedelt'a]
Quali sono i vincoli che uniscono la contraccezione all'infedeltà, all'aborto e al divorzio?
-What links are there between contraception, infidelity, abortion and divorce?

8419 **ululare** **howl|ululate**
vb
[ululare]
Hanno sentito ululare dei lupi da lontano.
-They heard wolves howling in the distance.

8420 **cecità** **blindness**
la
[tʃetʃit'a]
Vede, è questa inversione la probabile causa della cecità facciale.
-See, it's this reversal that's likely causing the face blindness.

8421 **carrozzina** **pram**
la
[karrottsina]
Il Martedì mattina abbiamo un servizio di carrozzine per le mamme ed i loro bambini pre-scolari.
-We have a pram service on Tuesday mornings for mums and their pre-school children.

8422 **sloggiare** **dislodge**
vb
[zloddʒare]
Quando il patrimonio sarà stabilito, dovremo sloggiare.
-When the estate was settled, we'd move out.

8423 **potassio** **potassium**
il
[potassjo]
Noi abbiamo il potassio nel nostro corpo.
-We have potassium in our bodies.

8424 **roditore** **rodent**
adj[roditore]
Il capibara è il roditore più grande del mondo. -The capybara is the world's largest rodent.

8425 **carriola** | **wheelbarrow**
la
[karrjola]
Ieri mi è stata rubata la carriola.
-Yesterday, my wheelbarrow was stolen.

8426 **superstizioso** | **superstitious**
adj
[superstittsjozo]
Circa 15 anni fa andai da un amico a Hong Kong a quell'epoca ero molto superstizioso.
-. ~~~ And at the time I was very superstitious.

8427 **visconte** | **viscount**
il
[viskonte]
La guarnigione si è arresa per salvare il visconte Trencavel.
-The garrison has surrendered to save Viscount Trencavel's life.

8428 **inoffensivo** | **harmless**
adj
[inoffensivo]
Questo è inoffensivo in sé.
-This is harmless in itself.

8429 **risoluto** | **resolute**
adj
[rizoluto]
A questo punto è importantissimo un passo risoluto per raggiungere gli obiettivi di Kyoto.
-An energetic step to achieve the Kyoto targets is now of major importance.

8430 **affrettare** | **hasten|expedite**
vb
[affrettare]
Mi affretterò nel dire che queste superfici sono completamente artificiali.
-I hasten to say that these surfaces are completely artificial.

8431 **annotare** | **note**
vb
[annotare]
Se vuoi annotare qualche indirizzo, ecco la mia matita.
-If you want to write down any addresses, here's my pencil.

8432 **lampione** | **lamp**
il
[lampjone]
Si trovava qui, proprio vicina al lampione.
-It was here, right next to this lamppost.

8433 **incrociatore** | **cruiser**
il
[iŋkrotʃatore]
Un incrociatore romulano ci ha visti.
-We've been spotted by a Romulan cruiser.

8434 **cappellaio** | **hatter**
il
[kappellajo]
No, io faccio il cappellaio a Nimes.
-No, I'm a hatter from Nîmes.

8435 **illimitato** | **unlimited|unrestricted**
adj
[illimitato]
L'elenco è illimitato.
-The list is limitless.

8436 **pomata** | **ointment|pomade**
la
[pomata]
Io sono felice che la pomata che ha raccomandato il medico funziona davvero.
-I am happy the ointment the doctor has recommended really works.

8437 **rappresentanza** | **representation**
la
[rapprezentantsa]
Non esiste alcuna rappresentanza invece in alcune popolari destinazioni turistiche.
-There is no representation whatsoever in certain popular tourist destinations.

8438 **pancreas** | **pancreas**
lo
[paŋkreas]
Il vostro pancreas produce insulina per riportarlo alla normalità, come è bene che sia.
-Your pancreas makes insulin to bring it back down, which is good.

8439 **diabetico** | **diabetic; diabetic**

adj; il | Joe è diabetico.
[djabetiko] | -Joe's diabetic.

8440 **dodicesimo** **twelfth|twelfth**
adj
[doditʃezimo]
Il dodicesimo membro della giuria è mancante.
-The twelfth juror is missing.

8441 **pitone** **python**
il
[pitone]
Non è facile come sembra catturare un pitone.
-It's not as easy as you think to capture a python.

8442 **diagnosticare** **diagnose**
vb
[djaɲɲostikare]
Questo aiuterà i responsabili ASHA a diagnosticare l'anemia nei luoghi di cura.
-This will help ASHA workers diagnose anemia at the point of care.

8443 **agrimensore** **surveyor**
il
[agrimensore]
È molto seccante per me, signor agrimensore...
-It's very unpleasant for me, mister land surveyor...

8444 **falce** **sickle**
la
[faltʃe]
Gli uomini cadono come granoturco sotto la falce.
-Men go down like corn before the scythe.

8445 **sollevato** **relieved**
i
[sollevato]
Sono sicura che Joe sarà sollevato.
-I'm sure Joe will be relieved.

8446 **congelamento** **freezing|frostbite**
il
[kondʒelamento]
Qual è il punto di congelamento dell'acqua?
-What's the freezing point of water?

8447 **nitrire** **neigh**
vb
[nitrire]
È la quinta volta che vengo e non l'ho mai sentito nitrire.
-It's the fifth time I come here, and I've never heard neighing.

8448 **discriminazione** **discrimination**
la
[diskriminattsjone]
Voi sapete qual è la prima causa di discriminazione in Italia?
-Do you know what is the first cause of discrimination in Italy?

8449 **proclamare** **proclaim|declare**
vb
[proklamare]
Dobbiamo proclamare i diritti fondamentali di ciascuno di noi.
-We must proclaim the fundamental rights of each and every one of us.

8450 **omero** **humerus**
il
[omero]
Se fosse stato un piccione viaggiatore, si sarebbe potuto chiamarlo l'"Odissea di Omero".
-If it was a homing pigeon, it would be called "Homer's Odyssey."

8451 **gerarchia** **hierarchy**
la
[dʒerarkja]
Vorrei soprattutto sottolineare l'inclusione della gerarchia divergente dei rifiuti.
-I particularly wish to emphasise the inclusion of the divergent waste hierarchy.

8452 **immigrare** **immigrate**
vb
[immigrare]
Le opportunità per i cittadini stranieri non rifugiati di immigrare in Europa come lavoratori migranti dovrebbero essere ampliate.
-The opportunity for foreign citizens who are not refugees to immigrate to Europe as migrant workers should be expanded.

8453 **beatitudine** **bliss**
la
[beatitudine]
Ho vissuto in uno stato di beatitudine scribacchina.
-I've been in a state of writerly bliss these past weeks.

8454 **spastico** **spastic; spastic**

adj; lo [spastiko] Lo capisco dal tuo scatto spastico e dallo sguardo bisognoso.
-I can tell by your spastic sprint and your needy stare.

8455 **sanguinario** **bloodthirsty|slaughterous**
adj [saŋgwinarjo] Stai parlando di un sanguinario estremista, che minaccia la vita dei tuoi compatrioti.
-We're talking about a bloodthirsty extremist threatening the lives of your countrymen.

8456 **gladiatore** **gladiator**
il [gladjatore] Conosco solo le vie del gladiatore.
-I know only the ways of a gladiator.

8457 **detersivo** **detergent; detergent**
adj; il [detersivo] Se la stessa quantità di detersivo necessaria per lavare cinque chilogrammi di biancheria viene utilizzata per lavarne uno solo, qui sorge il vero problema dell'inquinamento ambientale.
-If the same amount of washing powder is used for one kilo of laundry as for five kilos, this is where the real environmental pollution arises.

8458 **statuto** **statute**
lo [statuto] Purtuttavia è ancora previsto dallo statuto.
-And yet it's still on the statute books.

8459 **cicerone** **guide**
il [tʃitʃerone] Il relatore ha citato Cicerone, ciò si addice a un parlamentare.
-The rapporteur quoted Cicero, which is appropriate for a Member of Parliament.

8460 **casata** **house**
la [kazata] E quello che ha detto, Lakshmi, è assolutamente vero: non è solo Ratan Tata, è la casata di Tata nel tempo.
-And what you said, Lakshmi, is absolutely true: it's not just Ratan Tata, it's the house of Tatas over time.

8461 **identikit** **identikit**
gli [identikit] Assomigliava abbastanza all'identikit per convincere Daren.
-He looked enough like the sketch to fool Daren.

8462 **detector** **detector**
il [detektor] (Applause) And the detector then transmits the image to the computer.
-(applauso) E il rilevatore trasmette quindi l'immagine al computer.

8463 **detonare** **detonate**
vb [detonare] Potrebbe farlo detonare in ogni momento.
-She could detonate it at any second. No.

8464 **scroto** **scrotum**
lo [skroto] E poi un'altra fascetta viene applicata allo scroto, in modo stretto.
-And then another band is applied to the scrotum, tightly.

8465 **fiduciario** **trustee; fiduciary**
il; adj [fidutʃarjo] Parere della BCE sul finanziamento del contributo austriaco a un fondo fiduciario dell'FMI
-ECB Opinion on the financing of the Austrian contribution to an IMF trust fund

8466 **lirico** **lyrical|operatic**
adj [liriko] Gus, sono un gangster lirico...
-Gus, I'm a lyrical gangster.

8467 **feudo** **feud|fief**
il [feudo] Prima di abbandonarmi, trovami un feudo.
-Before dumping me, find me a fief.

8468 **sottosegretario** **undersecretary**
il
[sottozegretarjo]
È vice sottosegretario per l'Europa Orientale.
-He's a deputy undersecretary on the eastern European desk.

8469 **plurale** **plural; plural**
adj; il
[plurale]
"Qual è il plurale di nazi?" "Stronzi."
-"What is the plural of Nazi?" - "Assholes."

8470 **confederazione** **confederation|union**
la
[konfederattsjone]
Alegria, Coordinatrice della Confederazione spagnolo-portoghese, e di sr.
-Alegria, Spanish and Portugues Confederation's Coordinator, and of sr.

8471 **incombere** **impend**
vb
[iŋkombere]
Sentendo incombere su di sé una minaccia sempre più terribile, gruppi ogni giorno più numerosi di tibetani decidono di abbandonare il paese.
-An ever-greater number of Tibetans are choosing to leave the country because they feel increasingly threatened.

8472 **zelo** **zeal|zealousness**
lo
[dzelo]
Qui si attinge, giorno dopo giorno, anche lo zelo per l'evangelizzazione.
-In personal prayer they draw daily zeal for evangelization.

8473 **saporito** **tasty|savory**
adj
[saporito]
E' saporito.
-It's savory.

8474 **esaudire** **fulfill|grant**
vb
[ezaudire]
Ecco perché la Repubblica ceca ha deciso di fare da sola e di esaudire il desiderio dei suoi cittadini.
-That is why the Czech Republic has decided to go it alone and grant its citizens their wish.

8475 **protesto** **protest**
il
[protesto]
Intendo dunque protestare ed esprimere la mia viva opposizione a tale decisione.
-I therefore protest and wish to register my vehement objection to your decision.

8476 **carnefice** **executioner**
il
[karnefitʃe]
Il carnefice è un membro della Resistenza.
-The executioner, he is a member of the Resistance!

8477 **trombone** **trombone**
il
[trombone]
Non avevo idea che voi sapeste suonare il trombone.
-I had no idea you knew how to play the trombone.

8478 **calcolatore** **computer; calculating**
il; adj
[kalkolatore]
Per piacere, notificami tramite e-mail qualsiasi bug trovato o funzioni mancanti che vuoi che siano incluse nelle versioni future dal calcolatore IMC.
-Please notify me by e-mail about any bugs found or missing functions that you want to be included in future versions of the BMI calculator.

8479 **pulsazione** **pulsation|throbbing**
la
[pulsattsjone]
Il paramedico che la doveva dichiarare morta, ha sentito una pulsazione.
-Paramedic went to pronounce her, found a pulse.

8480 **vizioso** **vicious**
adj
[vittsjozo]
Joe è vizioso.
-Joe is depraved.

8481 **prodigo** **prodigal|lavish**

adj
[prodigo]
Il mio compagno di stanza è prodigo quando si tratta di spendere soldi per i film; li compra il giorno che escono, indipendentemente dal prezzo.
-My roommate is prodigal when it comes to spending money on movies; he buys them the day they're released, regardless of price.

8482 **irreversibile** **irreversible**
adj
[irreversibile]
Secondo, considerare l' immigrazione come un fenomeno positivo e irreversibile.
-Two, to consider immigration as a positive and irreversible phenomenon.

8483 **predecessore** **predecessor**
il
[predetʃessore]
Questo candidato è notevolmente migliore rispetto al suo predecessore.
-This candidate is significantly better compared to his predecessor.

8484 **tropico** **tropic**
il
[tropiko]
La stagione del Tropico è cominciata e Mendoza, il nostro uomo dentro... ...dice che l'hotel sarà pieno in una settimana.
-The tropical season is just starting, and Mendoza, he's our inside man... he says that the hotel will be full up in another week.

8485 **babbuino** **baboon**
il
[babbwino]
Lei assomiglia a un babbuino.
-You look like a baboon.

8486 **oste** **host|publican**
il
[oste]
L'oste è un giovane garzone serve del vino dalle anfore.
-The host is a young boy serving wine from amphoras.

8487 **tredicesimo** **thirteenth|thirteenth**
adj
[treditʃezimo]
Il tredicesimo emendamento ha liberato tutti gli schiavi afroamericani.
-The Thirteenth Amendment freed all Negro slaves.

8488 **grandine** **hailstorm**
la
[grandine]
I chicchi di grandine erano grandi come palle da tennis.
-The hailstones were as big as tennis balls.

8489 **tonalità** **tonality|tone**
le
[tonalitˈa]
È la tonalità esatta che volevo per il nostro matrimonio.
-This is the exact shade I wanted for our wedding.

8490 **rigenerazione** **regeneration**
la
[ridʒenerattsjone]
Queste sono le stimolanti iniziative di rigenerazione che dovremmo sostenere.
-These are the exciting urban regeneration initiatives that we should be supporting.

8491 **gironzolare** **roam|wander about**
Vb
[dʒirontsolare]
E, francamente, a gironzolare qui non sei al sicuro.
-And, frankly, you're not safe to walk around.

8492 **dotto** **learned; scholar**
adj; il
[dotto]
L'avevo ricordato qualche mese fa dicendo: "Ci sono grandi dotti, grandi specialisti, grandi teologi, maestri della fede, che ci hanno insegnato molte cose.
-I made this reminder a few months ago saying: "There have been great scholars, great experts, great theologians, teachers of faith who have taught us many things.

8493 **impetuoso** **impetuous|dashing**
adj
[impetwozo]
Era un cavallo spaventoso e impetuoso, al quale gli altri cavalli obbedivano.
-He was a fiery and fearsome horse to whom the other horses obeyed.

8494 **spinale** **spinal**

adj
[spinale]
Abbiamo il tronco encefalico in mezzo alla corteccia cerebrale, e il midollo spinale.
-There is the brain stem in between the cerebral cortex and the spinal cord.

8495 **sassone**
adj; il
[sassone]
Saxon; Saxon
L'Irlanda si colloca tra il modello sociale europeo continentale e il modello anglo-sassone.
-Ireland fits somewhere between the continental European social model and the Anglo-Saxon model.

8496 **sepolcro**
il
[sepolkro]
tomb|sepulcher
Prima erano venute la notte del Monte degli Ulivi, l'eclissi solare della passione e morte di Gesù, la notte del sepolcro.
-The night on the Mount of Olives, the solar eclipse of Jesus' passion and death, the night of the grave had all passed.

8497 **effettivo**
adj; il
[effettivo]
actual; strength
Molte persone pensano che le auto d'epoca abbiano un prezzo superiore al loro valore effettivo.
-Many people think that antique cars are overpriced.

8498 **ungere**
vb
[undʒere]
anoint|grease
Ci serve qualcosa per ungere la faccia.
-We need to get something to grease his face.

8499 **fortino**
il
[fortino]
blockhouse
Joe e i suoi amici costruirono un fortino di neve.
-Joe and his friends built a snow fort.

8500 **straccione**
lo
[strattʃone]
ragamuffin
Mink mi derubava in combutta con lo straccione.
-Mink was robbing me with the ragamuffin.

8501 **ingrossare**
vb
[iŋgrossare]
swell|enlarge
Appena gli uomini della Walrus vedranno i limiti del signor Singleton, avremo una serie di talentuosi disertori pronti ad ingrossare le nostre fila.
-Once the Walrus's men realize Mr. Singleton's limitations, we'll have a host of talented defectors eager to swell our ranks.

8502 **bambinone**
il
[bambinone]
baby
Non volevo... e non sono emotivamente represso, né un bambinone.
-I wasn't, and I'm not emotionally stunted or a man–child.

8503 **fantoccio**
il
[fantottʃo]
puppet
È un fantoccio dei nuovi ricchi di Cleveland.
-He's a puppet for the fast-money boys in Cleveland.

8504 **nettare**
il; vb
[nettare]
nectar; clean
Bevono questo favoloso nettare e poi rimangono tutti un po' appiccicaticci.
-They drink this fabulous nectar and then they're all a bit sticky.

8505 **cipria**
la
[tʃiprja]
powder
Su un problema così delicato e serio, che attiene alla sicurezza alimentare, non è accettabile una "spruzzatina di cipria" per farsi belli agli occhi dei consumatori.
-On such a sensitive and serious food safety issue, it is not acceptable just to dab on a touch of face powder to look good to the consumers.

8506 **irraggiungibile**
adj
[irraddʒundʒibile]
unattainable
Poiché questo obiettivo è irraggiungibile, l'UE si condanna a una presenza a tempo indeterminato in quel paese.

-Since this goal is unattainable, the EU condemns itself to an indefinite presence in that country.

8507 **batosta** **blow**
la
[batosta]
Abbiamo preso una bella batosta nella finale.
-We took a pounding in the final.

8508 **monarchia** **monarchy**
la
[monarkja]
Il movimento militare rovescia la monarchia e proclama la Repubblica del Brasile.
-A military movement overthrows the monarchy and proclaims the Republic in Brazil.

8509 **notevolmente** **considerably**
adv
[notevolmente]
Le giornate stanno diventando notevolmente più corte ora che è arrivato l'autunno.
-The days are getting noticeably shorter now that autumn has arrived.

8510 **rullare** **roll**
vb
[rullare]
Autorizzazioni e istruzioni ad entrare, atterrare, decollare, attendere al suolo in prossimità di, attraversare, rullare ed effettuare contropista su qualsiasi pista; nonché
-Clearances and instructions to enter, land on, take off from, hold short of, cross, taxi and backtrack on any runway; and

8511 **frizzante** **crisp**
adj
[friddzante]
La maggior parte delle persone riconoscerebbero che lui era un giovane frizzante.
-Most would acknowledge that he was a sparkling young man.

8512 **archeologo** **archaeologist|archaeologian**
il
[arkeologo]
Un importante archeologo e scrittore europeo, Valerio Massimo Manfredi, ha scritto: "Roma era soprattutto un grande ideale".
-An important European archaeologist and writer, Valerio Massimo Manfredi, wrote: 'Rome was above all a great ideal.'

8513 **controspionaggio** **counterintelligence**
il
[kontrospjonaddʒo]
Lavora nella task force del controspionaggio della CIA a Langley.
-He's detailed to a CIA Counterintelligence task force at Langley.

8514 **per lo più** **mostly**
adv
[per lo pju]
Senta, questa roba è per lo più zuccheri e colorante.
-Listen, this stuff is mostly sugar and food coloring.

8515 **parità** **equality|parity**
la
[parit'a]
Il principio di parità e cooperazione deve sostituire questo approccio.
-The principle of parity and cooperation should replace such an approach.

8516 **riordinare** **rearrange|tidy**
vb
[rjordinare]
Io voglio riordinare il mio appartamento.
-I want to declutter my apartment.

8517 **incalzante** **pressing**
adj
[iŋkaltsante]
Signor Commissario, mi attendo che lei ponga tale domanda incalzante quando si recherà a Pechino.
-Commissioner, I expect that you will be asking this pressing question in Beijing.

8518 **nutrimento** **nourishment|food**
il
[nutrimento]
L'Eucaristia è nutrimento, è cibo e bevanda.
-The Eucharist is nourishment; it is food and drink.

8519 **formicaio** **anthill**

il | La Microsoft è un formicaio enorme?
[formikajo] | -Is Microsoft a great big anthill?

8520 **zenzero** **ginger**
lo
[dzentsero]
Questa è una bevanda allo zenzero.
-This is a ginger drink.

8521 **appendice** **appendix**
la
[appenditʃe]
L'appendice è lunga circa 10 cm.
-The appendix is about 10 cm long.

8522 **buffonata** **farce|tomfoolery**
la
[buffonata]
Erin, le Risorse Umane sono una buffonata.
-Erin, HR is a joke.

8523 **lebbra** **leprosy**
la
[lebbra]
La Commissione ha già lanciato iniziative volte a combattere la lebbra?
-Has the Commission already launched various initiatives in order to combat leprosy?

8524 **intonare** **intone|tone**
vb
[intonare]
Viva, saremmo lieti se tu potessi intonare l'inno che abbiamo imparato al coro dell'ultimo anno.
-Viva, we'd all love it if you could sing the hymn we've been learning in senior choir?

8525 **imprecare** **curse|swear**
vb
[imprekare]
Joe ha cominciato a imprecare.
-Joe started swearing.

8526 **insufficienza** **insufficiency|lack**
la
[insuffitʃentsa]
Causa del decesso: arresto cardiaco causato da insufficienza respiratoria.
-Cause of death: Cardiac arrest, brought on by respiratory failure.

8527 **antifurto** **antitheft; antitheft**
adj; gli
[antifurto]
Speravo di trovare qualche segnale antifurto prima che finisca in qualche sfasciacarrozze.
-I'm just hoping we can pick up her car's anti–theft signal before it ends up in a chop shop.

8528 **assessore** **assessor**
gli
[assessore]
La Prima Sezione della Segreteria di Stato è diretta da un Arcivescovo, il Sostituto per gli Affari Generali, coadiuvato da un Prelato, l'Assessore per gli Affari Generali.
-The First Section of the Secretariat of State is headed by an Archbishop, the Substitute for General Affairs, assisted by a Prelate, the Assessor for General Affairs.

8529 **quoziente** **quotient**
il
[kwottsjente]
Non conosco il mio quoziente intellettivo.
-I don't know my IQ.

8530 **barboncino** **poodle**
il
[barbontʃino]
Non vorrai assomigliare ad un barboncino.
-You don't want to look like a poodle.

8531 **scavalcare** **climb over**
vb
[skavalkare]
Troppo vecchio per scavalcare muri o nascondermi nei panni sporchi.
-I'm too old to climb over walls or hide in laundry baskets.

8532 **interazione** **interaction**
la
[interattsjone]
Le domande e le risposte giocano un enorme ruolo nell'interazione.
-Questions and answers play an enormous role in interaction.

8533 **ritoccare** **retouch**

vb L'onorevole Sterckx afferma che non dovremmo ritoccare accordi internazionali che sono già soddisfacenti.
[ritokkare] -Mr Sterckx says that we should not tinker with international agreements which are already satisfactory.

8534 **deportare** **deport**
vb Come può un governo,secondo il diritto internazionale, deportare uno dei suoi stessi cittadini?
[deportare] -How, in international law, can a government deport one of its own citizens?

8535 **freccetta** **dart**
la Joe lanciò la freccetta.
[frettʃetta] -Joe threw the dart.

8536 **nasale** **nasal**
adj Questo sono io, durante un lavaggio nasale.
[nazale] -That's me, getting a nasal lavage.

8537 **ginnasta** **gymnast**
il/la Ma puoi essere una ginnasta diversa.
[dʒinnasta] -But, you can be a different kind of gymnast.

8538 **continentale** **continental**
adj L'ICE rappresenta un nuovo strumento di democrazia partecipativa su scala continentale.
[kontinentale] -The ECI is a new instrument of participatory democracy on a continental scale.

8539 **crocifiggere** **crucify**
vb I romani là fuori cercano persone da crocifiggere.
[krotʃifiddʒere] -Romans are out there looking for people to crucify.

8540 **variare** **vary|range**
vb L'attuazione tecnica di tali valori potrebbe ovviamente variare.
[varjare] -The technical implementation of those values may vary, of course.

8541 **biopsia** **biopsy**
la Quando non si sa che altro fare, si fa la biopsia polmonare a cielo aperto.
[bjopsja] -You do an open lung biopsy when you've got no other options.

8542 **opuscolo** **brochure**
il Ha visto questo opuscolo?
[opuskolo] -Have you seen this pamphlet?

8543 **autobiografia** **autobiography**
le Le mie amiche mi hanno spinto a scrivere un'autobiografia.
[autobjografja] -My friends pushed me to write a memoir.

8544 **centralinista** **operator**
il/la Dottor Kakel, chiami il centralinista.
[tʃentralinista] -WOMAN (over P.A.): Dr. Kakel, call the operator.

8545 **titano** **titan**
il Ho sentito dire che le "rocce" su Titano in realtà sono fatte di ghiaccio, non di pietra.
[titano] -I hear that the "rocks" on Titan are actually made of ice, not rock.

8546 **eccessivamente** **excessively|over**
adv Klava semplifica eccessivamente tutto.
[ettʃessivamente] -Klava oversimplifies everything.

8547 **prospero** **prosperous|bonanza**
adj Quest'anno sarà prospero.
[prospero] -This year is going to be prosperous.

8548 **restituzione** **return|rebate**
la
[restituttsjone]
Altrimenti, per quale motivo i Greci esigono la restituzione dei Marmi di Elgin?
-Why else do Greeks demand the return of the Elgin Marbles?

8549 **alcolismo** **alcoholism**
il
[alkolismo]
A motivare questi comportamenti non sono né i divorzi, né l'alcolismo, né altro.
-It is not divorce, alcoholism or anything else that encourages this behaviour.

8550 **agghiacciante** **dreadful**
adj
[aggjattʃante]
E' agghiacciante constatare che si possa abitare letteralmente l'uno accanto all'altro, eppure vivere in una pericolosa ignoranza e paura l'uno dell'altro.
-It is chilling to realise that people can live literally right next door to one another and yet live in dangerous ignorance and fear of one another.

8551 **avanzamento** **progress|promotion**
il
[avantsamento]
Sicuramente esso impedisce l'avanzamento e la mobilità delle persone di provate capacità.
-It certainly blocks the advance and mobility of people with proven capabilities.

8552 **tonsilla** **tonsil**
la
[tonsilla]
È stata osservata anche infezione delle tonsille.
-An infection of the tonsils has also been observed.

8553 **inquieto** **restless|worried**
adj
[iŋkwjeto]
Sono inquieto.
-I'm restless.

8554 **ruffiano** **pander**
il
[ruffjano]
Ha detto che non la vende ad un ruffiano.
-He said he wouldn't sell it to a pimp.

8555 **interrogativo** **questioning; interrogative**
il; adj
[interrogativo]
E'stato sollevato un interrogativo, ma più che di un interrogativo, si tratta di una scelta.
-The question has been raised, and it is more than a question, it is a choice.

8556 **perlustrazione** **patrol**
la
[perlustrattsjone]
Hal e Maggie sono appena tornati dalla perlustrazione.
-Hal and Maggie just got back from patrol.

8557 **stanzetta** **room**
la
[stantsetta]
In un certo senso, la stanza stessa è l'elefante nella stanza, ma non lo vediamo.
-In a sense, the room itself is the elephant in the room, but we don't see it.

8558 **radioso** **radiant**
adj
[radjozo]
Altrimenti non ha senso parlare di futuro radioso.
-If it cannot, there is no sense talking about a bright future.

8559 **aia** **farmyard**
le
[aja]
Non menare il can per l'aia.
-Don't beat around the bush.

8560 **ingrandimento** **magnification|aggrandizement**
il
[iŋgrandimento]
Aumenta il fattore di ingrandimento dell'immagine attuale.
-Increase the zoom factor on the current image.

8561 **recapito** **delivery**
il
[rekapito]
L'ultimo recapito noto era rue Hadat 7 a Damasco. E spero che porti con sé al suo ritorno una risposta.
-The last known address was 7, rue Hadat, and I expect you to bring a reply back with you.

8562 **funzionale** **functional**
adj
[funtsjonale]
Penso che tutto sia funzionale.
-I think everything is functional.

8563 **clamore** **clamor|outcry**
il
[klamore]
Suscitò molto clamore.
-It caused quite a commotion.

8564 **scarpone** **boot**
lo
[skarpone]
Se risultasse compatibile con l'impronta dello scarpone, sarebbe utilissimo.
-If this is an exact match to the boot prints, this'll be very helpful.

8565 **sovversivo** **subversive**
adj
[sovversivo]
Parlateci della macchina per stampare materiale sovversivo.
-Tell us about the machine to print subversive material.

8566 **esaurito** **spent**
adj
[ezaurito]
Ha esaurito la carta.
-She ran out of paper.

8567 **tunica** **tunic**
la
[tunika]
Mi piace indossare una tunica.
-I like to wear a tunic.

8568 **fissato** **fixed|set**
adj
[fissato]
L'hanno fissato.
-They fixed it.

8569 **vanitoso** **vain**
adj
[vanitozo]
Non sono così vanitoso come sembra.
-I'm not nearly as vain as it looks.

8570 **guardiamarina** **midshipman**
il
[gwardjamarina]
Il guardiamarina McCarty vi mostrerà l'ufficio comunicazioni.
-Ensign McCarty will show you to the communications department.

8571 **compresso** **bowsprit**
lo
[kompresso]
Mandamelo come un file compresso.
-Send it to me as a compressed file.

8572 **boccale** **mug**
il
[bokkale]
Per questo il boccale utilizzato per servire la birra viene chiamato anche Maß , ossia «misura».
-In Bavaria, for example, beer is drunk in a measured way - and that is why we call the mug from which we drink it a 'measure' .

8573 **castità** **chastity**
la
[kastit'a]
Come una cintura di castità maschile.
-It's like a male chastity device.

8574 **ghianda** **acorn**
la
[gjanda]
Ho cominciato nel centro con una ghianda per la civiltà indiana degli Ohlone.
-So I started in the center with the acorn for the Ohlone Indian civilization.

8575 **rondine** **swallow**

la
[rondine]
La rondine è un segno dell'estate.
-The swallow is a sign of summer.

8576 **accampare**
vb
[akkampare]
camp
Qualcuno si è accampato nella tua testa.
-Somebody is camping in your head.

8577 **contrazione**
la
[kontrattsjone]
contraction
Dimmi quando hai un'altra contrazione.
-Just let me know when you're having another contraction.

8578 **collezionare**
vb
[kollettsjonare]
collect
Il mio hobby è collezionare gli insetti.
-My hobby is collecting insects.

8579 **serrata**
la
[serrata]
lockout
E le è stata addossata personalmente la colpa della serrata.
-And you are being blamed personally for this government shutdown.

8580 **fusibile**
il; adj
[fuzibile]
fuse; fusible
Digli che dovevi cambiare un fusibile.
-Tell them that you needed to change a fuse.

8581 **nitrato**
il
[nitrato]
nitrate
Un penultimo punto è stato quello relativo al nitrato di potassio.
-My penultimate point concerns potassium nitrate.

8582 **fabbricante**
il/la
[fabbrikante]
manufacturer
Infatti, come potremmo pensare di fabbricare veicoli con un motore "pulito» se questo dovesse funzionare con carburante inquinante?
-How could we build vehicles with a "clean' engine which would have to operate using pollutant fuel?

8583 **tallone**
il
[tallone]
heel
Il mio tallone sinistro è infiammato.
-My left heel is inflamed.

8584 **acrobazia**
le
[akrobattsja]
stunt
(Risate) Qualche volta le nostre macchine diventano talmente matte, che fanno anche qualche acrobazia.
-(Laughter) Sometimes our cars get so crazy, they even do little stunts.

8585 **porcospino**
il
[porkospino]
porcupine|urchin
Io vivo con un porcospino.
-I live with a porcupine.

8586 **residenziale**
adj
[rezidentsjale]
residential
Lui vive in una comunità residenziale chiusa.
-He lives in a gated community.

8587 **portamento**
il
[portamento]
bearing|deportment
Si, ma le tue ragazze trasudavano portamento e sicurezza.
-Yes, but your girls exuded such poise and confidence.

8588 **malto**
il
[malto]
propulsion
E vi prego di passarmi il pane al malto.
-And I'll thank you to hand me the malt loaf.

8589 **problematico**
adj
[problematiko]
problematic
Joe era un bambino problematico.
-Joe was a troubled child.

8590 **compatibile**
adj
[kompatibile]
compatible
Il mio software non è compatibile con Windows.
-My software isn't compatible with Windows.

8591 **rocca** **fortress**
la
[rokka]
Devi essere di pietra, come la rocca del giudizio.
-You've got to be like stone, like the rock of judgement.

8592 **soggezione** **awe**
la
[soddʒettsjone]
La premiazione è stata così commovente che siamo ancora tutti un po' in soggezione dopo quanto abbiamo udito.
-I think the last award was so moving that we are still a little in awe of what has happened.

8593 **sodio** **sodium**
il
[sodjo]
Il sale da tavola, composto principalmente da cloruro di sodio, può essere usato sia per insaporire che per conservare gli alimenti.
-Table salt, primarily composed of sodium chloride, can be used both to season and to preserve food.

8594 **incoraggiante** **cheering**
adj
[iŋkoraddʒante]
Io lo trovo molto incoraggiante.
-I find it very encouraging.

8595 **tossicodipendente** **addict**
il/la
[tossikodipendente]
Non sono un tossicodipendente.
-I'm not a drug addict.

8596 **fazione** **faction**
la
[fattsjone]
Non so nulla di nessuna fazione.
-I don't know anything about a faction.

8597 **trans-** **trans-**
pfx
[trans-]
I grassi trans fanno male alla salute.
-Trans fats are bad for your health.

8598 **treccia** **braid|pigtail**
la
[trettʃa]
(Risate) Si stanno facendo delle trecce ai capelli.
-(Laughter) And they are plaiting hair.

8599 **califfo** **caliph**
il
[kaliffo]
Zufiqar era la famosa spada di Hazret-i Ali, quarto califfo dell'Islam.
-Zulfiqar was the famous sword of Hazret-i Ali, fourth caliph of Islam.

8600 **moltitudine** **multitude|crowd**
la
[moltitudine]
Tutta la complessità dell'impresa è illustrata dalla moltitudine di emendamenti depositati.
-The full complexity of the undertaking is illustrated by the multitude of amendments tabled.

8601 **impasto** **dough**
lo
[impasto]
In realtà gli antichi egizi... facevano la pasta stendendo l'impasto con i piedi.
-Actually, the ancient Egyptians made pasta by flattening the dough with their feet.

8602 **esibire** **show|show off**
vb
[ezibire]
Devono "esibire il corpo".
-They have to produce the body.

8603 **piedino** **toothsie**
il
[pjedino]
Dammi quel piedino, sembra squisito.
-Give me that foot, it looks delicious.

8604 **disertare** **desert|bolt**
vb
[dizertare]
Se ti preoccupa così tanto potremmo disertare anche noi.
-Well, if you're that worried about him, maybe we could just defect ourselves.

8605 **riporre** **put**
vb
[riporre]
Vien da chiedersi se l'Unione europea non riponga troppa fiducia nella sorveglianza e nell'amministrazione.
-The question is, does the European Union repose too much confidence in monitoring and administration?

8606 **paletto** **stake|pole**
il
[paletto]
Dobbiamo solo portargli via quel paletto.
-All we need is to take that stake away from him.

8607 **pertinente** **relevant**
adj
[pertinente]
Chiese qualche domanda pertinente.
-He asked a few pertinent questions.

8608 **retroguardia** **rearguard**
la
[retrogwardja]
I tuoi Immortali hanno distrutto la retroguardia greca fino all'ultimo uomo.
-Your Immortals have destroyed the Greek rearguard to the last man.

8609 **vegetare** **vegetate**
vb
[vedʒetare]
Centinaia di cristiani pakistani vegetano in carcere per anni senza un valido processo.
-Hundreds of Pakistani Christians vegetate in prison for years without access to any legal process.

8610 **callo** **callus**
il
[kallo]
C'è un callo esteso sulla clavicola.
-There's a large callus on the clavicle.

8611 **aviatore** **aviator**
il
[avjatore]
Lo specchietto retrovisore da aviatore include un altimetro e un indicatore della temperatura dell'aria.
-The aviator's rear–view mirror incorporates an altimeter and an air temperature gauge.

8612 **obiettare** **object**
vb
[objettare]
Io devo obiettare.
-I must object.

8613 **parabola** **parabola**
la
[parabola]
And after that first parabola, you know, the doc said everything is great.
-E dopo quella prima parabola il dottore disse che tutto andava bene.

8614 **molteplice** **multiple|manifold**
adj
[molteplitʃe]
Le cause dell'obesità sono molteplici ed estremamente complesse, e non è imponendo ulteriori proibizioni che riusciremo ad affrontarle.
-The causes of obesity are multifarious and highly complex, and it is not by imposing more bans that we will successfully address them.

8615 **serietà** **seriousness|reliability**
la
[serjet'a]
Mi preoccupa molto la serietà del festival.
-I am very concerned about the seriousness of the festival.

8616 **lineamento** **feature|outline**
il
[lineamento]
Sui volti degli "sconfitti della vita" si stagliano i lineamenti del volto di Cristo morente sulla croce.
-On the faces of those who have been "defeated by life" there appear the features of the face of Christ dying on the Cross.

8617 **progenie** **progeny**
la
[prodʒenje]
È perché tu... sei la mia sola progenie.
-It's because you are my only progeny.

8618 **complessità** **complexity**

	la [komplessit'a]	Ciò comporterà una nuova complessità legislativa ed un inquinamento normativo. -This will bring about a new legislative complexity and a prescriptive pollution.
8619	**cherosene**	**kerosene**
	il [kerozene]	Che cosa succede quando parliamo di tassare il cherosene, il combustibile utilizzato in aviazione? -What happens when we talk in terms of taxing kerosene, the fuel used in aircraft?
8620	**sciagura**	**disaster**
	la [ʃagura]	Lei porterà la sciagura che ho profetizzato. -She will bring the disaster I have prophesied.
8621	**intenzionale**	**intentional**
	adj [intentsjonale]	Io penso che fosse intenzionale. -I think it was intentional.
8622	**nullo**	**null|insignificant**
	adj [nullo]	Il testamento venne dichiarato nullo dalla corte. -The will was declared void by the court.
8623	**tramonto**	**sunset|setting**
	il [tramonto]	Joe ha paura di andare fuori dopo il tramonto, vero? -Joe is afraid to go out after dark, isn't he?
8624	**letargo**	**hibernation**
	il [letargo]	Perché le persone non vanno in letargo? -Why don't people hibernate?
8625	**stellina**	**starlet**
	la [stellina]	Questa e' una stella, questa e' una stella, tutte le altre sono galassie, d'accordo? -This is a star, this is a star, everything else is a galaxy, OK?
8626	**insaziabile**	**insatiable**
	adj [insattsjabile]	Joe ha un appetito insaziabile. -Joe has an insatiable appetite.
8627	**doloso**	**malicious**
	adj [dolozo]	L'incendio doloso è un atto criminale. -Arson is a criminal act.
8628	**calmante**	**calming; sedative**
	adj; il [kalmante]	Gli hanno dato un calmante per farlo riposare meglio. -They gave him a sedative so he can rest easier.
8629	**indebito**	**undue**
	adj [indebito]	I datori di lavoro si appellano al fatto che l'assunzione di disabili comporta quello che si definisce un onere indebito. -The employers then claim that hiring disabled people represents what is called undue hardship.
8630	**disdire**	**cancel|unsay**
	vb [dizdire]	The consequences are dire for the residents of entire areas. -Le conseguenze sono disastrose per tutti i residenti di quelle zone.
8631	**cilecca**	**misfire**
	la [tʃilekka]	Se le avessi mai usate prima sapresti che funzionano male, fanno cilecca, rompono le zampe del castoro. -If you ever used those things before you'd know that they malfunction, misfire, break the beaver's legs.
8632	**scoria**	**slag|waste**

la
[skorja]
Quindi noi siamo una scoria chimica diversa. Questa scoria chimica possiede l'universalità.
-So we are a chemical scum that is different. This chemical scum has universality.

8633 **tralasciare** **omit|give up**
vb
[tralaʃʃare]
Le persone non devono tralasciare la questione a causa dell'inattività delle istituzioni e del ritardo nel processo decisionale.
-People should not miss out because of the institutions' inactivity and delayed decision-making.

8634 **recipiente** **container**
il
[retʃipjente]
Il recipiente è pieno.
-The container is full.

8635 **grugnire** **grunt**
vb
[gruɲɲire]
Sto fermo qui praticamente grugnendo e sperando di costruire un'idea simile, confusa e articolata nella vostra testa che somigli un po' alla mia.
-I'm sitting here making grunting sounds basically, and hopefully constructing a similar messy, confused idea in your head that bears some analogy to it.

8636 **raffineria** **refinery**
la
[raffinerja]
Ma ciò che secondo me è davvero inquietante in questo cartello è la raffineria sullo sfondo.
-But what's really, to me, frightening about the picture and about this billboard is the refinery in the background.

8637 **imprimere** **give|impress**
vb
[imprimere]
Come in tutti i sacramenti che imprimono il carattere, la grazia ha una virtualità permanente.
-Just as in all sacraments which imprint character, grace has a permanent virtuality.

8638 **benestante** **well-off**
adj
[benestante]
Il dottore, che è benestante, non è soddisfatto.
-The doctor, who is well off, is not satisfied.

8639 **scoraggiare** **discourage|be discouraged**
vb
[skoraddʒare]
Joe non vuole scoraggiare Jane.
-Joe doesn't want to discourage Jane.

8640 **liquirizia** **licorice**
la
[likwirittsja]
Adoro la liquirizia come adoro donne.
-I like my licorice like I like my women.

8641 **oroscopo** **horoscope**
il
[oroskopo]
Mia sorella non riesce a iniziare la giornata senza leggere il suo oroscopo.
-My sister can't start the day without reading her horoscope.

8642 **lusinga** **flattery**
la
[luziŋga]
Prevede la ricerca di compromessi attraverso conversazioni e lunghe colazioni e, se necessario, qualche gentile lusinga per raggiungere un risultato.
-It involves the search for compromises through conversations and long lunches and, if necessary, a bit of gentle cajoling in the interests of achieving a result.

8643 **incurabile** **incurable**
adj
[iŋkurabile]
Joe ha una malattia incurabile.
-Joe has an incurable disease.

8644 **traversata** **crossing**

la
[traversata]
Ma le libellule non sono le uniche creature che effettuano la traversata.
-But dragonflies are not the only creatures that make the crossing.

8645 **saponetta** **soap**
la
[saponetta]
Gli acquisti quotidiani di una famiglia irachena, persino quello di una sola saponetta, erano imposti e controllati dal potere politico.
-The ordinary Iraqi family's purchase, even of one bar of soap, was politically directed and controlled.

8646 **mastino** **mastiff**
il
[mastino]
Il suo unico errore è essere un mastino tibetano che pochi mesi dopo pesa circa 40 chili.
-His one mistake is he's a Tibetan mastiff, and a few months later, he weighs, you know, 80 pounds.

8647 **seggio** **seat**
il
[seddʒo]
Invito l' onorevole deputato a occupare il seggio presidenziale.
-I call on Mr Cox to take the Chair.

8648 **nafta** **naphtha**
la
[nafta]
(Combinazione complessa di idrocarburi ottenuta stabilizzando la nafta riformata cataliticamente.
-(A complex combination of hydrocarbons obtained from stabilisation of catalytic reformed naphtha.

8649 **sarcastico** **sarcastic|derisive**
adj
[sarkastiko]
Joe era sarcastico.
-Joe was sarcastic.

8650 **gratificare** **gratify**
vb
[gratifikare]
Signor Presidente, è stato gratificante ascoltare il Commissario Vitorino.
-Mr President, it was gratifying to listen to Commissioner Vitorino.

8651 **bengala** **Bengal light**
il
[beŋgala]
Un aspetto forse più significativo è la scoperta di riserve di gas naturale nel Golfo del Bengala.
-Perhaps more significantly, reserves of natural gas have now been discovered in the Bay of Bengal.

8652 **risplendere** **shine|sparkle**
vb
[risplendere]
Questa è la luce più luminosa che possiamo far risplendere oggi negli angoli bui del continente europeo.
-That is the best light that we can shine in the dark corners of the European continent today.

8653 **empio** **impious**
adj
[empjo]
LUCAS: – metti in fuga l'empio tentatore.
-LUCAS: – Put the unholy tempter to flight.

8654 **orzo** **barley**
il
[ortso]
Siamo circondati da campi di orzo.
-And we're surrounded by fields of barley.

8655 **salvaguardare** **safeguard**
vb
[salvagwardare]
Disposizioni eccessivamente rigide talvolta sono servite a salvaguardare le spese.
-Unduly rigid provisions have sometimes served to safeguard expenditure.

8656 **rimanente** **remaining; leftovers**
adj; il
[rimanente]
Joe non aveva denaro rimanente.
-Joe had no money left.

8657 **falcone** **falcon**

il
[falkone]
C'è il mio, in qualche modo rovinato, Falcone di Scupley, perché ho dovuto tirarlo fuori dalla forma.
-There's my somewhat ruined Sculpey Falcon, because I had to get it back out of the mold.

8658 **acquisizione** **acquisition**
la
[akkwizittsjone]
Inoltre, stiamo cercando un consulente che ci possa aiutare a sfruttare le loro competenze di mercato per l'acquisizione del prodotto da parte dei produttori della zona.
-In addition, we are looking for an consultant who can assist us in leveraging their expertise of the market to acquire product from manufacturers in the area.

8659 **fermezza** **firmness**
la
[fermettsa]
Applicare questo grado di fermezza ora potrebbe servire a mantenere la pace in futuro.
-Using this degree of firmness now would help to maintain peace in the future.

8660 **mannaia** **cleaver|ax**
la
[mannaja]
I tagli sono compatibili con una mannaia.
-The gashes are consistent with a cleaver.

8661 **patriottico** **patriotic**
adj
[patrjottiko]
Vorrei formulare soltanto un commento patriottico in quest'Aula multinazionale.
-I should just like to make one patriotic comment in this multinational Chamber.

8662 **magnesio** **magnesium**
il
[maɲɲezjo]
Questo è il dettaglio di una sedia in magnesio che ho disegnato.
-This is a detail of a chair that I've designed in magnesium.

8663 **underground** **underground**
il
[underground]
There was an underground railroad of sorts that was going on during those years.
-C'era una sorta di percorso semi-clandestino che si poteva percorrere in quegli anni.

8664 **figlioccio** **godson**
il
[fiʎʎottʃo]
Marcus mi ha parlato del tuo figlioccio.
-Marcus was telling me about your godson.

8665 **ninfomane** **nymphomaniac**
adj
[ninfomane]
Tutti i sintomi più caratteristici di una ninfomane.
-All the standard symptoms of the nymphomaniac.

8666 **palese** **obvious|evident**
adj
[paleze]
Signor Presidente, intendo seguire il palese suggerimento dell'onorevole Nordmann e adottare l'emendamento a nome del gruppo del Partito popolare europeo.
-Mr President, I should like to follow the very broad hint given by Mr Nordmann and adopt the amendment on behalf of the Group of the European People's Party.

8667 **neutralizzare** **neutralize|counter**
vb
[neutraliddzare]
Un vaccino addestra il corpo preventivamente a riconoscere e neutralizzare un invasore specifico.
-Narrator: A vaccine trains the body in advance how to recognize and neutralize a specific invader.

8668 **infliggere** **inflict**

vb Infliggere una nota di biasimo a qcn.
[infliddʒere] -To give sb an official warning.

8669 **circoncidere** **circumcise**
vb Stanno aspettando di essere circoncisi.
[tʃirkontʃidere] -They're waiting to be circumcised.

8670 **caramello** **caramel**
il Accompagnare a piacere con salsa al cioccolato o caramello.
[karamello] -Add chocolate or caramel sauce according to taste.

8671 **mousse** **mousse**
la Io non ho ancora finito la mia mousse al cioccolato.
[mousse] -I still haven't finished my chocolate mousse.

8672 **densità** **density|thickness**
la Il Giappone ha una elevata densità di popolazione.
[densit'a] -Japan has a high population density.

8673 **sintonizzare** **tune**
vb Sintonizzare la radio su una stazione.
[sintoniddzare] -To tune in to a radio station.

8674 **sutura** **suture**
la E alcune delle graffette usate oggi per la sutura sono state disegnate proprio da Alexis.
[sutura] -He actually devised some of the same technologies used today for suturing blood vessels, and some of the blood vessel grafts we use today were actually designed by Alexis.

8675 **scricchiolio** **crunch|creaking**
lo Non l'avevo neanche notata finché non ho sentito lo scricchiolio sotto la scarpa.
[skrikkjoljo] -Until I Felt The Crunch Under My Shoe. Ew.

8676 **carreggiata** **track**
la Erano tutti sul lato sinistro della carreggiata.
[karreddʒata] -There were all on the left–hand side of the road.

8677 **clitoride** **clitoris**
la Io non riesco a trovare il clitoride della mia ragazza.
[klitoride] -I can't find my girlfriend's clitoris.

8678 **bustina** **sachet**
la Non potete superare quella busta, che rappresenta 100.000 rupie, 2,:,000 dollari.
[bustina] -You can't cross that envelope, which is 100,000 rupees, 2,000 dollars.

8679 **artefatto** **artifact; artificial**
il; adj Pensiamo che un artefatto di pace pura possa neutralizzarlo.
[artefatto] -We're thinking an artifact of pure peace might counteract it.

8680 **visionario** **visionary**
adj Lei è un visionario, signor Knox.
[vizjonarjo] -You're a visionary, Mr. Knox.

8681 **localizzazione** **location**
la Qui potrai scegliere lingua e localizzazione.
[lokaliddzattsjone] -You can select your language and location here.

8682 **neurale** **neural**
adj Un'altra cosa sulla compassione è che fa aumentare la cosiddetta integrazione neurale.
[neurale] -Another thing about compassion is that it really enhances what's called neural integration.

8683 **recupero** **recovery**
il
[rekupero]
C'è poca speranza per il suo recupero.
-There is little if any hope for his recovery.

8684 **cinismo** **cynicism**
il
[tʃinismo]
Il vostro cinismo dev'essere affettato.
-Then all of your cynicism must be nothing but a pose.

8685 **immondo** **unclean|filthy**
adj
[immondo]
Cercherò di capire come azionare questo immondo apparecchio.
-I will try to figure out how to operate this foul device.

8686 **risuonare** **ring**
vb
[rizwonare]
Se foste abbastanza vicini, le vostre orecchie risuonerebbero con la compressione e la dilatazione dello spazio.
-If you were standing near enough, your ear would resonate with the squeezing and stretching of space.

8687 **deridere** **mock|deride**
vb
[deridere]
Molti deridono questo concetto, come se si trattasse di una nozione legata al Medioevo.
-Many people deride the idea of food security as if such an idea belongs to the dark ages.

8688 **beffare** **mock|make fun of**
vb
[beffare]
Naturalmente coloro che non credono nell'Unione europea troveranno intelligenti scuse legali e pretesti politici allo scopo di beffare la Costituzione e hanno tutto il diritto di farlo.
-Those who do not believe in the European Union will naturally find clever legal excuses for political pretexts to deride the Constitution and they have every right to do so.

8689 **barlume** **glimmer|flicker**
il
[barlume]
Vedemmo il barlume di un faro distante.
-We saw the gleam of a distant lighthouse.

8690 **accarezzare** **caress|stroke**
vb
[akkarettsare]
Sarebbe splendido poter accarezzare un animale.
-It would be so good to just pet an animal today.

8691 **rinfrescante** **refreshing**
adj
[rinfreskante]
L'esperanto è diverso in modo rinfrescante.
-Esperanto is refreshingly different.

8692 **sorgente** **source; rising**
la; adj
[sordʒente]
Dov'è la sorgente di questo fiume?
-Where is the source of this river?

8693 **anticamera** **anteroom**
le
[antikamera]
In tale anticamera dell' Europa, va loro prospettata la possibilità di avvicinarsi ancora di più alla famiglia europea affinché l' Unione ponga infine termine alle loro tensioni secolari.
-This antechamber of Europe must offer them new prospects of even closer fellowship with the European family, so that the Union can ultimately snuff out their age-old tensions.

8694 **piovra** **octopus**
la
[pjovra]
La piovra è nel mare.
-The octopus is in the sea.

8695 **tappezzeria** **upholstery**
la
[tappettserja]
Ricoprire la tappezzeria precedente.
-To paper over the existing wallpaper.

8696 **scontato** | **discounted**
adj
[skontato]
Do per scontato che la mia risposta sia corretta.
-I take for granted that my answer is correct.

8697 **annientamento** | **annihilation**
il
[annjentamento]
E penso che in un certo modo siamo stati molto più duri con gli uomini nell'annientamento della cellula-ragazza che è in loro.
-And I think in some ways we've been much harsher to men in the annihilation of their girl cell.

X 8698 **successone** | **wow**
il
[suttʃessone]
Non l'ho mai visto nemmeno io ma è un successone.
-I haven't seen it either, but it's a big hit.

8699 **plancia** | **bridge**
la
[plantʃa]
Possiamo Variare i parametri direttamente dalla plancia.
-Now we can vary all the parameters directly from the bridge.

8700 **penisola** | **peninsula**
la
[penizola]
Siete mai state nella penisola coreana?
-Have you ever been to the Korean Peninsula?

8701 **lucciola** | **firefly**
la
[luttʃola]
Mi reincarnerò in una lucciola e tornerò qui.
-I'm going to turn into a firefly and come back here.

8702 **innegabile** | **undeniable**
adj
[innegabile]
È innegabile.
-That's undeniable.

8703 **imbottito** | **padded**
adj
[imbottito]
Un bersaglio dannatamente enorme, lento, imbottito.
-Ruddy great target, slow–moving, padded.

8704 **salina** | **saltern**
la
[salina]
Preparate salina calda e riscaldate delle coperte.
-Prep warm saline, and heat up some blankets.

8705 **propriamente** | **properly**
adv
[proprjamente]
Non credo che si tratti di una questione che riguarda propriamente il Consiglio.
-I do not think that is actually a question to the Council.

8706 **cuccetta** | **bunk|couchette**
la
[kuttʃetta]
Portate il capitano in una cuccetta.
-Let's get the Captain into a bunk.

8707 **idrante** | **hydrant**
il
[idrante]
Un agente di sicurezza lo ha definito particolarmente inefficace, come se si volesse riempire un bicchiere con un idrante.
-A security agent compared it aptly with filling a water glass with a fire hose, in other words, particularly inefficient.

8708 **larghezza** | **width|span**
la
[largettsa]
Per calcolare il volume, moltiplichi la lunghezza con la larghezza e la profondità.
-To calculate the volume, multiply the length by the width by the depth.

8709 **loquace** | **talkative|voluble**
adj
[lokwatʃe]
Lei non è loquace.
-She's not talkative.

8710 **ariano** | **Aryan; Aryan**
adj; il
[arjano]
Chissà se quel fantasma ariano comparirà stasera.
-I wonder if that Aryan ghost will even appear tonight.

8711 **pittoresco** adj [pittoresko] — **picturesque|colorful**
Il lato pittoresco di qcs.
-The picturesque quality of sth.

8712 **arringa** le [arriŋga] — **harangue**
Quella relazione è un'arringa a favore della concessione di una maggiore assistenza finanziaria alle piccole e medie imprese.
-This report is a plea to grant greater financial assistance to small– and medium–sized businesses.

8713 **infiammabile** adj [infjammabile] — **flammable|irascible**
Il legno è infiammabile.
-Wood is flammable.

8714 **schivo** adj [skivo] — **shy|reserved**
È sempre sembrato così... schivo e intimidito.
-He always seemed so... demure and cowed.

8715 **spezzatino** lo [spettsatino] — **stew**
Io ho mangiato dello spezzatino di manzo a pranzo.
-I had beef stew for lunch.

8716 **andamento** il [andamento] — **trend|progress**
Condivido le preoccupazioni dell'onorevole Schwab per l'andamento del debito pubblico.
-I share Mr Schwab's concern with regard to the progress of public debt.

8717 **zerbino** lo [dzerbino] — **mat**
Il gatto sedeva sullo zerbino.
-The cat sat on the mat.

8718 **ingelosire** vb [indʒelozire] — **make jealous**
Voglio farlo ingelosire.
-I want to make him jealous.

8719 **peschereccio** adj; il [peskerettʃo] — **fishing; fishing boat**
In Irlanda, ad esempio, è raro che trascorra un anno senza la perdita in mare di qualche peschereccio, con diversi pescatori feriti mentre sono al lavoro.
-Certainly, in Ireland alone, rarely does a year pass without some fishing boat being lost at sea, and many fishers are injured in their work.

8720 **dispaccio** il [dispattʃo] — **dispatch**
È arrivato questo dispaccio da Maggie Dubois.
-Boss, this dispatch just came in from Maggie Dubois.

8721 **rinnovo** il [rinnovo] — **renewal**
Essa mira in particolare a rinnovare il mandato del relatore speciale.
-This particularly aims to renew the mandate of the Special Rapporteur.

8722 **generosamente** adv [dʒenerozamente] — **generously**
Ringrazio tutti coloro che hanno contribuito così generosamente alla discussione.
-I thank everyone who has contributed so generously to this debate.

8723 **acclamare** vb [akklamare] — **acclaim**
Acclamiamo con gioia l'inizio della nostra salvezza.
-Let us joyfully acclaim the beginning of our salvation.

8724 **limitazione** la [limitattsjone] — **limitation|restraint**
Dissentiamo inoltre sulla limitazione delle copie protette proposta dalla relatrice.
-We disagree with the limitation on the protection of copies proposed by the rapporteur.

8725 **allentare** **loosen|slacken**
vb
[allentare]
Cosa faremo per allentare la morsa dell'FMI sul Presidente Lula?
-What are we going to do to loosen the IMF's vice-like grip on Mr Lula?

8726 **vicario** **vicar; vicarious**
il; adj
[vikarjo]
E' la realtà della comunione dei santi, il mistero della « realtà vicaria », della preghiera come via di unione con Cristo e con i suoi santi.
-This is the reality of the communion of saints, the mystery of vicarious life, of prayer as the means of union with Christ and his saints.

8727 **rialzo** **rise**
il
[rjaltso]
La tendenza è al rialzo; quindi si tratta, indubbiamente, di un settore molto importante.
-This tendency is on the increase, so it is indeed a very important sector.

8728 **deplorevole** **regrettable|deplorable**
adj
[deplorevole]
"Se qualcuno di voi sopravvive in questa notte fatale e ritorna in Giamaica dica all'ammiraglio che ero alla ricerca del pirata quando questo evento deplorevole ha avuto luogo; gli dica che spero di aver sempre fatto il mio dovere, e che io-."
-"If any of you survive this fatal night and return to Jamaica tell the admiral that I was in search of the pirate when this lamentable occurrence took place; tell him I hope I have always done my duty, and that I-."

8729 **retaggio** **heritage|survival**
il
[retaddʒo]
Ha inoltre ufficialmente rinunciato al suo retaggio islamico.
-Turkey has also officially renounced its Islamic inheritance.

8730 **riciclare** **recycle**
vb
[ritʃiklare]
Mi piace riciclare: questo protegge l'ambiente ed il mio portafoglio.
-I like to recycle, It protects the environment and my wallet.

8731 **teorico** **theoretical; theorist**
adj; il
[teoriko]
Il motivo è ovvio: vi è una grave crisi di fiducia nei confronti dei politici e dei teorici dei rapporti di lavoro.
-The reason is obvious: there is a serious crisis of confidence between politicians and employment relation theoreticians.

8732 **pozzanghera** **puddle**
la
[pottsaŋgera]
La Città Perduta era caratterizzata da queste incredibili formazioni calcaree e da pozzanghere sottosopra.
-And Lost City was characterized by these incredible limestone formations and upside down pools.

8733 **auricolare** **earphone; auricular**
il; adj
[aurikolare]
Mettiti l'auricolare.
-Put the headphone on.

8734 **roccioso** **rocky**
adj[rottʃozo]
Ma ciò che Galileo vide fu un mondo roccioso e arido che espresse attraverso la sua pittura ad acquerello. -But what Galileo saw was a rocky, barren world, which he expressed through his watercolor painting.

8735 **grattare** **scratch|scrape**
vb
[grattare]
Dovresti provare a non grattare i morsi degli insetti.
-You should try not to scratch insect bites.

8736 **lacrimogeno** **lachrymatory**
adj
[lakrimodʒeno]
Un lacrimogeno grande come una lattina di Pepsi mi sfiora la testa. Woosh!
-And a tear gas canister the size of a Pepsi can goes by my head. Whoosh!

8737 **persuadere** vb [perswadere] **persuade|convince**
Joe cercò di persuadere Jane ad andare alla festa di John.
-Joe tried to persuade Jane to go to John's party.

8738 **spruzzare** vb [spruttsare] **spray|sprinkle**
E se c'è un filo di vento, se si vuole minimizzare gli spruzzi, si può abbassare il tetto.
-And if there's a bit of wind, if you want to minimize splashing, you can actually lower the roof.

8739 **chalet** lo [kalet] **chalet**
Andò in quello chalet sulle montagne.
-So he went to this cabin in the mountains.

8740 **indeterminato** adj [indeterminato] **indeterminate**
La Commissione non ha assolutamente intenzione di sminuire l'importanza del contratto a tempo indeterminato.
-The Commission's intention is in no way to reduce the importance of the open-ended contract.

8741 **tridimensionale** adj [tridimensjonale] **tridimensional**
Possono essere disposte su un piano orizzontale o tridimensionale.
-They can be planar formations, they can be three-dimensional formations.

8742 **tristemente** adv [tristemente] **sorrowfully**
Il vecchio iniziò a ridere tristemente.
-The old man started to laugh sadly.

8743 **rivestimento** il [rivestimento] **coating|jacket**
Abbiamo trovato 800.000 dollari americani nascosti nel rivestimento della valigia di Khalid.
-We found $800,000 in U.S. bills stuffed into the lining of Khalid's suitcase.

8744 **evocare** vb [evokare] **evoke**
Potrei evocare un demone per ucciderla.
-You know, I could summon a demon that would kill her.

8745 **elettrodomestico** il [elettrodomestiko] **household appliance**
Tuttavia quell'elettrodomestico non era sicuro, probabilmente perché contraffatto.
-Nevertheless the appliance was not safe, probably because it was counterfeit.

8746 **rutto** il [rutto] **burp|retch**
Io rutto molto.
-I burp a lot.

8747 **sdolcinato** adj [zdoltʃinato] **sloppy**
L'Europa non ha più bisogno del moralismo sdolcinato dei cristiani che parlano di pace e cooperazione.
-Europe does not need any more mawkish, moralising Christers who speak of peace and cooperation.

8748 **squarciare** vb [skwartʃare] **rip|slash**
E non voglio guidare fino in Messico, per poi farmi squarciare la gola da te.
-And I don't feel like driving all the way down to Mexico just to have you rip my throat out.

8749 **inverosimile** adj [inverozimile] **unlikely|tall**
Spiegare i brogli elettorali come una conseguenza di differenze culturali sembra inverosimile e controproducente.

-Explaining electoral fraud as the result of cultural differences seems both far-fetched and self-defeating.

8750 **schizofrenico** adj [skiddzofreniko]
schizophrenic
Non sei schizofrenico.
-You're not schizophrenic.

8751 **cerchia** la [tʃerkja]
circle|ring
Ci sono due dottori nella sua cerchia di amici, un chirurgo e un oftalmologo.
-There are two doctors in his circle of friends, a surgeon and an ophthalmologist.

8752 **suicida** la; adj [switʃida]
suicide; suicidal
Dobbiamo operare una distinzione fra l'attentatore suicida e colui che lo recluta.
-We need to distinguish between the suicide bomber and his or her recruiter.

8753 **caricamento** il [karikamento]
loading
Il corretto caricamento e funzionamento dell'esplosivo quando è impiegato per lo scopo a cui è destinato.
-The correct loading and functioning of the explosive when used for its intended purpose.

8754 **clero** il [klero]
clergy
Gli appartenenti al clero sono vittime di torture particolarmente raffinate.
-Members of the clergy are victims of particularly insidious torture.

8755 **diocesi** la [djotʃezi]
diocese|see
Sarà insignito dell'onorificenza dalla diocesi...
-He has the St. Gregory award from the diocese.

8756 **malessere** il [malessere]
malaise|illness
Allora ho un malessere che mi uccide.
-Well, then I'm dying of malaise.

8757 **oscenità** le [oʃʃenit'a]
obscenity|filthiness
A me non piace l'oscenità.
-I don't like profanity.

8758 **sonnambulo** il [sonnambulo]
sleepwalker
Magari le hai fumate mentre eri sonnambulo.
-Maybe you smoked them while you were out sleepwalking.

8759 **allegramente** adv [allegramente]
cheerfully
Sita ha sorriso allegramente.
-Sita smiled pleasantly.

8760 **esultanza** la[ezultantsa]
exultation
A tale proposito, trovo divertente assistere all'esultanza di coloro che sono soddisfatti dell'esito del referendum in Irlanda. -By the way, it is amusing to see the rejoicing of those who are pleased with the result of the referendum in Ireland.

8761 **rognoso** adj [roɲɲozo]
mangy
Allora pagate voi, tirchio rognoso!
-So then pay up, you mangy codger!

8762 **vendicativo** adj [vendikativo]
vindictive
È essenziale mantenere questo tratto non-vendicativo e assicurarsi che perfino i peggiori criminali siano trattati con dignità, anche se non lo meritano.
-It is essential to maintain this non-vindictive provision and to ensure

that even the worst of criminals must be treated with dignity, even if they do not deserve it.

8763 **macellare** — **slaughter**
vb
[matʃellare]
Ora, il numero di queste amigdale mostra che non possono essere state fatte per macellare gli animali.
-Now, the sheer numbers of these hand axes shows that they can't have been made for butchering animals.

8764 **stimolare** — **stimulate|spur**
vb
[stimolare]
Credo che le discussioni che ora state per svolgere debbano essere uno stimolo in questa direzione.
-I think that the debates you are going to conduct now must be a spur in that direction.

8765 **qualora** — **if**
con
[kwalora]
Qualora gli svedesi cambiassero idea, probabilmente si ritornerebbe sulla questione.
-If the Swedish people change their minds, the question may possibly arise again.

8766 **pelare** — **skin|fleece**
vb
[pelare]
So pelare una mela.
-I can peel an apple.

8767 **corporatura** — **build**
la
[korporatura]
La sua corporatura massiccia.
-The compactness of his build.

8768 **giornaliero** — **daily; day-to-day**
adj; il
[dʒornaljero]
Ciò vale anche per i periodi di riposo giornaliero e per le pause brevi.
-This also applies to the daily rest periods and the short breaks.

8769 **allineamento** — **alignment**
lo
[allineamento]
La proposta si limita esclusivamente alle modifiche necessarie all'allineamento.
-The proposal is limited to modifications for the purpose of alignment only.

8770 **attitudine** — **attitude**
le
[attitudine]
E la chiave è promuovere un'attitudine positiva dell'Africa riguardo l'Africa.
-And the key is to promote a positive African attitude towards Africa.

8771 **balordo** — **stupid**
adj
[balordo]
Non ritengo di alcun interesse un balordo ubriacone.
-I take no interest in your mindless banter.

8772 **pancione** — **paunch**
il
[pantʃone]
Joe ha il pancione.
-Joe has a potbelly.

8773 **subbuglio** — **confusion**
il
[subbuʎʎo]
Qual è lo scopo di tutto questo subbuglio?
-What's the purpose of all this commotion?

8774 **cliché** — **cliche**
i
[klik'e]
And thirdly, the idea that machines are becoming biological and complex is at this point a cliche.
-In terzo luogo, l'idea che le macchine stiano diventando biologiche e complesse è a questo punto uno stereotipo.

8775 **morboso** — **morbid|unhealthy**
adj
[morbozo]
Leggendo il testo, si resta con la morbosa impressione che ogni gravidanza debba essere per forza un dramma.

-Reading this report, one is given the morbid impression that any pregnancy is necessarily a crisis.

8776 **destrezza** **dexterity**
la
[destrettsa]
E'di estrema importanza che i membri del Consiglio di sicurezza facciano ricorso a tutta la loro destrezza per raggiungere l'unanimità.
-It is extremely important that the Security Council members use all their skill to achieve unanimity.

8777 **rivendicare** **claim**
vb
[rivendikare]
Essa piuttosto dovrebbe avere l'orgoglio di rivendicare le proprie radici cristiane, specie di fronte al grave pericolo di un'islamizzazione strisciante.
-It should, instead, lay claim to its own Christian roots with pride, in particular in the face of the grave danger of creeping Islamicisation.

8778 **gemma** **gem|bud**
la
[dʒemma]
Forse questo mi guiderà alla gemma.
-Maybe this will lead me to the gem.

8779 **urna** **urn**
le
[urna]
Mettile in un urna in un mausoleo.
-Put them in an urn at a mausoleum.

8780 **avversità** **adversity|ill**
le
[avversit'a]
Abbiamo avuto molte avversità.
-We've had a lot of adversity.

8781 **figuraccia** **poor figure**
le
[figurattʃa]
Joe fece una figuraccia.
-Joe goofed.

8782 **insistenza** **insistence**
la
[insistentsa]
Questo è ciò che intendo per la mia costante insistenza sulla "moderazione" nel governo.
This is what I mean by my constant insistence upon "moderation" in government.

8783 **botanico** **botanist; botanic**
il; adj
[botaniko]
Così ho parlato con un botanico del Giardino Botanico di Pretoria, che mi ha spiegato che alcune specie di alberi si sono adattate a questa regione.
-So, I spoke to a botanist at the Pretoria Botanical Garden, who explained that certain species of trees have adapted to this region.

8784 **tettuccio** **canopy**
il
[tettuttʃo]
Chiuda lo sportello e mani sul tettuccio.
-Close the car door, put your hands on the roof.

8785 **beduino** **Bedouin; Bedouin**
adj; il
[bedwino]
I cammelli sono come gli angeli disse un beduino.
-"Camels are like angels," a Bedouin once said.

8786 **dissenso** **dissent|disagreement**
il
[dissenso]
Giusto, mostriamogli il nostro dissenso.
-Right, let's show them our dissent.

8787 **stipulare** **stipulate**
vb
[stipulare]
Va osservato che la proposta non stipula le condizioni per l'ammissione di cittadini di paesi terzi.
-It is important to note that this proposal does not stipulate the conditions for admitting third-country nationals.

8788 **altruismo** **altruism**

	il	Io rispetto il suo altruismo.
	[altrwismo]	-I respect her selflessness.
8789	**siamese**	**Siamese; Siamese**
	adj; il/la	Raymur e il suo gemello siamese, Flanigan.
	[sjameze]	-Raymour and his conjoined twin, Flanigan.
8790	**astrologia**	**astrology**
	la	Non confondere l'astrologia con l'astronomia.
	[astrolodʒa]	-Don't confuse astrology with astronomy.
8791	**forense**	**forensic**
	adj	II. della decisione del Consiglio che istituisce un sistema di analisi forense speciale del profilo delle droghe sintetiche.
	[forense]	-II. establishing a system of special forensic profiling analysis of synthetic drugs
8792	**spiedo**	**spit**
	lo	Sono uscito per preparare il terreno per lo spiedo.
	[spjedo]	-I came out to ready the ground for the spit.
8793	**latitante**	**absconding; abscond**
	adj; il	Sto cercando un Flessibile latitante di nome Malcolm Dawkins.
	[latitante]	-I'm looking for a fugitive folder by the name of Malcolm Dawkins.
8794	**poppante**	**suckling**
	il/la	Ha la stazza di un poppante.
	[poppante]	-He has the feet of a toddler.
8795	**letizia**	**joy**
	la	Gli dissi che, al contrario, lo facevo con grande letizia.
	[letittsja]	-I told him, on the contrary, it was my great joy to do this.
8796	**favoreggiamento**	**abetment**
	il	E' favoreggiamento.
	[favoreddʒamento]	-Buying people out of slavery is like paying a burglar to get your television back; it's abetting a crime.
8797	**radioattività**	**radioactivity**
	la	A cosa pensi quando senti la parola "radioattività"?
	[radjoattivit'a]	-What do you think of when you hear the word "radioactivity"?
8798	**fuggiasco**	**fugitive|escapee**
	il	Guarda, sei uno schiavo fuggiasco e io un avvocato.
	[fuddʒasko]	-Look, you are a runaway slave, and I am a lawyer.
8799	**maestoso**	**majestic|stately**
	adj	Come ricorderete, ad un certo punto del libro 2001, HAL si rende conto che l'universo è troppo grande e maestoso e ampio per quegli stupidissimi astronauti.
	[maestozo]	-As you remember, at some point in the book for "2001," HAL realizes that the universe is too big, and grand, and profound for those really stupid astronauts.
8800	**dentino**	**denticle**
	il	Sai, parlo di quando perdono il primo dentino o delle coccole quando sono malate.
	[dentino]	-You know, I'm talking about losing their first tooth, or holding them when they're sick.
8801	**secondare**	**comply**
	vb	Dar impulso al know–how e all'eccellenza in Europa, comparare e migliorare i sistemi esistenti e secondare la dimensione interpersonale.
	[sekondare]	

-Promote European know–how and excellence, compare and improve existing systems as well as support the people–to–people dimension.

8802 **civilizzare** **civilize**
vb
[tʃiviliddzare]
I giardini zoologici non sono affatto necessari nel cosiddetto mondo civilizzato odierno.
-Zoos are unessential in this so-called civilized world of today.

8803 **ghiacciaio** **glacier**
il
[gjattʃajo]
Sulle Ande: questo ghiacciaio è la fonte dell'acqua potabile di questa città.
-In the Andes, this glacier is the source of drinking water for this city.

8804 **confrontare** **compare**
vb
[konfrontare]
Ora dobbiamo solo confrontare il DNA.
-Now we just need to compare the DNA.

8805 **gesuita** **Jesuit**
il
[dʒezwita]
Lui divenne gesuita Si era convertito dalla confessione anglicana.
-He became a Jesuit. He converted from his Anglican faith.

8806 **pungente** **pungent; nippy**
adj; il
[pundʒente]
E ci ha ricoperti di foglie e di un odore pungente.
-It was frightening, and it showered us with leaves and a pungent smell.

8807 **degradare** **degrade**
vb
[degradare]
E' stupendo quando posso degradare il tessuto.
-And that's great when I can degrade the tissue.

8808 **reprimere** **repress|suppress**
vb
[reprimere]
E il popolo si può reprimere quanto si vuole, ma c'è sempre la possibilità che si ribelli.
-And you can repress people for so long and so much, but there is always the possibility that they will rebel.

8809 **patteggiare** **negotiate**
vb
[patteddʒare]
Patteggiare con il nemico.
-To negotiate with the enemy.

8810 **farmaceutico** **pharmaceutical**
adj
[farmatʃutiko]
Seguiranno altri settori, come quello alimentare, cosmetico, farmaceutico e dei servizi.
-Other sectors such as foodstuffs, cosmetics, pharmaceuticals and services will follow.

8811 **comunemente** **commonly**
adv
[komunemente]
La chiave inglese è uno strumento usato comunemente.
-A wrench is a commonly used tool.

8812 **trapelare** **leak|transpire**
vb
[trapelare]
Qualcuno ha fatto trapelare il segreto al nemico.
-Someone leaked the secret to the enemy.

8813 **aneurisma** **aneurysm**
il
[aneurisma]
E dobbiamo farlo prima che l'aneurisma si rompa, o potrebbe morire.
-And we need to do that before the aneurysm ruptures, or you will die.

8814 **incarcerare** **imprison**
vb
[iŋkartʃerare]
L'onorevole Pilip, è stato incarcerato ventisei giorni a Cuba, perché era in contatto con un gruppo di dissidenti.
-Mr Pilip was detained for 26 days in a Cuban jail for having established links with dissidents.

8815 **establishment** **establishment**

gli [establisment] Establishment of the European Criminal Records Information System (ECRIS)
-Istituzione del sistema europeo d'informazione sui casellari giudiziari (ECRIS)

8816 **eterosessuale** **heterosexual**
adj [eterozesswale]
(Risate) Agitate, e avrete una coppia eterosessuale.
-(Laughter) Shake it, and you have a heterosexual couple.

8817 **argenteo** **silvery**
adj [ardʒenteo]
E i testimoni hanno descritto un forte flash argenteo.
-And, eyewitnesses described a bright, silvery flash.

8818 **stilista** **stylist**
il/la [stilista]
È una stilista di moda.
-She's a fashion designer.

8819 **protone** **proton**
il [protone]
Devi solo prendere un protone, e lo scolpisci rapidamente con un elettrone.
-You simply take the proton, and you hit it really sharply with an electron.

8820 **trivellare** **drill**
vb [trivellare]
E' il foro geologico più profondo mai trivellato.
-So it's the deepest geological bore hole ever drilled.

8821 **motorizzazione** **motorization**
la [motoriddzattsjone]
Ho un contatto alla motorizzazione che può aiutarci.
-I got a contact at the DMV that can help us out.

8822 **quietare** **quiet|calm**
vb [kwjetare]
Le prove di stress proposte dalla Commissione non basteranno di per loro a quietare il pubblico.
-The stress tests proposed by the Commission will not be enough on their own to pacify the public.

8823 **nazionalità** **nationality**
la [nattsjonalit'a]
Di che nazionalità è?
-What is his nationality?

8824 **scontroso** **grumpy|surly**
adj [skontrozo]
È scontroso.
-He is unsociable.

8825 **fantasticare** **daydream**
vb [fantastikare]
Una specie che ama fantasticare sulla propria morte.
-A life form that loves to fantasize about its own demise.

8826 **speronare** **ram**
vb [speronare]
Perché ho sempre desiderato speronare qualcosa.
-Because I've always wanted to ram something.

8827 **cavalluccio** **hobbyhorse**
il [kavalluttʃo]
O meglio ancora... un cavalluccio marino.
-Or even better, a sea horse.

8828 **coraggiosamente** **courageously|gamely**
adv [koraddʒozamente]
Pinocchio, anche se da solo, si difese coraggiosamente.
-Pinocchio, although alone, defended himself bravely.

8829 **sorcio** **mouse**
il [sortʃo]
Tom, a quanto pare Bruce Vilanch si è presentato qui travestito da sorcio.
-It appears that Bruce Vilanch has arrived wearing a rat costume.

8830 **fasciatura** **bandage|dressing**

	la [faʃʃatura]	Credo proprio che servirà una fasciatura. -Well, I think we're definitely going to need a bandage.
8831	**rastrello** il [rastrello]	**rake** Questa è la storia di un mio rastrello. -This is the story of a rake in my backyard.
8832	**sanatorio** il [sanatorjo]	**sanatorium** Sono stato mandato qui per chiudere questo sanatorio. -I've been sent here to close down this sanatorium.
8833	**dolciume** il; adj [doltʃume]	**sweets; sweet** L'ha passata in giro come un dolciume mentre tu giocavi a golf. -Yes. He passed her around like a piece of candy while you were out playing golf.
8834	**versamento** il [versamento]	**payment** Gli onorevoli Rasmussen e Starkevičiūthanno parlato di versamenti di fondi nell'economia. -Mr Rasmussen and Mrs Starkevičiūttalked of pouring money into the economy.
8835	**bidello** il [bidello]	**janitor** Quel bidello... lo stava toccando. -That janitor was, like, touching him.
8836	**riassumere** vb [rjassumere]	**summarize|reassume** In tre parole riesco a riassumere tutto ciò che ho imparato riguardo alla vita: essa va avanti. -In three words I can sum up everything I've learned about life — It goes on.
8837	**naufragio** il [naufradʒo]	**shipwreck|sinking** E questo spinge il naufragio molto più verso Key West. -And that pulls the shipwreck way over toward Key West.
8838	**fuliggine** la [fuliddʒine]	**soot** Mancano altre emissioni quali quelle del carbone, ossia la fuliggine. -But what we're missing is also some other emissions like black carbon, that is soot.
8839	**insinuazione** le [insinwattsjone]	**insinuation|implication** Era più un'insinuazione, che un'accusa. -That was more of an insinuation than an accusation.
8840	**conservatorio** il; adj [konservatorjo]	**conservatory; conservative** Io sto studiando canto in un conservatorio. -I'm studying singing at a college of music.
8841	**repellente** adj [repellente]	**repellent|repulsive** La trovo repellente, mio signore. -I find it repellent, my liege.
8842	**galantuomo** il [galantwomo]	**gentleman** Riguarda quel galantuomo e mia moglie. -It's in reference to that gentleman and my wife.
8843	**nocca** la [nokka]	**knuckle** Un taglio netto, proprio alla nocca. -Clean cut right at the knuckle.
8844	**deduzione** la [deduttsjone]	**deduction** Potrebbe essere un esperimento di deduzione interessante per te. -If nothing else, it would be an interesting experiment in deduction for you.

8845 **affitto** **rent**
i
[affitto]
Sami ha preso in affitto un appartamento al Cairo.
-Sami rented an apartment in Cairo.

8846 **infrastruttura** **infrastructure**
le
[infrastruttura]
Infrastruttura per l'informazione territoriale nella Comunità (INSPIRE) (votazione).
-Infrastructure for Spatial Information in the European Community (INSPIRE) (vote).

8847 **tremante** **trembling|shaking**
adj
[tremante]
E' uscita di corsa dai rovi dirigendosi dritta verso di noi, ci si è seduta a fianco, tremante, con la schiena rivolta verso Derek e lo sguardo lontano.
-She came charging out of the thicket straight towards us, sat next to us, shivering, with her back towards Dereck, and looking out.

8848 **arricchire** **enrich**
vb
[arrikkire]
Questi due emendamenti arricchiscono la posizione comune.
-These two amendments enhance the common position.

8849 **elettrizzante** **electrifying**
adj
[elettriddzante]
Immagino sia un racconto piuttosto elettrizzante.
-I suppose it was quite a thrilling tale.

8850 **allarmare** **alarm**
vb
[allarmare]
Come politici abbiamo il compito di non suscitare paure e di non usare termini che possano allarmare.
-It behoves us, as politicians, not to be raising fears and using terms which alarm people.

8851 **esaltare** **exalt|celebrate**
vb
[ezaltare]
Per esaltare la virtù, così che tutti apprezzino lo spirito della gentilezza e della docilità, e che possano tutti beneficiare di un regno di pace eterna.
-To exalt virtue, so that all should cherish the spirit of kindness and meekness, and that they should all enjoy a reign of eternal peace.

8852 **presiedere** **preside**
vb
[prezjedere]
È proprio del parroco presiedere i consigli parrocchiali.
-It is for the Parish Priest to preside at parochial councils.

8853 **disinvolto** **casual**
adj
[dizinvolto]
Joe sembra disinvolto.
-Joe looks cool.

8854 **formulare** **formulate|express**
vb
[formulare]
Il concetto potrebbe essere formulato in maniera banale.
-I could phrase this loosely.

8855 **zavorra** **ballast**
la
[dzavorra]
Senza questa zavorra intellettuale, la relazione sarebbe stata nettamente migliore.
-The report would have been better without such intellectual ballast.

8856 **cloro** **chlorine**
il
[kloro]
Un aspetto importante è il contenuto di cloro.
-An important aspect in this connection is the high chlorine content.

8857 **pastello** **pastel; pastel**
adj; il
[pastello]
Lascia a papà il pastello viola.
-Save the purple crayon for daddy.

8858 **coltellata** **stab**
la
[koltellata]
La prima coltellata è sempre gratuita.
-First stab's always for free.

8859 **cognizione** **cognition|acquaintance**
la
[koɲɲittsjone]
Io persi la cognizione del tempo.
-I lost track of time.

8860 **attaccabrighe** **wrangler**
gli
[attakkabrige]
Terribile attaccabrighe... c'è rimasto ingarbugliato alla fine.
-Terrible scrapper... he got caught up in it at the end.

8861 **astronomia** **astronomy**
le
[astronomja]
L'astronomia è un hobby costoso.
-Astronomy is an expensive hobby.

8862 **provocante** **provocative**
adj
[provokante]
Jane è diventata molto provocante.
-Jane became very flirtatious.

8863 **adeguato** **adequate**
adj
[adegwato]
Era adeguato.
-It was adequate.

8864 **tassametro** **taximeter|meter**
il
[tassametro]
Il tassametro gira, Jeebs.
-The meter's running, Jeebs.

8865 **mormorio** **murmur|hum**
il
[mormorjo]
Che sia il mormorio della televisione di un vicino...
-Whether it's the murmur of a neighbor's television...

8866 **truffa** **fraud|swindle**
la
[truffa]
Te l'ho detto che era una truffa.
-I told you it was a scam.

8867 **devastazione** **devastation**
la
[devastattsjone]
Oggi, nel XXI secolo, l'obiettivo di una guerra non può più essere la devastazione o il massimo danno.
-Today, in the 21st century, making war can no longer be led by the idea of ravaging or by the idea of maximum damage.

8868 **concilio** **council**
il
[kontʃiljo]
La questione venne riproposta nella Commissione conciliare costituita nell'ottobre 1962.
-The question was raised again in the Conciliar Commission, set up in October 1962.

8869 **bollitore** **kettle|heater**
il
[bollitore]
Il bollitore sta fischiando sulla stufa.
-The kettle is whistling on the stove.

8870 **sciame** **swarm**
lo
[ʃame]
Uno sciame di calabroni attaccò i bambini.
-A swarm of hornets attacked the children.

8871 **contemporaneo** **contemporary**
adj
[kontemporaneo]
Possono benissimo rappresentare la sfida maggiore allo sport contemporaneo.
-They may well represent the greatest challenge to contemporary sport.

8872 **ricapitolare** **recap|summarize**
vb
[rikapitolare]
I tempi non permettono di ricapitolare l'intera discussione.
-Time does not allow me to summarize the entire debate.

8873 **oppresso** **oppressed**
il
[oppresso]
Inoltre, i funzionari locali hanno oppresso i, o popolo della tribù della collina.

-Moreover, local officials also oppressed in particular the Montagnard, or hill tribe people.

8874 **calabrone** — **hornet**
il
[kalabrone]
Joe è stato ucciso da un calabrone gigante.
-Joe was killed by a giant hornet.

8875 **sorvolare** — **fly over**
vb
[sorvolare]
Ho avuto il privilegio, se così si può dire, di sorvolare Haiti e il Cile, a un paio di settimane di distanza.
-I had the dubious privilege to fly over Haiti and Chile, within a couple of weeks of each other.

8876 **gettone** — **token**
il
[dʒettone]
So che per molti tossici è un... gettone prezioso.
-I know that to most addicts it's a treasured token.

8877 **macedonia** — **fruit salad**
la
[matʃedonja]
Vi piace la macedonia?
-Do you like fruit salad?

8878 **aggravare** — **aggravate | make worse**
vb
[aggravare]
La pratica della disinformazione ha contribuito soltanto ad aggravare il problema.
-The disinformation measures have only served to aggravate the problem.

8879 **permaloso** — **touchy | sensitive**
adj
[permalozo]
Joe è molto permaloso, vero?
-Joe is very touchy, isn't he?

8880 **moscio** — **soft**
adj
[moʃʃo]
Scusate, Don Giovanni... ...il vostro lucertolone sembra moscio.
-Excuse me, Don Giovanni... ...your lizard seems limp.

8881 **borghesia** — **bourgeoisie**
la
[borgezja]
Oggi, con il pretesto del "terrorismo", sono stati riesumati dai tempi oscuri della storia della borghesia in Europa.
-Today, on the pretext of 'terrorism', they are hauled in again from the darkest ages in the history of the bourgeoisie in Europe.

8882 **croissant** — **croissant**
i
[kroissant]
Prenda un croissant.
-Have a croissant.

8883 **vertebrale** — **vertebral**
adj
[vertebrale]
Da un lato, si pone il problema di dove estrarre la colonna vertebrale.
-Where should the vertebral column be removed.

8884 **spettrale** — **spectral | phantom**
adj
[spettrale]
Il videocomparatore spettrale dovrebbe poterci dire cosa c'era sopra.
-The Video Spectral Comparator should be able to tell us what was once on here.

8885 **assordare** — **deafen**
vb
[assordare]
Pietosa speranza all'interno, assordante silenzio all'esterno.
-Pious hope on the inside, deafening silence on the outside.

8886 **impotenza** — **impotence | impuissance**
le
[impotentsa]
Il fumo può causare l'impotenza.
-Smoking can cause impotence.

8887 **perforare** — **pierce | drill**
vb
[perforare]
Ucciderà mostri e perforare le armature samurai.
-It will kill monsters and pierce samurai armor.

8888 **limbo** **limbo**
il
[limbo]
Non è esplicitamente vietato, ma in realtà non è neanche permesso. È un limbo giuridico.
-It's not explicitly prohibited, but in fact it is not allowed either. It is a legal limbo.

8889 **olimpico** **Olympic**
adj
[olimpiko]
L'ippica è l'unico evento olimpico aperto a entrambi i sessi.
-Equestrian is the only mixed-gender Olympic event.

8890 **gnomo** **gnome|elf**
lo
[ɲomo]
Gli gnomi politici che ci governano permettono ai demagoghi di estrema destra e di estrema sinistra, compresi i nazionalsocialisti e altri separatisti, di demolire il sogno europeo.
-The political gnomes who govern us are allowing demagogues from the extreme Right and Left, including National Socialists and other separatists, to demolish the European dream.

8891 **rizzare** **raise**
vb
[riddzare]
Questo mi ha fatto rizzare i capelli.
-It made my hair stand on end.

8892 **ceretta** **waxing**
la
[tʃeretta]
Devo prenotare una ceretta brasiliana per domani a mezzogiorno.
-I need to book a Brazilian wax for noon tomorrow

8893 **stampante** **printer**
la
[stampante]
La stampante ha dell'inchiostro?
-Does the printer have any ink?

8894 **diversità** **diversity**
le
[diversit'a]
In ogni cuore umano ci sono una tigre, un maiale, un asino e un usignolo. La diversità di carattere è dovuta alla loro attività diseguale.
-In each human heart are a tiger, a pig, an ass and a nightingale. Diversity of character is due to their unequal activity.

8895 **pubertà** **puberty**
la
[pubert'a]
Dopo la pubertà cadiamo fuori dal grafico.
-After puberty, we fall off the map.

8896 **dedito** **dedicated**
adj
[dedito]
Sono dedito.
-I'm committed.

8897 **dannoso** **harmful|detrimental**
adj
[dannozo]
Fumare è dannoso per la vostra salute.
-Smoking is bad for your health.

8898 **accorgersi** **notice|realize**
vb
[akk'ɔrdʒersi]
Signor Presidente, mi sono appena accorto che alcuni osservatori, alzando la mano, stanno prendendo parte alla votazione.
-Mr President, I have just found out that some observers are taking part in votes by raising their hands.

8899 **garofano** **carnation**
il
[garofano]
Questo nastro bianco è un simbolo, com'è anche un simbolo il garofano che ricorda la lotta delle donne congolesi contro le sofferenze che subiscono ogni giorno: sono qui con noi proprio adesso.
-This white ribbon is a symbol, it is also the symbol of the carnation that recalls the fight of Congolese women against the suffering they undergo every day - they were here just now.

8900 **gazzetta** **gazette**

la Essere ladro come una gazza.
[gattsetta] -To be a thieving magpie.

8901 **civico** **civic**
adj Votare è il vostro dovere civico.
[tʃiviko] -It's your civic duty to vote.

8902 **indugio** **delay**
il Qualsiasi uomo di chiesa lascerebbe la nostra parrocchia senza ulteriore indugio.
[indudʒo] -Any Christian man would leave our parish without delay.

8903 **paesano** **villager; village**
il; adj C'è una bellissima storia riguardo un discorso con un paesano in India. ~~~ Uno dice, "Hai predo il tuo Dapsone?"
[paezano] -He has a wonderful story of talking to a villager in India and saying, "Have you taken your Dapsone?"

8904 **disturbato** **disturbed**
adj Mi ha disturbato per del denaro.
[disturbato] -He bothered me for money.

8905 **indaffarato** **busy**
adj Alcuni giorni dopo, il governo italiano è indaffarato ad attuare proprio queste misure.
[indaffarato] -Days later the Italian Government is busy enacting these very measures.

8906 **furibondo** **furious|wild**
adj Il mio George sarebbe furibondo.
[furibondo] -My George would be furious.

8907 **desolazione** **desolation**
la Ho osservato da vicino gli incendi che ancora infuriavano in Spagna e Portogallo, e poi il mare di desolazione che hanno lasciato dietro di sé.
[dezolattsjone] -I saw at close quarters the fires in Portugal and Spain while they were still raging, and also the widespread devastation they wreaked.

8908 **anguria** **watermelon**
la Mi piace l'anguria.
[aŋgurja] -I like watermelon.

8909 **prossimamente** **soon|in a short time**
adv Il prossimo dibattito, in seno al COREPER, sulla strategia futura avrà luogo venerdì prossimo.
[prossimamente] -The next discussion in Coreper on the future strategy will take place next Friday.

8910 **carceriere** **jailer|warder**
il Uccideremo il figlio del nostro carceriere.
[kartʃerjere] -We will kill the son of our jailer.

8911 **guadare** **wade**
vb Un uomo ha una volpe, un coniglio e un cavolo e vuole guadare il fiume, ma può caricarli sulla barca uno per volta.
[gwadare] -A man has a fox, a rabbit, and a cabbage, And he wants to get across the river, But his boat can only carry one of them at a time.

8912 **dirupo** **cliff**
il Ho intenzione di partire da un dirupo, catapultandomi da un dirupo.
[dirupo] -And I plan to start from a cliff, like catapulted from a cliff.

8913 **sanguinoso** **bloody**
adj Alziamo la voce, signor Commissario Figel, per impedire l'ennesimo, cruento, ingiusto, sanguinoso schiaffo al Tibet e ai tibetani.
[saŋgwinozo]

-Let us raise our voices, Commissioner Figel', to prevent the umpteenth bloody, unjust, gory insult to Tibet and the Tibetans.

8914 **calamità** **calamity|misfortune**
le
[kalamit'a]
Tuo fratello è una vera calamità!
-Your brother is a walking disaster!

8915 **attaccamento** **attachment|adhesion**
il
[attakkamento]
E' questo puro attaccamento al terrore che rende Hamas tanto inadatto a governare.
-It is this undiluted attachment to terror that makes Hamas so unfit to govern.

8916 **donzella** **damsel**
la
[dontsella]
Sfortunatamente, qualcuno con un po' di complesso dell'eroe decise che questa donzella fosse in pericolo e che avesse bisogno di essere salvata.
-Unfortunately, somebody with a bit of a hero complex decided that this damsel was in distress and needed saving.

8917 **fibbia** **buckle**
la
[fibbja]
Collegare la cinghia di carico alla fibbia simulata.
-The loading strap can be attached to the simulated buckle.

8918 **basilare** **basic**
adj
[bazilare]
Il principio basilare resta però il pari trattamento.
-These conditions must be included, but the basic principle is equal treatment.

8919 **progettazione** **design**
la
[prodʒettattsjone]
Joe ha scoperto una falla nella progettazione della nave.
-Joe discovered a flaw in the ship's design.

8920 **mortalità** **mortality**
la
[mortalit'a]
E comincia a riconoscere i pericoli della mortalità e perché dovrebbe allontanarsi dalla mortalità.
-And she's recognizing the dangers of mortality and why she should break away from mortality.

8921 **mutilazione** **mutilation**
la
[mutilattsjone]
Vale la pena di ricordare quale grave mutilazione è l'aborto per una donna.
-It is worth remembering what a serious mutilation an abortion is for a woman.

8922 **rinviare** **postpone|refer**
vb
[rinvjare]
Io penso che dobbiamo rinviare la riunione.
-I think we need to postpone the meeting.

8923 **magno** **great**
adj
[maɲɲo]
La prima volta che vennero in contatto fu all'epoca di Alessandro Magno.
-They first came into contact at the time of Alexander the Great.

8924 **cloche** **joystick**
la
[kloke]
Voglio subito in volo chiunque abbia mai tenuto in mano una cloche.
-Everybody that's ever held a stick, I want them up there now.

8925 **vaiolo** **smallpox**
il
[vajolo]
Ma vedere il vaiolo dal punto di vista di un sovrano è la prospettiva sbagliata.
-But to see smallpox from the perspective of a sovereign is the wrong perspective.

8926 **avocado** **avocado**
gli
[avokado]
Gli avocado sono ricchi di vitamina E.
-Avocados are rich in vitamin E.

√ 8927 **spartire** vb [spartire] **share**
E dato che Lucas è figlio unico, potrebbe piacergli spartire i giocattoli con qualcuno.
-And I think it's important for Lucas, as an only child, to have someone that he has to share his toys with.

8928 **saccheggio** il [sakkeddʒo] **plunder|sack**
Noi non tollereremo alcun saccheggio.
-We won't tolerate any looting.

8929 **modellino** il [modellino] **model**
Essi modellano il modo in cui penso e guardo al mondo.
-They fashion the way in which I think about and look at the world.

8930 **contemplare** vb [kontemplare] **contemplate**
Le conseguenze sarebbero talmente orribili che non si possono nemmeno contemplare.
-The consequences are too horrific to contemplate.

8931 **regolatore** il [regolatore] **regulator**
Per il buon funzionamento dei mercati è assolutamente essenziale il ruolo del regolatore.
-For markets to function well, the role of regulator is absolutely crucial.

8932 **insostenibile** adj [insostenibile] **unsustainable**
La vita sotto il tetto di Joe era insostenibile.
-Life under Joe's roof was unbearable.

8933 **cinquantina** la [tʃiŋkwantina] **about fifty**
È deplorevole, signor Presidente, ma magari con una cinquantina di morti in più…
-Pitiful, Mr President, but perhaps with fifty more deaths...

8934 **completamento** il [kompletamento] **completion**
Vi farà piacere sapere che il completamento...
-However, you'll be glad to know that the completion...

8935 **canino** adj [kanino] **canine**
Quindi, nell'addestramento canino abbiamo questa idea di dominanza, o di cane alfa — ne avrete già sentito parlare.
-So, we get in dog training this notion of dominances, or of the alpha dog.

8936 **melodrammatico** adj [melodrammatiko] **melodramatic**
Non sia così melodrammatico.
-Don't be so melodramatic.

8937 **spicciare** vb [spittʃare] **hurry up**
lo sono andato a far la spesa e a spicciare.
-I had to go shopping and rush through the housework

8938 **fuga** la [fuga] **escape|get-away**
Fadil ha finanziato la fuga di Layla.
-Fadil financed Layla's escape.

8939 **ampliare** vb [ampljare] **extend|enlarge**
Lei vuole ampliare l'area non fumatori.
-She wants to extend the no-smoking area.

8940 **elevato** adj [elevato] **high|elevated**
Il prezzo è elevato.
-The price is high.

8941 **sussurro** **whisper|murmur**

il
[sussurro]
Quanto proporremo alla Conferenza intergovernativa in tema di PESC è poco più di un flebile sussurro destinato a non far tremare neanche una foglia.
-What we are going to propose to the Intergovernmental Conference on the subject of the CFSP is little more than a plaintive murmur, before which not so much as a leaf will tremble.

8942 **rumeno** **Romanian**
adj
[rumeno]
Il mio nome è rumeno; il suo è americano.
-My name is Romanian; his is American.

8943 **scansafatiche** **loafer|shirker**
il/la
[skansafatike]
Joe non è uno scansafatiche.
-Joe is no slouch.

8944 **tulipano** **tulip**
il
[tulipano]
La Rivoluzione dei tulipani del 2005 ha destato, ancora una volta, immense speranze.
-The Tulip revolution in 2005 once again raised immense hope.

8945 **mascherina** **radiator grill**
la
[maskerina]
Credo si stia abituando alla mascherina.
-I think she's getting used to the mask.

8946 **ausiliario** **auxiliary|subsidiary**
adj
[auziljarjo]
L'estensione del controllo da parte del personale ausiliario nel caso della carne rossa ci causa particolari preoccupazioni.
-The extension of inspection by ancillary staff in the case of red meat causes us special concern.

8947 **premier** **premier**
il
[premjer]
Il premier ha annunciato la sua intenzione di intraprendere riforme drastiche in parlamento.
-The premier announced his intention to undertake drastic reforms in parliament.

8948 **accordarsi** **agree|arrange**
vb
[akkordarsi]
Ciò che manca loro è quello spazio sicuro per riunirsi, accordarsi e agire.
-What they lack is that safe space to come together, agree and move to action.

8949 **buccia** **peel|husk**
la
[buttʃa]
Siete mai scivolati su una buccia di banana?
-Have you ever slipped on a banana peel?

8950 **indigestione** **indigestion**
la[indidʒestjone]
Il ragazzo ebbe un'indigestione dopo aver mangiato troppo. -The boy had indigestion after eating too much.

8951 **fagiano** **pheasant**
il
[fadʒano]
Quello è un fagiano.
-That's a pheasant.

8952 **schedare** **file|record**
vb
[skedare]
Era stata incaricata di separare e schedare le singole prove...
-She was assigned to sort and file the individual trace elements...

8953 **pedaggio** **toll**
il
[pedaddʒo]
Si erano accampati nei boschi vicino al ponte a pedaggio.
-They were camping in the woods near the toll bridge.

8954 **albino** **albino**
il
[albino]
Joe è albino.
-Joe is an albino.

8955 **rimando** **return**
il
[rimando]
Perciò, dovremo attenerci al Regolamento del Parlamento e rimandare la votazione alla seduta che si terrà a Strasburgo.
-We will therefore have to respect the rules of this House and adjourn the vote until the Strasbourg sitting.

8956 **procreare** **procreate**
vb
[prokreare]
Perché avvertire le donne prima e durante la gravidanza e ignorare gli effetti sugli uomini in grado di procreare?
-Why warn women before and during pregnancy and ignore the effect of alcoholism on the men procreating?

8957 **bruciapelo** **point-blank**
adj
[brutʃapelo]
Mi avrà ucciso più di cento volte, a bruciapelo.
-He has executed me over 100 times at point–blank range.

8958 **imperativo** **imperative**
adj
[imperativo]
È imperativo che Cunth non ottenga quei codici.
-It is imperative that Cunth does not get those codes.

8959 **amplificatore** **amplifier**
il
[amplifikatore]
L'amplificatore deve trovarsi su quello.
-Amplifier's got to be on that one.

8960 **appaltare** **contract**
vb
[appaltare]
Per di più, il governo spagnolo continua ad appaltare nuove linee dell'AVE.
-Nonetheless, the Spanish Government continues to tender for new sections of the AVE.

8961 **carisma** **charisma**
il
[karisma]
Sottovalutate il vostro carisma.
-You underestimate your charisma.

8962 **occasionalmente** **occasionally|by chance**
adv
[okkazjonalmente]
Fadil lavorava occasionalmente lì.
-Fadil occasionally worked there.

8963 **fertilizzare** **fertilize**
vb
[fertiliddzare]
Non è riuscita a fertilizzare altri ovuli.
-She hasn't been able to fertilize any more eggs.

8964 **estinguere** **extinguish**
vb
[estiŋgwere]
Non lasciate estinguere il fuoco.
-Don't let the fire burn out.

8965 **ossessivo** **obsessive**
adj
[ossessivo]
Io penso che Joe sia ossessivo.
-I think Joe is obsessive.

8966 **masochista** **masochist**
il/la
[mazokista]
Io sono un masochista.
-I'm a masochist.

8967 **sincronizzare** **synchronize|time**
vb
[siŋkroniddzare]
In questo caso, potrai solo sincronizzare la tua versione con le modifiche presenti in Google Documenti.
-In this case, you'll be able to only sync changes down from Google Docs.

8968 **ambedue** **both**
adj
[ambedwe]
Chiedo dunque di inserire ambedue questi punti nella valutazione.
-I would therefore ask for both these points to be looked at in the evaluation.

8969 **suppliziare** **torment**
vb
[supplittsjare]
Che bello vederti supplicare, McManus.
-I like it when you beg, McManus.

8970 **inaccessibile** **inaccessible**
adj
[inattʃessibile]
Li potete trovare in ogni villaggio inaccessibile del mondo.
-You find them in any inaccessible village around the world.

8971 **ghiacciolo** **icicle**
il
[gjattʃolo]
.Mi piace come lecchi quel ghiacciolo, tesoro.
-I love the way you work that popsicle, babe.

8972 **variante** **variant**
la
[varjante]
E' una variante che gli euroscettici non devono essere i soli a criticare.
-It is a variant which the EU's critics should not be alone in criticising.

8973 **femminista** **feminist**
il/la
[femminista]
Le conseguenze del movimento femminista hanno colpito sia gli uomini che le donne.
-The changes resulting from the women's movement have affected both women and men.

8974 **assalitore** **assailant**
il
[assalitore]
L'assalitore è arrivato a bordo di una BMW e se né andato dopo aver rubato una borsa.
-The attacker came from a BMW and got away with a bag.

8975 **agricolo** **agricultural**
adj
[agrikolo]
Anni di lavoro agricolo hanno indurito il suo corpo.
-Years of farm work have hardened his body.

8976 **strangolamento** **strangling**
lo
[straŋgolamento]
Saremmo morti tutti di fame, peggio dello strangolamento.
-We would all die of hunger here, a fate worse than strangulation.

8977 **consistenza** **consistency|texture**
la
[konsistentsa]
La consistenza granulosa di questo purè è profondamente sgradevole.
-The grainy texture of these mashed potatoes is deeply unpleasant.

8978 **sovranità** **sovereignty**
la
[sovranit'a]
Nessuna distinzione sarà inoltre stabilita sulla base dello statuto politico, giuridico o internazionale del paese o del territorio cui una persona appartiene, sia che tale territorio sia indipendente, o sottoposto ad amministrazione fiduciaria o non autonomo, o soggetto a qualsiasi altra limitazione di sovranità.
-Furthermore, no distinction shall be made on the basis of the political, jurisdictional or international status of the country or territory to which a person belongs, whether it be independent, trust, non-self-governing or under any other limitation of sovereignty.

8979 **barchetta** **small boat**
la
[barketta]
Forza piccola Barchetta, vediamo che sai fare.
-Come on then, little Barchetta, let's see what you've got.

8980 **convalescenza** **convalescence**
la
[konvaleʃʃentsa]
Le serve una cura, ha bisogno di un primo intervento, di terapie a lungo termine e infine di un periodo di convalescenza.
-It needs a cure, it needs first aid, it needs long-term care and it needs a period of convalescence.

8981 **fandonia** **humbug**
la
[fandonja]
La storia dei kamikaze è una fandonia.
-All this kamikaze stuff is a load of bull.

8982 **medesimo** **same**
adj
[medezimo]
Il medesimo discorso vale per gli onorevoli deputati degli altri gruppi politici.
-The same applies to the honourable Members from the other political groups.

8983 **futile** **futile|trivial**
adj
[futile]
Non disturbare i tuoi genitori con una cosa così futile.
-Don't bother your parents with such a trivial thing.

8984 **interminabile** **endless**
adj
[interminabile]
L'elenco delle violazioni commesse è interminabile e la situazione non sembra migliorare.
-The list of human rights violations is endless and the situation does not appear to be improving.

8985 **aristocratico** **aristocratic; aristocrat**
adj; il
[aristokratiko]
Le sue lunghe ciglia nere compensavano il pallore aristocratico delle sue guance.
-Her very long, black eyelashes set off the aristocratic pallor of her cheeks.

8986 **sartoria** **tailoring**
la
[sartorja]
Ho mandato i vestiti in sartoria.
-I sent my cloth for tailoring.

8987 **vigoroso** **vigorous|strong**
adj
[vigorozo]
Come sei vigoroso!
-How vigorous you are!

8988 **violinista** **violinist**
il/la
[vjolinista]
La violinista ha una tecnica eccellente.
-The violinist has excellent technique.

8989 **tricheco** **walrus**
il
[trikeko]
Come un tricheco che nuota e finisce nel motore di una barca.
-Like a walrus swimming into a boat motor.

8990 **codardia** **cowardice**
la
[kodardja]
La codardia politica esiste e contro di essa non c'è nulla da fare.
-Political cowardice does exist, and there is nothing to be done about it.

8991 **inesperto** **inexperienced|inexpert**
adj
[inesperto]
Lui è ancora inesperto negli affari.
-He is still green in business.

8992 **staffetta** **relay**
la
[staffetta]
Benvenuti alla Corsa campestre a staffetta della Baia di Mobile.
-Welcome to the Mobile Bay Cross–Country Relay Race.

8993 **schivare** **dodge|avoid**
vb
[skivare]
Bel modo di schivare la domanda, Danny.
-Way to dodge the question, Danny.

8994 **proibizionismo** **prohibition**
il
[proibittsjonismo]
E' una buona soluzione, che non modifica in sostanza la politica e che evita gli eccessi del proibizionismo morale, come ha giustamente sottolineato l'onorevole Guardans Cambó.
-It is a solution that does not alter the thrust of the policy and that avoids the excesses of moral prohibitionism, as Mr Guardans Cambó rightly pointed out.

8995 **suscitare** **arouse|elicit**

vb
[suʃʃitare]
La decisione del Parlamento ha suscitato una reazione particolarmente negativa nei nuovi paesi membri.
-This parliamentary decision has met with a particularly negative response in the new Member States.

8996 **svaligiare** **rob**
vb
[zvalidʒare]
Hai scelto la casa sbagliata da svaligiare.
-You picked the wrong house to rob.

8997 **dirigibile** **airship; dirigible**
il; adj
[diridʒibile]
Hai mai volato in dirigibile?
-Have you ever flown in a blimp?

8998 **sottoveste** **petticoat**
la
[sottoveste]
Quindi la sottoveste indica la spia donna che Mozzie vuole incontrare.
-So the petticoat is the female spy Mozzie wants to meet.

8999 **corallino** **coral**
adj
[korallino]
Adesso vedrete un bel fondale corallino.
-In the next scene, you're going to see a nice coral bottom.

9000 **cromo** **chrome**
il
[kromo]
L'aggiunta di un agente riduttore, in genere il solfato di ferro, contribuisce a ridurre il cromo VI a una forma chimica innocua.
-The addition of a reducing agent, usually ferrous sulphate, reduces chromium VI to a harmless chemical form.

9001 **risucchiare** **suck**
vb
[rizukkjare]
E se venissero a risucchiare gli oceani per l'idrogeno?
-What if they come to, you know, suck up our oceans for the hydrogen?

9002 **premonizione** **premonition**
la
[premonittsjone]
La premonizione di Dan era corretta.
-Dan's premonition was correct.

9003 **scenografo** **set designer**
lo
[ʃenografo]
Tom Harrison, il nostro scenografo.
-Tom Harrison, our art director.

9004 **eretico** **heretic**
adj
[eretiko]
Non è infinita questo è chiaro, non intendo essere eretico, però rasenta la grandezza dell'infinito.
-She is not infinite, this is clear, I don't mean to be heretical, but She grazes the greatness of infinity.

9005 **convincente** **convincing**
adj
[konvintʃente]
Joe è convincente.
-Joe is persuasive.

9006 **rallegrare** **cheer|brighten**
vb
[rallegrare]
È con questo spirito che la Commissione presenta oggi la direttiva e mi rallegra particolarmente constatare il sostanziale accordo del Parlamento sugli obiettivi della stessa.
-That is the spirit in which the Commission presents the directive today, and I am very heartened by Parliament's support in broad terms for the objectives of the directive.

9007 **biblico** **biblical**
adj
[bibliko]
Questo approccio biblico alla vecchiaia colpisce per la sua disarmante oggettività.
-This biblical approach to old age is striking for its disarming objectivity.

9008 **letterale** **literal**

adj Loro possono aggiungere una traduzione letterale.
[letterale] -They can add a literal translation.

9009 **torso** **torso**
il Nessuna cicatrice da proiettile sul torso.
[torso] -No scar from a bullet wound on her torso.

9010 **innescare** **trigger**
vb È... un tentativo di innescare ricordi piacevoli.
[inneskare] -It's an attempt to trigger a fond memory.

9011 **temprare** **anneal**
vb Lui pensa di poter temprare un giovane prete in questa città.
[temprare] -He thinks of a young priest to temper him in this town.

9012 **oltremare** **overseas**
adv Se volessi investire oltremare, comprerei un fondo dei mercati emergenti.
[oltremare] -If I want to invest overseas, I will buy an emerging markets fund.

9013 **amministrativo** **administrative**
adj È un problema amministrativo, non medico.
[amministrativo] -It's an administrative problem, not a medical one.

9014 **cagnetto** **doggy**
il Questo piccolo cagnetto, invece, non mi ha fatto niente.
[kaɲɲetto] -This little dog, on the other hand, didn't do nothing to me.

9015 **temerario** **reckless|daredevil**
adj Giusto per dimostrarvi quanto appena detto, ho portato con me del plankton bioluminescente, in quello che è indubbiamente un tentativo temerario di una dimostrazione dal vivo.
[temerarjo] -But just to try to prove that fact to you, I've brought along some bioluminescent plankton in what is undoubtedly a foolhardy attempt at a live demonstration.

9016 **rincorrere** **run after**
vb Sono interessati ad annusarsi a vicenda, a rincorrere gli scoiattoli.
[riŋkorrere] -They have interest sniffing each other, chasing squirrels.

9017 **pedina** **pawn|piece**
la Non voglio essere una pedina del loro gioco, capito?
[pedina] -I just don't want to be another piece in their game, you know?

9018 **stucco** **stucco**
lo Tutti questi adattamenti sono sepolti sotto lo stucco.
[stukko] -Adaptations all get buried under the stucco.

9019 **berlina** **sedan|limousine**
la È l'elefante nella... berlina accartocciata.
[berlina] -It's the elephant in the... crumpled Sedan.

9020 **contestare** **challenge|contest**
vb Non intendiamo contestare nemmeno noi la lista decisa sino al 2004, anche se le relative procedure si sono comunque rivelate problematiche.
[kontestare] -We do not wish to quarrel with the list as decided up to 2004, despite the fact that here too the procedures were rather problematic.

9021 **beneficiario** **beneficiary**
il Resta altresì da verificare se il beneficiario chieda effettivamente uno stanziamento addizionale.
[benefitʃarjo] -Also it remains to be verified if the beneficiary is in fact asking for any additional funding at all.

9022 **menomare** **impair|maim**

vb Essendo cresciuto nell'Irlanda del nord ho visto fin troppe persone menomate e assassinate nel perseguimento di obiettivi politici.
[menomare] -Growing up in Northern Ireland, I saw too many people maimed and murdered in the pursuit of political goals.

9023 **focaccia** **cake**
la Ora mi devi mostrare la focaccia.
[fokattʃa] -Now it's time for you to show me the tat.

9024 **rupe** **cliff**
la E mentre partiva, vide un uccello fare il nido sul bordo di una rupe.
[rupe] -And as he's leaving, he sees a bird making a nest on a cliff ledge.

9025 **vaglio** **screen**
il Non è possibile che detti aspetti vengano rimossi senza il vaglio del Parlamento.
[vaʎʎo] -It cannot be that those issues are transferred without proper parliamentary scrutiny.

9026 **prevalere** **prevail|overbear**
vb La ragion di Stato non deve prevalere sulle ragioni del popolo.
[prevalere] -The discretion of the State must not take precedence over that of the people.

9027 **corsetto** **corset**
il E indosserò il mio corsetto di pelle.
[korsetto] -And I'll wear my leather corset.

9028 **collaudare** **test**
vb Significa pilota incaricato di collaudare l'aeromobile durante il volo.
[kollaudare] -It means the pilot who tests the aircraft during flight.

9029 **sgobbare** **slog|work hard**
vb Devo sgobbare un bel po' prima che arrivi.
[zgobbare] -I have a lot to cram in before he gets here.

9030 **spumante** **sparkling; sparkling wine**
adj; lo Vado a prendere un po' di spumante.
[spumante] -I'm going to get some sparkling wine.

9031 **fotocopia** **photocopy**
la Si è limitata a fotocopiare il messaggio dell'élite al popolo.
[fotokopja] -It has just photocopied the message of the elite to the people.

9032 **meteorologico** **weather**
adj Non voglio parlare del tempo meteorologico.
[meteorolodʒiko] -I don't want to talk about the weather.

9033 **confezionare** **pack|manufacture**
vb Tutte le mie bevande sono confezionate con la plastica, persino nei negozi salutisti.
[konfettsjonare] -All of my beverages are packaged in plastic, even at the health food market.

9034 **uscio** **door**
il Gli Ottomani hanno appena portato la prossima Guerra Santa sul mio uscio.
[uʃʃo] -The Ottomans just brought the next Holy War to my doorstep.

9035 **discretamente** **discreetly**
adv Sei discretamente un eroe.
[diskretamente] -You're quite a hero.

9036 **rappresaglia** **retaliation**

la
[rappreza ʎʎa]
Indicando i paesi che presumibilmente violano i diritti umani, li esponiamo al pericolo di rappresaglie e vendette da parte dei terroristi.
-By naming countries that allegedly infringe human rights, we are exposing them to the danger of reprisals and revenge attacks by terrorists.

9037 **privilegiato** **privileged**
adj
[priviledʒato]
Mi sento privilegiato, e curiosamente orgoglioso.
-I'm feeling privileged, and oddly, I'm proud.

9038 **presidio** **garrison|defense**
il
[prezidjo]
Lord Bolton terrà un presidio qui finché non ritorneremo.
-Lord Bolton will garrison here until we return.

9039 **incompleto** **incomplete**
adj
[iŋkompleto]
Era incompleto.
-It was incomplete.

9040 **bagnino** **lifeguard**
il
[baɲɲino]
Lui è un bagnino.
-He's a lifeguard.

9041 **appiccicare** **stick**
vb
[appittʃikare]
Avevo solo bisogno di qualcosa su cui appiccicare la mia gomma.
-I just needed somewhere to stick my gum.

9042 **eludere** **circumvent|bypass**
vb
[eludere]
Voglio dire in modo assolutamente chiaro che nessuno Stato membro può eludere questa responsabilità.
-I want to make it absolutely clear that no Member State can evade this responsibility.

9043 **issare** **hoist**
vb
[issare]
Se il coordinamento e la complementarità dovessero aver luogo nei paesi beneficiari, anche in questo caso i paesi donatori preferirebbero issare la bandiera nazionale.
-If coordination and complementarity were already in place in the recipient countries, donor countries would prefer to hoist their national flags there too.

9044 **araldo** **herald**
il
[araldo]
Sono Terrax, araldo del Divoratore!
-I'm Terrax. Herald of the Devourer.

9045 **correttezza** **correctness**
la
[korrettettsa]
Questo per quanto riguarda la correttezza dei dati di fatto.
-So much for factual accuracy.

9046 **slogare** **dislocate|sprain**
vb
[zlogare]
Mi si potrebbe slogare il polso.
-- my wrist might fall off.

9047 **fertilità** **fertility**
la
[fertilit'a]
Una condizione essenziale di tale controllo è la vita sessuale e la fertilità delle donne.
-One of the prerequisites of this is control of women' s sexuality and fertility.

9048 **artefice** **maker**
il
[artefitʃe]
Dio ha, dunque, chiamato all'esistenza l'uomo trasmettendogli il compito di essere artefice.
-God therefore called man into existence, committing to him the craftsman's task.

9049 **commestibile** **edible**
adj
[kommestibile]
QUESTO è commestibile?
-Is THIS edible?

9050 **mascherata** **masquerade**
la
[maskerata]
Qual è il ruolo del cittadino europeo in questa mascherata?
-What place is there for the European public in this masquerade?

9051 **convivenza** **cohabitation**
la
[konviventsa]
La convivenza della comunità nazionale con le minoranze etniche è stata ben organizzata.
-Coexistence between national and ethnic communities has also been well organised.

9052 **cozzare** **clash|butt**
vb
[kottsare]
Il cozzare delle onde non lo inquietò.
-The dashing of the waves disturbeth him not.

9053 **trampolino** **trampoline**
il
[trampolino]
Andate al trampolino e parlatene prima di darmi un'altra risposta affrettata.
-Go over by that trampoline and talk it through before you give me another quick answer.

9054 **reciso** **flat**
adj
[retʃizo]
Distruggendo questo patrimonio, una nazione taglia i suoi legami ancestrali, recide le sue radici.
-By destroying this heritage, a nation severs its ancestral ties and tears up its roots.

9055 **galeotto** **convict**
il
[galeotto]
Anche un galeotto ha diritto di respirare.
-Even a convict's got a right to breathe.

9056 **ghiaia** **gravel**
la
[gjaja]
Venuta la sera, dato che era un po' stanca, volle sedersi di fronte a una nuova caffetteria situata all'angolo di un nuovo boulevard, ancora pieno di ghiaia e già mostrante i suoi splendori incompiuti.
-Evening come, since you were slightly tired, you wished to sit in front of a new Café located on the corner of a new boulevard, still full of gravel and already showing its unfinished splendors.

9057 **sbandare** **slide|disperse**
vb
[zbandare]
Gli spari l'hanno mancato, ma lo hanno fatto sbandare e scontrarsi.
-Shots went wide, but they caused him to swerve and crash.

9058 **ipnotizzare** **hypnotize**
vb
[ipnotiddzare]
Walter, potresti ipnotizzare Emily per farle ricordare la visione dell'evento del disegno.
-Walter, I think you can hypnotize Emily to recover her vision of the event in that drawing.

9059 **giogo** **yoke**
il
[dʒogo]
E' stata raggiunta la libertà dal giogo di una terribile tirannia.
-Freedom from the yoke of a terrible tyranny has been achieved.

9060 **caldamente** **warmly**
adv
[kaldamente]
Lo consiglio caldamente.
-I highly recommend him.

9061 **consorzio** **consortium**
il
[konsortsjo]
Il consorzio svolge tale compito sotto la responsabilità dell'AR.
-The Consortium shall perform this task under the responsibility of the HR.

9062 **innesco** **trigger**
il
[innesko]
Ciò che abbiamo qui è un autentico innesco, che descrive la via verso la liberalizzazione di tutti i servizi, compresi i servizi pubblici, che chiama "esigenze di interesse pubblico e generale".
-What we have here is an authentic primer laying out the road towards liberalisation of all services, including public services, which it dubs 'public and general interest needs'.

9063 **steward** **steward**
gli
[stevard]
L'epidemia ha fatto il suo ingresso negli USA tramite uno steward maschio su un volo aereo, che si prese la malattia in Africa e la portò indietro con sé.
-The epidemic was introduced to the US by actually one male steward on an airline flight, who got the disease in Africa and brought it back.

9064 **sostare** **stop|pause**
vb
[sostare]
Ma in particolare mi piacerebbe poter sostare in meditazione anche in due città legate in modo speciale alla vicenda di Paolo, l'apostolo delle Genti.
-But in particular I would also like to be able to pause in meditation in two cities linked especially to the story of Paul, the Apostle of the Gentiles.

9065 **cranico** **cranial**
adj
[kraniko]
Lo sciatore subì un trauma cranico.
-The skier suffered a head trauma.

9066 **accumulo** **backlog**
il
[akkumulo]
Tutto questo è necessario per scongiurare un accumulo degli squilibri.
-This is needed to prevent an accumulation of imbalances.

9067 **molestatore** **molester; molesting**
il; adj
[molestatore]
Nessuno sapeva che Joe era un pericoloso molestatore di bambini.
-Nobody knew that Joe was a dangerous child molester.

9068 **programmatore** **programmer**
il
[programmatore]
Lei lo assunse come programmatore.
-She hired him as a programmer.

9069 **lare** **lares**
il
[lare]
Ma che ti alleni a lare'!
-What are you still practicing for?

9070 **input** **input; input**
gli; vb
[imput]
Dicono, bene, abbiamo una cosa in una scatola, abbiamo i suoi input i suoi output.
-They say, well, we have a thing in a box, and we have its inputs and its outputs.

9071 **bisnonna** **great grandmother**
la
[biznonna]
Lei è la mia bisnonna.
-She's my great-grandmother.

9072 **mercanzia** **merchandise**
la
[merkantsja]
Ora, andiamo a dividerci la mercanzia.
-Now, let's go split up the merchandise.

9073 **corallo** **coral**
il
[korallo]
Questo è un corallo scolorito, un corallo che è morto durante El Nino del 1982-83.
-This is a bleached coral, coral that died during the 1982-'83 El Nino.

9074 **ingordo** **greedy**

adj | Lui è ingordo e pigro.
[iŋgordo] -He is greedy and lazy.

9075 **forgiare** **forge|tilt**
vb
[fordʒare]
Facciamo quindi in modo che il Regno Unito sia un partner positivo, forgiato dal modello europeo.
-So let Britain be a positive partner, cast in the European mould.

9076 **aringa** **herring**
la
[ariŋga]
Oggi ho mangiato un po' di aringa affumicata per colazione.
-Today I had some kipper for breakfast.

9077 **ascendente** **ascending; influence**
adj; il/la
[aʃʃendente]
La paralisi da botulismo è discendente, non ascendente.
-Botulism paralysis is descending, not ascending.

9078 **dopobarba** **aftershave; aftershave**
adj; il
[dopobarba]
Usate il dopobarba?
-Do you use aftershave?

9079 **avarizia** **avarice**
la
[avarittsja]
I problemi finanziari dell'Unione sono in gran parte dovuti all'avarizia dei vecchi Stati membri.
-The Union's financial problems are largely due to meanness of the old Member States.

9080 **cordialmente** **cordially**
adv
[kordjalmente]
Vi invito cordialmente a riproporvi di svolgere insieme a noi quest'opera di convinzione.
-I cordially invite you to join with us in carrying on this work of persuasion together.

9081 **ventriloquo** **ventriloquist**
il
[ventrilokwo]
Il ventriloquo deve prima di tutto farci credere che tiene seduto in grembo un bambino piccolo.
-The ventriloquist must first make us believe that a small boy is sitting on his lap.

9082 **caffettiera** **coffeepot**
la
[kaffettjera]
Lui fa bollire dell'acqua in una caffettiera.
-He boils water in a coffee pot.

9083 **arpa** **harp**
la
[arpa]
Il violino, il pianoforte e l'arpa sono strumenti musicali.
-Violin, piano and harp are musical instruments.

9084 **fante** **knave|infantryman**
il
[fante]
No, non sei un fante.
-No, you're no Knave.

9085 **volgarità** **vulgarity|gaudiness**
la
[volgarit'a]
Noi ci scusiamo per la sua volgarità.
-We apologize for his rudeness.

9086 **bretella** **suspender|strap**
la
[bretella]
Si è rotta la bretella!
-The strap has broken!

9087 **corteggiamento** **courtship|lovemaking**
il
[korteddʒamento]
L'ipocrisia di Lukashenko nel suo recente corteggiamento dell'Occidente è inequivocabile.
-Lukashenka's hypocrisy in his recent courting of the West is unmistakable.

9088 **discreto** **discreet**

	adj	Ha subito un discreto trauma.
	[diskreto]	-You've had quite a shock.
9089	**setacciare**	**sift|search**
	vb	Il mandato per setacciare l'ufficio di De Soto è finalmente arrivato.
	[setattʃare]	-Search warrant for De Soto's office finally came through.
9090	**insicurezza**	**insecurity**
	la	Simili scelte che hanno prodotto morte, insicurezza e maggiore instabilità.
	[insikurettsa]	-Such decisions have led to death, insecurity and greater instability.
9091	**incesto**	**incest**
	il	Ne poteva prevedere che avresti commesso incesto.
	[intʃesto]	-Nor could he have predicted that you would commit incest.
9092	**facilitare**	**facilitate**
	vb	Sono qui per aiutare a facilitare un dialogo, se possibile.
	[fatʃilitare]	-What I'd like to do here is maybe help facilitate a dialogue.
9093	**puntualità**	**punctuality**
	la	È fiero della sua puntualità.
	[puntwalit'a]	-He is proud of his punctuality.
9094	**borraccia**	**water bottle**
	la	Ha preso la borraccia che ho raccolto alla Roccia Sanguinante.
	[borrattʃa]	-He took the canteen I collected at the Bleeding Stone.
9095	**violino**	**violin|fiddlefamiliare**
	il	È sicuro che Joe suoni il violino?
	[vjolino]	-Are you sure that Joe plays the violin?
9096	**timpano**	**tympanum|eardrum**
	il	– Commozione cerebrale e timpano rotto.
	[timpano]	-Well, she's got a concussion and a broken eardrum.
9097	**furtivo**	**furtive|slinky**
	adj	Penso che Joe sia furtivo.
	[furtivo]	-I think Joe is sneaky.
9098	**ronzare**	**hum|whir**
	vb	Basterà ronzare per fagli sapere che siamo qui.
	[rontsare]	-I'll just buzz and let them know we're here.
9099	**duplice**	**dual|duplex**
	adj	Le strutture di informazione devono riflettere questo fondamentale duplice obiettivo.
	[duplitʃe]	-The information structures should reflect this fundamental dual objective.
9100	**pipa**	**pipe**
	la	Joe sta fumando la sua pipa.
	[pipa]	-Joe is smoking his pipe.
9101	**usciere**	**usher**
	il	Se desiderate modificare il vostro voto, chiedete all'usciere una nuova scheda di voto e consegnate la vecchia.
	[uʃʃere]	-If you want to change your vote, ask the usher for a new ballot paper and surrender the old one.
9102	**provento**	**income**
	il	La rettifica è rilevata come provento o onere nel conto economico.
	[provento]	-The adjustment is recognised as income or expense in profit or loss.
9103	**comicità**	**comicality**

la
[komitʃit'a]
Il grado di comicità è lo stesso.
-The degree of humor is the same.

9104 **attesa** **waiting|expectation**
la
[atteza]
L'attesa vale la pena?
-Is the wait worth it?

9105 **pensatore** **thinker**
il
[pensatore]
Lui era un libero pensatore.
-He was a freethinker.

9106 **cooperativo** **cooperative**
adj
[kooperativo]
Joe è cooperativo.
-Joe is cooperative.

9107 **starnuto** **sneeze**
lo
[starnuto]
Reprimere uno starnuto.
-To hold back a sneeze.

9108 **legalità** **legality**
la
[legalit'a]
Ai fornitori non viene richiesto di dimostrare la legalità dei loro prodotti.
-Suppliers are not required to prove the legality of their products.

9109 **anarchico** **anarchist; anarchic**
il; adj
[anarkiko]
Gli autori di questi attacchi sono invece anarchici che usano impropriamente il nome dell' per l'obiettivo anarchico che perseguono di reinsediare la dittatura con loro al potere.
-Those who are carrying out these assaults are anarchists: they misuse the name of Islam for their anarchical aim to restore dictatorship with themselves in power.

9110 **torchio** **press**
il
[torkjo]
Queste sono state stampate da un torchio da stampa con dei veri cliché.
-These were printed in a press with real plates.

9111 **clip** **clip**
le
[klip]
Potreste mandare la seconda clip per favore?
-Could I have the second little video clip?

9112 **pendolare** **pendular**
adj
[pendolare]
Lo scrittore e pendolare, James Baldwin, rilasciò un intervista del 1984 in cui gli fu ripetutamente domandato della sua omosessualità.
-The writer and commuter James Baldwin gave an interview in 1984 in which he was repeatedly asked about his homosexuality.

9113 **lavapiatti** **dishwasher**
il/la
[lavapjatti]
Abbiamo un lavapiatti.
-We have a dishwasher.

9114 **cronico** **chronic**
adj
[kroniko]
Qui vedete le aree del dolore di un paziente affetto da dolore cronico.
-What you're seeing here is, we've selected the pathways in the brain of a chronic pain patient.

9115 **cinguettio** **chirping|twittering**
il
[tʃiŋgwettjo]
Avevamo paura ad accendere la stufa quando abbiamo sentito il cinguettio.
-We were afraid to light the stove When we heard the chirping.

9116 **duraturo** **lasting|enduring**
adj
[duraturo]
Adesso abbiamo l'opportunità di trovare una soluzione duratura al cronico conflitto nel Timor Orientale.
-We now have an opportunity to arrive at a durable solution to this lingering conflict in East Timor.

9117 **malumore** **bad mood**
il
[malumore]
Una tassazione sociale meno pesante comporta però, per le imprese, vantaggi concorrenziali a breve termine, i quali creano malumore tra le imprese dei paesi dove l'onere fiscale è maggiore.
-Lower social taxation, however, gives enterprises a competitive advantage in the short term, and this leads to discontentment among enterprises in countries with higher taxation levels.

9118 **rompicapo** **puzzle**
il
[rompikapo]
La morte è il contrario di un rompicapo interessante.
-Death is the opposite of a cool puzzle.

9119 **pomposo** **pompous**
adj
[pompozo]
Joe è pomposo.
-Joe is pompous.

9120 **sradicare** **eradicate|root up**
vb
[zradikare]
Loro provarono a sradicare la mia cultura.
-They tried to eradicate my culture.

9121 **trattoria** **tavern**
la
[trattorja]
Il padre aveva una piccola trattoria in Toscana.
-Her father owned a little trattoria in Tuscany.

9122 **arrampicata** **climbing|scramble**
le
[arrampikata]
Perché si è arrampicata sul tetto di casa sua?
-Why did you climb up on the roof of her house?

9123 **comperare** **buy**
vb
[komperare]
C'è qualcosa che vuole comperare?
-Is there something you want to buy?

9124 **castagna** **chestnut**
la
[kastaɲɲa]
Mi andrebbe molto una castagna dacqua.
-I'd love a water chestnut.

9125 **sintetico** **synthetic**
adj
[sintetiko]
Primo, c'è una differenza tra il DHA sintetico e il DHA presente nel latte materno.
-First, there is a difference between synthetic DHA and DHA in breast milk.

9126 **bestemmiare** **blaspheme**
vb
[bestemmjare]
Non bere, non bestemmiare e cerca di tenere la bocca chiusa.
-Don't drink, don't swear and try to keep your mouth shut.

9127 **psicanalista** **psychoanalyst**
il/la
[psikanalista]
E' il mio psicanalista.
-He is my psychoanalyst.

9128 **tintura** **dyeing**
la
[tintura]
Ovviamente c'è il problema della tintura.
-And, of course, there's the question of dyeing.

9129 **sarta** **seamstress**
la
[sarta]
Lavandaia, infermiera, sarta o schiava domestica.
-Laundry lady, nurse, seamstress, or domestic slave.

9130 **Rinascimento** **Renaissance**
il
[rinaʃʃimento]
Urbanizzazione, integrazione, insieme, portano a un nuovo rinascimento.
-Urbanization, integration, coming together, leads to a new renaissance.

9131 **percossa** **blow**

la
[perkossa]
L'ho percossa, ha cercato di mordermi.
-I beat her, she tried to bite me.

9132 **nonnino** **grandpa**
il
[nonnino]
No, lascia il nonnino qui.
-No, you kids go have a good time, leave Grandpa here.

9133 **genovese** **Genoese**
adj
[dʒenoveze]
Io sono un genovese e chiedo e credo che sarebbe bene impiegare più danaro per queste ispezioni negli aeroporti.
-I am Genoese and I suggest and believe it would be better to use more money for these airport inspections.

9134 **captare** **pick up**
vb
[kaptare]
Sto cercando di captare un segnale.
-I'm trying to pick up a signal.

9135 **esplicito** **explicit**
adj
[esplitʃito]
Io penso che Joe sia troppo esplicito.
-I think Joe is too outspoken.

9136 **intossicazione** **intoxication**
le
[intossikattsjone]
All'inizio penserebbero ad una semplice intossicazione alimentare.
-At first, you would probably think it was just food poisoning.

9137 **foulard** **scarf**
il
[foulard]
Signor Presidente, oggi indosso il mio foulard irlandese.
-Mr President, I am wearing my Irish scarf today.

9138 **unisono** **unison**
il
[unizono]
Notate, le mie labbra e il suono che voi percepite sono stati sincronizzati in perfetto unisono.
-Note how my lips and the sound issuing from them... are synchronized together... in perfect unison.

9139 **timidezza** **shyness**
la
[timidettsa]
Amo la sua mancanza di timidezza.
-I love your lack of shyness.

9140 **Plutone** **Pluto**
lo
[plutone]
La Russia è più grande di Plutone.
-Russia is larger than Pluto.

9141 **sommozzatore** **diver|scuba diver**
il
[sommottsatore]
Quindi, ho deciso che sarei diventato un sommozzatore all'età di 15 anni.
-So, I decided I was going to become a scuba diver at the age of 15.

9142 **toppa** **patch**
la
[toppa]
Domattina dovremo riuscire a montare la toppa.
-Well, we ought to be able to fit the patch tomorrow morning.

9143 **ostetrico** **obstetrician; obstetric**
il; adj
[ostetriko]
L'OMS stima che l'88-98 per cento di tutti i decessi in conseguenza del parto sarebbero evitabili se le donne avessero accesso a servizi riproduttivi e ostetrico-sanitari adeguati.
-The WHO estimates that 88-98% of all maternal deaths are avoidable if women have access to proper reproductive and obstetric health services.

9144 **branchia** **gill**
la
[braŋkja]
Ma hanno due tipi di branchie.
-But they have two types of gill structures.

9145 **replicare** **replicate|reply**

vb Ha quindi senso replicare questa politica anche per le altre istituzioni.
[replikare] -It therefore makes sense to replicate this policy for other institutions as well.

9146 **triciclo** **tricycle**
il Ha detto, oh, probabilmente costruirà un triciclo con ruote stepney.
[tritʃiklo] -He said, oh, probably he is going to build a three-wheeler with stepney.

9147 **diminutivo** **diminutive**
adj Jim è il diminutivo di James.
[diminutivo] -Jim is short for James.

9148 **lampone** **raspberry**
il Questo non è lampone, è rossetto.
[lampone] -That's not raspberry, it's lipstick.

9149 **perfezionare** **perfect|refine**
vb Occorre pertanto perfezionare l'accordo e stabilire regole precise.
[perfettsjonare] -We need to improve the situation and establish rules.

9150 **briefing** **briefing**
il Yesterday, Madam President, if I have understood correctly, the Conference of Presidents wanted me to make a brief statement to update Parliament on the latest news.
[brjefiŋg] -Ieri, signora Presidente, se ho ben capito, la Conferenza dei presidenti desiderava che rilasciassi una breve dichiarazione al fine di aggiornare il Parlamento sulle ultime notizie.

9151 **condottiero** **leader**
il Ed è il condottiero.
[kondottjero] -And he is the leader.

9152 **progettista** **designer**
il/la Sono Kevin Freeman, progettista di videogiochi.
[prodʒettista] -I'm Kevin Freeman, video game designer.

9153 **ricucire** **sew up**
vb Fatti ricucire quella ferita dalla dottoressa Shannon.
[rikutʃire] -Have Dr. Shannon stitch up that gash.

9154 **finanziatore** **financier**
il E 'il principale finanziatore al nord sudanese.
[finantsjatore] -He's the main financier to the northern Sudanese Army.

9155 **fulcro** **fulcrum**
il Tale decisione non può essere rinviata; essa è il fulcro e il perno di tutta la strategia.
[fulkro] -It cannot be delayed; it is the fulcrum and pivot of the whole strategy.

9156 **balestra** **crossbow**
la La balestra... non funziona davvero.
[balestra] -The crossbow – it doesn't actually work.

9157 **eminente** **eminent**
adj Il più eminente tra i mammografi statunitensi ha rilasciato questa dichiarazione al Washington Post.
[eminente] -The pre-eminent mammographer in the United States issued the following quote to the Washington Post.

9158 **infortunarsi** **get injured**
vb Infortunarsi facendo la capriola sul fusto è stata la cosa migliore che gli sia successa.
[infortunarsi] -getting injured in that keg stand was the best thing that ever happened to him.

9159 **prosperare** **thrive|prosper**
vb
[prosperare]
In un clima di questo genere, possono prosperare corruzione, nepotismo e irregolarità.
-In such a climate, corruption, nepotism and irregularities can thrive.

9160 **boccia** **bowl**
la
[bottʃa]
Adesso dobbiamo cambiare l'acqua alla boccia.
-And now we need to change the water in the bowl.

9161 **gnocco** **dumpling**
lo
[ɲokko]
Eri soffice e tonda... come uno gnocco.
-You were soft and round, like a dumpling.

9162 **prognosi** **prognosis**
la
[proɲɲozi]
Avremo una discussione riguardante la prognosi.
-We will have a discussion concerning the prognosis.

9163 **massone** **mason**
il
[massone]
Rocco Buttiglione, uomo libero di fede cattolica, è stato sostituito nella carica di Commissario da Franco Frattini, bell'esempio di massone.
-Mr Buttiglione, a free man of Catholic faith, has been replaced by Mr Frattini, a model freemason.

9164 **isolante** **insulating; insulator**
adj; il
[izolante]
L'isolante è stato strappato qui.
-The insulation's stripped off these.

9165 **fornicazione** **fornication**
la
[fornikattsjone]
Quale è il disordine morale racchiuso nella fornicazione e negli stessi rapporti pre-matrimoniali?
-What is the moral disorder involved in fornication and pre-marital relations?

9166 **grizzly** **grizzly**
i
[griddzl]
Mi trovavo in una riserva di grizzly, anche se nessuno me lo aveva detto prima di andarci.
-It was in a grizzly bear preserve, although no one told me that before we went.

9167 **prescrizione** **prescription**
la
[preskrittsjone]
Perciò, le farò una prescrizione.
-So, I'm going to write you a prescription.

9168 **conficcare** **stick|drive**
vb
[konfikkare]
Avevi la possibilità di conficcare un coltellino nel petto di una donna.
-You had the chance to stick a pen knife in a woman's chest.

9169 **piranha** **piranha**
i
[pirana]
Non ho paura della donna piranha.
-I'm not afraid of the piranha women.

9170 **iraniano** **Iranian**
adj
[iranjano]
Il popolo iraniano è abbastanza intelligente per prendere da solo una decisione.
-The Iranian people are intelligent enough to make the decision for themselves.

9171 **coccinella** **ladybug**
la
[kottʃinella]
Pare sia richiesta la coccinella elettrica.
-Someone sounds like he wants the Electric Ladybug.

9172 **deterrente** **deterrent**
adj
[deterrente]
Un'azione più mirata sarebbe quella di dare un esempio che funga da deterrente.

-Providing a deterrent example for the future, that would be better targeted.

9173 **commiato** **leave-taking**
il
[kommjato]
Sto scrivendo il mio commiato per voi tutti.
-I'm just composing my farewell to you all.

9174 **espiazione** **atonement**
la
[espjattsjone]
Tutti i suoi sensi sono colpiti e crocifissi, al fine di offrire espiazione per ogni genere di umano peccato.
-Thus, all His senses are mortified and crucified, that He may make atonement for every kind of human sin.

9175 **abracadabra** **abracadabra**
la
[abrakadabra]
Quando si raffredda, gocciola da qui... e abracadabra.
-As it all cools down, drips out here, and abracadabra.

9176 **riaccompagnare** **take back**
vb
[rjakkompaɲɲare]
Stavo per riaccompagnare Syd a casa.
-I was just about to take Syd home.

9177 **pendio** **slope|hillside**
il
[pendjo]
Scalammo un ripido pendio.
-We climbed a sharp slope.

9178 **dominatore** **ruler**
il
[dominatore]
Sono Lrrr, dominatore del pianeta...
-I am Lrrr, ruler of the planet...

9179 **gioioso** **joyful**
adj
[dʒojozo]
Joe non è così gioioso.
-Joe is not so bright.

9180 **segatura** **sawdust**
la
[segatura]
Le donne balinesi locali cucinano su bruciatori di segatura usando segreti che conoscono solo le loro nonne.
-Local Balinese women cook the food on sawdust burners using secrets that only their grandmothers know.

9181 **sbadato** **careless; scatterbrain**
adj; lo
[zbadato]
"Dannazione! Ho dimenticato l'ombrello sul treno." "Sbadato!"
-"Damn it! I forget my umbrella on the train." "Scatterbrain!"

9182 **reumatismo** **rheumatism**
il
[reumatismo]
Se vuoi, posso avere "L'esistenzialismo è un reumatismo" in sciroppo.
-If you like, I can get "Existentialism is Rheumatism" in syrup form.

9183 **aratro** **plow**
il
[aratro]
Noi che un giorno abbiamo messo mano all'aratro, facilmente guardiamo indietro.
-At the onset of difficulty, the temptation we feel is to abandon the struggle and look back as we place our hand to the plough.

9184 **longitudine** **longitude**
la
[londʒitudine]
Non si basa su longitudine o latitudine, ma sull'altitudine.
-It's not based on longitude or latitude, it's altitude.

9185 **impadronirsi** **seize|master**
vb
[impadronirsi]
Udito ciò, i suoi vennero per impadronirsi di lui, poiché dicevano: ?E' fuori di sé'.
-And when his friends heard it, they went out to seize him, for they said, 'He is beside himself.'

9186 **tesoriere** **treasurer**

il
[tezorjere]
Oltre a non avere alcuna esperienza nelle mansioni affidatele, ha un passato molto discutibile come tesoriere nazionale del CND.
-Besides having no experience of the required tasks, she has a highly dubious past as National Treasurer of CND.

9187 **aspro** **sour|harsh**
adj
[aspro]
E' un paesaggio aspro e brullo, eppure qui vivono alcuni tipi di ragni. -This is a rugged and barren landscape, yet there are quite a few spiders here.

9188 **vendicatore** **avenger**
il
[vendikatore]
Da molti era considerato uno spietato vendicatore, benché fosse assetato di giustizia, non di vendetta.
-He had been known as a merciless avenger by many, even though he had been seeking justice, not revenge.

9189 **trionfare** **triumph**
vb
[trjonfare]
Il benessere di ogni individuo e il diritto alla vita e alla pace devono trionfare.
-The well-being of every individual and his or her right to life and peace must triumph.

9190 **inflessibile** **inflexible|adamant**
adj
[inflessibile]
Joe è inflessibile.
-Joe is inflexible.

9191 **controverso** **controversial**
adj
[kontroverso]
È molto controverso.
-That's very controversial.

9192 **monarca** **monarch**
il
[monarka]
Pianta questo semino; aspetta 2000 anni, e otterrai questo: il Monarca Perduto.
-Plant this small seed, wait 2,000 years, and you get this: the Lost Monarch.

9193 **impudente** **impudent; jackanapes**
adj; il/la
[impudente]
Questa donna impudente è fuori di sé.
-This impudent woman is out of her mind.

9194 **venerare** **venerate|worship**
vb
[venerare]
San Francesco di Assisi è oggi venerato non solo dai cristiani ma anche da molti seguaci di altre tradizioni religiose.
-St Francis of Assisi is revered today not only by Christians but also by many followers of other religious traditions.

9195 **imperfetto** **imperfect**
adj
[imperfetto]
Immagina quest'uomo, secondo te così imperfetto...
-So this man who, according to you, is so imperfect...

9196 **trailer** **trailer**
il
[trailer]
È il trailer di Cherie Redfern.
-That's Cherie Redfern's trailer.

9197 **bronchite** **bronchitis**
la
[broŋkite]
La bronchite l'ha costretto a letto.
-Bronchitis kept him in bed.

9198 **ingiunzione** **injunction**
le
[indʒuntsjone]
Bene, andremo dal giudice a chiedere i danni, avrò un'ingiunzione e ricominceremo.
-Fine, we'll go to the judge, move for costs, get an order, and do it all over again.

9199 **ammaccare** **dent|bruise**

vb
[ammakkare]
Non vorrete ammaccare la merce di scambio.
-You don't want to bruise the merchandise.

9200 **immutabile** **immutable**
adj
[immutabile]
Molto bene: questa è la regola immutabile.
-Very well: that is to be the unchanging rule.

9201 **ammoniaca** **ammonia**
la
[ammonjaka]
L'ammoniaca è una base.
-Ammonia is a base.

9202 **redditizio** **profitable**
adj
[redditittsjo]
In numerosi settori il commercio elettronico è destinato a diventare più redditizio rispetto al commercio tradizionale.
-Electronic shopping is going to prove more lucrative in many sectors than traditional shopping.

9203 **comodamente** **comfortably|easily**
adv
[komodamente]
Goditi il piacere musicale comodamente seduto sul tuo divano
-Experience the enjoyment of music - comfortably sitting on your couch

9204 **bile** **bile**
la
[bile]
Se la bile continua ad accumularsi, potrebbe causare cirrosi o insufficienza epatica.
-And if the bile continues to build up, then we're looking at cirrhosis or possible liver failure.

9205 **provetto** **proficient**
adj
[provetto]
Un cuoco provetto.
-An expert cook.

9206 **nevrotico** **neurotic**
adj
[nevrotiko]
A volte sa essere un po' nevrotico.
-He can be a little neurotic.

9207 **verosimile** **likely|plausible**
adj
[verozimile]
Penso che la prima probabilità sia più verosimile della seconda.
-At the moment I see the second possibility as the most likely.

9208 **diavoletto** **imp**
il
[djavoletto]
Lui è un diavoletto.
-He's a little devil.

9209 **finimondo** **pandemonium**
il
[finimondo]
Noi entriamo e combiniamo il finimondo.
-We go in, blow the place to bits.

9210 **eguale** **compeer**
il
[egwale]
In secondo luogo, manca il principio di un eguale trattamento.
-Secondly, the principle of equal treatment does not seem to count for much.

9211 **alleggerire** **lighten|ease**
vb
[alleddʒerire]
Riconosco nondimeno il merito di voler alleggerire il fisco.
-Even so, you are trying to lighten the tax burden, I grant you that.

9212 **sciabola** **saber**
la
[ʃabola]
E' una sciabola di luce verde.
-It's a saber of green light.

9213 **poro** **pore**
il
[poro]
Questo poro può aprirsi e chiudersi.
-Now, this pore can open and close.

9214 **giaccone** **short coat**

il C'è scritto che il giaccone di Danny era ricoperto di trementina.
[dʒakkone] -Said that Danny's turnout coat was doused in turpentine.

9215 **nuotatore** **swimmer**
il Joe è un nuotatore molto veloce.
[nwotatore] -Joe is a very fast swimmer.

9216 **fermaglio** **clip**
il Ho appena trovato un paio di miei orecchini e un fermaglio di corallo.
[fermaʎʎo] -I've just found a pair of my earrings, and one coral dress clip.

9217 **gazzella** **gazelle**
la Gazzella, ti ho uccisa per il tocco squisito della tua pelle, per come è facile incunearla in una tavola esposta alle intemperie come un grezzo foglio bianco di beccheria.weathered raw as white butcher paper.
[gattsella] -Gazelle, I killed you for your skin's exquisite touch, for how easy it is to be nailed to a board.

9218 **abitualmente** **usually**
adv Non vi sono dubbi che si compiano abitualmente attività aberranti.
[abitwalmente] -There is no question that abhorrent activities are habitually taking place.

9219 **infatuazione** **infatuation**
la Era solo un'infatuazione passeggera.
[infatwattsjone] -It was just a passing infatuation.

9220 **acciuga** **anchovy**
la La pesca dell'acciuga nel Golfo di Biscaglia riveste una notevole importanza sociale ed economica.
[attʃuga] -The anchovy fishery in the Bay of Biscay is of considerable social and economic importance.

9221 **soffocante** **suffocating|stifling**
adj La stanza è soffocante.
[soffokante] -The room is stuffy.

9222 **rattristare** **sadden**
vb Un'altra cosa che mi rattrista quest'anno è ciò a cui ha fatto riferimento l'on. Fabre-Aubrespy, la dichiarazione di affidabilità.
[rattristare] -Another thing that depresses me this year was referred to by Mr Fabre-Aubrespy, namely the statement of assurance.

9223 **infilzare** **stick**
vb Però cerca di non infilzare tua sorella.
[infiltsare] -Try not to stab your sister with it.

9224 **arido** **arid**
adj Sono scritte nello stile arido della vecchia burocrazia.
[arido] -They're written in the dry style of the old bureaucracy.

9225 **gioire** **rejoice**
vb Ma c'è anche la gioia dei malvagi, si può gioire anche per la sofferenza di qualcuno.
[dʒoire] -But there's also wicked joy, you can rejoice in someone's suffering.

9226 **quintale** **quintal**
il Da vent'anni il prezzo al quintale del grano è diminuito del 40 percento mentre i costi di produzione sono aumentati del 20 percento e oltre in taluni settori.
[kwintale] -In twenty years, the price of a metric quintal of wheat has fallen by 40 % whereas production costs have increased by 20 % and more in certain sectors.

9227 **droghiere** **grocer**

il
[drogjere]
Signora Presidente, domani mattina presto mi recherò dal droghiere per acquistare acqua potabile in bottiglia.
- Madam President, early tomorrow morning I am going to the grocer's to buy bottled drinking water.

9228 **acero** **maple**
il
[atʃero]
Il somiere di legno d'acero è composto da 7 strati di acero tagliato trasversalmente, le fibre di ogni strato formano rispettivamente un angolo di 90 gradi.
-The hardwood maple pinblock is made of 7 layers of quarter-sawn maple, at a 90-degree grain angle on each layer.

9229 **infiltrarsi** **infiltrate**
vb
[infiltrarsi]
Cercheranno di infiltrarsi nell'area di sicurezza.
-They will try to infiltrate the security area.

9230 **gonfiore** **swelling|distension**
il
[gonfjore]
Joe è stato brutalmente pestato e medici lo hanno dovuto mettere in un coma indotto per alleviare il gonfiore nel suo cervello.
-Joe was viciously bashed and doctors had to put him into an induced coma to relieve the swelling on his brain.

9231 **nitro** **nitre**
il
[nitro]
We're not hauling nitro through the Andes, either.
-Non stiamo neanche trasportando nitroglicerina nelle Ande.

9232 **bolide** **fireball|meteor**
il
[bolide]
Within five, 10 million years of the bolide impact we had a whole variety of animals going into the water.
-Entro cinque, 10 milioni di anni dall'impatto con il bolide una grande varietà di animali si spostarono in acqua.

9233 **camomilla** **chamomile**
la
[kamomilla]
Io penso che farò una tripla camomilla.
-I think I'm going to make a triple camomile.

9234 **riabilitare** **rehabilitate**
vb
[rjabilitare]
Fatto ciò, puoi riabilitare le applicazioni.
-Once you've done so, you can then re-enable the applications.

9235 **sbocciare** **bloom|open**
vb
[zbottʃare]
A volte puoi trovare un fiore e aiutarlo a sbocciare.
-Sometimes you find a flower you can help to bloom.

9236 **meritevole** **worthy|deserving**
adj
[meritevole]
Se l'iniziativa avrà successo, sarà meritevole di un premio per la pace.
-If success is achieved in this, it will be worthy of a peace prize.

9237 **ripiano** **shelf|terrace**
il
[ripjano]
Il ripiano cadde e tutti i libri crollarono addosso a Vasya.
-The shelf fell off and all the books went tumbling down on Vasya.

9238 **indescrivibile** **indescribable**
adj
[indeskrivibile]
La sua bellezza è indescrivibile.
-Her beauty is indescribable.

9239 **profilo** **profile**
il
[profilo]
Visiti il mio profilo di Facebook.
-Visit my Facebook profile.

9240 **interstellare** **interstellar**
adj
[interstellare]
Mentre ci allontaniamo dalle stelle, ora stiamo andando in uno spazio interstellare, e abbiamo un senso dello spazio intorno alla stella.
-As we pull away from the star here, we're actually going now out into

interstellar space, and we're getting a sense of the space around our home star.

9241 **bustarella** **bribe**
la
[bustarella]
Hai accettato o no la bustarella?
-Did you or did you not accept the bribe?

9242 **esplicitamente** **roundly**
adv
[esplitʃitamente]
L'immigrato dice le cose esplicitamente.
-The immigrant says things explicitly.

9243 **recessione** **recession**
la
[retʃessjone]
Siamo in recessione.
-We're in a recession.

9244 **paghetta** **pocket money**
la
[pagetta]
Per quanto mi riguarda, non affiderei alla Commissione europea, né passata né attuale, la custodia della paghetta dei miei nipotini.
-Personally I would not trust the European Commission, past or present, to look after my grandchildren's pocket money.

9245 **pollame** **poultry**
il
[pollame]
In merito al pollame, la direttiva IPPC già controlla 40 000 posti pollame.
-On poultry, the IPPC already controls 40 000 poultry places.

9246 **fluire** **flow; flow**
il; vb
[flwire]
Lasciale fluire dalla mano al quaderno.
-Let them flow through you... from your hand to the pad.

9247 **sottomettere** **submit|subdue**
vb
[sottomettere]
Un bersaglio ubriaco è più facile da sottomettere.
-A drunk target would be easier to subdue.

9248 **maggiolino** **cockchafer**
il
[maddʒolino]
Scommetto che guida un maggiolino.
-I bet she drives a beetle.

9249 **purificare** **purify|cleanse**
vb
[purifikare]
Possiamo purificare la resina e fare polvere di frattale.
-We can purify the resin and make fractal dust.

9250 **mormone** **mormon**
adj
[mormone]
Dissero: "Noi crediamo anche che se sei un Mormone e sei in pace con la chiesa, quando muori potrai andare in paradiso e stare con la tua famiglia per l'eternità."
-They said, "Well, we also believe that if you're a Mormon and if you're in good standing with the church, when you die you get to go to heaven and be with your family for all eternity."

9251 **frigido** **frigid**
adj
[fridʒido]
Ah, non importa, sono frigido.
-Ah, no matter, I'm frigid.

9252 **vibrare** **vibrate|thrill**
vb
[vibrare]
Joe sentì vibrare il suo telefono.
-Joe felt his phone vibrate.

9253 **simulatore** **simulator**
il
[simulatore]
E lo ha usato come componente IT di un meccanismo che azionava un simulatore di volo.
-And he used that as the IT piece of a mechanism which ran a flight simulator.

9254 **antidepressivo** **antidepressant; antidepressive**

il; adj
[antidepressivo]
Quindi pensate che i topi abbiano assunto da soli degli antidepressivi?
-So do you think the mice self-administered antidepressants?

9255 **toscano**
adj; il
[toskano]
Tuscan; Tuscan
Iniziamo dal nostro vino scadente, poi passeremo a questo toscano.
-Let's start with our poor wine, and then we'll move on to this tuscany.

9256 **degradante**
adj
[degradante]
degrading
Questa canzone è degradante per le donne.
-This song is degrading to women.

9257 **ergersi**
vb
[erdʒersi]
rise
Non riteniamo che l'Unione europea debba ergersi a giudice di alcuno Stato in Europa e neppure nel resto del mondo.
-We do not believe that the EU should sit in judgment on individual states in Europe; or the world, for that matter.

9258 **monotono**
adj
[monotono]
monotonous|monotone
Io penso che Joe sia monotono.
-I think Joe is uninteresting.

9259 **spalancare**
vb
[spalaŋkare]
open wide
Chiedo quindi all'Europa di spalancare le porte.
-I would urge Europe to throw the doors open wide.

9260 **mongolfiera**
la
[moŋgolfjera]
hot-air balloon
Le persone nella mongolfiera hanno reagito.
-People in the hot air balloon fought back.

9261 **stock**
lo
[stokk]
stock
Lo stock dell'anguilla europea, che è uno stock comune, si è ridotto del 40 per cento dal 2007.
-The European eel stock, one common stock, has declined by 40% since 2007.

9262 **focolare**
il; il
[fokolare]
hearth; astronomer
Una casa non è un focolare.
-A house is not a home.

9263 **schiaffeggiare**
vb
[skjaffeddʒare]
slap
Certe volte mi sembra che tu voglia schiaffeggiare anche me.
-Sometimes I feel like you want to slap me.

9264 **decretare**
vb
[dekretare]
decree|enact
Tuttavia, l'Unione dovrebbe iniziare in un'area di evidente incoerenza che richiede più di un decreto ministeriale per essere risolta.
-But the Union should start in one area of glaring inconsistency which requires little more than ministerial fiat to fix.

9265 **prossimità**
la
[prossimit'a]
proximity|closeness
Joe ebbe un'esperienza di prossimità alla morte.
-Joe had a near-death experience.

9266 **colmare**
vb
[kolmare]
fill|bridge
Tali sovvenzioni sono destinate a colmare il deficit di bilancio, equivalente al 14 per cento del PIL.
-This aid is intended to cover the budget deficit equivalent to 14% of GDP.

9267 **invitante**
adj
[invitante]
inviting
Sembri molto invitante al momento.
-You are looking quite inviting at the moment.

9268 **stuzzicadenti**
toothpick

lo [stuttsikadenti] — Joe stava masticando uno stuzzicadenti.
-Joe was chewing on a toothpick.

9269 **Balcani** — **Balkans**
i
[balkani]
In particolare, contribuiranno a stabilizzare la situazione politica nei Balcani.
-In particular, they will help stabilise the political situation in the Balkans.

9270 **capriccioso** — **capricious|whimsical**
adj
[kaprittʃozo]
Joe è piuttosto capriccioso.
-Joe is quite temperamental.

9271 **duplicato** — **duplicate**
il
[duplikato]
Questa frase è stata eliminata perché era un duplicato.
-This sentence has been deleted because it was a duplicate.

9272 **cannonata** — **cannon shot**
la
[kannonata]
Quindi visto che i muri sono di cemento armato, l'onda d'urto ha rimbalzato ed è tornata indietro con la forza di una cannonata.
-So, since the walls are actually solid concrete, the blast wave bounced off them and shot out like a cannon.

9273 **rigo** — **line|staff**
il
[rigo]
I miei non hanno mai letto un rigo di poesia.
-My parents never read a line of poetry – in their lives.

9274 **tipografia** — **typography**
la
[tipografja]
Il signor Lewis lavora di notte in una tipografia del quartiere.
-Mr. Lewis works at a print shop overnight in the neighborhood.

9275 **circostante** — **surrounding**
adj
[tʃirkostante]
È in netto contrasto con l'ambiente circostante.
-It contrasts sharply with its surroundings.

9276 **buonumore** — **good mood**
il
[bwonumore]
Era di buonumore.
-He was in good spirits.

9277 **insegna** — **signboard|banner**
le
[inseɲɲa]
Joe mi insegna il francese.
-Joe teaches me French.

9278 **sopportabile** — **bearable**
adj
[sopportabile]
Parallelamente, il problema della disoccupazione ha raggiunto il limite del sopportabile, le nostre industrie sono deboli e notevoli i rischi di una grave crisi.
-Along with this, the problem of unemployment has reached the limit of what is bearable, our industries are fragile and there are grave risks of a major crisis.

9279 **ristoro** — **refreshment**
il
[ristoro]
Lei offre ristoro quando vuole qualcosa.
-You offer refreshment when you want something.

9280 **thriller** — **thriller**
il
[triller]
Permettetemi di ricordare la notte artica del gennaio 1968, ancora all'epoca della guerra fredda - in effetti, i fatti di questa storia sembrano un thriller internazionale.
-Let me take you back to an Arctic night in January 1968, still the era of the Cold War - indeed the facts of this story sound like an international thriller.

9281 **premiato** — **prize; prizewinner**

adj; il
[premjato]
E io penso che un buon lavoro vada premiato.
-And I think good work should be rewarded.

9282 **congiunto** **joined; kinsman**
adj; il
[kondʒunto]
In merito alle mie osservazioni sul fatto di trattare le due proposte congiuntamente, vorrei dire che si è trattato di un'osservazione procedurale.
-In relation to my comments on taking both motions together: that was a procedural comment.

9283 **subacqueo** **underwater**
adj
[subakkweo]
Questo orologio subacqueo è un po' troppo costoso.
-This diver's watch is a little too expensive.

9284 **evolvere** **evolve**
vb
[evolvere]
Chi di noi è a favore vuole che continui a evolvere e a dare risultati positivi.
-Those of us who support it want it to continue to evolve and yield positive results.

9285 **istantaneamente** **instantly**
adv
[istantaneamente]
Romeo si è innamorato istantaneamente di Giulietta.
-Romeo instantly fell in love with Juliet.

9286 **commemorazione** **commemoration**
la
[kommemorattsjone]
Signori, non andrò alla commemorazione di Gurjit.
-Gentlemen, I am not going to Gurjit's memorial...

9287 **lodevole** **commendable**
adj
[lodevole]
Ciò riduce la credibilità di quello che è essenzialmente un lodevole approccio.
-This diminishes the credibility of what is essentially a commendable approach.

9288 **fervore** **fervor|zeal**
il
[fervore]
L'entusiasta non cambia il colore delle cose; ma semplicemente se ne serve col fervore che l'amore domanda e merita.
-The enthusiastic does not change the color of things; But if it simply serves with the fervor that love demand and deserve.

9289 **broker** **broker**
il
[broker]
Siete un broker.
-You are a broker.

9290 **trachea** **trachea**
la
[trakea]
She regrew her own trachea, and 72 hours later it was implanted.
-La "sua" trachea ricrebbe, e 72 ore dopo la reimpiantarono.

9291 **istruttivo** **instructive**
adj
[istruttivo]
Questo è un libro istruttivo.
-This is an instructive book.

9292 **sorpassare** **overtake|surpass**
vb
[sorpassare]
Hei, è pericoloso sorpassare in curva.
-Hey, it's dangerous to overtake on bends.

9293 **galletto** **cockerel**
il
[galletto]
È rossa con un galletto d'argento sul coperchio.
-From last night. It's red with a silver rooster on it.

9294 **ottocento** **eight hundred**
num
[ottotʃento]
Ci sono quarantuno insegnanti e circa ottocento studenti in questa scuola.
-There are forty-one teachers and about eight hundred students in this school.

9295 **ormeggiare** vb [ormeddʒare] **moor**
Ho parlato dei porti di rifugio e degli ormeggi sicuri in una delle mie precedenti relazioni.
-I mentioned airports and safe berthing places in one of my previous reports.

9296 **arcangelo** il [arkandʒelo] **archangel**
Perché l'arcangelo chiama così la Vergine di Nazareth?
-Why does the archangel address the Virgin of Nazareth in this way?

9297 **paladino** il [paladino] **paladin**
Tu sei un paladino della gente comune, lord Snow.
-You're a champion of the common people, Lord Snow.

9298 **finezza** la [finettsa] **fineness|finesse**
Ho bi5ogno che questo lavoro venga eseguito con finezza.
-I need this job executed with a perfect... finesse.

9299 **vigneto** il [viɲɲeto] **vineyard**
Tuttavia egli rimane contrario alle nostre proposte sul rinnovamento del vigneto e sul miglioramento dell'attrezzatura per la vinificazione.
-Nevertheless, he remains opposed to our proposals on the regeneration of vineyards and the improvement of wine-making facilities.

9300 **radiare** vb [radjare] **expel**
In tutti gli altri casi la Commissione considera la possibilità di radiare il peschereccio dall'elenco soltanto se sono soddisfatte le seguenti condizioni:
-In all other cases, the Commission shall only consider removing the fishing vessel from the list if the following conditions are fulfilled:

9301 **pignolo** adj; il [piɲɲolo] **finicky; fastidious person**
Lui è pignolo con le regole.
-He's a stickler for the rules.

9302 **donnola** la [donnola] **weasel**
Lasciaci in pace, piccola donnola.
-Leave us alone, you little weasel.

9303 **insufficiente** adj [insuffitʃente] **insufficient|inadequate**
Ciò è insufficiente.
-This is insufficient.

9304 **moderazione** la [moderattsjone] **moderation**
È meglio bere con moderazione.
-It's best to drink in moderation.

9305 **percussione** la [perkussjone] **percussion**
L'immagine che vi sto mostrando è di Leopoldo Auenbrugger che, alla fine del 1700, scoprì la percussione.
-The picture I'm showing you is of Leopold Auenbrugger who, in the late 1700s, discovered percussion.

9306 **irrigazione** la [irrigattsjone] **irrigation**
Portate un kit per irrigazione e iniziate a pulirlo.
-Let's get an irrigation tray and start cleaning this up.

9307 **disegnatore** il [dizeɲɲatore] **designer|draftsman**
Io sono un disegnatore.
-I'm a cartoonist.

9308 **intraprendente** adj [intraprendente] **enterprising**
Joe sembra intraprendente.
-Joe seems resourceful.

9309 **ghigno** **fleer**
il
[giɲɲo]
Tutto quello che si ottiene è un ghigno irritato di Mosca.
-All that achieves is an irritated sneer in Moscow.

9310 **spartito** **score**
lo
[spartito]
Questo é lo spartito del pezzo di Dan.
-In fact, this is the score for Dan's piece, completely composed by Dan in Hyperscore.

9311 **nutriente** **nutritious|feeding**
adj
[nutrjente]
È molto nutriente.
-It's very nutritious.

9312 **trascurato** **neglected|careless**
adj
[traskurato]
Forse abbiamo trascurato qualcosa.
-Perhaps we overlooked something.

9313 **decompressione** **decompression**
la
[dekompressjone]
Così facendo, talvolta emergono con rapidità dagli abissi marini e subiscono una mortale sindrome da decompressione, e/o si arenano sulle spiagge vicine, per trovarvi una misera fine.
-In so doing, they may rise very quickly from deep waters, thus suffering a form of fatal decompression sickness and/or they may be stranded on nearby beaches where they meet their demise.

9314 **tassì** **taxi**
i
[tass'i]
È andata al museo in tassì.
-She went to the museum by cab.

9315 **croupier** **croupier**
i
[kroupjer]
Non credo che il Presidente della Repubblica abbia la stoffa del croupier.
-I do not think the President of the Republic has a croupier's temperament.

9316 **piattino** **saucer**
il
[pjattino]
Appoggiate sul piattino c'erano due bustine di zucchero.
-Resting on the saucer were two packets of sugar.

9317 **eutanasia** **euthanasia**
la
[eutanazja]
L'aborto e l'eutanasia appaiono allora facilmente come «soluzioni» accettabili.
-Abortion and euthanasia then rapidly come to be seen as acceptable "solutions".

9318 **spergiuro** **perjury**
lo
[sperdʒuro]
È spergiuro, puoi andare in prigione.
-That's perjury, you can go to jail! – You don't understand.

9319 **epico** **epic**
adj
[epiko]
Questo è un romanzo epico.
-This is an epic novel.

9320 **stratagemma** **stratagem|trick**
lo
[stratadʒemma]
Ancora non abbiamo escluso lo stratagemma.
-We still haven't ruled out a ruse.

9321 **irriconoscibile** **unrecognizable**
adj
[irrikonoʃʃibile]
Alla fine voglio che sia irriconoscibile.
-By the time you're finished, I want him unrecognizable.

9322 **saccheggiare** **plunder|loot**
vb
[sakkeddʒare]
Vieni con me a saccheggiare la più grande città del Continente Occidentale.
-Come with me and plunder the greatest city in Westeros.

9323 **rinforzare** **strengthen|reinforce**
vb
[rinfortsare]
Ciò permetterà sia di rinforzare la sicurezza che aumentare il prestigio internazionale dell'Unione europea.
-This will manage to both reinforce security and raise the international prestige of the European Union.

9324 **costituzionale** **constitutional**
adj
[kostituttsjonale]
Stanno intralciando un diritto costituzionale basilare.
-They are interfering with a basic constitutional right.

9325 **impiantare** **implant|establish**
vb
[impjantare]
Su nostra iniziativa, sono stati installati in loco alcuni impianti d'allarme.
-On our initiative several warning devices have been installed there.

9326 **coordinato** **coordinate**
adj
[koordinato]
Noi abbiamo bisogno di uno sforzo coordinato.
-We need a coordinated effort.

9327 **boccetta** **small bottle**
la
[bottʃetta]
Sulla toletta una boccetta di profumo.
-On the dressing table, a bottle of perfume.

9328 **crocchetta** **croquette**
la
[krokketta]
La crocchetta è solo l'inizio...
-The croquette is only the beginning...

9329 **espiare** **atone|pay**
vb
[espjare]
Cercavo di espiare il mio peccato.
-I was trying to atone for my sin.

9330 **scassinatore** **burglar**
lo
[skassinatore]
È l'ingresso perfetto per uno scassinatore.
-It's the perfect entry point for a burglar.

9331 **donnaccia** **slut**
la
[donnattʃa]
È una donnaccia.
-She is a harlot.

9332 **emissario** **emissary**
il
[emissarjo]
Sua è stata la proposta di nominare la onorevole Garaud (a cui rivolgo le mie condoglianze), ma ero stato io a suggerire l' invio di un emissario.
-Specifically, the nomination of Mrs Garaud, and I add my condolences for her situation, was your proposal, but the proposal to send an emissary was mine.

9333 **sommerso** **black**
adj
[sommerso]
Sono stato solo sommerso dal lavoro.
-No! I've just been swamped with work.

9334 **anticristo** **Antichrist**
il
[antikristo]
Frits Bolkestein è diventato il salvatore per gli uni e l'anticristo per gli altri.
-Mr Bolkestein has become the saviour for some, and the Antichrist for others.

9335 **saldamente** **securely|tight**
adv
[saldamente]
Tieni saldamente questa scala.
-Hold this ladder steady.

9336 **menzione** **mention**
la
[mentsjone]
Non farebbe menzione del piano.
-He wouldn't mention the plan.

9337 **impavido** **fearless**

adj [impavido] Sono impavido.
-I'm fearless.

9338 **sottufficiale** **non-comissioned officer**
il/la
[sottuffitʃale]
Poi arriva l'istruttore di lanci, un sottufficiale con esperienza nelle operazioni in paracadute.
-And then a jumpmaster comes, and he's an experienced NCO in parachute operations.

9339 **artigiano** **artisan|workman**
il
[artidʒano]
Una fabbrica di integrati da 10 miliardi di dollari usa un procedimento che un artigiano di villaggio riconoscerebbe -- si spande del materiale e lo si cuoce.
-A 10-billion-dollar chip fab uses a process a village artisan would recognize -- you spread stuff around and bake it.

9340 **montacarichi** **elevator**
il
[montakariki]
Non sapevo ci fosse una telecamera sul montacarichi.
-I didn't know they'd put a camera on the freight elevator.

9341 **trabocchetto** **trap**
il
[trabokketto]
Quella è una domanda trabocchetto?
-Is that a trick question?

9342 **forziere** **coffer**
il
[fortsjere]
Era solo un piccolo forziere e non certo stracolmo.
-It was one small chest, hardly overflowing.

9343 **simboleggiare** **symbolize|epitomize**
vb
[simboleddʒare]
Questo simbolo vuole rappresentare perfezione, complementarietà e solidarietà nonché simboleggiare l'unità dell'Europa.
-The flag is intended to represent perfection, complementarity and solidarity and to symbolise Europe's unity.

9344 **ricognitore** **scout**
il
[rikoɲɲitore]
Servirà un ricognitore, un traduttore.
-You'll need a scout, a translator.

9345 **rivelatore** **detector**
il
[rivelatore]
L'uso di grammatica e ortografia errate nella e-mail che chiedeva a Joe di aggiornare il suo conto bancario era un segno rivelatore che si trattava di una truffa.
-The use of bad grammar and spelling in the email asking Joe to update his bank account details was a telltale sign that it was a scam.

9346 **eventualmente** **in case**
adv
[eventwalmente]
Faremo una verifica ed eventualmente apporteremo la correzione del caso.
-We shall check all this and correct the Minutes, if necessary.

9347 **rally** **rally**
il
[rall]
Gugu Dlamini in un rally a Johannesburg nel dicembre scorso ha annunciato di essere sieropositiva.
-Gugu Dlamini announced in a rally in Johannesburg last December that she was HIV positive.

9348 **casato** **stock|family**
il
[kazato]
Insieme state perpetuando i legami che uniscono il vostro casato al vostro popolo e state proseguendo sulla strada aperta da suo padre, coniugando tradizione e modernità.
-Together you are perpetuating the links uniting your family with your people and continuing along the path opened up by your father, reconciling tradition and modernity.

9349 **autonomo** adj [autonomo] **autonomous**
Abbiamo bisogno di un Presidente della Commissione indipendente, autonomo e dinamico.
-We need an independent, autonomous and dynamic President of the Commission.

9350 **cremazione** la [kremattsjone] **cremation**
Vorrei concludere con alcuni versi che ho scritto alla cremazione di mio padre.
-I'd like to end with a few verses of what I wrote at my father's cremation.

9351 **disapprovazione** la [dizapprovattsjone] **disapproval|disapprobation**
Spregiativo è una parola che esprime disprezzo o disapprovazione.
-Pejorative is a word that expresses contempt or disapproval.

9352 **vandalismo** il [vandalismo] **vandalism**
Fra coloro che arrivarono all'aeroporto di Manchester c'erano cittadini belgi, alcuni dei quali forse non erano nemmeno coinvolti in atti di vandalismo.
-Among those arriving in Manchester airport were Belgian nationals, some of whom may not have been involved in any hooliganism at all.

9353 **invecchiamento** il [invekkjamento] **aging**
Pertanto occorre un approccio esauriente e non frammentario all'invecchiamento.
-Therefore we need a comprehensive, not a fragmented approach to ageing.

9354 **indire** vb [indire] **call|announce**
The consequences are dire for the residents of entire areas.
-Le conseguenze sono disastrose per tutti i residenti di quelle zone.

9355 **militante** adj[militante] **militant**
In primo luogo, intende egli parlarci in qualità di militante, la prossima volta? -Firstly, will he come and speak to us as a militant on a future occasion?

9356 **vischio** il [viskjo] **mistletoe**
L'ho bevuto sotto il vischio.
-I drank that under the mistletoe.

9357 **smistamento** lo [smistamento] **sorting**
Forse l'ufficio di smistamento di Cambridge è stato bombardato.
-Maybe the Cambridge sorting office has been hit.

9358 **mortadella** la [mortadella] **mortadella**
La mortadella non la mangio più.
-I don't eat bologna no more.

9359 **smantellare** vb [smantellare] **dismantle**
E' giunto il momento di pensare seriamente a smantellare questi vecchi reattori nucleari.
-It is time to plan seriously to decommission these older nuclear reactors.

9360 **coordinatore** il [koordinatore] **coordinator**
Una seconda domanda complementare riguarda il coordinatore del programma SENSUS.
-A second supplementary question concerns the coordinator of the Sensus programme.

9361 **rielezione** **re-election**

la
[rjelettsjone]
Non hanno da pensare alla rielezione.
-They don't need to worry about re–election.

9362 **frullatore** **mixer**
il
[frullatore]
Joe versò del latte nel frullatore.
-Joe poured milk into the blender.

9363 **carpentiere** **carpenter**
il
[karpentjere]
Lui è un bravo carpentiere.
-He is a good carpenter.

9364 **aerobico** **aerobic**
adj
[aerobiko]
Si trattava di sostanze che non venivano completamente eliminate nel trattamento aerobico e in alcuni casi limitavano l'eliminazione di altra materia organica.
-They were not fully removed in the aerobic treatment and in some cases limited the removal of other organic matter.

9365 **sparviero** **hawk**
lo
[sparvjere]
Lo sparviero è il maschio e il primo ballerino di questa danza.
-The sparrow hawk is the male and the main dancer in this ballet.

9366 **calce** **lime**
la
[kaltʃe]
Erano parole che, secondo me, andrebbero scritte in calce alla posizione comune del Consiglio.
-These are words, I believe, that should be placed at the bottom of the Council's common position.

9367 **ingenuità** **naivety|ingenuousness**
le[indʒenwit'a]
E così c'è qualcosa da dire sull'ingenuità. -And so there's something to be said about naivete.

9368 **autunnale** **autumnal**
adj
[autunnale]
Colgo questa opportunità per porgervi il benvenuto alla sessione autunnale.
-I should like to take the opportunity to welcome everyone back for the autumn session of our work.

9369 **disumano** **inhuman**
adj
[dizumano]
Dimmi, come può questo rendermi disumano?
-Tell me, how does that make me inhuman?

9370 **primaverile** **vernal**
adj
[primaverile]
Oggi è una splendida giornata primaverile.
-It's a bright, beautiful spring day.

9371 **illeso** **unharmed|uninjured**
adj
[illezo]
Il Sindaco, anche se illeso, è enormemente scosso dall'inimmaginabile tragedia.
-The Mayor himself, though unharmed, is greatly shaken by the unimaginable tragedy.

9372 **diminuzione** **decrease|reduction**
la
[diminuttsjone]
Il petrolio greggio ha subito una diminuzione di prezzo.
-Crude oil has been falling in price.

9373 **familiarità** **familiarity**
la
[familjarit'a]
Io ho familiarità con l'argomento.
-I'm familiar with the subject.

9374 **contingente** **contingent**
adj
[kontindʒente]
"Va sottolineato che tale contingente avrà principalmente la funzione di deterrente".

-'It should be emphasised that this contingent will mainly act as a deterrent'.

9375 **vittorioso** **victorious**
adj
[vittorjozo]
Joe era vittorioso.
-Joe was victorious.

9376 **fraterno** **fraternal|sisterly**
adj
[fraterno]
Ci aspettiamo amore fraterno, invece assistiamo a rivalità tra fratelli, poi a omicidio, fratricidio.
-We expect brotherly love. Instead there is sibling rivalry and then murder, fratricide.

9377 **intolleranza** **intolerance**
la
[intollerantsa]
Le vostre dichiarazioni riflettono la vostra intolleranza.
-Your declarations reflect your intolerance.

9378 **iodio** **iodine**
lo
[jodjo]
Non ho né bende né tintura di iodio.
-I don't have any bandages or tincture of iodine.

9379 **irritazione** **irritation|annoyance**
le
[irritattsjone]
Raramente può essere osservata anche un'irritazione transitoria locale.
-Very rarely, there is also temporary irritation at the application site.

9380 **calciare** **kick**
vb
[kaltʃare]
BF: Dal mio piede, cercherò di calciare il settimo birillo.
-BF: From my foot, I'll attempt to kick the seventh club.

9381 **burlone** **joker**
il
[burlone]
Mi dispiace invece che un qualche burlone si sia permesso di modificare il titolo della risoluzione.
-I am sorry that some joker has taken the liberty of changing the title of the resolution.

9382 **display** **display**
il
[displa]
Con l'evolvere della tecnologia, man mano che arrivano display full immersion e cose simili, questo tipo di cose potrà solo crescere.
-As the technology evolves, as you get full immersive displays and whatnot, this sort of thing will only grow.

9383 **martirio** **martyrdom|torture**
il
[martirjo]
L'esperienza del martirio ha accomunato cristiani di differenti confessioni presenti in Romania.
-The experience of martyrdom joined Christians of different denominations in Romania.

9384 **mecenate** **patron**
il/la
[metʃenate]
Non è neppure un mecenate ingenuo disposto a pagare gli Stati Uniti per aver fatto il 'lavoro sporco?.
-Neither is the EU a naïve Maecenas, who pays up once the United States has done the dirty work.

9385 **tombino** **manhole**
il
[tombino]
Hanno visto Wells uscire dal tombino.
-They're bound to have seen Wells come through the manhole.

9386 **esonerare** **exempt|exonerate**
vb
[ezonerare]
I sistemi tecnici di filtraggio, del tipo V-chip per esempio, non possono esonerare genitori, educatori ed insegnanti dalle loro responsabilità.
-Technical security means, such as the V chip, should not be allowed to relieve parents and teachers of their responsibility.

9387 **riluttanza** **reluctance**

	la [riluttantsa]	Joe non capisce la riluttanza di Jane ad uscire con suo fratello. -Joe doesn't understand Jane's reluctance to go out with his brother.
9388	**serbare** vb [serbare]	**keep|remain** Ma, soprattutto, vorrei sapere da lui se è favorevole a un modal-shift e quali misure abbia in serbo per raggiungere tale obiettivo. -But above all I should like to know if he favours a modal shift and what measures he has in store to that end.
9389	**tumulto** il [tumulto]	**tumult|turmoil** Allora Pilato, vedendo che non otteneva nulla, ma che anzi il tumulto cresceva sempre più, prese dell'acqua e si lavò le mani davanti alla folla, dicendo: "Io sono innocente del sangue di questo giusto; pensateci voi." -And Pilate having seen that it profiteth nothing, but rather a tumult is made, having taken water, he did wash the hands before the multitude, saying, 'I am innocent from the blood of this righteous one.'
9390	**acrobata** il/la [akrobata]	**acrobat** Questo acrobata lavora senza rete! -This acrobat performs without a safety net!
9391	**irreparabile** adj [irreparabile]	**irreparable** Questo vaso rotto è irreparabile. -This broken vase is irreparable.
9392	**fioraio** il[fjorajo]	**florist** Solo qualche libro e uno scontrino del fioraio per una dozzina di rose, pagamento in contanti. -Just a bunch of books and a receipt from a flower shop for a dozen roses, but she paid in cash.
9393	**papero** il [papero]	**gander** Prendiamo tutti in giro il papero. -Let's all laugh at the duck.
9394	**dissenteria** la [dissenterja]	**dysentery** La dissenteria e la diarrea si stanno diffondendo in tutto il Bangladesh a causa dell'acqua inquinata. -There is a major spread of dysentery and diarrhoea right across Bangladesh because of the impure water.
9395	**bevitore** il [bevitore]	**drinker** Il padre di Joe era un bevitore. -Joe's father was a drinker.
9396	**ciabatta** la [tʃabatta]	**slipper** Sembri un cucciolo con una ciabatta. -You look like a puppy with a slipper.
9397	**provocatorio** adj [provokatorjo]	**provocative** L'altro giorno ero ospite ad un talk show e uno dei presenti mi ha chiesto in tono provocatorio: "Cosa fa un pastore per tutelare l'ambiente?" -I was debating the other day on a talk show, and the guy was challenging me and go, "What's a pastor doing on protecting the environment?"
9398	**ode** le [ode]	**ode** Si chiama 'Ode al Tamburo' e proverò a leggerla nel modo in cui Yusef sarebbe orgoglioso di sentirla leggere. -It's called "Ode to the Drum," and I'll try and read it the way Yusef would be proud to hear it read.
9399	**profano** adj; il [profano]	**profane; layman** Come profano, se dovessi usare un prodotto del genere, sono queste le domande che mi farei.

-As a layman, if I had to use a device like this, these are the questions that I would ask myself.

9400 **supplementare** adj [supplementare]
additional|supplementary
Una Carta supplementare, foss'anche europea, non risponderà ad una tale esigenza.
-An additional charter, European or not, will certainly not provide them.

9401 **ambientazione** la [ambjentattsjone]
setting
Mi è piaciuta molto l'ambientazione a Felixstowe.
-I really liked the setting, Felixstowe.

9402 **suggestione** la [suddʒestjone]
suggestion
Lo so, ma è il potere della suggestione.
-I know, but that's the power of suggestion.

9403 **restringere** vb [restrindʒere]
restrict|narrow
Dunque noi pensiamo che possiamo ampliare o restringere i genomi, dipendentemente dal punto di vista, fino a 300 forse o 400 geni da un minimo di 500.
-So we think that we can expand or contract genomes, depending on your point of view here, to maybe 300 to 400 genes from the minimal of 500.

9404 **raggirare** vb [raddʒirare]
circumvent|deceive
Ciò che state facendo è prendere in giro le persone; è un raggiro e la gente se ne sta accorgendo.
-What you are doing is conning people; it is a scam and the people are finding you out.

9405 **avvincere** adj [avvintʃere]
compelling|fascinating
Questo enigma delle feci dovrebbe avvincerti...
-I thought you'd really be into that feces puzzle.

9406 **branca** la [braŋka]
branch
In quale branca delle forze armate eri?
-Which branch of the armed forces were you in?

9407 **tweed** il [tveed]
tweed
Una giacca di tweed.
-A tweed jacket.

9408 **riscontrare** vb [riskontrare]
find|verify
Gli aeroporti regionali potrebbero riscontrare difficoltà a sostenere i costi aggiuntivi dell'aggiornamento dei sistemi.
-Regional airports may find it very hard to sustain the added costs of updating their systems.

9409 **villetta** la [villetta]
chalet
Ho una piccola villetta estiva a Long Island, è tutta vostra.
-I have a little summer cottage out on the island. It's all yours.

9410 **arsenico** il; adj [arseniko]
arsenic; arsenical
E scrissero "Adultera maniaca dello shopping ingoia arsenico dopo una frode creditizia".
-And they wrote "Shopaholic Adulteress Swallows Arsenic After Credit Fraud."

9411 **maltese** adj [malteze]
Maltese
Perché manca il maltese nella lista delle lingue?
-Why's Maltese absent from the languages list?

9412 **impugnatura**
handle|grip

	la [impuɲɲatura]	Il sudore sull'impugnatura corrisponde al DNA sul bicchiere. -But sweat around the handle matched the DNA on the glass.
9413	**dentale** adj [dentale]	**dental** È un tipo di placca dentale fossilizzata ufficialmente denominata calcolo dentale. -It's a type of fossilized dental plaque that is called officially dental calculus.
9414	**nientemeno** con [njentemeno]	**no less than** E nientemeno che nel mio giorno libero. -And on my day off no less.
9415	**berciare** vb [bertʃare]	**jangle** Dovremmo cercare la tossicità in qualcos'altro. -Then we should look for toxic exposures from something else.
9416	**raddrizzare** vb [raddriddzare]	**straighten|right** Una volta ribaltato, un catamarano è impossibile da raddrizzare senza aiuto. -Once capsized, a catamaran is impossible to straighten without help.
9417	**strangolatore** o [straŋgolatore]	**choker** E lo strangolatore gli risponde, come niente fosse: "Oh no. -And the strangler says very matter-of-factly, "Oh no.
9418	**frenesia** la [frenezja]	**frenzy** Emozionante, il nostro negozietto ai margini di una frenesia dei media. -That's a bit exciting, a little shop on the fringes of a media frenzy.
9419	**fisarmonica** la [fizarmonika]	**accordion** Suonavo la fisarmonica. -I played the accordion.
9420	**egizio** adj [edʒittsjo]	**Egyptian** Sono tornato al dipartimento egizio del Louvre questa mattina. -I went to the Egyptian department at the Louvre this morning.
9421	**filastrocca** la [filastrokka]	**doggerel** La filastrocca era un diversivo per tenerci occupati. -The nursery rhyme was a diversion to keep us busy.
9422	**obsoleto** adj [obsoleto]	**obsolete** È obsoleto. -It's outdated.
9423	**socializzare** vb [sotʃaliddzare]	**socialize** Lui è stufo di socializzare. -He's fed up with socializing.
9424	**tonico** adj; il [toniko]	**tonic; tonic** Devo preparare un tonico alle erbe. -I need to prepare an herbal tonic.
9425	**esecutore** il [ezekutore]	**performer** Ho ricevuto una lettera dall'esecutore testamentario di mio padre. -I got a letter from the executor of my father's estate.
9426	**cocomero** il [kokomero]	**watermelon** Mi piace mangiare il cocomero. -I like to eat watermelon.
9427	**strizzare** vb [striddzare]	**wring|squeeze** Tutti sanno che bisogna strizzare le mammelle per far uscire il latte. -Everybody know you got to squeeze the teat to produce the milk.

9428 **somministrare** **administer|give**
vb
[somministrare]
In primo luogo dobbiamo somministrare una terapia d'urto per far uscire il paziente dal suo attuale coma.
-Firstly, we must administer a shock treatment to bring the patient out of his current coma.

9429 **sostanziale** **substantial**
adj
[sostantsjale]
Avrei bisogno di un sostanziale anticipo, vossignoria.
-It would have to be a substantial advance, your Lordship.

9430 **bacheca** **showcase**
la
[bakeka]
Non hai nulla sulla tua bacheca.
-You have nothing on your wall.

9431 **scacchiera** **chessboard**
la
[skakkjera]
E se guardate alle loro estremità adesive, quei segmentini di DNA, potete vedere che formano una scacchiera.
-And if you look at their sticky ends, these little DNA bits, you can see that they actually form a checkerboard pattern.

9432 **perdutamente** **hopelessly**
adv
[perdutamente]
Lui è perdutamente innamorato.
-He's head over heels in love.

9433 **arrangiare** **arrange**
vb
[arrandʒare]
Credo di poter arrangiare la cosa con il coroner.
-I guess I can arrange it with the coroner.

9434 **supplemento** **supplement|extra charge**
il
[supplemento]
Posso avere un supplemento di riso e verza?
-Can I have seconds on rice and cabbage?

9435 **coccio** **earthenware|shard**
il
[kottʃo]
Prese un coccio di qualcosa e si tagliò un pezzo di carne dalla coscia e la pose a terra.
-And he took a shard of something, and cut a piece of flesh from his thigh, and he placed it on ground.

9436 **mollusco** **shellfish|clam**
il
[mollusko]
Lascerò questo mollusco nella spazzatura là fuori.
-I'll leave this mollusk in the garbage... outside.

9437 **pigrizia** **laziness|idleness**
la
[pigrittsja]
La mia pigrizia sarà la mia rovina.
-My idleness will become my doom.

9438 **molotov** **molotov cocktail**
il
[molotov]
Per amor del cielo, non ti avvicinare così, al fuoco, o esploderai come una bomba molotov.
-For heavens' sake, don't get so close to the fire, or you'll explode like a Molotov cocktail.

9439 **amaca** **hammock**
la
[amaka]
Julio sta oscillando sull'amaca che ho appeso sotto la vecchia quercia.
-Julio is swinging in the hammock that I hung under the old oak tree.

9440 **manopola** **knob|handle**
la
[manopola]
Si può mettere una manopola al centro e si ottiene un piccolo dimmer.
-You can put a knob in between and now you've made a little dimmer.

9441 **desiderabile** **desirable**
adj
[deziderabile]
E' un fatto che la soluzione desiderabile sarebbe un accordo tra le parti interessate.

-It is a fact that the desirable solution would be an agreement between the parties involved.

9442 **inconsapevole** **unaware|oblivious**
adj
[iŋkonsapevole]
Lui sembrava inconsapevole della mia presenza.
-He seemed unconscious of my presence.

9443 **sibilo** **hiss|hissing**
il
[sibillo]
Credevo che la parola "sibilo" fosse abbastanza esplicita.
-I thought the word "hissing" kind of covered that nicely.

9444 **dardo** **dart**
il
[dardo]
Joe lanciò il dardo.
-Joe threw the dart.

9445 **scopa** **broom**
la
[skopa]
Non riesco a trovare la scopa.
-I can't find the broom.

9446 **rasare** **shave|mow**
Vb
[razare]
Mi sono fatta rasare e tagliare i capelli.
-I got a shave and a haircut.

9447 **cardiologo** **cardiologist**
il
[kardjologo]
Lo dovete portare da un cardiologo.
-You need to have him see a cardiologist.

9448 **scrivano** **scribe|clerk**
lo
[skrivano]
I cittadini possono scrivere al Parlamento e ricevere una risposta in queste lingue.
-Citizens can write to Parliament and receive a response in these languages.

9449 **diffidente** **suspicious|distrustful**
adj
[diffidente]
Joe sembra diffidente.
-Joe looks suspicious.

9450 **innato** **innate|inborn**
adj
[innato]
Gauss aveva un talento innato per i problemi matematici.
-Gauss had an innate talent for mathematical problems.

9451 **spasmo** **spasm**
lo
[spasmo]
Qualcosa avrà causato uno spasmo arterioso mentre controllavamo il flusso sanguigno.
-Maybe something caused an arterial spasm while we were checking the function of the blood supply.

9452 **insuccesso** **failure**
il
[insuttʃesso]
Signor Presidente, onorevoli colleghi, non intendo associarmi al lamento per l'insuccesso di Bali e non mi soffermerò sui punti che sono già stati trattati.
-Mr President, ladies and gentlemen, I do not want right now to join in the weeping and wailing over the fiasco in Bali, and I also propose to leave out the points that have already been addressed.

9453 **addebito** **charge**
il
[addebito]
Nessun addebito su carte di credito o prepagate.
-No credit card or debit card charges, no cell phone usage.

9454 **consecutivo** **consecutive|running**
adj
[konsekutivo]
E' il settimo anno consecutivo che ho il piacere di accogliere questo Consiglio.
-This is the seventh consecutive year that I have the pleasure of receiving this Council.

9455 **ambiguo** | **ambiguous|devious**
adj
[ambigwo]
Il significato di questa frase è ambiguo.
-The meaning of this sentence is ambiguous.

9456 **guaire** | **yelp**
vb
[gwaire]
Faresti meglio a correre prima di guaire.
-You'd better run before you yelp.

9457 **schiacciata** | **smash**
la
[skjattʃata]
Tossicodipendenti come lui usano la loro instabilità percepita come capitale sociale per mantenere la loro fiducia e la buona fede viva a lungo dopo che è stata schiacciata più e più volte per la loro crudeltà e perversione.
-Abusers like him use their perceived instability as social capital to keep their trust and good faith alive long after it's been crushed again and again by their cruelty and perversion.

9458 **risaia** | **paddy field**
la
[rizaja]
E ogni anno, il 99,:,9 percento delle risaie è trapiantato a mano.
-And every year, 99,:,9 percent of the paddy is transplanted manually.

9459 **posizionare** | **position**
vb
[pozittsjonare]
Non abbiamo un gruppo di venditori e di operatori di marketing che può dirci come posizionare questo farmaco contro un altro.
-We don't have a team of salespeople and marketeers that can tell us how to position this drug against the other.

9460 **tiepido** | **warm|lukewarm**
adj
[tjepido]
La relazione di quest'anno è più equilibrata, tuttavia anch'essa manda un messaggio piuttosto tiepido.
-This year's report is more balanced, but it still sends a lukewarm message.

9461 **argomentazione** | **argumentation**
le
[argomentattsjone]
La tua argomentazione non è basata sulla realtà.
-Your argument is not based in reality.

9462 **smaltire** | **dispose of**
vb
[smaltire]
Tuttavia, sono ingenti capitali da smaltire.
-Nonetheless, there are considerable assets to dispose of.

9463 **sensualità** | **sensuality**
la
[senswalit'a]
Vuole parlarti della tua perdita di sensualità.
-He wants to talk about your loss of sensuality.

9464 **ingannevole** | **misleading|tricky**
adj
[iŋgannevole]
Come hanno applicato la direttiva sulla pubblicità ingannevole e comparativa?
-How have they applied the directive on misleading and comparative advertising?

9465 **gelsomino** | **jasmine**
il
[dʒelsomino]
La rivoluzione del gelsomino si è fondata principalmente su valori quali la dignità e l'uguaglianza.
-The Jasmine Revolution was very much about dignity and equity.

9466 **anticorpo** | **antibody**
gli
[antikorpo]
E se un anticorpo è attaccato ad una di queste cose sulla cellula, significa "è cibo".
-And if an antibody is stuck to one of these things on the cell, it means "that's food."

9467 **smuovere** | **move|shift**

vb Trova un uomo talmente potente da smuovere tuo padre, e sposalo.
[smwovere] -Find a man with power to shake your father and marry him.

9468 **inceppare** **clog|obstruct**
vb Mike, dobbiamo inceppare la ventola con qualcosa che non verrà triturata.
[intʃeppare] -Mike, we got to jam the fan with something that won't get cut to bits.

9469 **apprendimento** **learning**
il Io non sono contraria al vostro apprendimento dell'inglese per acquisire conoscenza o per guadagnare il vostro sostentamento, ma mi oppongo al vostro dare tanta importanza all'inglese e dare un posto basso alla vostra lingua nazionale, l'hindi.
[apprendimento] -I do not object to your learning English for the sake of acquiring knowledge or for the sake of earning your livelihood but I object to your giving so much importance to English and giving a low place to your national language, Hindi.

9470 **ventola** **fan**
la Ho trovato la ventola di un trattore, un ammortizzatore, dei tubi di plastica.
[ventola] -I found a tractor fan, shock absorber, PVC pipes.

9471 **ostruzione** **obstruction**
le Avevano stabilito di accusarlo di ostruzione e... comportamento minaccioso.
[ostruttsjone] -They were all set to charge him with obstruction and threatening behaviour.

9472 **melanzana** **eggplant**
la Quando sono fortunato, è un cetriolo o una melanzana.
[melantsana] -When I'm lucky, it's a cucumber or eggplant.

9473 **seppia** **cuttlefish**
la Quella seppia con gli asparagi non è molto stabile.
[seppja] -That cuttlefish and asparagus is not sitting well.

9474 **dosaggio** **dosage**
il Se il farmaco non funziona, forse dovremmo aumentare il dosaggio.
[dozaddʒo] -If the medicine isn't working, maybe we should up the dosage.

9475 **imperialismo** **imperialism**
il Sarebbe una forma di imperialismo culturale.
[imperjalismo] -That would be a form of cultural imperialism.

9476 **antigas** **antigas**
il Le maschere antigas saranno fornite dalle autorità locali.
[antigas] -Gas masks will be issued to you by your local authority.

9477 **ambra** **amber**
la Qualcuno ricrea i dinosauri estraendo il DNA dall'ambra preistorica.
[ambra] -Someone is re-engineering dinosaurs by extracting their DNA from prehistoric amber.

9478 **pacifista** **pacifist**
il/la È una pacifista.
[patʃifista] -She's a pacifist.

9479 **dirottatore** **hijacker**
il Niente prova del DNA, ma furono raccolti capelli e fibre dai vestiti del dirottatore.
[dirottatore] -There's no DNA evidence, even though they pulled hairs and fibers from the hijacker's clothing.

9480 **vaselina** **vaseline**

	la [vazelina]	Avete mai provato a vederlo con della vaselina davanti agli occhi? -Have you ever tried to see that if you have Vaseline in front of your eyes?
9481	**prevenzione**	**prevention|prophylaxis**
	la [preventsjone]	La prevenzione è la chiave. -Prevention is the key.
9482	**squilibrio**	**imbalance**
	lo [skwilibrjo]	Ha uno squilibrio enzimatico nel cervelletto. -He says you have a slight enzymatic imbalance in your cerebellum.
9483	**orda**	**horde**
	la [orda]	Erano nude, trascinate a terra per i capelli, circondate da un'orda di membri della CRS. -They were stripped naked and dragged along the floor by their hair, surrounded by a horde of state security police.
9484	**cifrario**	**code**
	il [tʃifrarjo]	Un cifrario, uno strumento algoritmico per criptare informazioni. -A cipher, an algorithmic tool for performing encryption.
9485	**filantropo**	**philanthropist**
	il [filantropo]	Un pezzo di me potrebbe ispirare un commediografo o uno scrittore di romanzi o uno scienziato, e questo a sua volta può essere il seme che ispirerà un dottore o un filantropo o una babysitter. -So a piece of mine may inspire a playwright or a novelist or a scientist, and that in turn may be the seed that inspires a doctor or a philanthropist or a babysitter.
9486	**lugubre**	**dismal|lugubrious**
	adj [lugubre]	Joe è lugubre. -Joe is grim.
9487	**trionfante**	**triumphant**
	adj [trjonfante]	Il benessere di ogni individuo e il diritto alla vita e alla pace devono trionfare. -The well-being of every individual and his or her right to life and peace must triumph.
9488	**sdegno**	**indignation|disdain**
	lo [zdeɲɲo]	L'editore disse, con enorme sdegno, "L'ho letto. -The editor said, with enormous disdain, "I read this.
9489	**pennuto**	**fledged**
	adj [pennuto]	Allora, infila la mano dentro il pennuto e tira fuori le frattaglie. -So reach your hand inside the bird and pull out the giblets.
9490	**afflitto**	**sad**
	adj [afflitto]	Sono afflitto. -I am woebegone.
9491	**armistizio**	**armistice**
	il [armistittsjo]	Ecco perché credo che si sia raggiunto un armistizio, più che una vittoria. -Therefore I think we have reached an armistice, rather than that the battle is won.
9492	**assenzio**	**absinthe**
	il [assentsjo]	È assenzio, rum e analgesico. -It's absinthe, rum, and paregoric.
9493	**rinomato**	**renowned**
	adj [rinomato]	Un rinomato chirurgo cardiotoracico. Io sono... -I am Preston Burke, a widely renowned cardiothoracic surgeon.

9494 **gengiva** **gum**
la
[dʒendʒiva]
Ieri avevo un quintetto di ottoni sotto la gengiva.
-(sighs) yesterday, I had a 5–piece brass band underneath my gum.

9495 **edicola** **newsstand**
le
[edikola]
Ogni mattina compro un giornale in un'edicola.
-Every morning I buy a newspaper at a newsstand.

9496 **trapezio** **trapeze**
il
[trapettsjo]
Pattinaggio, trapezio e ginnastica ritmica.
-Varsity figure skating, trapeze and rhythmic dance.

9497 **pompelmo** **grapefruit**
il
[pompelmo]
Ho mangiato mezzo pompelmo per colazione.
-I had half a grapefruit for breakfast.

9498 **emarginare** **marginalize**
vb
[emardʒinare]
Perché mi vuole emarginare?
-Why do you want to outcast me?

9499 **incarnazione** **incarnation**
le
[iŋkarnattsjone]
Sei l'incarnazione vivente della bellissima Principessa Panchali.
-You are the living embodiment of the beautiful Princess Panchali.

9500 **affabile** **affable|amiable**
adj
[affabile]
La ragazza che lavora nella panetteria è affabile.
-The girl who works in the bakery is affable.

9501 **lenza** **line**
la
[lentsa]
Proprio come la lenza, quella da pesca.
-It's basically like a fisherman's line, a fishing line.

9502 **criniera** **mane**
la
[krinjera]
E i tuoi capelli sono come la criniera di un unicorno.
-And your hair is like a unicorn's mane.

9503 **giovare** **profit**
vb
[dʒovare]
Concordo con l'onorevole Adamou, in situazioni come queste si impongono ragionevolezza e realismo, mentre il panico non giova a nessuno.
-I agree with Mr Adamou that everybody should be as reasonable and realistic as possible in this situation - panicking does not help anybody.

9504 **confisca** **confiscation**
la
[konfiska]
Essi sono esenti da perquisizioni, requisizioni, confisca o espropriazione.
-They shall be exempt from search, requisition, confiscation or expropriation.

9505 **attuare** **carry out**
vb
[attware]
Il mio primo messaggio è "attuare, attuare, attuare".
-My first message is, 'implement, implement, implement'.

9506 **bellico** **war-; warlike**
pfx; adj[belliko]
In tal senso, stiamo per varcare la soglia del conflitto bellico. -In this respect, things are close to exceeding the threshold of war.

9507 **lustrino** **spangle**
il
[lustrino]
Ok, allora potrà spiegarci perché abbiamo trovato questo... lustrino rotto della sua giacca... sul corpo di Amber.
-Okay, well, then maybe you can explain why we found this broken sequin from your jacket on her body.

9508 **malta** **mortar**
le
[malta]
Io abito a Malta.
-I live in Malta.

9509 **londinese** **Londoner; London's**
il/la; adj
[londineze]
Lei era nata e cresciuta londinese.
-She was a born and bred Londoner.

9510 **quattromila** **four thousand**
num
[kwattromila]
Mi servono più di quattromila minuti.
-I need more than four thousand minutes.

9511 **selvaggina** **game**
la
[selvaddʒina]
In molte parti del mondo è illegale sparare a della selvaggina come cervi, alci o fagiani.
-In many parts of the world it is illegal to shoot wild game such as deer, moose or pheasant.

9512 **legittimare** **legitimize|justify**
vb
[ledʒittimare]
Il dramma che stiamo vivendo dovrebbe essere sufficiente per legittimare questo esercizio inusuale.
-The problems that we are experiencing would justify this unusual step.

9513 **automobilistico** **automotive**
adj
[automobilistiko]
Martiniano Martin non è più nel sindacato automobilistico…
-Martiniano Martin is no longer on the committee of the car factory.

9514 **moltiplicare** **multiply**
vb
[moltiplikare]
Questo rapporto sbilanciato non fa altro che moltiplicare i contenziosi.
-This unbalanced relationship can only multiply disputes.

9515 **piastrina** **platelet**
la
[pjastrina]
La difficoltà sorge se viene impedita la distribuzione con altri Stati membri dei componenti labili, per esempio gli eritrociti, le piastrine o il plasma prima del frazionamento.
-But the difficulty arises when labile components, for example red blood cells, platelets or plasma prior to fractionation, are prevented from being shared with other Member States.

9516 **cinematografo** **cinema**
il
[tʃinematografo]
Vedi, Guido, il cinematografo è una delle forze più pericolose nella nostra società.
-You see, Guido, cinema has a very dangerous influence on our society.

9517 **striscio** **scratch**
lo
[striʃʃo]
E appena c'è silenzio strisciano fuori.
-And as soon as it's silent, they sort of creep out.

9518 **momentaneamente** **at the moment**
adv
[momentaneamente]
Lydia tornerà, ma solo momentaneamente.
-Lydia will be returning, but only momentarily.

9519 **sfrontato** **cheeky**
adj
[sfrontato]
Poteva essere un po' più sfrontato.
-It could stand to be a little more bold.

9520 **vagabondare** **wander|stroll**
vb
[vagabondare]
Quando sono andato via per vagabondare, restavo sempre vicino al mare.
-After I left to wander, I always stayed near the sea.

9521 **luccicante** **shimmering**
adj
[luttʃikante]
Joe vide qualcosa di luccicante nell'acqua.
-Joe saw something shiny in the water.

9522 **impuro** **impure**
adj
[impuro]
Nessuna ribellione, o pensiero impuro.
-She never had a rebellious or impure thought.

9523 **impigliare** **entangle**

vb Ti si può impigliare nei capelli.
[impiʎʎare] -It may get tangled in your hair.

9524 **fabbricazione** **manufacture**
la La data di fabbricazione viene mostrata sul coperchio.
[fabbrikattsjone] -The date of manufacture is shown on the lid.

9525 **dizione** **diction**
la So sputare ogni parola con precisione, dizione e chiarezza.
[dittsjone] -I can spit my words out with precision, diction, and clarity.

9526 **trasferta** **transfer**
la Mi piacete quando andate in trasferta in Toscana.
[trasferta] -I like you when you go away to Tuscany.

9527 **isterismo** **hysteria**
gli Abbiamo abbastanza potenziale isterismo anche senza il ragazzo di Fortune.
[isterismo] -We've enough potential for hysteria without the boyfriend.

9528 **rimorchiatore** **tug**
il Poi trovai un rimorchiatore abbandonato, molto più economico.
[rimorkjatore] -Then I found an abandoned tugboat, and it was way cheaper.

9529 **festino** **party**
il Quando riesci a capirlo, puoi fare un figurone alle feste.
[festino] -Once you figure this out, you can really impress people at parties.

9530 **installazione** **installation**
la Questa installazione ha un certo valore.
[installattsjone] -This installation has a substantial dollar value attached to it.

9531 **affanno** **breathlessness**
il Da mezz'ora accusa dolori al petto, nausea, affanno.
[affanno] -He's had 30 minutes of chest pains, nausea, shortness of breath.

9532 **sfinge** **sphinx**
la Veramente intelligente quella Sfinge!
[sfindʒe] -Really smart, that Sphinx!

9533 **bozzolo** **cocoon**
il Sembra una piccola farfalla in un bozzolo.
[bottsolo] -She looks like a little butterfly in a cocoon.

9534 **lavastoviglie** **dishwasher**
la Noi non abbiamo una lavastoviglie.
[lavastoviʎʎe] -We don't have a dishwasher.

9535 **contrabbasso** **contrabass**
il Ho provato il contrabbasso e deciso per la batteria.
[kontrabbasso] -I tried the double bass and settled on the drums.

9536 **Trinità** **Trinity**
la Lui venne dagli irlandesi con tutti i segni di un apostolo, e quando la gente gli chiese di spiegare la Santissima Trinità, si chinò a terra e prese un trifoglio.
[trinit'a] -He came to the Irish with all the signs of an apostle, and when the people asked him to explain the Blessed Trinity, he reached down to the ground and picked up a shamrock.

9537 **valente** **talented**
adj Potenzialmente questo mercato può valere miliardi di euro.
[valente] -Potentially that market is worth billions of euros.

9538 **filone** **vein**

il
[filone]

Ma il secondo filone è diverso: pur sostenendo l'Unione europea, esso nutre alcuni timori per i suoi orientamenti e le sue azioni.
-But the second strand is different: it can support the European Union but it worries about its directions and its actions.

9539 **girovagare** — **wander|wander about**
vb
[dʒirovagare]
Fino ad allora, questa gattona dovrà girovagare.
-Until then, this big cat's got to roam.

9540 **candore** — **candor|whiteness**
il
[kandore]
Tutto quello che vogliamo è un certo candore in questo dibattito.
-All we want now is a certain candour in that matter in this debate.

9541 **clic** — **click**
i
[klik]
È meno della metà di un clic.
-It's less than half a click.

9542 **competitivo** — **competitive**
adj
[kompetitivo]
Qual è il vantaggio competitivo della società?
-What is the company's competitive advantage?

9543 **disfunzione** — **dysfunction**
la
[disfuntsjone]
Credo che abbia una disfunzione somatica neuro–muscolare–scheletrica.
-I think he's experiencing somatic skeletal neuromuscular dysfunction.

9544 **innovativo** — **innovative**
adj
[innovativo]
Joe era innovativo.
-Joe was innovative.

9545 **cigolare** — **creak|grate**
vb
[tʃigolare]
Il suo peso ha fatto cigolare le assi del pavimento.
-His weight made the floorboards creak.

9546 **ricompensa** — **reward|award**
la
[rikompensa]
C'è una ricompensa?
-Is there a reward?

9547 **tappa** — **stage|stop**
la
[tappa]
L'ultima tappa del nostro viaggio sarà la più difficile.
-The last leg of our journey will be the most difficult.

9548 **respiratore** — **respirator**
il
[respiratore]
Io so cosa succede quando staccano una persona dal respiratore.
-I know what happens when they take someone off of life support.

9549 **glassa** — **icing**
la
[glassa]
Se proprio devo, mangio solo la glassa.
-If I absolutely have to, I'll just eat the frosting.

9550 **alpino** — **alpine**
adj
[alpino]
L'ordine del giorno reca il proseguimento della discussione congiunta sul traffico alpino.
-The next item is the continuation of the joint debate on Alpine transit.

9551 **basco** — **Basque; Basque**
adj; il
[basko]
Ci sono oltre 800,000 parlanti di basco nel mondo.
-There are over 800,000 Basque speakers in the world.

9552 **capostazione** — **stationmaster**
il
[kapostattsjone]
Thomax Fallfresh, il capostazione di Diss, anticipava 4.730 treni l'anno.
-Thomax Fallfresh, the Diss stationmaster, could expect 4,730 trains a year.

9553 **questionario** — **questionnaire**

il | Compili il questionario.
[kwestjonarjo] | -Fill out the questionnaire.

9554 **rettilineo** **straight; straight**
adj; il
[rettilineo]
Ovviamente, sul rettilineo, potrei batterti facilmente.
-Obviously on the straight, I could easily have you.

9555 **doge** **doge**
il
[dodʒe]
Ed è un no al nipote del doge.
-That's no to the doge's nephew.

9556 **subdolo** **sneaky; seismic**
adj; adj
[subdolo]
Tu sei subdolo.
-You're sneaky.

9557 **mimo** **mime**
il
[mimo]
Ma prima di creare giocattoli sono stato un artista di strada, un mimo.
-And before I was a toy designer, oh, I was a mime, a street mime, actually.

9558 **prosa** **prose**
la
[proza]
Quel poema mescola la prosa con la poesia.
-That poem mixes prose with poetry.

9559 **coniuge** **spouse|consort**
il
[konjudʒe]
E sorprendentemente, il 22% ha detto di aver tenuto nascosto l'aborto al proprio coniuge.
-And astoundingly, 22 percent said they would hide a miscarriage from their spouse.

9560 **perenne** **perennial|perpetual**
adj
[perenne]
Antonio La vede, è Lei, l'Immacolata Madre che sconfigge il dolore del tramonto con la luce dell'inizio della perenne vita.
-Antonio La seen, it is she, the Immaculate Mother who conquers the pain of the sunset with the light to the start of the perennial life.

9561 **contrastante** **conflicting**
adj
[kontrastante]
Si tratta infatti di un "no" a più facce, con motivazioni confuse e talvolta contrastanti.
-It is actually a multiple 'no', with mixed and sometimes conflicting motives.

9562 **statico** **static**
adj
[statiko]
Il carico verticale statico massimo è fissato dal costruttore.
-The maximum static vertical load is laid down by the manufacturer.

9563 **sarcofago** **sarcophagus**
il
[sarkofago]
Come mai non disponiamo ancora di un'analisi del rischio sul sarcofago I?
-Why is it that we still do not have a risk analysis for Sarcophagus I?

9564 **nascente** **rising**
adj
[naʃʃente]
Il sole nascente visto dalla cima era bello.
-The rising sun seen from the top was beautiful.

9565 **brevettare** **patent**
vb
[brevettare]
Nessuno ammette apertamente di voler brevettare il.
-Nobody is openly admitting that they want to patent software.

9566 **destare** **arouse|kindle**
vb
[destare]
Come giunse l'alba andò incontro al suo destino, lasciò ai posteri una pila di fogli sul tavolo.
-And as the dawn came up and he went to meet his destiny, he left this pile of papers on the table for the next generation.

9567 **inquietudine** **restlessness**
le
[iŋkwjetudine]
A noi sembra che l'inquietudine dell'opinione pubblica europea sia logica.
-We think the anxiety manifested in European public opinion is reasonable.

9568 **possedimento** **possession**
il
[possedimento]
Seguo con rammarico le controversie sui possedimenti nuovi e storici.
-I follow with displeasure the disputes over both new and historical possessions.

9569 **combattivo** **combative**
adj
[kombattivo]
In altri termini, sarà un "sì" combattivo, che deve essere un inizio, non una fine.
-In other words, it will be a combative 'yes', which should signal a beginning and not an end.

9570 **catacomba** **catacomb**
la
[katakomba]
Sembrava più una catacomba che una fognatura.
-It looked more like a catacomb than a sewer line.

9571 **crostaceo** **crustacean; shellfish**
adj; il
[krostatʃo]
Non dimenticate l'illegale contrabbando di un crostaceo senza una licenza.
-Don't forget illegal poaching of a crustacean without a license.

9572 **assegnazione** **assignment|allocation**
la
[asseɲɲattsjone]
Dobbiamo assolutamente garantire condizioni più rigorose sull'assegnazione dei finanziamenti.
-It is very important for us to ensure that tougher conditions are attached to the allocation of funding.

9573 **medicare** **medicate**
vb
[medikare]
A victor in a thousand contests, three great civil rights laws, Medicare, aid to education.
-Un vincitore in migliaia di competizioni, tre grandi leggi sui diritti civili, assistenza sanitaria, aiuti alla scuola.

9574 **wurstel** **frankfurter**
i
[vurstel]
I Beatles hanno suonato 2 anni negli strip club tedeschi schivando wurstel.
-The Beatles spent two years playing German strip bars, dodging bratwurst.

9575 **importunare** **bother|importune**
vb
[importunare]
Così non dovrò più importunare né te né Pufflandia.
-That way I never have to bother you or Smurf Village again.

9576 **auspicio** **omen**
il
[auspitʃo]
L'auspicio di vedere l'adesione di un'isola riunificata non si è concretizzato.
-Our hope of seeing a reunited island joining the Union has not materialised.

9577 **accusatore** **accuser**
il
[akkuzatore]
Di conseguenza, l'accusatore ha intentato il procedimento penale contro l'onorevole Tamás Deutsch.
-Accordingly, the accuser brought the criminal proceedings against Tamás Deutsch.

9578 **instabilità** **instability**

le
[instabilit'a]
Per questa lacuna dobbiamo sopportare una instabilità climatica molto estesa.
-We are suffering widespread climate instability because of that failure.

9579 **tessile**
adj
[tessile]
textile
Gli esempi possono indubbiamente essere desunti dal settore tessile.
-Examples of this can certainly be seen within the textile sector.

9580 **bancarella**
la
[baŋkarella]
stall|stand
Lasciamogli un biglietto per spiegargli perché abbiamo dovuto chiudere la bancarella.
-Let's leave a note explaining why we needed to shut the stall.

9581 **mendicare**
vb
[mendikare]
beg
Che ho dovuto mendicare per mangiare.
-That I had to beg for food.

9582 **sacerdotessa**
la
[satʃerdotessa]
priestess
Ti ho salvato da Hilda, la grande sacerdotessa vudu'.
-I saved you from Hilda the high voodoo priestess.

9583 **eccezionalmente**
adv
[ettʃettsjonalmente]
exceptionally
Abbiamo suonato eccezionalmente bene.
-We played exceptionally well.

9584 **bavarese**
adj; il/la
[bavareze]
Bavarian; Bavarian
Spero che non vi dispiaccia se, come cittadino bavarese, traccio un parallelo.
-I hope you will not mind if a Bavarian like myself draws a parallel.

9585 **patrono**
il
[patrono]
patron|patron saint
Qualora ce ne dimenticassimo, il nostro comune santo patrono, São Jorge, ce lo ricorderebbe.
-If we forget, our mutual patron saint, São Jorge, is there to remind us.

9586 **appaiare**
vb
[appajare]
pair|brace
Quindi un punto qui è il comportamento di una coppia di giocatori, uno che cerca di appaiare, uno che cerca di disappaiare.
-So a point here is the behavior by a pair of players, one trying to match, one trying to mismatch.

9587 **banalità**
la
[banalit'a]
banality|triviality
Se si confronta il comportamento di HAL con la banalità delle persone sulle astronavi, si può vedere cos'è scritto tra le righe.
-If you contrast HAL's behavior with the triviality of the people on the spaceship, you can see what's written between the lines.

9588 **ricattatore**
il
[rikattatore]
blackmailer
Joe è il ricattatore.
-Joe is the blackmailer.

9589 **lealmente**
adv
[lealmente]
loyally
Non ho alcuna intenzione di scusarmi per aver lavorato lealmente a fianco di questi capi di Stato e di governo.
-I make no apology for having loyally worked alongside these Heads of State or Government.

9590 **pedalare**
vb
[pedalare]
pedal
È davvero difficile pedalare!
-It's really difficult to pedal!

9591 **scremare**
vb
[skremare]
skim
L'obiettivo perseguito è quello di scremare i settori più redditizi a vantaggio delle grandi imprese private, riducendo il servizio pubblico al minimo, entro il concetto di« servizio universale».

-The aim is to cream off the most profitable sectors for the benefit of large private companies, reducing the public service to a minimum level, as expressed by the notion of a 'universal service '.

9592 **piroscafo** **steamer**
il
[piroskafo]
Tre cabine sul piroscafo Carnatic, prego.
-Three cabins on the steamer Carnatic, please. Yes, sir.

9593 **tresca** **affair**
la
[treska]
Forse Madhuri aveva ragione sulla tresca.
-You know, maybe Madhuri was right about the affair.

9594 **tuffare** **dive|dip**
vb
[tuffare]
Mi voglio andare a tuffare dalla scogliera.
-I want to dive off the cliff.

9595 **lungi** **far**
adv
[lundʒi]
La sua idea è ben lungi dall'essere soddisfacente per noi.
-His idea is far from satisfactory to us.

9596 **spifferare** **blurt out|blab**
vb
[spifferare]
Almeno io so di non dover spifferare a una ragazza che qualcuno sta flirtando con il suo ragazzo.
-At least I know not to blab to a girl about somebody flirting with her boyfriend.

9597 **totem** **totem**
i
[totem]
And there is a gharial looking at us from the river. And these are powerful water totems.
-E c'è un Gaviale che ci controlla dal fiume Sono simboli acquatici potenti.

9598 **giostra** **carousel|joust**
la
[dʒostra]
Questa é una giostra, progettata dalla Roundabout, che pompa l'acqua man mano che i bambini giocano.
-This is a merry-go-round invented by the company Roundabout, which pumps water as kids play.

9599 **giugulare** **jugular vein**
la
[dʒugulare]
Un taglio netto di esofago, trachea, carotide e giugulare.
-One cut clean through the esophagus, trachea, carotid artery, and jugular.

9600 **gratifica** **bonus**
la
[gratifika]
Signor Presidente, è stato gratificante ascoltare il Commissario Vitorino.
-Mr President, it was gratifying to listen to Commissioner Vitorino.

9601 **panetteria** **relic**
la
[panetterja]
La panetteria è in via Pino.
-The bakery is on Pino Street.

9602 **cimelio** **relic**
il
[tʃimeljo]
Volevo un cimelio di mio padre.
-I wanted an heirloom of my father's.

9603 **ringhio** **snarl**
il
[riŋgjo]
Ma con me sembra più un ringhio.
-But all I'm hearing is a growl.

9604 **mascara** **mascara**
il
[maskara]
Pure in rossetto e mascara, i capelli fluenti, non potevano che starsene a mani strette, a supplicare pace.
-Even in lipstick and mascara, their hair aflow, could only stand wringing their hands, begging for peace.

9605 **capogiro** **dizziness**
il
[kapodʒiro]
Ho avuto un capogiro.
-I was dizzy.

9606 **scorza** **rind|peel** buccia
la
[skortsa]
Dividetevi quella scorza di arancia, e vi darò questa.
-Share that orange peel, and I'll give you this.

9607 **argano** **winch|capstan**
il
[argano]
Forse... tireranno su questa barca con un argano.
-Probably just winch this boat up.

9608 **spensierato** **carefree|light-hearted**
adj
[spensjerato]
All'inizio di Giugno, disse che voleva viaggiare in modo spensierato.
-Early in June, he said he wanted to travel in a carefree manner.

9609 **cerbiatto** **fawn**
il
[tʃerbjatto]
L'amore è venuto a farmi visita, timido come un cerbiatto.
-Love came to visit me, shy as a fawn.

9610 **asfissia** **asphyxiation**
le
[asfissja]
Dan è morto di asfissia.
-Dan died of asphyxiation.

9611 **preferibile** **preferable**
adj
[preferibile]
La morte è preferibile a tale sofferenza.
-Death is preferable to such suffering.

9612 **convenevole** **fitting**
adj
[konvenevole]
Buon Master Silence, ben convenevole che siate giudice di pace.
-Good Master Silence, it well befits you'd be of the peace.

9613 **spassoso** **amusing|entertaining**
adj
[spassozo]
Il discorso di Joe era spassoso.
-Joe's speech was hilarious.

9614 **scagionare** **exonerate**
vb
[skadʒonare]
Pertanto sembra che il traduttore volesse a tutti costi scagionare il governo spagnolo e i suoi sostenitori greci.
-It would therefore appear that the translator wanted to exonerate the Spanish Government and its Greek supporters, come what may.

9615 **disordinato** **messy|disorderly**
adj
[dizordinato]
Sono disordinato.
-I'm messy.

9616 **domatore** **tamer**
il
[domatore]
Ora vedrete un domatore di donne.
-Now you'll see a woman tamer.

9617 **setaccio** **sieve**
il
[setattʃo]
Gli Stati membri dovranno quindi passare al setaccio i rispettivi ordinamenti e incrementare la trasparenza nel processo di recepimento.
-Member States must therefore screen their legal systems and increase the clarity of the transposition process.

9618 **attestare** **attest|vouch**
vb
[attestare]
Signor Commissario, cari colleghi, siamo tutti d'accordo che dovrebbe esistere un marchio finalizzato ad attestare la sicurezza dei prodotti.
-Mr. Commissioner, dear colleagues, we all agree that there should be a marking to attest the product safety.

9619 **ibernazione** **hibernation**
la
[ibernattsjone]
Infine oggi saltiamo fuori con questa ingiustificabile ibernazione.
-Finally today we are coming out of this unjustifiable hibernation.

9620 **fettina** **chip; rudeness**
la; la
[fettina]
Ci ho messo dentro una fettina di mela.
-I put a slice of apple in it.

9621 **brioche** **muffin**
il
[brjoke]
Oggi nessuno dovrebbe dire: "Qu'ils mangent de la brioche" ("Che mangino brioche").
-Today nobody should say 'Qu'ils mangent de la brioche' ('Let them eat cake').

9622 **lavorativo** **working**
adj
[lavorativo]
Organizzeranno un sindacato lavorativo.
-They will organize a labor union.

9623 **cottimo** **piece rate system**
il
[kottimo]
Lulù, la causa è regolamentare quello cottimo, non fare una rivoluzione.
-You see Lulu', the situation is about regulating the piecework... here it's not about making a revolution... you are always doing somersaults

9624 **sottostante** **below; underlying**
adv; adj
[sottostante]
Il secondo criterio riguarda la struttura economica sottostante a ciascuna area.
-The second criterion concerns the underlying economic structure in each area.

9625 **stracciare** **tear|shred**
vb
[strattʃare]
E se pagavano con la carta di credito... poteva stracciare le ricevute.
-And if they pay with a credit card, he'd just tear up the transaction.

9626 **falena** **moth**
la
[falena]
♫ Dall'ape dell'uccello della falena.
-♫ From the bee of the bird of the moth.

9627 **psicanalisi** **psychoanalysis**
la
[psikanalizi]
Quindi, che Dio ci guardi dal demonizzare queste pratiche, come un tempo si fece con la psicanalisi.
-It is quite ridiculous to denigrate these practices just as psychoanalysis was when it made its appearance.

9628 **quantico** **quantum**
adj
[kwantiko]
Stiamo per fare il salto quantico.
-We're about to make the quantum leap.

9629 **spazzaneve** **snowplow**
gli
[spattsaneve]
Ero stato investito da uno spazzaneve del comune e vivevo coi soldi del risarcimento.
-I got hit by a city snowplow, and I was living off the settlement money, man.

9630 **capovolgere** **invert|reverse**
vb
[kapovoldʒere]
Assicurandosi che lo stantuffo della siringa sia ancora completamente spinto in basso, capovolgere il flaconcino.
-Ensuring that the syringe plunger rod is still fully depressed, invert the vial.

9631 **rimproverare** **reproach|blame**
vb
[rimproverare]
Ho voluto solo mettere in guardia contro alcuni passi che si stanno compiendo e non volevo dunque assolutamente rimproverare nessuno.
-I really did not want to teach anyone a lesson.

9632 **stanzino** **closet**
lo
[stantsino]
Vorrei sapere come intende stanziare i fondi.
-I would like to know how you intend to ring-fence.

9633 **configurazione** **configuration|layout**

la | La configurazione corrisponde alla naVe di Ohniaka III.
[konfigurattsjone] | -It matches the configuration of the ship at Ohniaka ill.

9634 **esteriore** | **external|exterior**
adj | La tutela dei disegni protegge solo l'aspetto esteriore dei prodotti.
[esterjore] | -Design protection covers only the outward appearance of products.

9635 **bambolotto** | **doll**
il | Mi sembra di aver visto un bambolotto avvocato.
[bambolotto] | -I think I saw a lawyer doll.

9636 **druido** | **Druid**
il | Vuole aiutare la ragazza druido a fuggire.
[drwido] | -He's going to help the Druid girl escape.

9637 **pomiciare** | **neck**
vb | Questo perché vuoi pomiciare con me.
[pomitʃare] | -That's because you want to make out with me.

9638 **algoritmo** | **algorithm**
il | Il mio algoritmo ha un tasso di successo del 99%.
[algoritmo] | -My algorithm has a 99% success rate.

9639 **clistere** | **enema**
il | Comunque, ecco il tuo clistere.
[klistere] | -Anyway, here is your enema.

9640 **pube** | **pubis**
il | Sto facendo una incisione dallo sterno al pube.
[pube] | -I'm making a midline incision from sternum to pubis.

9641 **faglia** | **fault**
la | Quei pozzi si trovano nella faglia di Hayward.
[faʎʎa] | -Those wells are in the Hayward fault.

9642 **runa** | **rune**
la | La runa che Sayorlean ha posto all'interno della tua collana d'argento.
[runa] | -The rune placed Sayorlean inside of your silver necklace.

9643 **lineare** | **linear|straightforward**
adj | Kathleen sta studiando l'algebra lineare.
[lineare] | -Kathleen is studying linear algebra.

9644 **centrifugo** | **centrifugal**
adj | Noi ne eravamo molto orgogliosi, specialmente del titolo che era "Frullino come Centrifuga."
[tʃentrifugo] | -We were very proud of this, particularly the title, which was "Eggbeater as Centrifuge."

9645 **virale** | **viral**
adj | È diventato virale.
[virale] | -It went viral.

9646 **asportare** | **remove**
vb | Ho dovuto asportare una delle ovaie.
[asportare] | -I had to remove one of Tracy's ovaries.

9647 **expo** | **exhibition**
le | E abbiamo ottenuto l'appalto per progettare un edificio all'ingresso dell'expo.
[ekspo] | -And we got a commission to design a building at the entrance of the expo.

9648 **eugenetico** | **eugenic**

	adj [eudʒenetiko]	Nessun intervento deve invece essere finalizzato alla selezione o alla manipolazione a scopo eugenetico. -No intervention should have the purpose of eugenic selection or manipulation.
9649	**impossibilità**	**impossibility**
	la [impossibilit'a]	L'elemento dell'impossibilità non sta quindi nella direttiva, ma nella realtà odierna. -The impossibility lies, therefore, not in the directive but in the current situation.
9650	**infamare**	**defame**
	vb [infamare]	Centinaia di migliaia di persone loro parenti sono state uccise durante quegli anni bui, spesso con l'etichetta infamante di emarginati sociali. -Hundreds of thousands of their relatives were murdered during those dark years, often having been disgracefully branded as social outcasts.
9651	**commemorare**	**commemorate**
	vb [kommemorare]	Vogliamo qui commemorare le vittime ed esprimere ai loro congiunti le nostre condoglianze. -We remember the victims and express our condolences to their relatives.
9652	**progressista**	**progressive**
	il/la [progressista]	Credo che in tale ambito dovremmo unire le nostre forze per convincere il Consiglio a mettere in atto una politica più aperta, più progressista e rivolta verso il futuro. -I believe we must join forces to this end, in order to try and persuade the Council to frame policy in this area that is more transparent, progressive and forward-looking.
9653	**tisana**	**tisane**
	la [tizana]	Salome... mi ha detto di portarti questa tisana. -Salome... told me to bring you this herbal tea.
9654	**indugiare**	**linger|delay**
	vb [indudʒare]	Cercano di indugiare il più possibile, ma si sentono osservate e allora vanno via. -They try to loiter as it is, but they feel conspicuous, so they leave.
9655	**arbusto**	**shrub**
	il [arbusto]	Monk, non andrò dal procuratore sventolando un arbusto. -Monk, I'm not going to the D.A. waving a shrub.
9656	**loggia**	**invulnerable**
	adj [loddʒa]	Credo facesse parte della loggia di Chessani. -Part of Chessani's lodge, I think.
9657	**rapidità**	**speed|rapidity**
	la [rapidit'a]	Ammiro e stimo la dedizione l' impegno da lui profusi e apprezzo molto la sua rapidità. -I admire and value his dedication and commitment, and I also very much appreciate his rapidity.
9658	**scolpire**	**sculpt|carve**
	vb [skolpire]	Alcune di queste storie le scolpisco un po' qua e un po' là. -Some of these stories I sculpt a little, here and there.
9659	**genuino**	**genuine|authentic**
	adj [dʒenwino]	Era genuino. -It was genuine.
9660	**commilitone**	**fellow soldier**

il Di sicuro fai un sacco di domande, commilitone.
[kommilitone] -You sure do ask a lot of questions, comrade.

9661 **recapitare** **deliver**
vb
[rekapitare]
Anche gli operatori privati potranno recapitare lettere, ad un prezzo pari a quattro volte la tariffa per una lettera ordinaria.
-Private operators will also be able to deliver letters at four times the price of a normal letter.

9662 **sconfinare** **trespass**
vb
[skonfinare]
In terzo luogo, l'agenzia non deve sconfinare nella gestione dei rischi e nel potere regolamentare.
-Thirdly, the Agency must not encroach upon the management of risks and regulatory power.

9663 **sbando** **drift**
lo
[zbando]
Giorni amari, di sbando, furono i successivi.
-Bitter days of disarray, were the next.

9664 **esile** **slender|thin**
adj
[ezile]
Penso che Joe sia esile.
-I think Joe is thin.

9665 **stendardo** **standard**
lo
[stendardo]
L'anno prossimo porterò lo stendardo scolastico.
-Next year I'll be carrying the school banner.

9666 **anatroccolo** **duckling**
il
[anatrokkolo]
In quarto luogo, il "brutto anatroccolo" del bilancio comunitario: le azioni esterne.
-Fourthly, the 'ugly duckling' of the Community budget: external actions.

9667 **solfare** **sulphurise**
vb
[solfare]
Abbiamo subito un bombardamento di protoni da brillamento solare.
-We've experienced a massive proton field upset sequel to a solar flare.

9668 **negligente** **negligent|careless**
adj
[neʎʎidʒente]
Joe è estremamente negligente.
-Joe is extremely careless.

9669 **serenata** **serenade**
la
[serenata]
Questo gentiluomo ha richiesto una serenata per la sua deliziosa ragazza.
-The gentleman pre–requested a serenade for the lovely lady.

9670 **zappa** **hoe**
la
[tsappa]
Nel frattempo, come dite in Slovenia, "preghi per un buon raccolto, ma continui a zappare".
-But in the mean time, as you say in Slovenia, 'pray for a good harvest, but keep on hoeing'.

9671 **rumba** **rumba**
la
[rumba]
Okay, I like the rumba.
-Ok, mi piace la rumba.

9672 **brontolone** **growler**
il
[brontolone]
Perché Joe è così brontolone oggi?
-Why is Joe so grouchy today?

9673 **raccordo** **junction**
il
[rakkordo]
Se riusciamo a raccordare i rimanenti 14 chilometri di questa linea ferroviaria, la Corea del Sud e l'Europa saranno finalmente congiunte.
-If we manage to link the remaining 14 kilometres of this railway, South Korea and Europe will finally be connected.

9674 **represso** adj [represso]
repressed
Un delirio psicotico causato da un ricordo represso.
-It eased the pain, a psychotic delusion brought on by a repressed memory.

9675 **contraddire** vb [kontraddire]
contradict
Quindi, tale simbolo potrebbe dar adito ad abusi per trarre in inganno il consumatore e contraddire così lo scopo della direttiva.
-Such a symbol, therefore, could be misused in order to deceive the consumer, and would be contrary to the aim of the proposal.

9676 **diminuendo** lo [diminwendo]
diminuendo
Il costo della vita in Giappone sta diminuendo.
-The cost of living in Japan is going down.

9677 **impudenza** le [impudentsa]
impudence|nerve
Io sono infastidita dalla loro impudenza.
-I'm annoyed by their impudence.

9678 **gallese** adj; il [galleze]
Welsh; Welsh
Io ho insegnato al mio pappagallo a parlare in gallese.
-I've taught my parrot to speak Welsh.

9679 **freddezza** la [freddettsa]
coldness|cold shoulder
Ma seriamente, penso che quella freddezza sia parte del problema.
-But truthfully, that coldness, I think, is part of the problem.

9680 **moscerino** il [moʃʃerino]
gnat
La malattia, causata da un virus trasmesso dal culicoides imicola, un tipo di moscerino, colpisce particolarmente mucche e pecore.
-Cattle and sheep are particularly badly affected by the disease, which is caused by a virus transmitted by the gnat, a type of midge.

9681 **bocciolo** il [bottʃolo]
bud
Roz, mio tenero e purulento bocciolo, stai da favola.
-Roz, my tender, oozing blossom, you're looking fabulous today.

9682 **abolizione** la [abolittsjone]
abolition
L'abolizione della schiavitù in Siam.
-The abolition of slavery in Siam.

9683 **miraggio** il [miraddʒo]
mirage
E' come se la frenetica smania di Charles Clarke di intervenire sulla questione fosse un miraggio.
-It is as if Charles Clarke's frenzy of activity on this topic was a mirage.

9684 **borsellino** il [borsellino]
purse
Non si è accorta di non avere il borsellino fino a quando non è tornata.
-She didn't miss her purse till she got back.

9685 **ripasso** il [ripasso]
revision
Ripasso le mie lezioni quasi ogni giorno.
-I revise my lessons almost every day.

9686 **fruttare** vb [fruttare]
yield|fruit
In tale prospettiva dobbiamo ora comprendere che le risoluzioni sono uno strumento troppo angusto per fruttare risultati concreti.
-In this sense, we now need to realise that the resolution system is too limited to bring in results.

9687 **specificare** vb [spetʃifikare]
specify|state
È innanzitutto necessario specificare le informazioni sulla sala riunioni, quali nome, indirizzo di posta elettronica e ubicazione.

-First, you provide the conference room information, such as the name, e-mail address, and location.

9688 **erroneamente** **wrongly**
adv
[erroneamente]
Le conseguenze della politica di plurilinguismo sono evidenti e di ampia portata, ma se erroneamente applicata, essa può sortire effetti fortemente negativi.
-The effects of the policy of multilingualism are far-reaching and obvious, but if erroneously applied the results can be pitiful.

9689 **pistacchio** **pistachio**
il
[pistakkjo]
Amo gelato al pistacchio.
-I love pistachio ice cream.

9690 **villeggiatura** **holiday**
la
[villeddʒatura]
Signor Presidente, mi limiterò a parlare di una sola isola: l'isola di Wight al largo della costa meridionale dell'Inghilterra, l'isola preferita dalla Regina Vittoria come luogo di villeggiatura.
-Mr President, I will confine myself to just one island - the Isle of Wight off the south coast of England - the favourite holiday island of Queen Victoria.

9691 **versato** **versed**
adj
[versato]
Lei ha versato del brandy nei bicchieri.
-She poured brandy into the glasses.

9692 **nordovest** **northwest**
il
[nordovest]
Si sta muovendo in direzione nordovest.
-It's on the move... Heading northwest.

9693 **promotore** **promoter; promotive**
il; adj
[promotore]
Per avviare l'iter referendario, il comitato promotore deve consegnare il testo del quesito sottoscritto da sessanta elettori.
-To activate referendum procedures the promoting committee must present the text of the topic under question, subscribed to by sixty electors.

9694 **requiem** **requiem**
il
[rekwjem]
Invece è diventato il mio requiem.
-Instead, it ended up becoming my requiem.

9695 **vigliaccheria** **cowardice**
la
[viʎʎakkerja]
Per vigliaccheria di fronte al nemico.
-For cowardice in the face of the enemy.

9696 **portuale** **roustabout**
lo
[portwale]
Yokohama è una bella città portuale.
-Yokohama is a beautiful port town.

9697 **sfiducia** **distrust**
la
[sfidutʃa]
Un altro gruppo di cittadini guarda all'integrazione europea con sfiducia.
-Another group of citizens look at European integration with distrust.

9698 **boschetto** **grove**
il
[bosketto]
In pratica, qualsiasi boschetto rientrerebbe nel campo di applicazione del regolamento.
-Practically every grove of trees would fall within the scope of the regulation.

9699 **campagnolo** **hillbilly**
il
[kampaɲɲolo]
Primo, campagnolo, devi imparare un po' di rispetto.
-First, hillbilly, you have got to learn some respect.

9700 **sfrattare** **evict**

	vb [sfrattare]	Le stesse persone che allora furono allontanate alla stregua di spazzatura, oggi si vedono nuovamente sfrattare con la forza. -The same people who were cleaned out as trash last time are being evicted now.
9701	**polemico** adj [polemiko]	**polemical|controversial** Sei polemico. -You're being contentious.
9702	**inceneritore** il [intʃeneritore]	**incinerator** Perché un inceneritore sia efficace, deve essere adeguatamente riempito. -For an incinerator to be efficient, it must be suitably filled.
9703	**ribasso** il [ribasso]	**fall|decline** Il ciclo economico e i prezzi sono ormai avviati a un ribasso. -The business cycle, as well as prices, are now projected to decline.
9704	**sud-ovest** il [sudovest]	**southwest** 200 000 ettari di foresta sono andati distrutti nel sud-ovest della Francia. -200 000 hectares of forest have been destroyed in the south west of France.
9705	**angolino** il [aŋgolino]	**nook** Meriti di avere il tuo angolino privato. -Because you deserve your own nook.
9706	**attivamente** adv [attivamente]	**actively** La Commissione continua a dedicarsi attivamente alla dimensione settentrionale. -The Commission continues to work actively on the Northern Dimension.
9707	**desideroso** adj [desiderozo]	**eager|desirous** Mi chinai in avanti, desideroso di cogliere ogni parola che diceva. -I leaned forward, eager to catch every word he spoke.
9708	**sfasciare** vb [sfaʃʃare]	**smash up** Penso che dovrò sfasciare la caldaia. -Guess I'll have to smash the boiler.
9709	**appello** gli [appello]	**appeal** Fiduciosa come sono che non scherziate con questo appello, il mio cuore affonda e la mia mano trema al pensiero nudo e crudo di una tale possibilità. -Confident as I am that you will not trifle with this appeal, my heart sinks and my hand trembles at the bare thought of such a possibility.
9710	**tutelare** vb [tutelare]	**protect** Dobbiamo inoltre tutelare i consumatori particolarmente vulnerabili. -Moreover, we have to protect consumers who are particularly vulnerable.
9711	**consultazione** la [konsultattsjone]	**consultation|counsel** Sul contenuto della relazione sarà effettuata una consultazione aperta. -An open consultation on the content of the report will be carried out.
9712	**indennizzare** vb [indenniddzare]	**indemnify** Si devono trovare i fondi per indennizzare le reti di transito per i loro servizi. -There are to be funds to compensate transit networks for their services.
9713	**milza** la [miltsa]	**spleen** Della stessa stregua, tanto per appiattire tutto, anche gli altri provvedimenti proposti, come l'asportazione obbligatoria di alcuni organi (milza, cervello, midollo spinale ecc.).

-This same spirit, this "lowest common denominator" approach, pervades the rest of the proposed measures, such as the mandatory removal of various organs (spleen, brain, spinal cord, etc.).

9714 **durezza** la [durettsa]
hardness|toughness
Preferirò sempre la durezza del pavimento.
-I will always prefer the hardness of the floor.

9715 **attendente** il [attendente]
orderly
Se mi permettete di citare le sagge parole del Primo Ministro, non dobbiamo limitarci ad attendere un momento migliore.
-If I can quote the wise words of the Prime Minister, we should not just wait around for a better time to come.

9716 **umanitario** adj [umanitarjo]
humanitarian
Intelligente, sensibile, umanitario... tutti nella stessa frase.
-Intelligent, sensitive, caring - all in the same sentence, I bet you.

9717 **affiancare** vb [affjaŋkare]
help
Il Consiglio può affiancare a tale autorizzazione istruzioni negoziali.
-The Council may complement such authorisation by negotiating directives.

9718 **vulcanico** adj [vulkaniko]
volcanic
E c'è il Monte Olimpo su Marte, che è tipo un enorme scudo vulcanico di quel pianeta.
-And that's Mount Olympus on Mars, which is a kind of huge volcanic shield on that planet.

9719 **barbarie** la [barbarje]
barbarism
Non bisogna mai rispondere alla barbarie con la barbarie.
-Barbarism should never be answered with barbarism.

9720 **impacchettare** vb [impakkettare]
pack|package
Non potrò aiutarvi a impacchettare il nonno.
-I won't be able to help you pack up Grampa.

9721 **alfiere** lo [alfjere]
bishop
In Turchia io ero come questo alfiere, aiutavo le persone.
-In Turkey, I was like this bishop, helping people.

9722 **inumare** vb [inumare]
bury
Bene. Sapete dove inumarli?
-You know where to bury?

9723 **giaguaro** il [dʒagwaro]
jaguar
Che verrà divorato dallo spirito del giaguaro.
-That they would be devoured by the jaguar spirit.

9724 **arpione** il [arpjone]
harpoon
Fammi indovinare, l'ha ucciso l'arpione.
-Let me guess, the harpoon killed him.

9725 **smanceria** la [smantʃerja]
affectation
Una smanceria, tipo "Vorrei essere lì con te",
-Say you wanted to text me a sweet nothing like,

9726 **arrostire** vb [arrostire]
roast
Sapete, con il solare ci vogliono 4 giorni per arrostire un pollo.
-You know, with solar power, it takes four days to roast a chicken.

9727 **molesto** adj [molesto]
troublesome
È Artie, il nostro vicino molesto.
-He's our annoying neighbor Artie.

9728 **allusione**
allusion

	le [alluzjone]	La prego però di lasciarmi rispondere alla sua allusione musicale con una citazione letteraria. -However, please let me respond to your musical allusion with a literary quotation.
9729	**intenzionato** adj [intentsjonato]	**intentional** Anche se Joe è ammalato, è intenzionato di andare a scuola. -Although Joe is sick, he's planning on going to school.
9730	**astemio** adj; il [astemjo]	**abstemious; teetotaler** Lui è astemio. -He's a teetotaller.
9731	**quindicesimo** num [kwinditʃezimo]	**fifteenth** Lubiana fu fondata nel quindicesimo anno del calendario giuliano. -Ljubljana was founded in year fifteen of the Julian calendar.
9732	**onta** le [onta]	**shame|offense** E'un'onta per la loro reputazione affermare che le loro cifre non danno un'immagine veritiera. -It is a slur on their reputation to suggest their figures do not give a true picture.
9733	**sbavare** vb [zbavare]	**drool|smudge** Senti, stai cominciando a sbavare. -Okay, you're starting to drool.
9734	**appetitoso** adj [appetitozo]	**appetizing|palatable** E lo chiamo metodo epossidico perché... non è molto appetitoso. -And I call it an epoxy method because -- it's not very appetizing.
9735	**tangente** la; adj [tandʒente]	**tangent; cut** Joe partì per la tangente. -Joe went off on a tangent.
9736	**separatista** il/la [separatista]	**separatist** L'accusa è sempre la stessa: propaganda separatista. -Over and over again, the charge is 'separatist propaganda'.
9737	**termonucleare** adj [termonukleare]	**thermonuclear** Sul punto "Fusione termonucleare controllata, fusione nucleare controllata» ci asteniamo dal voto. -We are abstaining on controlled thermonuclear fusion, controlled nuclear fusion.
9738	**condiscendente** adj [kondiʃʃendente]	**condescending** Molti allora schernirono il progetto con un atteggiamento piuttosto condiscendente. -There were many who laughed in a rather indulgent way then.
9739	**epilettico** adj [epilettiko]	**epileptic** Io sono epilettico. -I'm epileptic.
9740	**antropologia** le [antropolodʒa]	**anthropology** Davvero la cristologia sta a fondamento di ogni antropologia ed ecclesiologia. -Truly Christology is at the basis of every anthropology and ecclesiology.
9741	**diffida** la [diffida]	**warning** Diffida delle imitazioni. -Beware of imitations.
9742	**infiltrazione**	**infiltration**

	le [infiltrattsjone]	Mi riferisco ad una cooperazione più intensa tra i nostri servizi segreti e all'infiltrazione in reti terroristiche. -For example, a higher level of cooperation among our secret services and the infiltration of terrorist networks spring to mind.
9743	**papavero** il [papavero]	**poppy** Ti porterò il latte del papavero. -I'll get you milk of the poppy.
9744	**diagnostico** adj [djaɲɲostiko]	**diagnostic** La strategia di Lisbona è sia uno strumento diagnostico sia un programma di obiettivi da realizzare. -The Lisbon strategy is both a diagnostic and a list of tasks to perform.
9745	**ripensamento** il [ripensamento]	**afterthought** Joe sta avendo un ripensamento. -Joe is having second thoughts.
9746	**pettorale** adj [pettorale]	**pectoral** Vola nell'acqua poggiandosi sulle pinne pettorali, si solleva, imprime energia ai suoi movimenti con la pinna caudale lunata. -It flies through the ocean on its pectoral fins, gets lift, powers its movements with a lunate tail.
9747	**lievemente** adv [ljevemente]	**slightly|lightly** L'Austria: un paese confinante, lievemente simile e lievemente diverso. -Austria, a neighboring country, slightly similar, slightly different.
9748	**cedimento** il [tʃedimento]	**subsidence** Un cedimento meccanico non provocherebbe un'esplosione vicino alla porta. -No. A mechanical failure wouldn't cause an explosion by the door.
9749	**classificato** adj [klassifikato]	**classified** Quel libro è classificato come "romanzo". -That book is classified as "fiction."
9750	**alchimista** il [alkimista]	**alchemist** Questa è nel cortile di un alchimista del dodicesimo secolo. -This is in the courtyard of a twelfth-century alchemist.
9751	**équipe** le [ˈekwipe]	**team** La fusione ha creato una équipe multidisciplinare capace di enucleare le molteplici componenti della strategia dello sviluppo sostenibile. -The outcome is a multidisciplinary team capable of tackling the many facets of sustainable development strategy.
9752	**elaborazione** la [elaborattsjone]	**processing** I progetti dovrebbero comprendere l'elaborazione di piani di gestione che riducano l'impatto delle attività economiche sull'ambiente. -Projects are expected to include the development of management plans which reduce the environmental impacts of economic activities.
9753	**tappetino** il [tappetino]	**mat** Il gatto era seduto sul tappetino. -The cat sat on the mat.
9754	**fondamentalista** il [fondamentalista]	**fundamentalist** I responsabili sono motivati dall'ideologia islamica fondamentalista ed estremista. -Those responsible are motivated by fundamentalist and extremist Islamist ideology.
9755	**lappone**	**Lapp; Laplander**

adj; il Penso in lappone, quindi lo sono.
[lappone] -I think in Saami, therefore I am.

9756 **rurale** **rural**
adj Tu hai mai abitato in una zona rurale?
[rurale] -Have you ever lived in a rural area?

√ 9757 **bracciante** **laborer|worker**
il/la La straordinaria conquista di questo movimento di massa di 10 milioni di lavoratori, braccianti e intellettuali è stata una rivoluzione pacifica.
[brattʃante] -The amazing achievement of this mass movement of 10 million workers, farm labourers, and members of the intelligentsia was a peaceful revolution.

9758 **manovale** **laborer|hand**
il Sono un umile manovale, lo sai bene.
[manovale] -Well, I'm a labourer and you know that.

9759 **ignaro** **unaware**
adj Joe sembra ignaro.
[iɲɲaro] -Joe seems oblivious.

9760 **camelia** **camellia**
la Questa è il mio giardino delle camelia per la mia compagnia del tè.
[kamelja] -This is my camellia garden for my tea company.

9761 **tubetto** **tube**
il Volevamo entrambi lo stesso tubetto di formaggio.
[tubetto] -We were reaching for the same tube of cheese.

9762 **barbiturico** **barbiturate; barbituric**
il; adj Il corpo di Donald Everton conteneva alte concentrazioni di un barbiturico.
[barbituriko] -Donald Everton's body contained high concentrations of a barbiturate.

9763 **epicentro** **epicenter|focus**
lo Ero improvvisamente nel epicentro di Popolarland.
[epitʃentro] -I was suddenly in the epicenter of Popularland.

9764 **minerario** **mining**
adj E' il caso del settore turistico, minerario, agricolo, dei trasporti e della pesca.
[minerarjo] -These sectors include tourism, transportation, mining, agriculture and fisheries.

9765 **incendiario** **arsonist; incendiary**
il; adj E all'interno contiene un piccolo congegno incendiario, così che, se l'aereo si schianta, il mirino verrà distrutto e il nemico non avrà alcun modo di metterci sopra le mani.
[intʃendjarjo] -And there's a little incendiary device inside of it, so that, if the plane ever crashes, it will be destroyed and there's no way the enemy can ever get their hands on it.

√ 9766 **racimolare** **glean**
vb Si tratta, ovviamente, di un eccellente rimedio politico al livellamento dal basso ed un buon mezzo per racimolare alcuni ecu e metterli da parte.
[ratʃimolare] -It is evidently an excellent political remedy to the policy of levelling down and a good way of gleaning a few ECUs to round off your month end.

√ 9767 **faida** **feud**
la La nostra faida risale agli anni dell'infanzia.
[faida] -Our feud traces back to our childhood.

9768 **epilogo** **epilogue**
il
[epilogo]
Possiamo confidare che non ci sarà nessun epilogo indesiderato?
-Can we be confident that there will be no unwanted epilogue?

9769 **suola** **sole**
la
[swola]
Notate l'argilla sotto la suola.
-You notice the clay on the soles of her feet.

9770 **manovella** **crank**
la
[manovella]
Ora, se si gira la manovella una volta, poi due, due, vengono fuori le meraviglie.
-Now you turn the crank once, twice: twice, marvels come out.

9771 **corredo** **kit|equipment**
il
[korredo]
Mio padre mi ha tolto la macchina, dopo aver trovato la mia collezione di diademi nel mio cassettone del corredo.
-My dad took my baby away... after he found my tiara collection in my hope chest.

9772 **birreria** **brasserie**
la
[birrerja]
Il signor Cameron dimenticò sua figlia in birreria.
-Mr. Cameron forgot his daughter at the pub.

9773 **introvabile** **not to be found**
adj
[introvabile]
Lei era introvabile.
-She was nowhere to be seen.

9774 **fluttuare** **fluctuate|float**
vb
[fluttware]
L'euro fluttuerà per molto tempo rispetto al dollaro. Non potrebbe essere altrimenti.
-The euro will fluctuate against the dollar for a long period - there can be no alternative to that.

9775 **incorreggibile** **incorrigible**
adj
[iŋkorreddʒibile]
Joe è incorreggibile.
-Joe is unrepentant.

9776 **addomesticare** **tame**
vb
[addomestikare]
In altre parole suggerisce che potremmo addomesticare questi organismi.
-In other words, this suggests that we could domesticate these organisms.

9777 **bicarbonato** **bicarbonate**
il
[bikarbonato]
Si consiglia pertanto un attento controllo dei livelli di bicarbonato sierico.
-Closer monitoring of serum bicarbonate levels is therefore recommended.

9778 **risaltare** **stand out|show up**
vb
[rizaltare]
Dobbiamo insistere nei nostri sforzi per dare un risalto permanente a questo tema.
-We must be more forceful in our efforts to put the issue of debt relief for Third World countries on a permanent footing.

9779 **scollatura** **neckline**
la
[skollatura]
Le stava fissando la scollatura.
-He was staring at her cleavage.

9780 **integrante** **integral**
adj
[integrante]
Un libro tradizionale è parte integrante della nostra cultura, come il teatro o l'arte.
-A traditional book is an integral part of our culture, just like theatre or art.

9781 **illegittimo** **illegitimate**

adj
[illedʒittimo]
Tale sistema è operativamente rigido, politicamente chiuso e moralmente illegittimo.
-Such a system is operationally rigid, politically closed, and morally illegitimate.

9782 **montatore**
il
[montatore]
fixer
Okay. abbiamo due video da montare e solo un montatore.
-We got two packages to cut and only one editor.

9783 **alchimia**
la
[alkimja]
alchemy
Per lunghi secoli, il mercurio ha svolto un ruolo cruciale nell'alchimia e nelle scienze occulte.
-For many centuries, mercury had a crucial role in alchemy and the secret sciences.

9784 **voltaggio**
il
[voltaddʒo]
voltage
Gli adattatori non modificano il voltaggio, ma permettono soltanto il collegamento del dispositivo.
-Plug adapters do not change the voltage but merely enable connecting the device.

9785 **schieramento**
lo
[skjeramento]
array
Derek aiuta a addestrare reclute per lo schieramento.
-Derek helps train recruits for deployment.

9786 **rifilare**
vb
[rifilare]
trim|foist
Il vice Primo Ministro del Regno Unito – un uomo sventurato come pochi – sta tentando di rifilare la regionale al nostro elettorato.
-The UK Deputy Prime Minister a hapless fellow if ever there was one is trying to foist regional governance upon our own electorate.

9787 **judo**
il
[dʒudo]
judo
Faccio judo.
-I'm practising judo.

9788 **fuorché**
prp
[fwork'e]
except
Quel ponte è tutto fuorché sicuro.
-That bridge is anything but safe.

9789 **sociologia**
la
[sotʃolodʒa]
sociology
Sto cercando dei libri di testo sulla sociologia femminista.
-I'm looking for textbooks on feminist sociology.

9790 **mensola**
la
[mensola]
shelf
La tua mensola è piena di libri.
-Your shelf is full of books.

9791 **lentiggine**
la
[lentiddʒine]
freckle
Perché ogni volta che spiego qualcosa guadagno una lentiggine.
-Because every time I show up and explain something, I earn a freckle.

9792 **irrispettoso**
adj
[irrispettozo]
disrespectful
Joe è irrispettoso.
-Joe is disrespectful.

9793 **malanno**
il
[malanno]
illness
Stupido, prenderai ancora un malanno.
-Silly, you'll catch a cold again.

9794 **miope**
adj; il/la
[mjope]
myopic; myope
Sono miope e non riesco a leggere cosa c'è scritto su quel cartello.
-I am near-sighted, so I cannot make out what is written on that signboard.

9795 **vudù**
voodoo

il
[vudu]

La gente crede ancora nel Vudù.. cardiopatie, difetti del setto ventricolare e atriale, tetralogie.
-People still believe in Voodoo. Heart disease, VSD, hole in the heart, tetralogies.

9796 **mortorio**
adj
[mortorjo]
funeral
Alleluia, questo posto è un mortorio.
-Hallelujah, this place is dead.

9797 **turchino**
adj; il
[turkino]
blue; deep blue
Queste problematiche vengono sollevate periodicamente con le autorità turche.
-These issues are raised regularly with the Turkish authorities.

9798 **struzzo**
lo
[struttso]
ostrich
Lo struzzo ha le ali ma non può volare.
-The ostrich has wings, but it cannot fly.

9799 **energico**
adj
[enerdʒiko]
energetic
Questo è un uomo energico.
-This is an energetic man.

9800 **mondano**
adj
[mondano]
worldly
Uno come Tony, estroverso, talentuoso, mondano.
-Like Tony – outgoing, talented, worldly.

9801 **nylon**
il
[nlon]
nylon
Questa è stata fatta usando un etichetta di nylon della mia maglietta.
-But this one was made out of a nylon tag out of my shirt.

9802 **antiquario**
il; adj
[antikwarjo]
antique dealer; antiquarian
Va da Osvaldo, l'antiquario.
-He's going to Osvaldo's, the antique dealer.

9803 **demoniaco**
adj
[demonjako]
demoniac|fiendish
Ho l'ordine di eseguire il sacro rito dell'esorcismo demoniaco.
-My orders are to execute the holy rites for demonic exorcism.

9804 **caporeparto**
il
[kaporeparto]
shopwalker
Il caporeparto è sempre in calore.
-That the foreman is always on heat.

9805 **rigorosamente**
adv
[rigorozamente]
rigorously
Esortiamo vivamente gli Stati membri ad applicare rigorosamente questo principio.
-We strongly urge the Member States to ensure that this principle is strictly upheld.

9806 **pilone**
il
[pilone]
pylon
No, il mio posto è qui dentro al pilone.
-No. My place is here in the pylon.

9807 **attizzatoio**
il
[attiddzatojo]
poker
Un'idea intelligente, piegare l'attizzatoio.
-A clever idea, that bend in the poker.

9808 **clavicola**
la
[klavikola]
clavicle
Beh, il dottore può programmare un livello di voltaggio di questa elevazione TS che lancerà un allarme di emergenza, una vibrazione come quella del telefonino, ma proprio sull'osso della clavicola.
-Well, the doctor can program a level of this ST elevation voltage that will trigger an emergency alarm, vibration like your cell phone, but right by your clavicle bone.

9809 **indignazione**
indignation|warmth

le | Malgrado la nostra indignazione, queste tragedie si ripetono ogni anno.
[indiɲɲattsjone] -In spite of our indignation, every year these tragedies are repeated.

9810 **ammaliare** **charm**
vb
[ammaljare]
Se tu potessi darmi cinque minuti, da solo, fuori, quando torno, potrei ammaliare di brutto Dean Whitman.
-If you were to give me just 5 minutes alone outside, I will come back, and I will charm the pants off Dean Whitman.

9811 **zoppicare** **limp|halt**
vb
[tsoppikare]
Forza, non dimenticarti di zoppicare.
-Go on, don't forget to limp.

9812 **revocare** **revoke|reverse**
vb
[revokare]
Di conseguenza è opportuno revocare l'approvazione del fenbutatin ossido.
-Consequently, it is appropriate to withdraw the approval of fenbutatin oxide.

9813 **anticarro** **antitank**
il
[antikarro]
Mine anticarro, che hanno integrato le mine antiuomo.
-Anti-tank mines which have anti-personnel mines integrated in them.

9814 **boscaglia** **bush|brush**
la
[boskaʎʎa]
La boscaglia lacera gli abiti e c'è molto fango dovunque.
-The bush will tear clothing, and the mud is very deep in places.

9815 **crocevia** **crossroads**
le
[krotʃevja]
Fin da tempi antichissimi, il Kashmir è un punto di passaggio e un crocevia tra il Medio Oriente, l'Asia centrale e l'Asia meridionale.
-Since time immemorial, Kashmir has been a bridging point and intersection between the Near East, Central Asia and South Asia.

9816 **riacquistare** **regain|buy back**
vb
[rjakkwistare]
Essi però volevano farci pagare una compensazione, ovvero che pagassimo per riacquistare le nostre denominazioni di origine.
-Yet they wanted us to buy back – to pay in order to buy back – our designations of origin.

9817 **ortica** **nettle**
la
[ortika]
Ti costerà solo un brandy all'ortica.
-It'll only cost you a nettle brandy.

9818 **trama** **plot|weft**
la
[trama]
Questo film segue esattamente la trama del libro.
-This movie follows the book's plot exactly.

9819 **desistere** **desist**
vb
[dezistere]
I quattro articoli sono chiarissimi nell'invitarvi a desistere.
-The four articles are very clear in calling on you to desist.

9820 **mercatino** **flea market**
il
[merkatino]
Karen ha comprato molte cose al mercatino delle pulci.
-Karen bought a lot of things at the flea market.

9821 **apparecchiare** **lay**
vb
[apparekkjare]
Prima che David arrivasse Samantha cominciò ad apparecchiare.
-Before David arrived, Samantha started to lay the table.

9822 **tabù** **taboo**
il
[tabu]
Nelle forze speciali la tortura è un tabù.
-In special forces, torture is a taboo.

9823 **espediente** **expedient|device**

il E' ancora più preoccupante che, per paura di perdere un voto o di non
[espedjente] riceverne nemmeno uno, lei si avvalga di un espediente procedurale per evitare il dibattito.
-More disturbing is that, fearful of losing a vote or perhaps fearful of having a vote at all, you resort to a procedural device to prevent debate.

9824 **caritatevole** **charitable**
adj
[karitatevole]
Il carattere caritatevole: I gruppi di beneficenza in Canada non sono autorizzati a patrocinare.
-Charitable status: Groups who have charitable status in Canada aren't allowed to do advocacy.

9825 **lustrascarpe** **shoeshine|bootblack**
i
[lustraskarpe]
Non si tratta mai di un lustrascarpe quattordicenne per le strade di Londra, morto di stenti.
-Nothing is ever said about a 14 year-old bootblack in the streets of London who died of consumption.

9826 **argine** **embankment|bank**
il
[ardʒine]
Io vivo vicino all'argine.
-I live near the levee.

9827 **irrequieto** **restless**
adj
[irrekwjeto]
Joe sta diventando irrequieto.
-Joe is getting frantic.

9828 **sillabare** **syllabify**
vb
[sillabare]
I ricercatori alla Gorilla Foundation devono sillabare parole come 'c-a-n-d-y' e 'g-u-m' quando Koko è nelle vicinanze.
-Researchers at the Gorilla Foundation have to spell out words like "c-a-n-d-y" and "g-u-m" when Koko is nearby.

9829 **prezzemolo** **parsley**
il
[prettsemolo]
Se è besciamella perché non usate prezzemolo o macis?
-If that's Bechamel, why don't you use parsley or mace?

9830 **portinaio** **porter|concierge**
il
[portinajo]
Il portinaio mi ha detto che ci sei.
-The doorman told me you were.

9831 **cencio** **rag**
il
[tʃentʃo]
È bianca come un cencio.
-You are as white as a sheet.

9832 **convenienza** **convenience|advantage**
la
[konvenjentsa]
L' onestà e la trasparenza sono state sacrificate alla convenienza.
-Honesty and transparency have been sacrificed to expedience.

9833 **cialda** **waffle**
la
[tʃalda]
Questa è una cialda di silicone, ed essenzialmente è solo un gruppo di strati di materiale bidimensionale, come stratificato.
-This is a silicon wafer, and essentially that's just a whole bunch of layers of two-dimensional stuff, sort of layered up.

9834 **aderire** **join|adhere**
vb
[aderire]
La Croazia dovrebbe poter aderire all'Unione europea quando è pronta per farlo.
-Croatia should be allowed to accede when it is completely ready.

9835 **orrido** **horrid|dreadful**
adj
[orrido]
Dopo non sembrerai più così trasandato e orrido.
-Then you won't look so scruffy and horrid.

9836 **monaca** **nun**

	la [monaka]	Madre Teresa era una monaca cattolica che viveva e lavorava a Calcutta, in India. -Mother Teresa was a Catholic nun who lived and worked in Calcutta, India.
9837	**pepita** la [pepita]	**nugget** Ma la cosa positiva è, con l'innovazione, non esiste l'ultima pepita. -But the good thing is, with innovation, there isn't a last nugget.
9838	**melassa** la [melassa]	**molasses** Per motivi economici i produttori hanno preferito continuare ad utilizzare alcol distillato da cereali o melassa di barbabietola da zucchero. -For economic reasons, producers preferred to stick with alcohol produced from grain or sugar beet molasses.
9839	**cantastorie** i [kantastorje]	**ballad singer** In realtà sono un regista, un cantastorie. -And I'm not a dancer, I'm not a choreographer -- I'm actually a filmmaker, a storyteller.
9840	**covare** vb [kovare]	**hatch|sit** Il Consiglio ha forse intenzione di covare ancora per molto le direttive ricordate dall'onorevole Hughes? -Does the Council intend to brood much longer over the directives mentioned by Mr Hughes?
9841	**corteggiare** vb [korteddʒare]	**court** Quelle risposte non debbono servire a corteggiare l'opinione popolare, ma essere responsabili e ragionevoli. -These answers are not about courting popular opinion, but about being responsible and sensible.
9842	**compressione** la [kompressjone]	**compression** Quindi la tavola armonica in legno di abete bianco è più resistente alla compressione -This gives the white spruce soundboard better resistance to compression.
9843	**disputa** la [disputa]	**dispute|argument** Prendiamo un caso contemporaneo di disputa sulla giustizia. -Let's take a contemporary example of the dispute about justice.
9844	**cornetto** il [kornetto]	**cornet** Prendete un cornetto. -Have a croissant.
9845	**attribuire** vb [attribwire]	**attribute|award** A lui piaceva attribuire la maggior parte dei suoi errori e delle sfortune della sua vita a un padre tirannico. -He liked to blame most of his faults and misfortunes of his life on a tyrannical father.
9846	**alluvione** le [alluvjone]	**flood|flooding** L'alluvione ha fatto un sacco di danni alle colture. -The flood did a lot of harm to the crops.
9847	**leva** la [leva]	**lever|draft** Un sorriso al giorno leva il medico di torno! -One smile a day keeps the doctor away!
9848	**incuriosire** vb [iŋkurjozire]	**excite curiosity** Questo mi fa incuriosire. -This makes me curious.
9849	**infermo**	**infirm**

adj C'è qualcuno infermo fra voi? Chiami gli anziani della chiesa...
[infermo] -Is any sick among you, let him call for the elders of the church...

9850 **orbitale** **orbital**
adj Stiamo puntando a un concorso orbitale.
[orbitale] -We're going after an orbital prize.

9851 **inondare** **flood|overflow**
vb Possiamo sciogliere le calotte glaciali, inondare il mondo.
[inondare] -I mean we can melt the ice caps, flood the world.

9852 **figliastra** **stepdaughter**
la Turista: Ho portato la mia figliastra qui da Indianapolis.
[fiʎʎastra] -Tourist: I've taken my step-daughter here from Indianapolis.

9853 **lignaggio** **lineage|kin**
il È di lignaggio nobile.
[liɲɲaddʒo] -He is of noble ancestry.

9854 **osseo** **bone|bony**
adj Sono i tonni più grandi, al secondo posto per dimensioni tra i pesci a scheletro osseo.
[osseo] -They're the largest of the tunas, the second-largest fish in the sea -- bony fish.

9855 **meticcio** **mestizo**
il È un meticcio, una minaccia per la nostra sopravvivenza.
[metittʃo] -It is a mongrel, a threat to our survival.

9856 **savana** **savannah**
la Non era la savana, e nemmeno l'acqua, era questo!"
[savana] -It was not the savanna, it was not the water, it was this!"

9857 **sferrare** **launch**
vb Come sottolineato dall'onorevole Dominique Souchet, poiché la scomparsa del franco sferra un colpo mortale anche al franco CFA, l'intera Africa francofona ne risulta lesa.
[sferrare] -As Dominique Souchet noted, given that the death of the franc is a fatal blow to the CFA franc, it is thus also a fatal blow to the whole of French-speaking Africa.

9858 **sincronizzazione** **synchronization|timing**
la Inoltre, vorrei aggiungere un'osservazione riguardo alla sincronizzazione e al coordinamento.
[siŋkroniddzattsjone] Furthermore, I would like to add something which has to do with synchronisation and coordination.

9859 **tamponare** **dab|stop**
vb Tamponare leggermente una ferita.
[tamponare] -To dab a wound gently.

9860 **fotocopiatrice** **photocopier**
la Abbiamo esaurito la carta per la fotocopiatrice.
[fotokopjatritʃe] -We've run out of paper for the photocopier.

9861 **pluviale** **pluvial; waterspout**
adj; il Il Casinò Mediterranean ha un giardino pluviale.
[pluvjale] -The Mediterranean Casino has a rainforest garden.

9862 **camaleonte** **chameleon**
il E può mimetizzarsi come un camaleonte.
[kamaleonte] -And he can blend into his surroundings like a chameleon.

9863 **elettrocardiogramma** **electrocardiogram**

il Desidero farle un prelievo ed anche un elettrocardiogramma.
[elettrokardjogramma] -I would like to draw some blood and do an EKG as well.

9864 **autenticità** **authenticity|genuine**
la Il problema con le citazioni su Internet è che è difficile verificarne l'autenticità.
[autentitʃit'a] -The problem with quotes on the Internet is that it is hard to verify their authenticity.

9865 **galattico** **galactic**
adj E vi sono altri pericoli avvicinandosi al nucleo galattico.
[galattiko] -And there are other dangers the closer you get to the galactic core.

9866 **telecomunicazione** **telecommunication**
la Ad essi deve essere garantito un accesso privo di ostacoli ai mezzi di telecomunicazione.
[telekomunikattsjone] -They must be ensured unimpeded access to means of telecommunication.

9867 **antigelo** **antifreeze**
gli Un meccanico che lavora con gli antigelo.
[antidʒelo] -A mechanic who works with antifreeze.

9868 **venereo** **venereal**
adj Fu diagnosticato come un tumore venereo trasmissibile, un cancro trasmesso sessualmente che colpisce i cani.
[venereo] -The vet diagnosed this as transmissible venereal tumor, a sexually transmitted cancer that affects dogs.

9869 **integrare** **integrate**
vb Dobbiamo integrare le politiche sociali ed economiche, non tenerle separate.
[integrare] -We have to integrate social and economic policies, not segregate them.

9870 **respiratorio** **respiratory**
adj Fondamentalmente inquinano il sistema respiratorio e circolatorio della Terra.
[respiratorjo] -They're basically fouling up Earth's respiratory and circulatory systems.

9871 **arredatore** **interior decorator**
il Sembra qualcosa che potrebbe vendervi un arredatore.
[arredatore] -Sounds like something that a decorator would make you buy.

9872 **narcisista** **narcissist**
il/la Joe è un narcisista maligno.
[nartʃizista] -Joe is a malignant narcissist.

9873 **ovaia** **ovary**
le Il campione di ovaia che avete mandato è normale.
[ovaja] -The ovary specimen you sent is normal.

9874 **pennarello** **pen**
il Non conosco nessun pennarello del genere.
[pennarello] -I don't know any marker like that.

9875 **silo** **silo**
il Guardate questa donna, Ram Timari Devi, su un silo granario, in Champaran, dove abbiamo fatto un Shodh Yatra.
[silo] -Look at this lady, Ram Timari Devi, on a grain bin.

9876 **borgo** **village|borough**
il Voglio visitare un borgo medievale.
[borgo] -I want to visit a medieval village.

9877 **rinnovamento** **renovation|regeneration**

il Le donne devono poter diventare protagoniste di questo rinnovamento.
[rinnovamento] -Women must be able to become the protagonists of this renewal.

9878 **gastrico** **gastric**
adj Facciamo un lavaggio gastrico con fluidi caldi.
[gastriko] -Let's do a gastric lavage with warm fluids.

9879 **sotterfugio** **subterfuge**
il Un tale sotterfugio giuridico non è degno della Commissione.
[sotterfudʒo] -That legal subterfuge is not worthy of the Commission.

9880 **avventuriero** **adventurer**
il Preferirei il termine "avventuriero".
[avventurjero] -I'd prefer the term "adventurer".

9881 **coke** **coke**
il In Tanzania and Uganda, they represent 90 percent of Coke's sales.
[koke] -In Tanzania ed in Uganda, costituiscono il 90% delle vendite della Coca-Cola.

9882 **equamente** **equally**
adv Con l'esperanto si può comunicare equamente con gente di altri paesi.
[ekwamente] -With Esperanto you can communicate equally with people from other countries.

9883 **tanfo** **stench**
il Ad un certo punto bastava camminare per Londra per essere sopraffatti dal tanfo.
[tanfo] -So, you would just walk around London at this point and just be overwhelmed with this stench.

9884 **beffa** **mockery|hoax**
la E' una beffa quando il governo sostiene di avere tutto sotto controllo!
[beffa] -It is a mockery for the government to allege it has everything under control.

9885 **briccone** **rascal; rascally; miscreant**
il; adv; adj Il briccone deve essersi nascosto in casa mia.
[brikkone] -The rascal must have gone to hide in my house again.

9886 **eiaculazione** **ejaculation**
la Questo è il macaco orsino al momento dell'eiaculazione.
[ejakulattsjone] -This is the ejaculation face of the stump-tailed macaque.

9887 **illustrazione** **illustration**
la Un'illustrazione del potere di trasformazione della tecnologia è a Kibera.
[illustrattsjone] -One illustration of the transformational power of technology is in Kibera.

9888 **malizia** **malice**
la Anime innocenti, bellissime... che non hanno mai conosciuto la malizia e la rabbia.
[malittsja] -Innocent, beautiful souls, who never knew malice or anger.

9889 **risentito** **resentful**
adj Lui ha risentito dell'azione della sua amica.
[rizentito] -He resented his friend's action.

9890 **cameratismo** **camaraderie**
il Tutto ciò che voglio è un po' di cameratismo.
[kameratismo] -All I want is some camaraderie.

9891 **slam** **slam**
lo It came in at speeds that were tremendous, slammed into the ground,
[zlam] blew up, and exploded with the energy of roughly a 20-megaton nuclear

bomb -- a very hefty bomb.
-Si avvicinò a velocità terrificanti, si schiantò contro il terreno, scoppiò ed esplose con l'energia di una bomba nucleare da 20 megatoni - una bomba davvero enorme.

9892 **scottante** **pressing**
adj
[skottante]
È un tema scottante perché ha provocato reazioni appassionate.
-It is a hot topic, because it has provoked passionate reactions.

9893 **sordomuto** **deaf and dumb; deaf mute**
adj; il
[sordomuto]
Gesù si conforma al linguaggio del sordomuto per farsi comprendere da lui.
-Jesus adapted to the language of the deaf-mute so as to be understood by him.

9894 **eschimese** **Eskimo; Eskimo**
adj; il/la
[eskimeze]
Ci ha quasi provato con un'eschimese.
-He tried to score with an Eskimo.

9895 **pece** **pitch**
la
[petʃe]
E voi tutti brucerete nella pece bollente!
-And you will all boil in boiling tar.

9896 **opportunista** **opportunist**
il/la
[opportunista]
Sei opportunista?
-Are you opportunistic?

9897 **autostoppista** **hitch-hiker**
il/la
[autostoppista]
Quello che dovrebbe preoccuparti è un autostoppista.
-What you should be worried about is a hitchhiker.

9898 **botteghino** **box office**
il
[bottegino]
In particolare il film "North Country" fu in realtà un pò un disastro al botteghino.
-One of these films in particular, called "North Country," was actually kind of a box office disaster.

9899 **amputare** **amputate**
vb
[amputare]
Posso darvi 15 minuti, dopodiché dovrò amputare.
-I can give you guys 15 minutes, and after that, I have to amputate.

9900 **impostare** **set up|set out**
vb
[impostare]
Devi impostare la sveglia prima di andare a letto.
-You've got to set the alarm clock before you go to bed.

9901 **dondolare** **swing|rock**
vb
[dondolare]
Fare dondolare un secchio all'estremità di una corda.
-To swing a bucket from the end of a rope.

9902 **inconfutabile** **irrefutable**
adj
[iŋkonfutabile]
Questo argomento è inconfutabile.
-This argument is irrefutable.

9903 **roccaforte** **stronghold**
la
[rokkaforte]
Mi ha detto che poteVa mostrarmi la roccaforte della Fratellanza Sengh.
-He said he could show me the Sengh Brotherhood stronghold.

9904 **pizzicato** **pizzicato**
lo
[piddzikato]
Joe mi ha pizzicato il braccio.
-Joe pinched my arm.

9905 **pregio** **quality|merit**
il
[predʒo]
Il grande pregio di questa direttiva è quello di racchiudere in un unico testo tutte le precedenti disposizioni in materia.

-The great merit of this directive is that it combines all the previous provisions on the subject in a single text.

9906 **simmetria** **symmetry**
la
[simmetrja]
La simmetria è noiosa.
-Symmetry is boring.

9907 **foschia** **mist**
la
[foskja]
Questa foschia è onnipresente e avvolge completamente Titano.
-This haze is ubiquitous. ~~~ It's completely global and enveloping Titan.

9908 **rettitudine** **rectitude**
la
[rettitudine]
Miei cari concittadini europei, optiamo tutti per la "rettitudine del cuore"!
-My fellow Europeans, let us all have 'righteousness in the heart'!

9909 **tenacia** **tenacity**
la
[tenatʃa]
Auguro al Commissario di dimostrare tenacia e pazienza nei negoziati con le sue controparti cinesi.
-I wish the Commissioner much perseverance in his negotiations with his Chinese opposite numbers.

9910 **cancellazione** **cancellation**
la
[kantʃellattsjone]
Al momento, gli utenti normali non possono eliminare le frasi, solo i responsabili del corpus possono. Un giorno aggiungeremo la possibilità per gli utenti di eliminare le proprie frasi, ma nel frattempo, se si vuole fare eliminare una frase, va aggiunto un commento alla frase per chiedere la cancellazione e spiegare perché la si vuole eliminare.
-At the moment, normal users cannot delete sentences, only corpus maintainers can. We will someday add the possibility for users to delete their own sentences, but in the meantime, if you want to have a sentence deleted, add a comment on the sentence asking for deletion and explain why you'd like to delete it.

9911 **assicuratore** **insurer**
il
[assikuratore]
Attualmente, l'assicuratore del paese di provenienza non è autorizzato a fornirgli tale copertura.
-Their current home insurer is not allowed to provide that cover.

9912 **inaugurare** **inaugurate**
vb
[inaugurare]
Per inaugurare questo nuovo ciclo della costruzione europea, liberiamo l' immaginazione, cominciamo col dire sì alla convenzione.
-In order to unveil this new round of European integration, let us allow our imagination to run free, and let us begin by saying 'yes' to the convention.

9913 **premeditazione** **premeditation|wilfulness**
la
[premeditattsjone]
Non li abbiamo convinti della premeditazione.
-Don't think we sold them on premeditation.

9914 **apprensione** **apprehension|anxiety**
la
[apprensjone]
I cavalli, come le persone, sentono l'apprensione, la paura e sanno fidarsi degli esseri umani.
-Horses, like people, feel apprehension, fear, and are able to trust humans.

9915 **calderone** **cauldron**
il
[kalderone]
Dovrei metterti nel calderone dal quale sei arrivato.
-I ought to put you in the cauldron from which you came.

9916 **spiaccicare** **mash**

	vb [spjattʃikare]	Che poi hai utilizzato per spiacciacare lo sceriffo Andy. -Which you then used to squish Sheriff Andy.
9917	**sazio** adj [sattsjo]	**full|sated** Quando il topo è sazio la farina è amara. -When the mouse is satiated, the flour is bitter.
9918	**gazza** la [gattsa]	**magpie** Essere ladro come una gazza. -To be a thieving magpie.
9919	**accanito** adj [akkanito]	**hard** Joe è un fumatore accanito. -Joe is a chain smoker.
9920	**scaraventare** vb [skaraventare]	**hurl** Questo posto sta per esplodere e scaraventare quintali di rocce su di noi. -This place is about to blow and drop a hundred feet of rock on us.
9921	**ricavo** il [rikavo]	**proceeds** Inoltre, il ricavo generato dal carbone vegetale è di 260 milioni di dollari. -In addition, the revenue generated from that charcoal is 260 million dollars.
9922	**scombussolare** vb [skombussolare]	**upset|mess up** Ma il piacere di uccidere ha iniziato a scombussolare la sua organizzazione. -But his enjoyment of killing is beginning to disrupt his organization.
9923	**pedana** la [pedana]	**footboard** Qui di seguito il termine porta comprende anche la pedana. -Hereafter, the word door includes the step as well.
9924	**ostello** il [ostello]	**hostel** C'è un ostello della gioventù da queste parti? -Is there a youth hostel around here?
9925	**vertebra** la [vertebra]	**vertebra** E così passo dopo passo, vertebra dopo vertebra, ho proseguito. -And so button by button, vertebrae by vertebrae, I built my way down.
9926	**ospitale** adj [ospitale]	**hospitable** Il nostro intestino è un ambiente ospitale per quei batteri. -Our gut is a wonderfully hospitable environment for those bacteria.
9927	**custodire** vb [kustodire]	**keep|guard** Essa non è un fine da raggiungere, ma uno strumento per custodire la vita in Dio. -This is not a goal to be reached, but a tool to guard life in God.
9928	**cassapanca** la [kassapaŋka]	**chest** Un cassetto della vecchia cassapanca di nostra madre, come per noi. -A drawer out of our mother's old chest, same as we did.
9929	**undicesimo** num [unditʃezimo]	**eleventh** Se Dio avesse dato un undicesimo comandamento mi chiedo cosa potesse essere stato. -If God had given an eleventh commandment, I wonder what it would have been.
9930	**celibe** adj; lo [tʃelibe]	**single; bachelor** Joe è ancora celibe. -Joe is still single.
9931	**clarinetto**	**clarinet**

il [klarinetto] | Joe ha rotto il clarinetto di Jane.
-Joe broke Jane's clarinet.

9932 **marca** — **brand|mark**
la
[marka]
Lui mi ha dato una marca selezionata di prodotti in scatola.
-He gave me a select brand of canned goods.

9933 **curatore** — **curator**
il
[kuratore]
Il governo britannico ritiene che la questione sia di competenza dei curatori del che, nel Regno Unito, sono indipendenti dal governo.
-The United Kingdom Government considers that this is a matter for the trustees of the British Museum, who are, in the case of the United Kingdom, independent of government.

9934 **precipitoso** — **hasty|precipitous**
adj
[pretʃipitozo]
Oggi, invece, sarebbe precipitoso pronunciarsi sulla sola base delle proposte elaborate dalla BCE.
-Today, it would be hasty to take a decision solely on the basis of the work of the European Central Bank.

9935 **encomio** — **praise**
il
[eŋkomjo]
Il suo documento di lavoro, che è stato la base della nostra relazione, è assai meritevole, è degno dell'encomio di questo Parlamento.
-He should have the commendation of this Chamber.

9936 **costanza** — **constancy**
la
[kostantsa]
Abbiamo bisogno di determinazione e di costanza.
-Determination and consistency are required.

9937 **rassegnazione** — **resignation**
la
[rasseɲɲattsjone]
Ma la disperazione, onorevole Wolf, non deve portare alla rassegnazione.
-But despair should not lead to resignation, Mr Wolf.

9938 **modestamente** — **lowly**
adv
[modestamente]
Il risultato raggiunto contribuisce altresì, seppure modestamente, alla felicità dell'uomo.
-It has added modestly to the sum total of human happiness as well.

9939 **involontario** — **involuntary|unintentional**
adj
[involontarjo]
E'possibile che talvolta commetta un errore, ma, in tal caso, credetemi, è del tutto involontario.
-I may make a mistake on the odd occasion, but in that case I assure you it is absolutely unintentional.

9940 **trasparenza** — **transparency**
la
[trasparentsa]
Il silenzio è l'opposto della trasparenza, e senza trasparenza non c'è democrazia.
-Silence is the opposite of transparency, and without transparency there is no democracy.

9941 **qualifica** — **qualification**
la
[kwalifika]
Non ritenete necessario mantenere una qualifica di alto livello?
-Do you not think that a high-level qualification should be maintained?

9942 **freschezza** — **freshness**
la
[freskettsa]
Come ti regala freschezza più a lungo -- più fresco, tre volte fresco.
-How do we keep you fresher longer -- better freshness, more freshness, three times fresher.

9943 **schiamazzo** — **noise|cackle**
lo
[skjamattso]
Ero calmo, volevo scusarmi, nessun schiamazzo, nessuna minaccia.
-I was calm, apologetic, no shouting, no threats.

9944 **congetturare** — **conjecture**

vb [kondʒetturare] Immagino che lei proteggerà l'Unione da questa congettura così ambigua e che i criteri politici continueranno ad essere al primo posto.
-I assume that you will be protecting Europe from such an indirect speculation and that the political criteria will simply continue to occupy prime position.

9945 **predone** **marauder**
il [predone] Se trapassi quella soglia un'altra volta, ti sparerò come fossi un predone qualsiasi.
-If you cross this threshold again, I'll shoot you like any other marauder.

9946 **sbarramento** **barrier**
lo [zbarramento] Poi incappiamo in uno sbarramento pieno di serpenti.
-And we run into a barrier full of snakes.

9947 **evolutivo** **evolutive**
adj [evolutivo] E' normale che la sua attività economica segua lo stesso andamento evolutivo.
-It is quite normal for its economic activity to follow the same evolutionary curve.

9948 **tabernacolo** **tabernacle**
il [tabernakolo] (Video) Richard Carter: Sono Richard Carter, e questo è il Coro 'Tabernacolo del Sashimi'.
-(Video) Richard Carter: I'm Richard Carter, and this is the Sashimi Tabernacle Choir.

9949 **termale** **thermal**
adj [termale] Secondo lui, il problema dell'equilibrio termale è che non possiamo viverci.
-He says, the problem with thermal equilibrium is that we can't live there.

9950 **fausto** **auspicious|fortunate**
adj [fausto] Nemmeno la fragorosa baldoria di Filemone e Bauci riusciva a distrarre Fausto dalle sue meditazioni.
-Not even the thunderous revelry of Philemon and Baucis could succeed in pulling Faust out of his meditations.

√ 9951 **amareggiare** **embitter**
vb [amareddʒare] Oggi vi sono meno domande e più dichiarazioni deluse e amareggiate, dichiarazioni che si basano sull'esperienza.
-Nowadays, there are fewer questions, there are more disillusioned, embittered statements and these statements are based on experience.

9952 **disappunto** **disappointment**
il [dizappunto] Joe ha provato a non mostrare il suo disappunto.
-Joe tried not to show his disappointment.

9953 **imitatore** **imitator**
il [imitatore] Non sappiamo se è un imitatore.
-We do not know if it is a copycat.

9954 **magnete** **magnet**
il [maɲɲete] In altre parole, il campo del magnete è vicino alla testa del piccione.
-In other words, the field of the magnet is near the pigeon's head.

9955 **claustrofobia** **claustrophobia**
la [klaustrofobja] Io soffro di claustrofobia.
-I've got claustrophobia.

√ 9956 **lordo** **gross|filthy**
adj [lordo] Ancora una volta è una frazione infinitesimale del prodotto nazionale lordo della Francia.

-Again, this is a fraction of a per mille of France's Gross National Product.

9957 **notificare** **notify**
vb
[notifikare]
Le autorità spagnole dovranno notificare il piano alla Commissione.
-The Spanish authorities must notify the plan to the Commission.

9958 **spalare** **shovel**
vb
[spalare]
Joe è fuori a spalare la neve.
-Joe is out shoveling snow.

9959 **circonferenza** **circumference**
la
[tʃirkonferentsa]
La circonferenza non dovrebbe essere in centimetri quadrati, per esempio.
-The circumference should not be in squared centimeters, for example.

9960 **salice** **willow**
la
[salitʃe]
Ed ecco il ruscello, e il pioppo, l'ontano e il salice.
-And here is the stream, and the aspen and the alder and the willow.

9961 **germano** **German**
adj
[dʒermano]
Il mio vero nome è Bob Germano.
-My real name is Bob Germano.

9962 **scaglia** **scale**
la
[skaʎʎa]
Numero tre: scaglia una lancia.
-Number three -- throw a spear.

9963 **ciancia** **babble**
la
[tʃantʃa]
Ok, per dieci secondi basta con questa ciancia fuori luogo sulla politica.
-Okay, can you stop throwing out the misplaced political babble for 10 seconds.

9964 **maltrattamento** **maltreatment|misuse**
il
[maltrattamento]
Oggetto: Maltrattamento degli animali durante il trasporto.
-Subject: Ill-treatment of animals in transit.

√ 9965 **stanare** **drive out**
vb
[stanare]
Vediamo se riusciamo a stanare Roger e Brock e a fargli cambiare idea.
-Let's see if we can smoke out Roger and brock and change their minds.

√ 9966 **spiccare** **stand out|issue**
vb
[spikkare]
Perché state per spiccare nel mondo.
-Because you are going to stand out to the world.

9967 **salmo** **psalm**
il
[salmo]
Così abbiamo poc'anzi ripetuto nel Salmo responsoriale.
-We repeated this a few moments ago in the responsorial psalm.

9968 **difatti** **in fact**
adv
[difatti]
Difatti, ci sono diversi punti della proposta con i quali non mi trovo d'accordo.
-There are in fact several points of the proposal with which I disagree.

9969 **ipotetico** **hypothetical|presumed**
adj
[ipotetiko]
Detto questo, non esprimerò un'opinione su un referendum ipotetico.
-That being said, I am not going to express an opinion on a hypothetical referendum.

9970 **annullo** **cancellation**
lo
[annullo]
Io, Seeley Joseph Booth di Washington, annullo il mio precedente testamento e i codicilli scritti su un post–it...
-...Seeley Joseph Booth, of Washington D.C., revoke my former Will and Codicils... written on a sticky note.

9971 **zotico** **boorish; churl**

adj; lo
[dzotiko]
Ma esce fuori che sei uno zotico.
-But it turns out you're an oaf.

9972 **intasare** **block|choke**
vb
[intazare]
Nelle nostre strade intasate ci sarebbe un'economia di spazio: due autotreni finlandesi ne occupano tanto quanto tre autotreni di altri paesi dell'Unione.
-The advantages here are obvious even to the layman. Space would be saved on our congested roads, since two Finnish lorries are the equivalent of three lorries from elsewhere in Europe.

9973 **simbolismo** **symbolism**
il
[simbolismo]
Faremo sapere all'assassino quanto apprezzi il suo simbolismo.
-We'll be sure to tell the killer how much you appreciate his symbolism.

9974 **relatività** **relativity**
la
[relativitˈa]
Fu iniziata con la scoperta della teoria della relatività e della teoria quantistica.
-It was begun with the invention of relativity theory and quantum theory.

9975 **bulgaro** **Bulgarian; Bulgarian**
adj; il
[bulgaro]
Vi piace il circo bulgaro?
-Do you like the Bulgarian circus?

9976 **moralista** **moralist; moralistic**
il/la; adj
[moralista]
Joe è un moralista.
-Joe is a prude.

9977 **angolare** **angular**
adj
[aŋgolare]
La natura angolare dell'orbita oculare indica che fosse caucasica.
-The angular nature of the orbital socket suggests she is Caucasian.

9978 **senile** **senile**
adj
[senile]
Probabilmente è confusa, forse anche un po' senile.
-She's probably confused, maybe even a little senile.

9979 **fugace** **fleeting|fugacious**
adj
[fugatʃe]
Cosa farò in così poco tempo così fugace?
-What am I going to do with this short amount of time that's just fleeting?

9980 **specificamente** **particularly**
adv
[spetʃifikamente]
Invece delle clausole generali, le competenze saranno conferite specificamente.
-Instead of more general clauses, powers will be specifically conferred.

9981 **afrodisiaco** **aphrodisiac; aphrodisiac**
adj; il
[afrodizjako]
Penseranno che doveva trattarsi di qualche tipo di afrodisiaco.
-They'll think it was some kind of aphrodisiac.

9982 **avversione** **aversion|dislike**
le
[avversjone]
Entrambe le personalità erano guidate dalla loro esperienza e dall'avversione per la guerra.
-What drove both men was their experience and their abhorrence of war.

9983 **accoppiare** **pair|join**
vb
[akkoppjare]
Voglio far accoppiare la regina con un maschio e conservare le uova.
-I intend to mate the queen with a male and preserve her eggs.

9984 **sedano** **celery**
il
[sedano]
Odio il sedano!
-I hate celery!

9985 **formicolio** **tingling|pins and needles**

il | – e il formicolio nella gamba.
[formikoljo] | -And that tingling in your leg.

9986 **elaborato** **elaborate; script**
adj; il
[elaborato]
Sembra che lui abbia elaborato una soluzione al suo problema.
-It appears that he has worked out a solution to his problem.

9987 **pallavolo** **volleyball**
la
[pallavolo]
Gli sport più comuni del mondo sono: calcio, basket, football, rugby, baseball, cricket, hockey su ghiaccio, pallavolo, beach volley, ping-pong, golf, boxe, wrestling, badminton e bowling.
-The most common sports games in the world are: Soccer, Basketball, Football, Rugby, Baseball, Cricket, Ice hockey, Volleyball, Beach volleyball, Tennis, Table tennis, Golf, Boxing, Wrestling, Badminton and Bowling.

9988 **catalizzatore** **catalyst**
il
[kataliddzatore]
Negli autocarri di nuova immatricolazione il catalizzatore è obbligatorio a partire dal 2008.
-Catalytic converters in lorries will be compulsory in 2008.

9989 **pediatra** **pediatrician|paediatrist**
il/la
[pedjatra]
Qual è dunque la funzione del pediatra?
-What, then, is the function of the paediatrician?

9990 **esclusione** **exclusion**
la
[eskluzjone]
Ciò inevitabilmente porterà all'ingiusta esclusione di molti siti importanti.
-This will inevitably lead to the unfair exclusion of many important sites.

9991 **catastrofico** **catastrophic**
adj
[katastrofiko]
Qualora riescano, il risultato sarebbe catastrofico.
-If they succeed, the results will be catastrophic.

9992 **dimensionale** **dimensional**
adj
[dimensjonale]
Prendiamo questo spazio curvo 12-dimensionale e lo trasformiamo in uno a 4 dimensioni.
-We take this curved 12-dimensional space and transform it into a flat four-dimensional space.

9993 **periferico** **peripheral**
adj
[periferiko]
E questo avviene per ogni nodo periferico.
-And that happens at every peripheral node.

9994 **economista** **economist**
il/la
[ekonomista]
Io sono una fottuta economista.
-I'm a fucking economist.

9995 **prerogativa** **prerogative|privelege**
la
[prerogativa]
Nessun parlamento può approvare una Costituzione che violi questa prerogativa.
-No parliament can agree to a constitution that violates this prerogative.

9996 **scorbutico** **scorbutic**
adj
[skorbutiko]
Sarebbe ora che ti sposassi... prima di diventare un vecchio scorbutico e solitario.
-It's about time you got married, Before you turn into a lonesome and bitter, old man.

9997 **indecenza** **indecency**
la
[indetʃentsa]
Lo stesso vale per i teppisti che danno fuoco ai loro quartieri perché la polizia commette l'indecenza di entrarvi per garantire la sicurezza delle persone oneste.

-The same is true of the young thugs who set the areas in which they live ablaze when the police commit the impropriety of entering them to ensure that decent people can live in safety.

9998 **uvetta** **raisin**
la
[uvetta]
Joe ha mangiato una manciata di uvetta.
-Joe ate a handful of raisins.

9999 **affezionato** **fond**
adj
[affettsjonato]
Nonostante molti colleghi ci siano affezionati, dobbiamo rinunciare a risoluzioni di routine che richiedono un notevole dispendio di tempo.
-We need to do without time-consuming routine resolutions, even though many Members have become attached to them.

10000 **strozzare** **throttle|choke**
vb
[strottsare]
Hai letto abbastanza romanzi fantasy da strozzare un ippogrifo.
-You've read enough fantasy novels – to choke a hippogriff.

10001 **inferiorità** **inferiority**
le
[inferjorit'a]
Ciò significa riconoscere, di fatto, la loro inferiorità.
-That simply amounts to acknowledging their inferiority.

10002 **ribollire** **boil|boil again**
vb
[ribollire]
Mi ha fatto ribollire il sangue.
-And it made my blood boil.

10003 **gruccia** **crutch**
la
[gruttʃa]
Cercò di uccidermi dentro di lei con una gruccia Ma sono sopravvissuta.
-She even tried to kill me inside her with a coat hanger, but I survived.

10004 **premettere** **premise**
vb
[premettere]
Come ministro irlandese, tuttavia, vorrei iniziare con il premettere che il PIL rileva la produzione, non i redditi.
-However, as an Irish Minister, I would start from the premise that GDP measures output, not incomes.

10005 **sprofondare** **collapse**
vb
[sprofondare]
Dobbiamo sprofondare in una fobia e in una deriva igieniste e regolamentari?
-Do we need to sink into a health and regulatory phobia and drift?

10006 **coltura** **culture**
la
[koltura]
In molte aziende agricole, essa costituisce ovviamente una coltura commerciale.
-On many farms it is clearly a cash crop.

10007 **scenetta** **sketch**
la
[ʃenetta]
La scena internazionale continua ad essere turbata da preoccupanti tensioni.
-The international scene continues to be disturbed by worrisome tensions.

10008 **mutevole** **changing|changeable**
adj
[mutevole]
Le modalità per quanto riguarda i fondi strutturali sono impraticabili: gli errori sorgono a causa delle norme eccessive ed estremamente mutevoli per i beneficiari di sussidi.
-The practicalities with regard to the structural funds are unmanageable: errors arise as a result of excessive and widely varying rules for recipients of subsidies.

10009 **amministrare** **administer|manage**
vb
[amministrare]
“di qualsiasi agenzia esecutiva istituita o ampliata per amministrare tale programma”.

-'any executive agency created or extended to administer this programme'

10010 **terrier** il [terrjer]
terrier
Phoebe non è un pitbull di tipo terrier.
-Phoebe is not a pit bull terrier type.

10011 **maestria** la [maestrja]
mastery
Presentano una maestria e un'accuratezza talmente elevate da lasciarci sovraffatti.
-There is a quality of craftsmanship and precision that is just astonishing and remarkable.

10012 **calcare** il; vb [kalkare]
limestone; emphasize
Ecco come moriremo... seppelliti dal calcare.
-This is how we die... buried in limestone.

10013 **satira** la [satira]
satire|lampoon
Tanto le belle intenzioni politiche quanto la satira beffarda stanno tentando di trasmetterci un messaggio.
-Both the fine policy intentions and mocking satire are trying to give us a message.

10014 **interagire** vb [interadʒire]
interact
Sappiamo che queste sostanze possono interagire in modo particolarmente negativo.
-We know that these substances can interact in a particularly unfortunate way.

10015 **rollare** vb [rollare]
roll
Tu eri il migliore a rollare uno spinello.
-You were the better at rolling a reefer.

10016 **amputazione** la [amputattsjone]
amputation
Todd Kuiken: Ok, e poi, dopo l'amputazione, pian piano ti sei ripresa.
-Todd Kuiken: Okay, so after your amputation, you healed up.

10017 **ultravioletto** adj; il [ultravjoletto]
ultraviolet; ultraviolet
Gli insetti vedono verde, blu e ultravioletto, e distinguono varie sfumature di ultravioletto.
-Insects see green, blue and ultraviolet, and they see various shades of ultraviolet.

10018 **lampante** adj [lampante]
glaring
Vi invitiamo a fare altrettanto e a porre termine a questa lampante coercizione.
-We call on you to do likewise and to stop this blatant coercion.

10019 **erotismo** il [erotismo]
eroticism
Lasciamo da parte l'erotismo che può essere legato in qualche modo all'arte.
-I am not talking about eroticism, which may have some connection with art.

10020 **disperare** vb [disperare]
despair
Ecco perché ritengo che non bisogna disperare.
-This is the reason why I believe we should not despair.

10021 **pressappoco** adv [pressappoko]
about
Questo dato è emerso nel 2008, pressappoco nel periodo in cui la crisi bancaria ha svelato che avevamo perso capitale finanziario per un importo pari a circa 2,5 trilioni di dollari.
-This came out in 2008, which was, of course, around the time that the

banking crisis had shown that we had lost financial capital of the order of two and a half trillion dollars.

10022 **origiliare** | **eavesdrop**

vb

[oriʎʎare]

Non dovrebbe origliare.

-You shouldn't eavesdrop.

10023 **radiofonico** | **radio**

adj

[radjofoniko]

Ha uno spettacolo radiofonico.

-He has a radio show.

10024 **carponi** | **on all fours**

adv

[karponi]

No, ma muoio dalla voglia di vederti camminare carponi qui dentro.

-No. It's just that I'm dying to watch you crawl through that hatch.

10025 **barattare** | **trade|barter**

vb

[barattare]

Non può essere l'oggetto di un baratto da parte dell'Unione europea, ma un atto spontaneo.

-This should not be the subject of bartering on the part of the European Union; this should be spontaneous.

Adjectives

Italian English Translation
Rank Part of Speech
galleggiante floating; float
7502 *adj; il*
filiale branch; filial
7504 *la; adj*
coerente consistent
7507 *adj*
accessibile accessible|attainable
7515 *adj*
residuo residue; residual
7516 *il; adj*
ammalato sick; sick person
7518 *adj; il*
colombiano Columbian
7523 *adj*
lucente shiny|lucent
7524 *adj*
sciolto loose|dissolved
7528 *adj*
affannoso labored|breathless
7530 *adj*
sfidante challenger; challenging
7531 *il/la; adj*
tecnologico technological
7540 *adj*
impenetrabile impenetrable
7549 *adj*
maldestro clumsy|maladroit
7550 *adj*
considerevole considerable|sizable
7558 *adj*
sbalorditivo amazing
7560 *adj*
estetico aesthetic
7564 *adj*
simbolico symbolic|token
7566 *adj*
rispettoso respectful
7580 *adj*
insicuro insecure
7582 *adj*
egocentrico egocentric; egotist
7585 *adj; il*
primordiale primordial
7586 *adj*
tibetano Tibetan; Tibetan
7589 *adj; il*
multinazionale multinational
7591 *adj*
islamico Islamic; Islam
7592 *adj; il*
capitolare capitulate; capitular
7595 *vb; adj*
colorito colorful; color
7600 *adj; il*
preventivo quote; preventive
7603 *il; adj*
ricorrente recurrent
7606 *adj*
inosservato unnoticed|unobserved
7608 *adj*
dignitoso decent
7620 *adj*
denso dense|full
7633 *adj*
razziale racial
7637 *adj*
minaccioso threatening|ugly
7644 *adj*
trionfale triumphal
7648 *adj*
indeciso undecided
7656 *adj*
abitato inhabited
7663 *adj*
adottivo adopted|foster
7664 *adj*
antiquato antiquated|outdated
7665 *adj*
strappato torn
7666 *adj*
innaturale unnatural
7673 *adj*
strepitoso resounding
7674 *adj*
napoletano Neapolitan; Neapolitan
7678 *adj; il*
arduo arduous|uphill
7681 *adj*
svariato varied

7696 *adj*
ortodosso orthodox

7698 *adj*
palestinese Palestinian; Palestinian

7704 *adj; il/la*
prematrimoniale premarital|prematrimonial

7705 *adj*
suscettibile susceptible|liable

7711 *adj*
indulgente indulgent|charitable

7713 *adj*
blasfemo blasphemous

7720 *adj*
dinamico dynamic

7721 *adj*
editoriale editorial; leader

7729 *adj; lo*
passivo passive; liabilities

7730 *adj; il*
distruttivo destructive

7737 *adj*
famigerato notorious

7738 *adj*
missionario missionary; missionary

7739 *adj; il*
idoneo suitable

7741 *adj*
ottuso obtuse; dolt

7743 *adj; il*
decappottabile convertible

7744 *adj*
incontrollabile uncontrollable

7747 *adj*
incline prone|inclined

7753 *adj*
educativo educational

7756 *adj*
confessionale confessional; confessional

7760 *adj; il*
scontento discontent; displeased

7768 *lo; adj*
bollente boiling

7771 *adj*
coniugale conjugal|marital

7772 *adj*
diffuso widespread

7773 *adj*
dettagliato detailed

7791 *adj*
attendibile reliable

7792 *adj*
inconcepibile inconceivable

7793 *adj*
docile docile|tame

7794 *adj*
variabile variable

7800 *adj*
socievole sociable

7801 *adj*
invadente intrusive; intruder

7803 *adj; il/la*
disabile disabled

7813 *adj*
patrizio patrician; patrician

7819 *adj; il*
ambulatorio surgery; ambulatory

7820 *il; adj*
bolscevico Bolshevik; Bolshevik

7823 *adj; il*
affrettato hurried|hasty

7828 *adj*
coloniale colonial

7829 *adj*
mero mere

7834 *adj*
alleato ally; allied

7843 *il; adj*
sconcertante disconcerting

7844 *adj*
proibito prohibited

7848 *adj*
perspicace perspicacious|discerning

7849 *adj*
terapeutico therapeutic

7851 *adj*
fiducioso confident

7856 *adj*
lasso period; weary

7857 *il; adj*
passante passing; passer-by

7859 *adj; il/la*
occasionale occasional|casual

7862 *adj*
contorto twisted
7864 *adj*
lussuoso luxurious
7870 *adj*
corporeo bodily
7871 *adj*
edilizio building
7881 *adj*
occulto occult|hidden
7882 *adj*
benevolo benevolent|benign
7883 *adj*
protestante Protestant; Protestant
7884 *adj; il/la*
profumato scented|fragrant
7885 *adj*
muscoloso muscular|muscled
7886 *adj*
fumante smoking
7888 *adj*
ennesimo umpteenth
7890 *adj*
gustoso tasty|savory
7895 *adj*
dolente sore|sorrowful
7899 *adj*
sconsiderato inconsiderate|thoughtless
7909 *adj*
moribondo dying; dying man
7911 *adj; il*
insensato senseless
7914 *adj*
belga Belgian; Belgian
7916 *adj; il/la*
texano Texan
7919 *adj*
planetario planetary; planetarium
7922 *adj; il*
emiliano emilian
7926 *adj*
aborigeno aboriginal; aborigine
7928 *adj; il*
geroglifico hieroglyph; hieroglyphic
7933 *il; adj*
distaccato detached
7934 *adj*
edile building; aedile
7935 *adj; il*
inarrestabile unrestrainable
7937 *adj*
alfabetico alphabetical|abecedarian
7944 *adj*
abbattuto down|dejected
7954 *adj*
irascibile irascible|cantankerous
7960 *adj*
eloquente eloquent|articulate
7962 *adj*
disarmato unarmed
7965 *adj*
competente competent
7967 *adj*
goffo clumsy; hobbledehoy
7968 *adj; il*
galante gallant
7969 *adj*
raggiungibile attainable
7978 *adj*
ripieno filling; stuffed
7984 *il; adj*
celestiale celestial
7985 *adj*
felino feline
7987 *adj*
glaciale glacial
7991 *adj*
conservatore conservator; Tory
8001 *il; adj*
narrativo narrative
8007 *adj*
mercantile merchant; merchantman
8011 *adj; il*
macabro macabre
8015 *adj*
ateo atheist; atheistic
8017 *il; adj*
sprovvisto devoid
8019 *adj*
imbattibile unbeatable
8024 *adj*
losco shady|sinister

8029 *adj*
informale informal
8032 *adj*
svitato nutty; screwball
8033 *adj; lo*
paragonabile comparable
8041 *adj*
evoluto advanced
8044 *adj*
balistico ballistic
8052 *adj*
prestigioso prestigious
8053 *adj*
eletto elect
8056 *adj*
strumentale instrumental
8058 *adj*
paterno paternal
8059 *adj*
implacabile implacable
8069 *adj*
vantaggioso advantageous|profitable
8080 *adj*
tagliente sharp|cutting
8086 *adj*
inesistente non-existent
8087 *adj*
presentabile presentable
8089 *adj*
sinonimo synonymous; synonym
8098 *adj; il*
virtuoso virtuous; virtuoso
8102 *adj; il*
emittente issuer; issuing
8107 *la; adj*
crasso crass
8109 *adj*
deforme deformed|crooked
8111 *adj*
gotico Gothic
8113 *adj*
limpido clear|limpid
8119 *adj*
globulare globular
8126 *adj*
derivato derivative; offshoot
8132 *adj; il*
indiscreto indiscreet|prying
8135 *adj*
acquatico aquatic
8136 *adj*
rivestito clad
8147 *adj*
lebbroso leper; leprous
8158 *il; adj*
unanime unanimous
8159 *adj*
mozzafiato breathtaking
8160 *adj*
compassionevole compassionate
8161 *adj*
bisognoso needy
8162 *adj*
danneggiato damaged
8164 *adj*
tetro gloomy|dark
8171 *adj*
ibrido hybrid
8174 *adj*
surrogato surrogate; ersatz
8178 *il; adj*
perplesso puzzled|perplexed
8183 *adj*
altruista selfless; altruist
8191 *adj; il/la*
austriaco Austrian; Austrian
8198 *adj; il*
casto chaste
8202 *adj*
imparziale impartial
8209 *adj*
fosco dark|gloomy
8210 *adj*
svergognato shameless
8211 *adj*
strategico strategic
8220 *adj*
direttivo directive|executive
8222 *adj*
organizzatore organizer; organizing
8226 *gli; adj*
polmonare pulmonary

8241 *adj*
portoricano Puerto Rican; Puerto Rican
8244 *adj; il*
psichico psychic|mental
8247 *adj*
termico thermal
8248 *adj*
benigno benign|genial
8250 *adj*
potabile drinking|potable
8257 *adj*
novello new|early
8260 *adj*
perpetuo perpetual
8261 *adj*
applicato applied; resign oneself
8271 *adj; vb*
sgarbato rude|impolite
8274 *adj*
sedicesimo sixteenth|sixteenth
8282 *adj*
tangibile tangible
8290 *adj*
appiccicoso sticky
8296 *adj*
stampato printed; printout
8301 *adj; lo*
trasparente transparent
8303 *adj*
soave sweet
8304 *adj*
avaro stingy; miser
8311 *adj; il*
corazzato armored
8316 *adj*
inammissibile inadmissible
8320 *adj*
birichino mischievous; cheeky youngster
8331 *adj; il*
interurbano interurban
8338 *adj*
generico generic
8346 *adj*
opprimente overwhelming|oppressive
8351 *adj*
scivoloso slippery
8356 *adj*
sudato sweaty
8360 *adj*
forestale forest
8364 *adj*
disastroso disastrous|shattering
8370 *adj*
inimmaginabile unimaginable
8373 *adj*
strutturale structural
8379 *adj*
manufatto artefact; manufactured
8381 *il; adj*
palmare palmar
8382 *adj*
straziante heartbreaking|harrowing
8383 *adj*
irritabile irritable|edgy
8384 *adj*
intoccabile untouchable; untouchable
8391 *adj; il/la*
assetato thirsty
8393 *adj*
oltraggioso offensive
8395 *adj*
ardito bold
8396 *adj*
dichiarato declared|avowed
8401 *adj*
fervido fervent
8404 *adj*
spilorcio stingy; miser
8407 *adj; lo*
cavallino pony; horsy
8414 *il; adj*
roditore rodent
8424 *adj*
superstizioso superstitious
8426 *adj*
inoffensivo harmless
8428 *adj*
risoluto resolute
8429 *adj*
illimitato unlimited|unrestricted

	8435	*adj*
diabetico		diabetic; diabetic
	8439	*adj; il*
dodicesimo		twelfth|twelfth
	8440	*adj*
spastico		spastic; spastic
	8454	*adj; lo*
sanguinario		bloodthirsty|slaughterous
	8455	*adj*
detersivo		detergent; detergent
	8457	*adj; il*
fiduciario		trustee; fiduciary
	8465	*il; adj*
lirico		lyrical|operatic
	8466	*adj*
plurale		plural; plural
	8469	*adj; il*
saporito		tasty|savory
	8473	*adj*
calcolatore		computer; calculating
	8478	*il; adj*
vizioso		vicious
	8480	*adj*
prodigo		prodigal|lavish
	8481	*adj*
irreversibile		irreversible
	8482	*adj*
tredicesimo		thirteenth|thirteenth
	8487	*adj*
dotto		learned; scholar
	8492	*adj; il*
impetuoso		impetuous|dashing
	8493	*adj*
spinale		spinal
	8494	*adj*
sassone		Saxon; Saxon
	8495	*adj; il*
effettivo		actual; strength
	8497	*adj; il*
irraggiungibile		unattainable
	8506	*adj*
frizzante		crisp
	8511	*adj*
incalzante		pressing
	8517	*adj*
antifurto		antitheft; antitheft
	8527	*adj; gli*
nasale		nasal
	8536	*adj*
continentale		continental
	8538	*adj*
prospero		prosperous|bonanza
	8547	*adj*
agghiacciante		dreadful
	8550	*adj*
inquieto		restless|worried
	8553	*adj*
interrogativo		questioning; interrogative
	8555	*il; adj*
radioso		radiant
	8558	*adj*
funzionale		functional
	8562	*adj*
sovversivo		subversive
	8565	*adj*
esaurito		spent
	8566	*adj*
fissato		fixed|set
	8568	*adj*
vanitoso		vain
	8569	*adj*
fusibile		fuse; fusible
	8580	*il; adj*
residenziale		residential
	8586	*adj*
problematico		problematic
	8589	*adj*
compatibile		compatible
	8590	*adj*
incoraggiante		cheering
	8594	*adj*
pertinente		relevant
	8607	*adj*
molteplice		multiple|manifold
	8614	*adj*
intenzionale		intentional
	8621	*adj*
nullo		null|insignificant
	8622	*adj*
insaziabile		insatiable
	8626	*adj*
doloso		malicious

	8627	*adj*
calmante		calming; sedative
	8628	*adj; il*
indebito		undue
	8629	*adj*
benestante		well-off
	8638	*adj*
incurabile		incurable
	8643	*adj*
sarcastico		sarcastic|derisive
	8649	*adj*
empio		impious
	8653	*adj*
rimanente		remaining; leftovers
	8656	*adj; il*
patriottico		patriotic
	8661	*adj*
ninfomane		nymphomaniac
	8665	*adj*
palese		obvious|evident
	8666	*adj*
artefatto		artifact; artificial
	8679	*il; adj*
visionario		visionary
	8680	*adj*
neurale		neural
	8682	*adj*
immondo		unclean|filthy
	8685	*adj*
rinfrescante		refreshing
	8691	*adj*
sorgente		source; rising
	8692	*la; adj*
scontato		discounted
	8696	*adj*
innegabile		undeniable
	8702	*adj*
imbottito		padded
	8703	*adj*
loquace		talkative|voluble
	8709	*adj*
ariano		Aryan; Aryan
	8710	*adj; il*
pittoresco		picturesque|colorful
	8711	*adj*
infiammabile		flammable|irascible
	8713	*adj*
schivo		shy|reserved
	8714	*adj*
peschereccio		fishing; fishing boat
	8719	*adj; il*
vicario		vicar; vicarious
	8726	*il; adj*
deplorevole		regrettable|deplorable
	8728	*adj*
teorico		theoretical; theorist
	8731	*adj; il*
auricolare		earphone; auricular
	8733	*il; adj*
roccioso		rocky
	8734	*adj*
lacrimogeno		lachrymatory
	8736	*adj*
indeterminato		indeterminate
	8740	*adj*
tridimensionale		tridimensional
	8741	*adj*
sdolcinato		sloppy
	8747	*adj*
inverosimile		unlikely|tall
	8749	*adj*
schizofrenico		schizophrenic
	8750	*adj*
suicida		suicide; suicidal
	8752	*la; adj*
rognoso		mangy
	8761	*adj*
vendicativo		vindictive
	8762	*adj*
giornaliero		daily; day-to-day
	8768	*adj; il*
balordo		stupid
	8771	*adj*
morboso		morbid|unhealthy
	8775	*adj*
botanico		botanist; botanic
	8783	*il; adj*
beduino		Bedouin; Bedouin
	8785	*adj; il*
siamese		Siamese; Siamese
	8789	*adj; il/la*
forense		forensic

8791 *adj*
latitante absconding; abscond

8793 *adj; il*
maestoso majestic|stately

8799 *adj*
pungente pungent; nippy

8806 *adj; il*
farmaceutico pharmaceutical

8810 *adj*
eterosessuale heterosexual

8816 *adj*
argenteo silvery

8817 *adj*
scontroso grumpy|surly

8824 *adj*
dolciume sweets; sweet

8833 *il; adj*
conservatorio conservatory; conservative

8840 *il; adj*
repellente repellent|repulsive

8841 *adj*
tremante trembling|shaking

8847 *adj*
elettrizzante electrifying

8849 *adj*
disinvolto casual

8853 *adj*
pastello pastel; pastel

8857 *adj; il*
provocante provocative

8862 *adj*
adeguato adequate

8863 *adj*
contemporaneo contemporary

8871 *adj*
permaloso touchy|sensitive

8879 *adj*
moscio soft

8880 *adj*
vertebrale vertebral

8883 *adj*
spettrale spectral|phantom

8884 *adj*
olimpico Olympic

8889 *adj*
dedito dedicated

8896 *adj*
dannoso harmful|detrimental

8897 *adj*
civico civic

8901 *adj*
paesano villager; village

8903 *il; adj*
disturbato disturbed

8904 *adj*
indaffarato busy

8905 *adj*
furibondo furious|wild

8906 *adj*
sanguinoso bloody

8913 *adj*
basilare basic

8918 *adj*
magno great

8923 *adj*
insostenibile unsustainable

8932 *adj*
canino canine

8935 *adj*
melodrammatico melodramatic

8936 *adj*
elevato high|elevated

8940 *adj*
rumeno Romanian

8942 *adj*
ausiliario auxiliary|subsidiary

8946 *adj*
bruciapelo point-blank

8957 *adj*
imperativo imperative

8958 *adj*
ossessivo obsessive

8965 *adj*
ambedue both

8968 *adj*
inaccessibile inaccessible

8970 *adj*
agricolo agricultural

8975 *adj*
medesimo same

8982 *adj*

futile futile|trivial
8983 *adj*
interminabile endless
8984 *adj*
aristocratico aristocratic; aristocrat
8985 *adj; il*
vigoroso vigorous|strong
8987 *adj*
inesperto inexperienced|inexpert
8991 *adj*
dirigibile airship; dirigible
8997 *il; adj*
corallino coral
8999 *adj*
eretico heretic
9004 *adj*
convincente convincing
9005 *adj*
biblico biblical
9007 *adj*
letterale literal
9008 *adj*
amministrativo administrative
9013 *adj*
temerario reckless|daredevil
9015 *adj*
spumante sparkling; sparkling wine
9030 *adj; lo*
meteorologico weather
9032 *adj*
privilegiato privileged
9037 *adj*
incompleto incomplete
9039 *adj*
commestibile edible
9049 *adj*
reciso flat
9054 *adj*
cranico cranial
9065 *adj*
molestatore molester; molesting
9067 *il; adj*
ingordo greedy
9074 *adj*
ascendente ascending; influence
9077 *adj; il/la*
dopobarba aftershave; aftershave
9078 *adj; il*
discreto discreet
9088 *adj*
furtivo furtive|slinky
9097 *adj*
duplice dual|duplex
9099 *adj*
cooperativo cooperative
9106 *adj*
anarchico anarchist; anarchic
9109 *il; adj*
pendolare pendular
9112 *adj*
cronico chronic
9114 *adj*
duraturo lasting|enduring
9116 *adj*
pomposo pompous
9119 *adj*
sintetico synthetic
9125 *adj*
genovese Genoese
9133 *adj*
esplicito explicit
9135 *adj*
ostetrico obstetrician; obstetric
9143 *il; adj*
diminutivo diminutive
9147 *adj*
eminente eminent
9157 *adj*
isolante insulating; insulator
9164 *adj; il*
iraniano Iranian
9170 *adj*
deterrente deterrent
9172 *adj*
gioioso joyful
9179 *adj*
sbadato careless; scatterbrain
9181 *adj; lo*
aspro sour|harsh
9187 *adj*
inflessibile inflexible|adamant
9190 *adj*

controverso controversial
9191 *adj*
impudente impudent; jackanapes
9193 *adj; il/la*
imperfetto imperfect
9195 *adj*
immutabile immutable
9200 *adj*
redditizio profitable
9202 *adj*
provetto proficient
9205 *adj*
nevrotico neurotic
9206 *adj*
verosimile likely|plausible
9207 *adj*
soffocante suffocating|stifling
9221 *adj*
arido arid
9224 *adj*
meritevole worthy|deserving
9236 *adj*
indescrivibile indescribable
9238 *adj*
interstellare interstellar
9240 *adj*
mormone mormon
9250 *adj*
frigido frigid
9251 *adj*
antidepressivo antidepressant; antidepressive
9254 *il; adj*
toscano Tuscan; Tuscan
9255 *adj; il*
degradante degrading
9256 *adj*
monotono monotonous|monotone
9258 *adj*
invitante inviting
9267 *adj*
capriccioso capricious|whimsical
9270 *adj*
circostante surrounding
9275 *adj*
sopportabile bearable
9278 *adj*
premiato prize; prizewinner
9281 *adj; il*
congiunto joined; kinsman
9282 *adj; il*
subacqueo underwater
9283 *adj*
lodevole commendable
9287 *adj*
istruttivo instructive
9291 *adj*
pignolo finicky; fastidious person
9301 *adj; il*
insufficiente insufficient|inadequate
9303 *adj*
intraprendente enterprising
9308 *adj*
nutriente nutritious|feeding
9311 *adj*
trascurato neglected|careless
9312 *adj*
epico epic
9319 *adj*
irriconoscibile unrecognizable
9321 *adj*
costituzionale constitutional
9324 *adj*
coordinato coordinate
9326 *adj*
sommerso black
9333 *adj*
impavido fearless
9337 *adj*
autonomo autonomous
9349 *adj*
militante militant
9355 *adj*
aerobico aerobic
9364 *adj*
autunnale autumnal
9368 *adj*
disumano inhuman
9369 *adj*
primaverile vernal
9370 *adj*
illeso unharmed|uninjured

9371 *adj*
contingente contingent
9374 *adj*
vittorioso victorious
9375 *adj*
fraterno fraternal|sisterly
9376 *adj*
irreparabile irreparable
9391 *adj*
provocatorio provocative
9397 *adj*
profano profane; layman
9399 *adj; il*
supplementare additional|supplementary
9400 *adj*
avvincere compelling|fascinating
9405 *adj*
arsenico arsenic; arsenical
9410 *il; adj*
maltese Maltese
9411 *adj*
dentale dental
9413 *adj*
egizio Egyptian
9420 *adj*
obsoleto obsolete
9422 *adj*
tonico tonic; tonic
9424 *adj; il*
sostanziale substantial
9429 *adj*
desiderabile desirable
9441 *adj*
inconsapevole unaware|oblivious
9442 *adj*
diffidente suspicious|distrustful
9449 *adj*
innato innate|inborn
9450 *adj*
consecutivo consecutive|running
9454 *adj*
ambiguo ambiguous|devious
9455 *adj*
tiepido warm|lukewarm
9460 *adj*
ingannevole misleading|tricky
9464 *adj*
lugubre dismal|lugubrious
9486 *adj*
trionfante triumphant
9487 *adj*
pennuto fledged
9489 *adj*
afflitto sad
9490 *adj*
rinomato renowned
9493 *adj*
affabile affable|amiable
9500 *adj*
bellico war-; warlike
9506 *pfx; adj*
londinese Londoner; London's
9509 *il/la; adj*
sfrontato cheeky
9519 *adj*
luccicante shimmering
9521 *adj*
impuro impure
9522 *adj*
valente talented
9537 *adj*
competitivo competitive
9542 *adj*
innovativo innovative
9544 *adj*
alpino alpine
9550 *adj*
basco Basque; Basque
9551 *adj; il*
rettilineo straight; straight
9554 *adj; il*
subdolo sneaky; seismic
9556 *adj; adj*
perenne perennial|perpetual
9560 *adj*
contrastante conflicting
9561 *adj*
statico static
9562 *adj*
nascente rising
9564 *adj*
combattivo combative

9569 *adj*
crostaceo crustacean; shellfish

9571 *adj; il*
tessile textile

9579 *adj*
bavarese Bavarian; Bavarian

9584 *adj; il/la*
spensierato carefree|light-hearted

9608 *adj*
preferibile preferable

9611 *adj*
convenevole fitting

9612 *adj*
spassoso amusing|entertaining

9613 *adj*
disordinato messy|disorderly

9615 *adj*
lavorativo working

9622 *adj*
sottostante below; underlying

9624 *adv; adj*
quantico quantum

9628 *adj*
esteriore external|exterior

9634 *adj*
lineare linear|straightforward

9643 *adj*
centrifugo centrifugal

9644 *adj*
virale viral

9645 *adj*
eugenetico eugenic

9648 *adj*
loggia invulnerable

9656 *adj*
genuino genuine|authentic

9659 *adj*
esile slender|thin

9664 *adj*
negligente negligent|careless

9668 *adj*
represso repressed

9674 *adj*
gallese Welsh; Welsh

9678 *adj; il*
versato versed

9691 *adj*
promotore promoter; promotive

9693 *il; adj*
polemico polemical|controversial

9701 *adj*
desideroso eager|desirous

9707 *adj*
umanitario humanitarian

9716 *adj*
vulcanico volcanic

9718 *adj*
molesto troublesome

9727 *adj*
intenzionato intentional

9729 *adj*
astemio abstemious; teetotaler

9730 *adj; il*
appetitoso appetizing|palatable

9734 *adj*
tangente tangent; cut

9735 *la; adj*
termonucleare thermonuclear

9737 *adj*
condiscendente condescending

9738 *adj*
epilettico epileptic

9739 *adj*
diagnostico diagnostic

9744 *adj*
pettorale pectoral

9746 *adj*
classificato classified

9749 *adj*
lappone Lapp; Laplander

9755 *adj; il*
rurale rural

9756 *adj*
ignaro unaware

9759 *adj*
barbiturico barbiturate; barbituric

9762 *il; adj*
minerario mining

9764 *adj*
incendiario arsonist; incendiary

9765 *il; adj*
introvabile not to be found

9773 *adj*
incorreggibile incorrigible
9775 *adj*
integrante integral
9780 *adj*
illegittimo illegitimate
9781 *adj*
irrispettoso disrespectful
9792 *adj*
miope myopic; myope
9794 *adj; il/la*
mortorio funeral
9796 *adj*
turchino blue; deep blue
9797 *adj; il*
energico energetic
9799 *adj*
mondano worldly
9800 *adj*
antiquario antique dealer; antiquarian
9802 *il; adj*
demoniaco demoniac|fiendish
9803 *adj*
caritatevole charitable
9824 *adj*
irrequieto restless
9827 *adj*
orrido horrid|dreadful
9835 *adj*
infermo infirm
9849 *adj*
orbitale orbital
9850 *adj*
osseo bone|bony
9854 *adj*
pluviale pluvial; waterspout
9861 *adj; il*
galattico galactic
9865 *adj*
venereo venereal
9868 *adj*
respiratorio respiratory
9870 *adj*
gastrico gastric
9878 *adj*
briccone rascal; rascally; miscreant
9885 *il; adv; adj*
risentito resentful
9889 *adj*
scottante pressing
9892 *adj*
sordomuto deaf and dumb; deaf mute
9893 *adj; il*
eschimese Eskimo; Eskimo
9894 *adj; il/la*
inconfutabile irrefutable
9902 *adj*
sazio full|sated
9917 *adj*
accanito hard
9919 *adj*
ospitale hospitable
9926 *adj*
celibe single; bachelor
9930 *adj; lo*
precipitoso hasty|precipitous
9934 *adj*
involontario involuntary|unintentional
9939 *adj*
evolutivo evolutive
9947 *adj*
termale thermal
9949 *adj*
fausto auspicious|fortunate
9950 *adj*
lordo gross|filthy
9956 *adj*
germano German
9961 *adj*
ipotetico hypothetical|presumed
9969 *adj*
zotico boorish; churl
9971 *adj; lo*
bulgaro Bulgarian; Bulgarian
9975 *adj; il*
moralista moralist; moralistic
9976 *il/la; adj*
angolare angular
9977 *adj*
senile senile
9978 *adj*

fugace fleeting|fugacious
9979 *adj*
afrodisiaco aphrodisiac; aphrodisiac
9981 *adj; il*
elaborato elaborate; script
9986 *adj; il*
catastrofico catastrophic
9991 *adj*
dimensionale dimensional
9992 *adj*
periferico peripheral
9993 *adj*
scorbutico scorbutic
9996 *adj*
affezionato fond
9999 *adj*
mutevole changing|changeable
10008 *adj*
ultravioletto ultraviolet; ultraviolet
10017 *adj; il*
lampante glaring
10018 *adj*
radiofonico radio
10023 *adj*

Italian English Translation
Rank Part of Speech
mediante through
7503 *prp*
contrariamente contrary to; in spite of
7966 *adv; prp*
fuorché except
9788 *prp*

Italian *English Translation*
Rank *Part of Speech*
mediante *through*
7503 *prp*
contrariamente *contrary to; in spite of*
7966 *adv; prp*
fuorché *except*
9788 *prp*
Italian *English Translation*
Rank *Part of Speech*
mediante *through*
7503 *prp*
contrariamente *contrary to; in spite of*
7966 *adv; prp*
fuorché *except*
9788 *prp*

Adverbs

Italian Rank	English Translation Part of Speech
parzialmente 7573	partly *adv*
dapprima 7609	at first *adv*
bruscamente 7661	short|brusquely *adv*
espressamente 7686	expressly *adv*
fedelmente 7712	faithfully *adv*
psicologicamente 7724	psychologically *adv*
violentemente 7761	violently *adv*
ampiamente 7818	widely *adv*
ciononostante 7946	nevertheless; in spite of this *adv; phr*
infuori 7948	out *adv*
contrariamente 7966	contrary to; in spite of *adv; prp*
doppiamente 7977	doubly *adv*
idem 8085	idem; ditto; ideally *prn; il; adv*
preferibilmente 8153	preferably *adv*
brevemente 8268	briefly *adv*
simultaneamente 8377	concurrently *adv*
appieno 8388	fully *adv*
notevolmente 8509	considerably *adv*
per lo più 8514	mostly *adv*
eccessivamente 8546	excessively|over *adv*
propriamente 8705	properly *adv*
generosamente 8722	generously *adv*
tristemente 8742	sorrowfully *adv*
allegramente 8759	cheerfully *adv*
comunemente 8811	commonly *adv*
coraggiosamente 8828	courageously|gamely *adv*
prossimamente 8909	soon|in a short time *adv*
occasionalmente 8962	occasionally|by chance *adv*
oltremare 9012	overseas *adv*
discretamente 9035	discreetly *adv*
caldamente 9060	warmly *adv*
cordialmente 9080	cordially *adv*
comodamente 9203	comfortably|easily *adv*
abitualmente 9218	usually *adv*
esplicitamente 9242	roundly *adv*
istantaneamente 9285	instantly *adv*
saldamente 9335	securely|tight *adv*
eventualmente 9346	in case *adv*
perdutamente 9432	hopelessly *adv*
momentaneamente 9518	at the moment *adv*
eccezionalmente 9583	exceptionally *adv*
lealmente 9589	loyally *adv*
lungi 9595	far *adv*
sottostante 9624	below; underlying *adv; adj*

erroneamente wrongly
9688 *adv*
attivamente actively
9706 *adv*
lievemente slightly|lightly
9747 *adv*

Conjunctions

Italian		English Translation
Rank		Part of Speech
qualora		if
	8765	*con*
nientemeno		no less than
	9414	*con*

Prepositions

Italian	English Translation
Rank	Part of Speech
mediante	through
7503	*prp*
contrariamente	contrary to; in spite of
7966	*adv; prp*
fuorché	except
9788	*prp*

Pronouns

Italian		English Translation
Rank		Part of Speech
noialtri		we
	8002	*prn*
idem		idem; ditto; ideally
	8085	*prn; il; adv*

Nouns

Italian	English Translation	Rank	Part of Speech
galleggiante	floating; float	7502	*adj; il*
filiale	branch; filial	7504	*la; adj*
cattedra	chair	7505	*la*
conquista	conquest	7508	*la*
negoziato	negotiation	7509	*il*
nume	numen	7511	*il*
pellegrinaggio	pilgrimage	7514	*il*
residuo	residue; residual	7516	*il; adj*
questura	police force	7517	*la*
ammalato	sick; sick person	7518	*adj; il*
orsetto	bear cub	7519	*il*
brama	craving|desire	7520	*la*
vallata	valley	7521	*la*
ciliegia	cherry	7522	*la*
ultimatum	ultimatum	7525	*gli*
relitto	wreck|wreckage	7526	*il*
maternità	maternity|parenthood	7527	*la*
rettile	reptile	7529	*il*
sfidante	challenger; challenging	7531	*il/la; adj*
creta	clay	7532	*la*
ristrutturazione	renovation	7533	*la*
armeria	armory	7534	*la*
manipolazione	handling|falsification	7535	*la*
mandibola	jaw|mandible	7536	*la*
napalm	napalm	7537	*il*
petrolifero	oil well	7538	*lo*
strillo	scream|squeal	7542	*lo*
frastuono	uproar	7543	*il*
colon	colon	7545	*lo*
curiosità	curiosity	7546	*la*
amarezza	bitterness	7547	*le*
periscopio	periscope	7548	*il*
contatore	counter|meter	7551	*il*
infamia	infamy	7552	*le*
popolarità	popularity	7553	*la*
fagotto	bassoon	7554	*il*
impazienza	impatience	7556	*le*
infelicità	unhappiness	7557	*le*
attentato	attempt	7561	*il*
soma	pack|burden	7562	*la*
bravura	cleverness	7565	*la*
fornace	furnace	7567	*la*
pirateria	piracy	7569	*la*
abbonamento	subscription	7574	*il*
candelina	taper		

7577 *la*
rimprovero reproach|rebuke
7578 *il*
superstrada highway|freeway
7583 *la*
mansione job|duty
7584 *la*
egocentrico egocentric; egotist
7585 *adj; il*
carie caries
7587 *la*
interfono intercom
7588 *gli*
tibetano Tibetan; Tibetan
7589 *adj; il*
attracco docking|mooring
7590 *il*
islamico Islamic; Islam
7592 *adj; il*
fascio beam|bundle
7594 *il*
conquistatore conqueror
7596 *il*
iena hyena
7598 *la*
pentimento repentance
7599 *il*
colorito colorful; color
7600 *adj; il*
flagello scourge|plague
7601 *il*
ghiandola gland
7602 *la*
preventivo quote; preventive
7603 *il; adj*
imbarcazione boat
7604 *le*
toga toga|robe
7605 *la*
diplomazia diplomacy
7607 *la*
patologia pathology
7610 *la*
nutrice nurse
7612 *la*
lampadario chandelier
7613 *il*
tomo tome
7615 *il*
metamorfosi metamorphosis
7617 *la*
manichino dummy
7618 *il*
congelatore freezer
7619 *il*
macelleria butcher's shop
7621 *la*
acquirente buyer|shopper
7622 *il/la*
laghetto pond
7623 *il*
travaglio labor|suffering
7624 *il*
carnagione complexion
7626 *la*
riconciliazione reconciliation
7627 *la*
placca plate
7629 *la*
posacenere ashtray
7631 *i*
motociclista motorcyclist
7634 *il/la*
ascella armpit|lath
7635 *le*
esibizionista exhibitionist
7636 *il/la*
spaccatura split
7638 *la*
seduzione seduction|allurement
7639 *la*
maga sorceress
7640 *la*
occultamento concealment|occultation
7641 *il*
variazione variation|change
7642 *la*
adunata gathering|muster
7643 *la*
brevetto patent
7645 *il*
statuetta statuette

7646 *la*
indomani next day
7647 *il*
reclusione imprisonment
7649 *la*
pavone peacock
7652 *il*
mandorla almond
7653 *la*
ricettatore fence
7654 *il*
funzionamento operation|working
7657 *il*
impiccio mess|hindrance
7658 *il*
segheria sawmill
7659 *la*
lanciatore thrower
7662 *il*
termometro thermometer
7667 *il*
algebra algebra
7668 *la*
bungalow bungalow
7669 *i*
zarina tsarina
7670 *la*
confessore confessor
7676 *il*
sostentamento sustenance|maintenance
7677 *il*
napoletano Neapolitan; Neapolitan
7678 *adj; il*
fornaio baker
7680 *il*
microbo microbe
7682 *il*
inquisizione inquisition
7683 *la*
muratore bricklayer
7684 *il*
persico perch
7685 *il*
tirocinio training
7687 *il*
bambinaia nanny
7688 *la*
virilità manhood|virility
7689 *la*
poltiglia mush
7690 *la*
bazooka bazooka
7691 *la*
arbitrio will
7694 *il*
bulldog bulldog
7697 *il*
beige beige
7699 *il*
conversione conversion
7700 *la*
santino holy picture
7701 *il*
jogging jogging
7703 *lo*
palestinese Palestinian; Palestinian
7704 *adj; il/la*
capote hood
7706 *la*
ottimismo optimism
7707 *lo*
cosacco Cossack
7708 *il*
carezza caress
7709 *la*
portacenere ashtray
7710 *il*
collocamento placement|placing
7715 *il*
avvento coming
7716 *il*
accompagnatrice chaperone
7717 *le*
bozza draft
7719 *la*
atrocità atrocity
7722 *le*
escursione excursion|hike
7723 *le*
ripercussione repercussion
7725 *la*
incoronazione coronation

7727 *le*
editoriale editorial; leader
7729 *adj; lo*
passivo passive; liabilities
7730 *adj; il*
pioniere pioneer
7732 *il*
bulldozer bulldozer
7734 *i*
archeologia archeology
7735 *le*
duo duo
7736 *il*
missionario missionary; missionary
7739 *adj; il*
cicca chewing gum
7740 *la*
sapientone wise guy|know-all
7742 *il*
ottuso obtuse; dolt
7743 *adj; il*
raffreddamento cooling
7745 *il*
tifone typhoon
7746 *il*
burattino puppet
7748 *il*
summit summit
7750 *il*
corridore runner
7751 *il*
combustione combustion
7752 *la*
rena sand
7754 *la*
inondazione flood|flooding
7755 *le*
involtino roulade
7757 *il*
autoradio car radio
7758 *le*
negoziatore negotiator
7759 *il*
confessionale confessional; confessional
7760 *adj; il*
seduttore seducer
7762 *il*
gestore manager
7763 *il*
consulto consultation
7764 *il*
mortaio mortar
7765 *il*
salvagente life buoy|life jacket
7766 *il*
scrigno casket
7767 *lo*
scontento discontent; displeased
7768 *lo; adj*
idealista idealist
7769 *il/la*
eventualità eventuality|possibility
7770 *le*
prole offspring|children
7774 *la*
catechismo catechism
7775 *il*
schiappa duffer
7776 *la*
infermità infirmity
7777 *le*
creditore creditor
7778 *il*
metabolismo metabolism
7780 *il*
chiatta barge
7782 *la*
vegetazione vegetation
7783 *la*
zimbello laughing stock
7784 *lo*
fiaba fairy tale
7785 *la*
stesura drawing up
7786 *la*
zeppelin zeppelin
7787 *lo*
groppa back
7788 *la*
fusto stem|drum
7789 *il*
pagnotta loaf

7790 *la*
rendita income

7796 *la*
minatore miner

7797 *il*
azoto nitrogen

7798 *il*
opossum opossum

7799 *gli*
appendicite appendicitis

7802 *la*
invadente intrusive; intruder

7803 *adj; il/la*
oasi oasis

7804 *le*
trazione traction|drive

7806 *la*
incompetenza incompetence

7812 *le*
gommone rubber dinghy

7814 *il*
grafica graphics

7815 *la*
ecografia echography

7816 *le*
analfabeta illiterate

7817 *il/la*
patrizio patrician; patrician

7819 *adj; il*
ambulatorio surgery; ambulatory

7820 *il; adj*
sacrilegio sacrilege

7821 *il*
sapienza wisdom

7822 *la*
bolscevico Bolshevik; Bolshevik

7823 *adj; il*
prefettura prefecture

7824 *la*
impeto impetus|fit

7825 *il*
sostituzione replacement

7827 *la*
peseta peseta

7830 *la*
bemolle flat

7831 *lo*
intrigo intrigue

7832 *il*
epica epic

7835 *le*
cartellone poster|program

7836 *il*
bernoccolo bump

7838 *il*
visone mink

7839 *il*
malocchio evil eye

7840 *il*
tendone marquee

7841 *il*
uguaglianza equality

7842 *la*
alleato ally; allied

7843 *il; adj*
persuasione persuasion

7845 *la*
falco hawk

7846 *il*
bava slime

7847 *la*
proroga extension

7850 *la*
squaw squaw

7852 *le*
sgabuzzino storage room

7853 *lo*
preferenza preference

7854 *la*
destriero steed

7855 *il*
lasso period; weary

7857 *il; adj*
teiera teapot

7858 *la*
passante passing; passer-by

7859 *adj; il/la*
esagerazione exaggeration|aggrandizement

7860 *le*
distorsione distortion

7861 *la*
pedone pedestrian|pawn

7863 *il*
guantone mitt
7865 *il*
calciatore soccer player
7866 *il*
megafono megaphone
7867 *il*
ventuno pontoon
7868 *i*
implicazione implication
7869 *le*
epilessia epilepsy
7872 *la*
riassunto summary|brief
7873 *il*
adolescenza adolescence
7874 *le*
carboidrato carbohydrate
7875 *il*
natica buttock
7876 *la*
tabulato printout
7877 *il*
ideologia ideology
7878 *la*
ostia host
7880 *la*
protestante Protestant; Protestant
7884 *adj; il/la*
divergenza divergence|difference
7887 *la*
manodopera labor|manpower
7889 *la*
sesamo sesame
7892 *il*
vertice summit|vertex
7893 *il*
maiuscola capital
7896 *la*
geometria geometry
7900 *la*
bivio fork
7901 *il*
biberon bottle
7902 *il*
lozione lotion
7903 *la*
garzone boy
7904 *il*
saga saga
7905 *la*
indice index|rate
7907 *i*
palombaro diver
7908 *il*
moribondo dying; dying man
7911 *adj; il*
patibolo scaffold
7912 *il*
carburatore carburetor|carburetter
7913 *il*
belga Belgian; Belgian
7916 *adj; il/la*
caparra deposit
7920 *la*
parentela relationship|kinship
7921 *la*
planetario planetary; planetarium
7922 *adj; il*
docente professor
7923 *il/la*
digestione digestion
7924 *la*
mangime fodder
7925 *il*
cortigiano courtier
7927 *il*
aborigeno aboriginal; aborigine
7928 *adj; il*
coalizione coalition|bloc
7929 *la*
fauna fauna
7930 *la*
stridio screech
7931 *lo*
geroglifico hieroglyph; hieroglyphic
7933 *il; adj*
edile building; aedile
7935 *adj; il*
supremazia supremacy
7936 *la*
scatolone carton

7939 *lo*
bombola cylinder

7940 *la*
accelerazione acceleration

7941 *la*
trasportatore conveyor|carrier

7942 *il*
chimera chimera

7943 *la*
purificazione purification|purifying

7945 *la*
balsamo balm|conditioner

7947 *il*
matricola freshman|number

7949 *la*
bestemmia blasphemy|curse

7950 *la*
mediatore mediator|broker

7951 *il*
banchina quay|wharf

7952 *la*
siepe hedge

7955 *la*
ricatto blackmail

7959 *il*
fondale backdrop|depth

7963 *il*
ballata ballad

7964 *la*
goffo clumsy; hobbledehoy

7968 *adj; il*
sintesi synthesis

7971 *la*
persecuzione persecution

7972 *la*
indole nature

7973 *il*
grammatica grammar

7976 *la*
amazzone horsewoman

7979 *la*
turbante turban

7980 *il*
secchione nerd

7981 *il*
passe-partout skeleton key

7982 *il*
ripieno filling; stuffed

7984 *il; adj*
guardone Peeping Tom

7986 *il*
ripetizione repetition|private lesson

7988 *la*
Mongolia Mongolia

7989 *la*
guaritore healer

7992 *il*
epatite hepatitis

7993 *le*
commodoro commodore

7995 *il*
trascrizione transcription

7996 *la*
estremista extremist

7997 *il/la*
influenza influence|influenza

7998 *la*
mammut mammoth

7999 *i*
soccorritore rescuer

8000 *il*
conservatore conservator; Tory

8001 *il; adj*
platea audience

8004 *la*
procione raccoon|procyon

8006 *il*
orchidea orchid

8008 *la*
internato internee

8009 *il*
mercantile merchant; merchantman

8011 *adj; il*
apprezzamento appreciation

8012 *lo*
maltempo bad weather

8013 *il*
icona icon

8014 *la*
spunto cue

8016 *lo*
ateo atheist; atheistic

8017 *il; adj*
nostromo boatswain
8018 *il*
iato hiatus
8021 *lo*
ingranaggio gear|cog
8022 *il*
apostolo apostle
8023 *il*
cocca nock
8025 *la*
fruscio rustling|swish
8026 *il*
sbruffone boaster
8027 *lo*
telaio frame|loom
8030 *il*
termite termite
8031 *la*
svitato nutty; screwball
8033 *adj; lo*
spessore thickness
8034 *lo*
autocontrollo restraint
8035 *il*
deficit deficit|deficiency
8037 *il*
olfatto smell
8038 *il*
capitalista capitalist
8040 *il/la*
avvistamento sighting
8042 *il*
infortunio accident
8043 *il*
metropoli metropolis
8045 *le*
bobina coil|reel
8046 *la*
reperto find
8047 *il*
attributo attribute
8048 *gli*
autonomia autonomy
8049 *la*
ducato duchy|ducat
8050 *il*
libellula dragonfly
8051 *la*
orca grampus
8054 *la*
criceto hamster
8055 *il*
ascensione ascension|mounting
8057 *la*
memoriale memorial
8060 *il*
sorellastra stepsister
8061 *la*
civilizzazione civilization
8062 *la*
scapolare scapulary
8064 *lo*
contagio contagion
8065 *il*
comfort comfort
8066 *il*
parodia parody|send-up
8067 *la*
piedistallo pedestal
8068 *il*
calzamaglia tights
8070 *la*
esiliato exile
8071 *il*
ippopotamo hippopotamus
8072 *il*
grammofono gramophone
8073 *il*
trasfusione transfusion
8074 *la*
lega alloy
8076 *la*
poligono polygon
8077 *il*
pasticcino pastry
8078 *il*
sdraio deckchair
8083 *le*
siccità drought
8084 *la*
idem idem; ditto; ideally

8085 *prn; il; adv*
ritaglio cut-out|clipping
8090 *il*
silenziatore silencer
8091 *il*
pulcino chick
8092 *il*
tempia temple
8093 *la*
penicillina penicillin
8094 *la*
germoglio bud|sprout
8096 *il*
leccapiedi toady|flunky
8097 *il/la*
sinonimo synonymous; synonym
8098 *adj; il*
remata row
8099 *la*
negazione denial
8101 *la*
virtuoso virtuous; virtuoso
8102 *adj; il*
rimedio remedy|help
8103 *il*
perseveranza perseverance
8104 *la*
bruciatura burn|scorch
8105 *la*
pressa press
8106 *la*
emittente issuer; issuing
8107 *la; adj*
malfunzionamento malfunction
8112 *il*
scolo drain
8114 *lo*
pesticida pesticide
8116 *il*
bandierina pennant
8118 *la*
stormo flock
8120 *lo*
larva larva
8121 *la*
contrabbandiere smuggler

8122 *il*
nervosismo nervousness|jitters
8123 *il*
tovaglia cloth
8124 *la*
barricata barricade
8125 *la*
strofa stanza
8127 *la*
targhetta plate
8128 *la*
scultore sculptor
8129 *lo*
fifa funk
8130 *la*
flashback flashback
8131 *i*
derivato derivative; offshoot
8132 *adj; il*
lavorazione processing
8133 *la*
infinità infinity
8134 *le*
lavata wash
8137 *la*
scarto waste
8138 *lo*
cucchiaino teaspoon
8139 *il*
sudiciume dirt|filth
8140 *la*
canzoncina ditty
8141 *la*
ingorgo jam
8142 *il*
nord-est northeast
8143 *il*
tribordo starboard
8144 *il*
estradizione extradition
8145 *le*
sassofono saxophone
8146 *il*
catrame tar
8148 *il*
fava bean

8149 *la*
citofono intercom
8150 *il*
merlo blackbird|merlon
8154 *il*
radiografia radiography|radiograph
8155 *la*
suonatore player
8157 *il*
lebbroso leper; leprous
8158 *il; adj*
euforia euphoria
8163 *le*
neutrone neutron
8165 *il*
tampone buffer|pad
8166 *il*
amianto asbestos
8167 *il*
empatia empathy
8168 *le*
diacono deacon
8169 *il*
rallentatore slow motion
8172 *il*
trivella auger
8173 *la*
condizionatore conditioner
8175 *il*
tossina toxin
8176 *la*
chemioterapia chemotherapy
8177 *la*
surrogato surrogate; ersatz
8178 *il; adj*
sfratto evicted
8179 *lo*
lucidità lucidity
8181 *la*
spargimento scatter
8182 *lo*
bracciale bracelet
8184 *il*
evenienza eventuality
8185 *la*
samaritano Samaritan

8186 *il*
quartetto quartet
8188 *il*
elogio praise
8189 *il*
altruista selfless; altruist
8191 *adj; il/la*
adorazione adoration|adorability
8192 *le*
morbillo measles
8194 *il*
fiorellino floret
8195 *il*
cero candle
8197 *il*
austriaco Austrian; Austrian
8198 *adj; il*
fotogramma still
8200 *il*
teologia theology
8201 *la*
tranello trap|game
8204 *il*
manto mantle
8205 *il*
compimento fulfillment|completion
8206 *il*
duetto duet
8207 *il*
manna manna
8213 *la*
diagramma diagram
8214 *il*
carillon carillon
8216 *il*
ritornello refrain
8217 *il*
lanciafiamme flame thrower
8218 *il*
indennità bonus
8221 *le*
organizzatore organizer; organizing
8226 *gli; adj*
brace embers
8227 *la*
assunto recruit

8228 *il*
miscuglio mixture|blend
8230 *il*
orologeria watchmaking
8232 *le*
chierichetto server
8233 *il*
altea marsh-mallow
8234 *la*
tanica tank
8235 *la*
proletariato proletariat
8236 *il*
fionda sling
8237 *la*
soldatino toy soldier
8238 *il*
sciacquone flushing device
8239 *lo*
cottura burning
8240 *la*
pestilenza pestilence
8242 *la*
svendita sale
8243 *la*
portoricano Puerto Rican; Puerto Rican
8244 *adj; il*
lingotto ingot
8245 *il*
zeta zed|zeta
8246 *la*
emiro emir
8249 *il*
diaframma diaphragm|baffle
8251 *il*
dormiglione sleepyhead
8252 *il*
supernova supernova
8253 *la*
ipermercato hypermarket
8254 *il*
rivoltella revolver
8255 *la*
elettrone electron
8256 *il*
traffico traffic
8258 *il*
renna reindeer
8262 *la*
ciocca lock
8263 *la*
pesco peach
8264 *il*
indulgenza indulgence|pardon
8265 *le*
davanzale sill
8267 *il*
brevemente briefly
8268 *adv*
autrice authoress
8270 *le*
birbante rascal
8275 *il*
bettola tavern
8276 *la*
scocciatura nuisance
8279 *la*
paletta scoop
8280 *la*
aspirazione suction|aspiration
8284 *le*
iarda yard
8285 *la*
lattaio milkman
8286 *il*
indumento garment
8287 *il*
ovile fold|pen
8288 *il*
baratto barter
8289 *il*
vettore vector
8292 *il*
juke-box jukebox
8293 *il*
distruttore destroyer
8294 *il*
cornicione cornice|eaves
8295 *il*
genesi genesis
8297 *la*
piastra plate

8298 *la*
racchetta racket
8299 *la*
improvvisazione improvisation|ad-lib
8300 *la*
stampato printed; printout
8301 *adj; lo*
papera gosling
8302 *la*
speculazione speculation|flutter
8305 *la*
annegamento drowning
8307 *il*
colpetto tap|flick
8308 *il*
baratro chasm
8309 *il*
avaro stingy; miser
8311 *adj; il*
unanimità unanimity
8312 *la*
fobia phobia
8313 *la*
garbo politeness
8318 *il*
megera shrew|harridan
8319 *la*
gioielliere jeweler
8322 *il*
sottomissione submission|subjection
8323 *la*
diffamazione defamation|libel
8324 *la*
linfa sap
8325 *la*
bossolo box
8326 *il*
stampella crutch
8327 *la*
latitudine latitude
8328 *la*
destinatario recipient|addressee
8330 *il*
birichino mischievous; cheeky youngster
8331 *adj; il*
scalpore sensation
8333 *lo*
coreografia choreography
8335 *la*
calunnia slander|libel
8337 *la*
giurisprudenza law
8339 *la*
sofà sofa
8340 *il*
diadema diadem
8341 *il*
marmaglia rabble|riffraff
8342 *la*
appropriazione appropriation
8343 *le*
figurina figurine
8344 *la*
sfumatura shade|nuance
8347 *la*
insubordinazione insubordination
8349 *la*
telepatia telepathy
8350 *la*
ciuffo tuft
8353 *il*
insetticida insecticide
8354 *lo*
potenzialità potentiality
8357 *le*
fornello stove
8359 *il*
calamaro squid
8361 *il*
versante side|slopes
8362 *il*
criterio criterion|principle
8363 *il*
scià shah
8365 *lo*
versetto verse
8366 *il*
bravata stunt
8367 *la*
secondino jailer|warder
8368 *il*

seggiolino seat
8369 *il*
inguine groin
8371 *il*
capannone shed
8372 *il*
crematorio crematory
8374 *il*
crema cream
8375 *la*
poppa stern
8376 *la*
contaminazione contamination
8378 *la*
dirottamento hijacking|diversion
8380 *il*
manufatto artefact; manufactured
8381 *il; adj*
proclama proclamation
8385 *lo*
strozzino usurer
8389 *lo*
intoccabile untouchable; untouchable
8391 *adj; il/la*
pensionamento retirement
8397 *il*
brocca pitcher
8398 *la*
cambiale draft|bill
8399 *la*
gruzzolo hoard
8400 *il*
valchiria Valkyrie
8402 *la*
realismo realism
8406 *il*
spilorcio stingy; miser
8407 *adj; lo*
masso boulder
8408 *il*
crocifissione crucifixion
8409 *la*
podio podium|platform
8410 *il*
smorfia grimace
8411 *la*
tacca notch|dent
8413 *la*
cavallino pony; horsy
8414 *il; adj*
importazione import
8415 *le*
duomo cathedral
8416 *il*
fondina holster
8417 *la*
infedeltà infidelity|disloyalty
8418 *le*
cecità blindness
8420 *la*
carrozzina pram
8421 *la*
potassio potassium
8423 *il*
carriola wheelbarrow
8425 *la*
visconte viscount
8427 *il*
lampione lamp
8432 *il*
incrociatore cruiser
8433 *il*
cappellaio hatter
8434 *il*
pomata ointment|pomade
8436 *la*
rappresentanza representation
8437 *la*
pancreas pancreas
8438 *lo*
diabetico diabetic; diabetic
8439 *adj; il*
pitone python
8441 *il*
agrimensore surveyor
8443 *il*
falce sickle
8444 *la*
sollevato relieved
8445 *i*
congelamento freezing|frostbite
8446 *il*

discriminazione discrimination
8448 *la*
omero humerus
8450 *il*
gerarchia hierarchy
8451 *la*
beatitudine bliss
8453 *la*
spastico spastic; spastic
8454 *adj; lo*
gladiatore gladiator
8456 *il*
detersivo detergent; detergent
8457 *adj; il*
statuto statute
8458 *lo*
cicerone guide
8459 *il*
casata house
8460 *la*
identikit identikit
8461 *gli*
detector detector
8462 *il*
scroto scrotum
8464 *lo*
fiduciario trustee; fiduciary
8465 *il; adj*
feudo feud|fief
8467 *il*
sottosegretario undersecretary
8468 *il*
plurale plural; plural
8469 *adj; il*
confederazione confederation|union
8470 *la*
zelo zeal|zealousness
8472 *lo*
protesto protest
8475 *il*
carnefice executioner
8476 *il*
trombone trombone
8477 *il*
calcolatore computer; calculating
8478 *il; adj*
pulsazione pulsation|throbbing
8479 *la*
predecessore predecessor
8483 *il*
tropico tropic
8484 *il*
babbuino baboon
8485 *il*
oste host|publican
8486 *il*
grandine hailstorm
8488 *la*
tonalità tonality|tone
8489 *le*
rigenerazione regeneration
8490 *la*
dotto learned; scholar
8492 *adj; il*
sassone Saxon; Saxon
8495 *adj; il*
sepolcro tomb|sepulcher
8496 *il*
effettivo actual; strength
8497 *adj; il*
fortino blockhouse
8499 *il*
straccione ragamuffin
8500 *lo*
bambinone baby
8502 *il*
fantoccio puppet
8503 *il*
nettare nectar; clean
8504 *il; vb*
cipria powder
8505 *la*
batosta blow
8507 *la*
monarchia monarchy
8508 *la*
archeologo archaeologist
8512 *il*
controspionaggio counterintelligence
8513 *il*
parità equality|parity
8515 *la*

nutrimento nourishment|food
8518 *il*
formicaio anthill
8519 *il*
zenzero ginger
8520 *lo*
appendice appendix
8521 *la*
buffonata farce|tomfoolery
8522 *la*
lebbra leprosy
8523 *la*
insufficienza insufficiency|lack
8526 *la*
antifurto antitheft; antitheft
8527 *adj; gli*
assessore assessor
8528 *gli*
quoziente quotient
8529 *il*
barboncino poodle
8530 *il*
interazione interaction
8532 *la*
freccetta dart
8535 *la*
ginnasta gymnast
8537 *il/la*
biopsia biopsy
8541 *la*
opuscolo brochure
8542 *il*
autobiografia autobiography
8543 *le*
centralinista operator
8544 *il/la*
titano titan
8545 *il*
restituzione return|rebate
8548 *la*
alcolismo alcoholism
8549 *il*
avanzamento progress|promotion
8551 *il*
tonsilla tonsil
8552 *la*
ruffiano pander
8554 *il*
interrogativo questioning; interrogative
8555 *il; adj*
perlustrazione patrol
8556 *la*
stanzetta room
8557 *la*
aia farmyard
8559 *le*
ingrandimento magnification
8560 *il*
recapito delivery
8561 *il*
clamore clamor|outcry
8563 *il*
scarpone boot
8564 *lo*
tunica tunic
8567 *la*
guardiamarina midshipman
8570 *il*
compresso bowsprit
8571 *lo*
boccale mug
8572 *il*
castità chastity
8573 *la*
ghianda acorn
8574 *la*
rondine swallow
8575 *la*
contrazione contraction
8577 *la*
serrata lockout
8579 *la*
fusibile fuse; fusible
8580 *il; adj*
nitrato nitrate
8581 *il*
fabbricante manufacturer
8582 *il/la*
tallone heel
8583 *il*
acrobazia stunt
8584 *le*

porcospino porcupine|urchin
8585 *il*
portamento bearing|deportment
8587 *il*
malto propulsion
8588 *il*
rocca fortress
8591 *la*
soggezione awe
8592 *la*
sodio sodium
8593 *il*
tossicodipendente addict
8595 *il/la*
fazione faction
8596 *la*
treccia braid|pigtail
8598 *la*
califfo caliph
8599 *il*
moltitudine multitude|crowd
8600 *la*
impasto dough
8601 *lo*
piedino toothsie
8603 *il*
paletto stake|pole
8606 *il*
retroguardia rearguard
8608 *la*
callo callus
8610 *il*
aviatore aviator
8611 *il*
parabola parabola
8613 *la*
serietà seriousness|reliability
8615 *la*
lineamento feature|outline
8616 *il*
progenie progeny
8617 *la*
complessità complexity
8618 *la*
cherosene kerosene
8619 *il*
sciagura disaster
8620 *la*
tramonto sunset|setting
8623 *il*
letargo hibernation
8624 *il*
stellina starlet
8625 *la*
calmante calming; sedative
8628 *adj; il*
cilecca misfire
8631 *la*
scoria slag|waste
8632 *la*
recipiente container
8634 *il*
raffineria refinery
8636 *la*
liquirizia licorice
8640 *la*
oroscopo horoscope
8641 *il*
lusinga flattery
8642 *la*
traversata crossing
8644 *la*
saponetta soap
8645 *la*
mastino mastiff
8646 *il*
seggio seat
8647 *il*
nafta naphtha
8648 *la*
bengala Bengal light
8651 *il*
orzo barley
8654 *il*
rimanente remaining; leftovers
8656 *adj; il*
falcone falcon
8657 *il*
acquisizione acquisition
8658 *la*
fermezza firmness
8659 *la*

mannaia cleaver|ax
8660 *la*
magnesio magnesium
8662 *il*
underground underground
8663 *il*
figlioccio godson
8664 *il*
caramello caramel
8670 *il*
mousse mousse
8671 *la*
densità density|thickness
8672 *la*
sutura suture
8674 *la*
scricchiolio crunch|creaking
8675 *lo*
carreggiata track
8676 *la*
clitoride clitoris
8677 *la*
bustina sachet
8678 *la*
artefatto artifact; artificial
8679 *il; adj*
localizzazione location
8681 *la*
recupero recovery
8683 *il*
cinismo cynicism
8684 *il*
barlume glimmer|flicker
8689 *il*
sorgente source; rising
8692 *la; adj*
anticamera anteroom
8693 *le*
piovra octopus
8694 *la*
tappezzeria upholstery
8695 *la*
annientamento annihilation
8697 *il*
successone wow
8698 *il*
plancia bridge
8699 *la*
penisola peninsula
8700 *la*
lucciola firefly
8701 *la*
salina saltern
8704 *la*
cuccetta bunk|couchette
8706 *la*
idrante hydrant
8707 *il*
larghezza width|span
8708 *la*
ariano Aryan; Aryan
8710 *adj; il*
arringa harangue
8712 *le*
spezzatino stew
8715 *lo*
andamento trend|progress
8716 *il*
zerbino mat
8717 *lo*
peschereccio fishing; fishing boat
8719 *adj; il*
dispaccio dispatch
8720 *il*
rinnovo renewal
8721 *il*
limitazione limitation|restraint
8724 *la*
vicario vicar; vicarious
8726 *il; adj*
rialzo rise
8727 *il*
retaggio heritage|survival
8729 *il*
teorico theoretical; theorist
8731 *adj; il*
pozzanghera puddle
8732 *la*
auricolare earphone; auricular
8733 *il; adj*
chalet chalet
8739 *lo*

rivestimento coating|jacket
8743 *il*
elettrodomestico household appliance
8745 *il*
rutto burp|retch
8746 *il*
cerchia circle|ring
8751 *la*
suicida suicide; suicidal
8752 *la; adj*
caricamento loading
8753 *il*
clero clergy
8754 *il*
diocesi diocese|see
8755 *la*
malessere malaise|illness
8756 *il*
oscenità obscenity|filthiness
8757 *le*
sonnambulo sleepwalker
8758 *il*
esultanza exultation
8760 *la*
corporatura build
8767 *la*
giornaliero daily; day-to-day
8768 *adj; il*
allineamento alignment
8769 *lo*
attitudine attitude
8770 *le*
pancione paunch
8772 *il*
subbuglio confusion
8773 *il*
cliché cliche
8774 *i*
destrezza dexterity
8776 *la*
gemma gem|bud
8778 *la*
urna urn
8779 *le*
avversità adversity|ill
8780 *le*
figuraccia poor figure
8781 *le*
insistenza insistence
8782 *la*
botanico botanist; botanic
8783 *il; adj*
tettuccio canopy
8784 *il*
beduino Bedouin; Bedouin
8785 *adj; il*
dissenso dissent|disagreement
8786 *il*
altruismo altruism
8788 *il*
siamese Siamese; Siamese
8789 *adj; il/la*
astrologia astrology
8790 *la*
spiedo spit
8792 *lo*
latitante absconding; abscond
8793 *adj; il*
poppante suckling
8794 *il/la*
letizia joy
8795 *la*
favoreggiamento abetment
8796 *il*
radioattività radioactivity
8797 *la*
fuggiasco fugitive|escapee
8798 *il*
dentino denticle
8800 *il*
ghiacciaio glacier
8803 *il*
gesuita Jesuit
8805 *il*
pungente pungent; nippy
8806 *adj; il*
aneurisma aneurysm
8813 *il*
establishment establishment
8815 *gli*
stilista stylist
8818 *il/la*

protone proton
8819 *il*
motorizzazione motorization
8821 *la*
nazionalità nationality
8823 *la*
cavalluccio hobbyhorse
8827 *il*
sorcio mouse
8829 *il*
fasciatura bandage|dressing
8830 *la*
rastrello rake
8831 *il*
sanatorio sanatorium
8832 *il*
dolciume sweets; sweet
8833 *il; adj*
versamento payment
8834 *il*
bidello janitor
8835 *il*
naufragio shipwreck|sinking
8837 *il*
fuliggine soot
8838 *la*
insinuazione insinuation|implication
8839 *le*
conservatorio conservatory; conservative
8840 *il; adj*
galantuomo gentleman
8842 *il*
nocca knuckle
8843 *la*
deduzione deduction
8844 *la*
affitto rent
8845 *i*
infrastruttura infrastructure
8846 *le*
zavorra ballast
8855 *la*
cloro chlorine
8856 *il*
pastello pastel; pastel
8857 *adj; il*
coltellata stab
8858 *la*
cognizione cognition|acquaintance
8859 *la*
attaccabrighe wrangler
8860 *gli*
astronomia astronomy
8861 *le*
tassametro taximeter|meter
8864 *il*
mormorio murmur|hum
8865 *il*
truffa fraud|swindle
8866 *la*
devastazione devastation
8867 *la*
concilio council
8868 *il*
bollitore kettle|heater
8869 *il*
sciame swarm
8870 *lo*
oppresso oppressed
8873 *il*
calabrone hornet
8874 *il*
gettone token
8876 *il*
macedonia fruit salad
8877 *la*
borghesia bourgeoisie
8881 *la*
croissant croissant
8882 *i*
impotenza impotence|impuissance
8886 *le*
limbo limbo
8888 *il*
gnomo gnome|elf
8890 *lo*
ceretta waxing
8892 *la*
stampante printer
8893 *la*
diversità diversity
8894 *le*

pubertà puberty
8895 *la*
garofano carnation
8899 *il*
gazzetta gazette
8900 *la*
indugio delay
8902 *il*
paesano villager; village
8903 *il; adj*
desolazione desolation
8907 *la*
anguria watermelon
8908 *la*
carceriere jailer|warder
8910 *il*
dirupo cliff
8912 *il*
calamità calamity|misfortune
8914 *le*
attaccamento attachment|adhesion
8915 *il*
donzella damsel
8916 *la*
fibbia buckle
8917 *la*
progettazione design
8919 *la*
mortalità mortality
8920 *la*
mutilazione mutilation
8921 *la*
cloche joystick
8924 *la*
vaiolo smallpox
8925 *il*
avocado avocado
8926 *gli*
saccheggio plunder|sack
8928 *il*
modellino model
8929 *il*
regolatore regulator
8931 *il*
cinquantina about fifty
8933 *la*
completamento completion
8934 *il*
fuga escape|get-away
8938 *la*
sussurro whisper|murmur
8941 *il*
scansafatiche loafer|shirker
8943 *il/la*
tulipano tulip
8944 *il*
mascherina radiator grill
8945 *la*
premier premier
8947 *il*
buccia peel|husk
8949 *la*
indigestione indigestion
8950 *la*
fagiano pheasant
8951 *il*
pedaggio toll
8953 *il*
albino albino
8954 *il*
rimando return
8955 *il*
amplificatore amplifier
8959 *il*
carisma charisma
8961 *il*
masochista masochist
8966 *il/la*
ghiacciolo icicle
8971 *il*
variante variant
8972 *la*
femminista feminist
8973 *il/la*
assalitore assailant
8974 *il*
strangolamento strangling
8976 *lo*
consistenza consistency|texture
8977 *la*
sovranità sovereignty
8978 *la*

barchetta small boat
8979 *la*
convalescenza convalescence
8980 *la*
fandonia humbug
8981 *la*
aristocratico aristocratic; aristocrat
8985 *adj; il*
sartoria tailoring
8986 *la*
violinista violinist
8988 *il/la*
tricheco walrus
8989 *il*
codardia cowardice
8990 *la*
staffetta relay
8992 *la*
proibizionismo prohibition
8994 *il*
dirigibile airship; dirigible
8997 *il; adj*
sottoveste petticoat
8998 *la*
cromo chrome
9000 *il*
premonizione premonition
9002 *la*
scenografo set designer
9003 *lo*
torso torso
9009 *il*
cagnetto doggy
9014 *il*
pedina pawn|piece
9017 *la*
stucco stucco
9018 *lo*
berlina sedan|limousine
9019 *la*
beneficiario beneficiary
9021 *il*
focaccia cake
9023 *la*
rupe cliff
9024 *la*
vaglio screen
9025 *il*
corsetto corset
9027 *il*
spumante sparkling; sparkling wine
9030 *adj; lo*
fotocopia photocopy
9031 *la*
uscio door
9034 *il*
rappresaglia retaliation
9036 *la*
presidio garrison|defense
9038 *il*
bagnino lifeguard
9040 *il*
araldo herald
9044 *il*
correttezza correctness
9045 *la*
fertilità fertility
9047 *la*
artefice maker
9048 *il*
mascherata masquerade
9050 *la*
convivenza cohabitation
9051 *la*
trampolino trampoline
9053 *il*
galeotto convict
9055 *il*
ghiaia gravel
9056 *la*
giogo yoke
9059 *il*
consorzio consortium
9061 *il*
innesco trigger
9062 *il*
steward steward
9063 *gli*
accumulo backlog
9066 *il*
molestatore molester; molesting
9067 *il; adj*

programmatore programmer
9068 *il*
lare lares
9069 *il*
input input; input
9070 *gli; vb*
bisnonna great grandmother
9071 *la*
mercanzia merchandise
9072 *la*
corallo coral
9073 *il*
aringa herring
9076 *la*
ascendente ascending; influence
9077 *adj; il/la*
dopobarba aftershave; aftershave
9078 *adj; il*
avarizia avarice
9079 *la*
ventriloquo ventriloquist
9081 *il*
caffettiera coffeepot
9082 *la*
arpa harp
9083 *la*
fante knave|infantryman
9084 *il*
volgarità vulgarity|gaudiness
9085 *la*
bretella suspender|strap
9086 *la*
corteggiamento courtship|lovemaking
9087 *il*
insicurezza insecurity
9090 *la*
incesto incest
9091 *il*
puntualità punctuality
9093 *la*
borraccia water bottle
9094 *la*
violino violin|fiddlefamiliare
9095 *il*
timpano tympanum|eardrum
9096 *il*

pipa pipe
9100 *la*
usciere usher
9101 *il*
provento income
9102 *il*
comicità comicality
9103 *la*
attesa waiting|expectation
9104 *la*
pensatore thinker
9105 *il*
starnuto sneeze
9107 *lo*
legalità legality
9108 *la*
anarchico anarchist; anarchic
9109 *il; adj*
torchio press
9110 *il*
clip clip
9111 *le*
lavapiatti dishwasher
9113 *il/la*
cinguettio chirping|twittering
9115 *il*
malumore bad mood
9117 *il*
rompicapo puzzle
9118 *il*
trattoria tavern
9121 *la*
arrampicata climbing|scramble
9122 *le*
castagna chestnut
9124 *la*
psicanalista psychoanalyst
9127 *il/la*
tintura dyeing
9128 *la*
sarta seamstress
9129 *la*
Rinascimento Renaissance
9130 *il*
percossa blow
9131 *la*

nonnino grandpa
9132 *il*
intossicazione intoxication
9136 *le*
foulard scarf
9137 *il*
unisono unison
9138 *il*
timidezza shyness
9139 *la*
Plutone Pluto
9140 *lo*
sommozzatore diver|scuba diver
9141 *il*
toppa patch
9142 *la*
ostetrico obstetrician; obstetric
9143 *il; adj*
branchia gill
9144 *la*
triciclo tricycle
9146 *il*
lampone raspberry
9148 *il*
briefing briefing
9150 *il*
condottiero leader
9151 *il*
progettista designer
9152 *il/la*
finanziatore financier
9154 *il*
fulcro fulcrum
9155 *il*
balestra crossbow
9156 *la*
boccia bowl
9160 *la*
gnocco dumpling
9161 *lo*
prognosi prognosis
9162 *la*
massone mason
9163 *il*
isolante insulating; insulator
9164 *adj; il*
fornicazione fornication
9165 *la*
grizzly grizzly
9166 *i*
prescrizione prescription
9167 *la*
piranha piranha
9169 *i*
coccinella ladybug
9171 *la*
commiato leave-taking
9173 *il*
espiazione atonement
9174 *la*
abracadabra abracadabra
9175 *la*
pendio slope|hillside
9177 *il*
dominatore ruler
9178 *il*
segatura sawdust
9180 *la*
sbadato careless; scatterbrain
9181 *adj; lo*
reumatismo rheumatism
9182 *il*
aratro plow
9183 *il*
longitudine longitude
9184 *la*
tesoriere treasurer
9186 *il*
vendicatore avenger
9188 *il*
monarca monarch
9192 *il*
impudente impudent; jackanapes
9193 *adj; il/la*
trailer trailer
9196 *il*
bronchite bronchitis
9197 *la*
ingiunzione injunction
9198 *le*
ammoniaca ammonia
9201 *la*

bile bile
9204 *la*
diavoletto imp
9208 *il*
finimondo pandemonium
9209 *il*
eguale compeer
9210 *il*
sciabola saber
9212 *la*
poro pore
9213 *il*
giaccone short coat
9214 *il*
nuotatore swimmer
9215 *il*
fermaglio clip
9216 *il*
gazzella gazelle
9217 *la*
infatuazione infatuation
9219 *la*
acciuga anchovy
9220 *la*
quintale quintal
9226 *il*
droghiere grocer
9227 *il*
acero maple
9228 *il*
gonfiore swelling|distension
9230 *il*
nitro nitre
9231 *il*
bolide fireball|meteor
9232 *il*
camomilla chamomile
9233 *la*
ripiano shelf|terrace
9237 *il*
profilo profile
9239 *il*
bustarella bribe
9241 *la*
recessione recession
9243 *la*
paghetta pocket money
9244 *la*
pollame poultry
9245 *il*
fluire flow; flow
9246 *il; vb*
maggiolino cockchafer
9248 *il*
simulatore simulator
9253 *il*
antidepressivo antidepressant; antidepressive
9254 *il; adj*
toscano Tuscan; Tuscan
9255 *adj; il*
mongolfiera hot-air balloon
9260 *la*
stock stock
9261 *lo*
focolare hearth; astronomer
9262 *il; il*
prossimità proximity|closeness
9265 *la*
stuzzicadenti toothpick
9268 *lo*
Balcani Balkans
9269 *i*
duplicato duplicate
9271 *il*
cannonata cannon shot
9272 *la*
rigo line|staff
9273 *il*
tipografia typography
9274 *la*
buonumore good mood
9276 *il*
insegna signboard|banner
9277 *le*
ristoro refreshment
9279 *il*
thriller thriller
9280 *il*
premiato prize; prizewinner
9281 *adj; il*
congiunto joined; kinsman

9282 *adj; il*
commemorazione commemoration
9286 *la*
fervore fervor|zeal
9288 *il*
broker broker
9289 *il*
trachea trachea
9290 *la*
galletto cockerel
9293 *il*
arcangelo archangel
9296 *il*
paladino paladin
9297 *il*
finezza fineness|finesse
9298 *la*
vigneto vineyard
9299 *il*
pignolo finicky; fastidious person
9301 *adj; il*
donnola weasel
9302 *la*
moderazione moderation
9304 *la*
percussione percussion
9305 *la*
irrigazione irrigation
9306 *la*
disegnatore designer|draftsman
9307 *il*
ghigno fleer
9309 *il*
spartito score
9310 *lo*
decompressione decompression
9313 *la*
tassì taxi
9314 *i*
croupier croupier
9315 *i*
piattino saucer
9316 *il*
eutanasia euthanasia
9317 *la*
spergiuro perjury
9318 *lo*
stratagemma stratagem|trick
9320 *lo*
boccetta small bottle
9327 *la*
crocchetta croquette
9328 *la*
scassinatore burglar
9330 *lo*
donnaccia slut
9331 *la*
emissario emissary
9332 *il*
anticristo Antichrist
9334 *il*
menzione mention
9336 *la*
sottufficiale non-comissioned officer
9338 *il/la*
artigiano artisan|workman
9339 *il*
montacarichi elevator
9340 *il*
trabocchetto trap
9341 *il*
forziere coffer
9342 *il*
ricognitore scout
9344 *il*
rivelatore detector
9345 *il*
rally rally
9347 *il*
casato stock|family
9348 *il*
cremazione cremation
9350 *la*
disapprovazione disapproval|disapprobation
9351 *la*
vandalismo vandalism
9352 *il*
invecchiamento aging
9353 *il*
vischio mistletoe
9356 *il*
smistamento sorting

9357 *lo*
mortadella mortadella
9358 *la*
coordinatore coordinator
9360 *il*
rielezione re-election
9361 *la*
frullatore mixer
9362 *il*
carpentiere carpenter
9363 *il*
sparviero hawk
9365 *lo*
calce lime
9366 *la*
ingenuità naivety|ingenuousness
9367 *le*
diminuzione decrease|reduction
9372 *la*
familiarità familiarity
9373 *la*
intolleranza intolerance
9377 *la*
iodio iodine
9378 *lo*
irritazione irritation|annoyance
9379 *le*
burlone joker
9381 *il*
display display
9382 *il*
martirio martyrdom|torture
9383 *il*
mecenate patron
9384 *il/la*
tombino manhole
9385 *il*
riluttanza reluctance
9387 *la*
tumulto tumult|turmoil
9389 *il*
acrobata acrobat
9390 *il/la*
fioraio florist
9392 *il*
papero gander
9393 *il*
dissenteria dysentery
9394 *la*
bevitore drinker
9395 *il*
ciabatta slipper
9396 *la*
ode ode
9398 *le*
profano profane; layman
9399 *adj; il*
ambientazione setting
9401 *la*
suggestione suggestion
9402 *la*
branca branch
9406 *la*
villetta chalet
9409 *la*
arsenico arsenic; arsenical
9410 *il; adj*
impugnatura handle|grip
9412 *la*
strangolatore choker
9417 *lo*
frenesia frenzy
9418 *la*
fisarmonica accordion
9419 *la*
filastrocca doggerel
9421 *la*
tonico tonic; tonic
9424 *adj; il*
esecutore performer
9425 *il*
cocomero watermelon
9426 *il*
bacheca showcase
9430 *la*
scacchiera chessboard
9431 *la*
supplemento supplement|extra charge
9434 *il*
coccio earthenware|shard
9435 *il*
mollusco shellfish|clam

9436 *il*
pigrizia laziness|idleness
9437 *la*
molotov molotov cocktail
9438 *il*
amaca hammock
9439 *la*
manopola knob|handle
9440 *la*
sibillo hiss|hissing
9443 *il*
dardo dart
9444 *il*
scopa broom
9445 *la*
cardiologo cardiologist
9447 *il*
scrivano scribe|clerk
9448 *lo*
spasmo spasm
9451 *lo*
insuccesso failure
9452 *il*
addebito charge
9453 *il*
schiacciata smash
9457 *la*
risaia paddy field
9458 *la*
argomentazione argumentation
9461 *le*
sensualità sensuality
9463 *la*
gelsomino jasmine
9465 *il*
anticorpo antibody
9466 *gli*
apprendimento learning
9469 *il*
ventola fan
9470 *la*
ostruzione obstruction
9471 *le*
melanzana eggplant
9472 *la*
seppia cuttlefish
9473 *la*
dosaggio dosage
9474 *il*
imperialismo imperialism
9475 *il*
antigas antigas
9476 *il*
ambra amber
9477 *la*
pacifista pacifist
9478 *il/la*
dirottatore hijacker
9479 *il*
vaselina vaseline
9480 *la*
prevenzione prevention|prophylaxis
9481 *la*
squilibrio imbalance
9482 *lo*
orda horde
9483 *la*
cifrario code
9484 *il*
filantropo philanthropist
9485 *il*
sdegno indignation|disdain
9488 *lo*
armistizio armistice
9491 *il*
assenzio absinthe
9492 *il*
gengiva gum
9494 *la*
edicola newsstand
9495 *le*
trapezio trapeze
9496 *il*
pompelmo grapefruit
9497 *il*
incarnazione incarnation
9499 *le*
lenza line
9501 *la*
criniera mane
9502 *la*
confisca confiscation

9504 *la*
lustrino spangle
9507 *il*
malta mortar
9508 *le*
londinese Londoner; London's
9509 *il/la; adj*
selvaggina game
9511 *la*
piastrina platelet
9515 *la*
cinematografo cinema
9516 *il*
striscio scratch
9517 *lo*
fabbricazione manufacture
9524 *la*
dizione diction
9525 *la*
trasferta transfer
9526 *la*
isterismo hysteria
9527 *gli*
rimorchiatore tug
9528 *il*
festino party
9529 *il*
installazione installation
9530 *la*
affanno breathlessness
9531 *il*
sfinge sphinx
9532 *la*
bozzolo cocoon
9533 *il*
lavastoviglie dishwasher
9534 *la*
contrabbasso contrabass
9535 *il*
Trinità Trinity
9536 *la*
filone vein
9538 *il*
candore candor|whiteness
9540 *il*
clic click
9541 *i*
disfunzione dysfunction
9543 *la*
ricompensa reward|award
9546 *la*
tappa stage|stop
9547 *la*
respiratore respirator
9548 *il*
glassa icing
9549 *la*
basco Basque; Basque
9551 *adj; il*
capostazione stationmaster
9552 *il*
questionario questionnaire
9553 *il*
rettilineo straight; straight
9554 *adj; il*
doge doge
9555 *il*
mimo mime
9557 *il*
prosa prose
9558 *la*
coniuge spouse|consort
9559 *il*
sarcofago sarcophagus
9563 *il*
inquietudine restlessness
9567 *le*
possedimento possession
9568 *il*
catacomba catacomb
9570 *la*
crostaceo crustacean; shellfish
9571 *adj; il*
assegnazione assignment|allocation
9572 *la*
wurstel frankfurter
9574 *i*
auspicio omen
9576 *il*
accusatore accuser
9577 *il*
instabilità instability

9578 *le*
bancarella stall|stand

9580 *la*
sacerdotessa priestess

9582 *la*
bavarese Bavarian; Bavarian

9584 *adj; il/la*
patrono patron|patron saint

9585 *il*
banalità banality|triviality

9587 *la*
ricattatore blackmailer

9588 *il*
piroscafo steamer

9592 *il*
tresca affair

9593 *la*
totem totem

9597 *i*
giostra carousel|joust

9598 *la*
giugulare jugular vein

9599 *la*
gratifica bonus

9600 *la*
panetteria relic

9601 *la*
cimelio relic

9602 *il*
ringhio snarl

9603 *il*
mascara mascara

9604 *il*
capogiro dizziness

9605 *il*
scorza rind|peel

9606 *la*
argano winch|capstan

9607 *il*
cerbiatto fawn

9609 *il*
asfissia asphyxiation

9610 *le*
domatore tamer

9616 *il*
setaccio sieve

9617 *il*
ibernazione hibernation

9619 *la*
fettina chip; rudeness

9620 *la; la*
brioche muffin

9621 *il*
cottimo piece rate system

9623 *il*
falena moth

9626 *la*
psicanalisi psychoanalysis

9627 *la*
spazzaneve snowplow

9629 *gli*
stanzino closet

9632 *lo*
configurazione configuration|layout

9633 *la*
bambolotto doll

9635 *il*
druido Druid

9636 *il*
algoritmo algorithm

9638 *il*
clistere enema

9639 *il*
pube pubis

9640 *il*
faglia fault

9641 *la*
runa rune

9642 *la*
expo exhibition

9647 *le*
impossibilità impossibility

9649 *la*
progressista progressive

9652 *il/la*
tisana tisane

9653 *la*
arbusto shrub

9655 *il*
rapidità speed|rapidity

9657 *la*
commilitone fellow soldier

9660 *il*
sbando drift
9663 *lo*
stendardo standard
9665 *lo*
anatroccolo duckling
9666 *il*
serenata serenade
9669 *la*
zappa hoe
9670 *la*
rumba rumba
9671 *la*
brontolone growler
9672 *il*
raccordo junction
9673 *il*
diminuendo diminuendo
9676 *lo*
impudenza impudence|nerve
9677 *le*
gallese Welsh; Welsh
9678 *adj; il*
freddezza coldness|cold shoulder
9679 *la*
moscerino gnat
9680 *il*
bocciolo bud
9681 *il*
abolizione abolition
9682 *la*
miraggio mirage
9683 *il*
borsellino purse
9684 *il*
ripasso revision
9685 *il*
pistacchio pistachio
9689 *il*
villeggiatura holiday
9690 *la*
nordovest northwest
9692 *il*
promotore promoter; promotive
9693 *il; adj*
requiem requiem
9694 *il*
vigliaccheria cowardice
9695 *la*
portuale roustabout
9696 *lo*
sfiducia distrust
9697 *la*
boschetto grove
9698 *il*
campagnolo hillbilly
9699 *il*
inceneritore incinerator
9702 *il*
ribasso fall|decline
9703 *il*
sud-ovest southwest
9704 *il*
angolino nook
9705 *il*
appello appeal
9709 *gli*
consultazione consultation|counsel
9711 *la*
milza spleen
9713 *la*
durezza hardness|toughness
9714 *la*
attendente orderly
9715 *il*
barbarie barbarism
9719 *la*
alfiere bishop
9721 *lo*
giaguaro jaguar
9723 *il*
arpione harpoon
9724 *il*
smanceria affectation
9725 *la*
allusione allusion
9728 *le*
astemio abstemious; teetotaler
9730 *adj; il*
onta shame|offense
9732 *le*
tangente tangent; cut

9735 *la; adj*
separatista separatist
9736 *il/la*
antropologia anthropology
9740 *le*
diffida warning
9741 *la*
infiltrazione infiltration
9742 *le*
papavero poppy
9743 *il*
ripensamento afterthought
9745 *il*
cedimento subsidence
9748 *il*
alchimista alchemist
9750 *il*
équipe team
9751 *le*
elaborazione processing
9752 *la*
tappetino mat
9753 *il*
fondamentalista fundamentalist
9754 *il*
lappone Lapp; Laplander
9755 *adj; il*
bracciante laborer|worker
9757 *il/la*
manovale laborer|hand
9758 *il*
camelia camellia
9760 *la*
tubetto tube
9761 *il*
barbiturico barbiturate; barbituric
9762 *il; adj*
epicentro epicenter|focus
9763 *lo*
incendiario arsonist; incendiary
9765 *il; adj*
faida feud
9767 *la*
epilogo epilogue
9768 *il*
suola sole
9769 *la*
manovella crank
9770 *la*
corredo kit|equipment
9771 *il*
birreria brasserie
9772 *la*
bicarbonato bicarbonate
9777 *il*
scollatura neckline
9779 *la*
montatore fixer
9782 *il*
alchimia alchemy
9783 *la*
voltaggio voltage
9784 *il*
schieramento array
9785 *lo*
judo judo
9787 *il*

Verbs

Italian English Translation
Rank Part of Speech
accertare ascertain
7501 *vb*
stirare iron|stretch
7506 *vb*
schierare deploy|line up
7510 *vb*
balzare jump|skip
7512 *vb*
premeditare premeditate
7513 *vb*
digitare type in
7539 *vb*
fendere cleave|slit
7541 *vb*
decaffeinare decaffeinate
7544 *vb*
arrossire blush|color
7555 *vb*
specializzare specialize
7559 *vb*
irrompere burst
7563 *vb*
aspirare aspire|suck
7568 *vb*
compiacere please|satisfy
7570 *vb*
confiscare confiscate|disendow
7571 *vb*
bonificare reclaim
7572 *vb*
rimbalzare bounce|bounce back
7575 *vb*
sparpagliare scatter
7576 *vb*
degenerare degenerate
7579 *vb*
predire predict
7581 *vb*
capitolare capitulate; capitular
7595 *vb; adj*
sgomberare clear
7597 *vb*
battezzare baptize|Christen
7611 *vb*
faticare labor|work hard
7614 *vb*
nuocere harm
7616 *vb*
calamitare magnetize
7625 *vb*
maltrattare abuse|mishandle
7628 *vb*
paragonare compare|confront
7630 *vb*
ostacolare hinder|hamper
7632 *vb*
burlare make fun of
7650 *vb*
approfondire deepen
7651 *vb*
ambientare set
7660 *vb*
conversare converse
7671 *vb*
appassionare thrill
7672 *vb*
sventolare wave
7675 *vb*
moderare moderate
7679 *vb*
filettare thread
7692 *vb*
assoldare engage
7693 *vb*
archiviare file
7695 *vb*
gravitare gravitate
7702 *vb*
seccare dry|bother
7714 *vb*
barricare barricade
7718 *vb*
remare row
7726 *vb*
predicare preach
7728 *vb*
travolgere overwhelm
7731 *vb*
scampare escape

	7733	*vb*
virare		turn
	7749	*vb*
squillare		ring
	7779	*vb*
pareggiare		equalize|balance
	7781	*vb*
intestare		head
	7795	*vb*
trafiggere		pierce
	7805	*vb*
espandere		expand|enlarge
	7807	*vb*
cronometrare		time|minute
	7808	*vb*
riconsiderare		reconsider
	7809	*vb*
meditare		meditate|brood
	7810	*vb*
motivare		motivate
	7811	*vb*
domare		tame
	7826	*vb*
sopprimere		abolish
	7833	*vb*
ricambiare		return|reciprocate
	7837	*vb*
stilare		draw up|draft
	7879	*vb*
sopravvalutare		overestimate|overvalue
	7891	*vb*
fronteggiare		face|cope
	7894	*vb*
disprezzare		despise|look down on
	7897	*vb*
ardere		burn|blaze
	7898	*vb*
azzeccare		hit|guess
	7906	*vb*
singhiozzare		sob
	7910	*vb*
scocciare		bother|be fed up
	7915	*vb*
ripiegare		fall back|fold up
	7917	*vb*
acchiappare		catch
	7918	*vb*
fulminare		fulminate
	7932	*vb*
prescrivere		prescribe
	7938	*vb*
addolorare		grieve|pain
	7953	*vb*
documentare		document
	7956	*vb*
disorientare		disorient|confuse
	7957	*vb*
indietreggiare		back|retreat
	7958	*vb*
gustare		enjoy|taste
	7961	*vb*
lastricare		pave
	7970	*vb*
accumulare		accumulate|store
	7974	*vb*
accorrere		rush
	7975	*vb*
rivoltare		turn over
	7983	*vb*
menare		lead
	7990	*vb*
combaciare		match|join
	7994	*vb*
vegliare		watch over
	8003	*vb*
inghiottire		swallow|gulp
	8005	*vb*
riscrivere		rewrite
	8010	*vb*
starnutire		sneeze
	8020	*vb*
fiaccare		sap|weaken
	8028	*vb*
contrattare		negotiate
	8036	*vb*
incrementare		increase
	8039	*vb*
emanare		issue|emanate
	8063	*vb*
allagare		flood
	8075	*vb*
consacrare		consecrate|devote

	8079	*vb*
manovrare		maneuver|handle
	8081	*vb*
contagiare		infect
	8082	*vb*
assaporare		savor
	8088	*vb*
disinfettare		disinfect
	8095	*vb*
soprannominare		nickname
	8100	*vb*
inquietare		worry
	8108	*vb*
coincidere		coincide
	8110	*vb*
poggiare		rest|lean
	8115	*vb*
situare		place|situate
	8117	*vb*
riconquistare		recapture
	8151	*vb*
rammollire		soften
	8152	*vb*
sculacciare		spank
	8156	*vb*
sabotare		sabotage
	8170	*vb*
molestare		harass|annoy
	8180	*vb*
illudere		deceive|delude oneself
	8187	*vb*
proiettare		project|screen
	8190	*vb*
pizzicare		pinch|pluck
	8193	*vb*
appiccare		set
	8196	*vb*
prosciugare		drain
	8199	*vb*
ricadere		fall|fall back
	8203	*vb*
allineare		align|line
	8208	*vb*
affliggere		afflict|plague
	8212	*vb*
rinfrescare		refresh|cool
	8215	*vb*
marchiare		mark|stamp
	8219	*vb*
ubbidire		obey
	8223	*vb*
insanguinare		bathe in blood
	8224	*vb*
adempiere		fulfill|perform
	8225	*vb*
sfogare		vent
	8229	*vb*
abbronzare		tan
	8231	*vb*
sterminare		exterminate
	8259	*vb*
strapazzare		scramble|mistreat
	8266	*vb*
affettare		slice|affect
	8269	*vb*
applicato		applied; resign oneself
	8271	*adj; vb*
rassegnare		resign oneself
	8272	*vb*
affumicare		smoke
	8273	*vb*
distogliere		divert|distract
	8277	*vb*
mutilare		mutilate
	8278	*vb*
rispedire		send back
	8281	*vb*
placare		appease|calm
	8283	*vb*
perlustrare		search|scour
	8291	*vb*
ingrandire		enlarge|expand
	8306	*vb*
convertire		convert
	8310	*vb*
designare		designate|appoint
	8314	*vb*
sotterrare		bury
	8315	*vb*
piombare		fall
	8317	*vb*
russare		snore

8321 *vb*
impicciare meddle

8329 *vb*
risposare remarry

8332 *vb*
indebolire weaken|impair

8334 *vb*
scomodare disturb|be inconvenient

8336 *vb*
ringhiare growl

8345 *vb*
gocciolare drip

8348 *vb*
spremere squeeze|squeeze out

8352 *vb*
sceneggiare dramatize

8355 *vb*
smascherare unmask

8358 *vb*
istituire establish|charter

8386 *vb*
contrastare counteract

8387 *vb*
celare conceal|be hidden

8390 *vb*
opprimere oppress|bully

8392 *vb*
invocare invoke|call upon

8394 *vb*
scarabocchiare doodle|scribble

8403 *vb*
simulare simulate|mimic

8405 *vb*
strofinare rub

8412 *vb*
ululare howl|ululate

8419 *vb*
sloggiare dislodge

8422 *vb*
affrettare hasten|expedite

8430 *vb*
annotare note

8431 *vb*
diagnosticare diagnose

8442 *vb*
nitrire neigh

8447 *vb*
proclamare proclaim|declare

8449 *vb*
immigrare immigrate

8452 *vb*
detonare detonate

8463 *vb*
incombere impend

8471 *vb*
esaudire fulfill|grant

8474 *vb*
gironzolare roam|wander about

8491 *vb*
ungere anoint|grease

8498 *vb*
ingrossare swell|enlarge

8501 *vb*
nettare nectar; clean

8504 *il; vb*
rullare roll

8510 *vb*
riordinare rearrange|tidy

8516 *vb*
intonare intone|tone

8524 *vb*
imprecare curse|swear

8525 *vb*
scavalcare climb over

8531 *vb*
ritoccare retouch

8533 *vb*
deportare deport

8534 *vb*
crocifiggere crucify

8539 *vb*
variare vary|range

8540 *vb*
accampare camp

8576 *vb*
collezionare collect

8578 *vb*
esibire show|show off

8602 *vb*
disertare desert|bolt

8604 *vb*
riporre put

8605 *vb*
vegetare vegetate
8609 *vb*
obiettare object
8612 *vb*
disdire cancel|unsay
8630 *vb*
tralasciare omit|give up
8633 *vb*
grugnire grunt
8635 *vb*
imprimere give|impress
8637 *vb*
scoraggiare discourage|be discouraged
8639 *vb*
gratificare gratify
8650 *vb*
risplendere shine|sparkle
8652 *vb*
salvaguardare safeguard
8655 *vb*
neutralizzare neutralize|counter
8667 *vb*
infliggere inflict
8668 *vb*
circoncidere circumcise
8669 *vb*
sintonizzare tune
8673 *vb*
risuonare ring
8686 *vb*
deridere mock|deride
8687 *vb*
beffare mock|make fun of
8688 *vb*
accarezzare caress|stroke
8690 *vb*
ingelosire make jealous
8718 *vb*
acclamare acclaim
8723 *vb*
allentare loosen|slacken
8725 *vb*
riciclare recycle
8730 *vb*
grattare scratch|scrape
8735 *vb*
persuadere persuade|convince
8737 *vb*
spruzzare spray|sprinkle
8738 *vb*
evocare evoke
8744 *vb*
squarciare rip|slash
8748 *vb*
macellare slaughter
8763 *vb*
stimolare stimulate|spur
8764 *vb*
pelare skin|fleece
8766 *vb*
rivendicare claim
8777 *vb*
stipulare stipulate
8787 *vb*
secondare comply
8801 *vb*
civilizzare civilize
8802 *vb*
confrontare compare
8804 *vb*
degradare degrade
8807 *vb*
reprimere repress|suppress
8808 *vb*
patteggiare negotiate
8809 *vb*
trapelare leak|transpire
8812 *vb*
incarcerare imprison
8814 *vb*
trivellare drill
8820 *vb*
quietare quiet|calm
8822 *vb*
fantasticare daydream
8825 *vb*
speronare ram
8826 *vb*
riassumere summarize|reassume
8836 *vb*
arricchire enrich

8848 *vb*
allarmare alarm
8850 *vb*
esaltare exalt|celebrate
8851 *vb*
presiedere preside
8852 *vb*
formulare formulate|express
8854 *vb*
ricapitolare recap|summarize
8872 *vb*
sorvolare fly over
8875 *vb*
aggravare aggravate|make worse
8878 *vb*
assordare deafen
8885 *vb*
perforare pierce|drill
8887 *vb*
rizzare raise
8891 *vb*
accorgersi notice|realize
8898 *vb*
guadare wade
8911 *vb*
rinviare postpone|refer
8922 *vb*
spartire share
8927 *vb*
contemplare contemplate
8930 *vb*
spicciare hurry up
8937 *vb*
ampliare extend|enlarge
8939 *vb*
accordarsi agree|arrange
8948 *vb*
schedare file|record
8952 *vb*
procreare procreate
8956 *vb*
appaltare contract
8960 *vb*
fertilizzare fertilize
8963 *vb*
estinguere extinguish
8964 *vb*
sincronizzare synchronize|time
8967 *vb*
suppliziare torment
8969 *vb*
schivare dodge|avoid
8993 *vb*
suscitare arouse|elicit
8995 *vb*
svaligiare rob
8996 *vb*
risucchiare suck
9001 *vb*
rallegrare cheer|brighten
9006 *vb*
innescare trigger
9010 *vb*
temprare anneal
9011 *vb*
rincorrere run after
9016 *vb*
contestare challenge|contest
9020 *vb*
menomare impair|maim
9022 *vb*
prevalere prevail|overbear
9026 *vb*
collaudare test
9028 *vb*
sgobbare slog|work hard
9029 *vb*
confezionare pack|manufacture
9033 *vb*
appiccicare stick
9041 *vb*
eludere circumvent|bypass
9042 *vb*
issare hoist
9043 *vb*
slogare dislocate|sprain
9046 *vb*
cozzare clash|butt
9052 *vb*
sbandare slide|disperse
9057 *vb*
ipnotizzare hypnotize

9058 *vb*
sostare stop|pause
9064 *vb*
input input; input
9070 *gli; vb*
forgiare forge|tilt
9075 *vb*
setacciare sift|search
9089 *vb*
facilitare facilitate
9092 *vb*
ronzare hum|whir
9098 *vb*
sradicare eradicate|root up
9120 *vb*
comperare buy
9123 *vb*
bestemmiare blaspheme
9126 *vb*
captare pick up
9134 *vb*
replicare replicate|reply
9145 *vb*
perfezionare perfect|refine
9149 *vb*
ricucire sew up
9153 *vb*
infortunarsi get injured
9158 *vb*
prosperare thrive|prosper
9159 *vb*
conficcare stick|drive
9168 *vb*
riaccompagnare take back
9176 *vb*
impadronirsi seize|master
9185 *vb*
trionfare triumph
9189 *vb*
venerare venerate|worship
9194 *vb*
ammaccare dent|bruise
9199 *vb*
alleggerire lighten|ease
9211 *vb*
rattristare sadden

9222 *vb*
infilzare stick
9223 *vb*
gioire rejoice
9225 *vb*
infiltrarsi infiltrate
9229 *vb*
riabilitare rehabilitate
9234 *vb*
sbocciare bloom|open
9235 *vb*
fluire flow; flow
9246 *il; vb*
sottomettere submit|subdue
9247 *vb*
purificare purify|cleanse
9249 *vb*
vibrare vibrate|thrill
9252 *vb*
ergersi rise
9257 *vb*
spalancare open wide
9259 *vb*
schiaffeggiare slap
9263 *vb*
decretare decree|enact
9264 *vb*
colmare fill|bridge
9266 *vb*
evolvere evolve
9284 *vb*
sorpassare overtake|surpass
9292 *vb*
ormeggiare moor
9295 *vb*
radiare expel
9300 *vb*
saccheggiare plunder|loot
9322 *vb*
rinforzare strengthen|reinforce
9323 *vb*
impiantare implant|establish
9325 *vb*
espiare atone|pay
9329 *vb*
simboleggiare symbolize|epitomize

9343 *vb*
indire call|announce
9354 *vb*
smantellare dismantle
9359 *vb*
calciare kick
9380 *vb*
esonerare exempt|exonerate
9386 *vb*
serbare keep|remain
9388 *vb*
restringere restrict|narrow
9403 *vb*
raggirare circumvent|deceive
9404 *vb*
riscontrare find|verify
9408 *vb*
berciare jangle
9415 *vb*
raddrizzare straighten|right
9416 *vb*
socializzare socialize
9423 *vb*
strizzare wring|squeeze
9427 *vb*
somministrare administer|give
9428 *vb*
arrangiare arrange
9433 *vb*
rasare shave|mow
9446 *vb*
guaire yelp
9456 *vb*
posizionare position
9459 *vb*
smaltire dispose of
9462 *vb*
smuovere move|shift
9467 *vb*
inceppare clog|obstruct
9468 *vb*
emarginare marginalize
9498 *vb*
giovare profit
9503 *vb*
attuare carry out
9505 *vb*
legittimare legitimize|justify
9512 *vb*
moltiplicare multiply
9514 *vb*
vagabondare wander|stroll
9520 *vb*
impigliare entangle
9523 *vb*
girovagare wander|wander about
9539 *vb*
cigolare creak|grate
9545 *vb*
brevettare patent
9565 *vb*
destare arouse|kindle
9566 *vb*
medicare medicate
9573 *vb*
importunare bother|importune
9575 *vb*
mendicare beg
9581 *vb*
appaiare pair|brace
9586 *vb*
pedalare pedal
9590 *vb*
scremare skim
9591 *vb*
tuffare dive|dip
9594 *vb*
spifferare blurt out|blab
9596 *vb*
scagionare exonerate
9614 *vb*
attestare attest|vouch
9618 *vb*
stracciare tear|shred
9625 *vb*
capovolgere invert|reverse
9630 *vb*
rimproverare reproach|blame
9631 *vb*
pomiciare neck
9637 *vb*
asportare remove

9646 *vb*
infamare defame
9650 *vb*
commemorare commemorate
9651 *vb*
indugiare linger|delay
9654 *vb*
scolpire sculpt|carve
9658 *vb*
recapitare deliver
9661 *vb*
sconfinare trespass
9662 *vb*
solfare sulphurise
9667 *vb*
contraddire contradict
9675 *vb*
fruttare yield|fruit
9686 *vb*
specificare specify|state
9687 *vb*
sfrattare evict
9700 *vb*
sfasciare smash up
9708 *vb*
tutelare protect
9710 *vb*
indennizzare indemnify
9712 *vb*
affiancare help
9717 *vb*
impacchettare pack|package
9720 *vb*
inumare bury
9722 *vb*
arrostire roast
9726 *vb*
sbavare drool|smudge
9733 *vb*
racimolare glean
9766 *vb*
fluttuare fluctuate|float
9774 *vb*
addomesticare tame
9776 *vb*
risaltare stand out|show up
9778 *vb*
rifilare trim|foist
9786 *vb*

Alphabetical order

A

abbattuto down|dejected
7954 *adj*
abbonamento subscription
7574 *il*
abbronzare tan
8231 *vb*
abitato inhabited
7663 *adj*
abitualmente usually
9218 *adv*
abolizione abolition
9682 *la*
aborigeno aboriginal; aborigine
7928 *adj; il*
abracadabra abracadabra
9175 *la*
accampare camp
8576 *vb*
accanito hard
9919 *adj*
accarezzare caress|stroke
8690 *vb*
accelerazione acceleration
7941 *la*
accertare ascertain
7501 *vb*
accessibile accessible|attainable
7515 *adj*
acchiappare catch
7918 *vb*
acciuga anchovy
9220 *la*
acclamare acclaim
8723 *vb*
accompagnatrice chaperone
7717 *le*
accoppiare pair|join
9983 *vb*
accordarsi agree|arrange
8948 *vb*
accorgersi notice|realize
8898 *vb*
accorrere rush
7975 *vb*
accumulare accumulate|store
7974 *vb*
accumulo backlog
9066 *il*
accusatore accuser
9577 *il*
acero maple
9228 *il*
acquatico aquatic
8136 *adj*
acquirente buyer|shopper
7622 *il/la*
acquisizione acquisition
8658 *la*
acrobata acrobat
9390 *il/la*
acrobazia stunt
8584 *le*
addebito charge
9453 *il*
addolorare grieve|pain
7953 *vb*
addomesticare tame
9776 *vb*
adeguato adequate
8863 *adj*
adempiere fulfill|perform
8225 *vb*
aderire join|adhere
9834 *vb*
adolescenza adolescence
7874 *le*
adorazione adoration|adorability
8192 *le*
adottivo adopted|foster
7664 *adj*
adunata gathering|muster
7643 *la*
aerobico aerobic
9364 *adj*
affabile affable|amiable
9500 *adj*
affanno breathlessness

9531 *il*
affannoso labored|breathless
7530 *adj*
affettare slice|affect
8269 *vb*
affezionato fond
9999 *adj*
affiancare help
9717 *vb*
affitto rent
8845 *i*
affliggere afflict|plague
8212 *vb*
afflitto sad
9490 *adj*
affrettare hasten|expedite
8430 *vb*
affrettato hurried|hasty
7828 *adj*
affumicare smoke
8273 *vb*
afrodisiaco aphrodisiac; aphrodisiac
9981 *adj; il*
agghiacciante dreadful
8550 *adj*
aggravare aggravate|make worse
8878 *vb*
agricolo agricultural
8975 *adj*
agrimensore surveyor
8443 *il*
aia farmyard
8559 *le*
albino albino
8954 *il*
alchimia alchemy
9783 *la*
alchimista alchemist
9750 *il*
alcolismo alcoholism
8549 *il*
alfabetico alphabetical|abecedarian
7944 *adj*
alfiere bishop
9721 *lo*
algebra algebra
7668 *la*
algoritmo algorithm
9638 *il*
allagare flood
8075 *vb*
allarmare alarm
8850 *vb*
alleato ally; allied
7843 *il; adj*
alleggerire lighten|ease
9211 *vb*
allegramente cheerfully
8759 *adv*
allentare loosen|slacken
8725 *vb*
allineamento alignment
8769 *lo*
allineare align|line
8208 *vb*
allusione allusion
9728 *le*
alluvione flood|flooding
9846 *le*
alpino alpine
9550 *adj*
altea marsh-mallow
8234 *la*
altruismo altruism
8788 *il*
altruista selfless; altruist
8191 *adj; il/la*
amaca hammock
9439 *la*
amareggiare embitter
9951 *vb*
amarezza bitterness
7547 *le*
amazzone horsewoman
7979 *la*
ambedue both
8968 *adj*
ambientare set
7660 *vb*
ambientazione setting
9401 *la*
ambiguo ambiguous|devious

9455 *adj*
ambra amber
9477 *la*
ambulatorio surgery; ambulatory
7820 *il; adj*
amianto asbestos
8167 *il*
ammaccare dent|bruise
9199 *vb*
ammalato sick; sick person
7518 *adj; il*
ammaliare charm
9810 *vb*
amministrare administer|manage
10009 *vb*
amministrativo administrative
9013 *adj*
ammoniaca ammonia
9201 *la*
ampiamente widely
7818 *adv*
ampliare extend|enlarge
8939 *vb*
amplificatore amplifier
8959 *il*
amputare amputate
9899 *vb*
amputazione amputation
10016 *la*
analfabeta illiterate
7817 *il/la*
anarchico anarchist; anarchic
9109 *il; adj*
anatroccolo duckling
9666 *il*
andamento trend|progress
8716 *il*
aneurisma aneurysm
8813 *il*
angolare angular
9977 *adj*
angolino nook
9705 *il*
anguria watermelon
8908 *la*
annegamento drowning
8307 *il*
annientamento annihilation
8697 *il*
annotare note
8431 *vb*
annullo cancellation
9970 *lo*
anticamera anteroom
8693 *le*
anticarro antitank
9813 *il*
anticorpo antibody
9466 *gli*
anticristo Antichrist
9334 *il*
antidepressivo antidepressant; antidepressive
9254 *il; adj*
antifurto antitheft; antitheft
8527 *adj; gli*
antigas antigas
9476 *il*
antigelo antifreeze
9867 *gli*
antiquario antique dealer; antiquarian
9802 *il; adj*
antiquato antiquated|outdated
7665 *adj*
antropologia anthropology
9740 *le*
apostolo apostle
8023 *il*
appaiare pair|brace
9586 *vb*
appaltare contract
8960 *vb*
apparecchiare lay
9821 *vb*
appassionare thrill
7672 *vb*
appello appeal
9709 *gli*
appendice appendix
8521 *la*
appendicite appendicitis
7802 *la*

appetitoso appetizing|palatable
9734 *adj*
appiccare set
8196 *vb*
appiccicare stick
9041 *vb*
appiccicoso sticky
8296 *adj*
appieno fully
8388 *adv*
applicato applied; resign oneself
8271 *adj; vb*
apprendimento learning
9469 *il*
apprensione apprehension|anxiety
9914 *la*
apprezzamento appreciation
8012 *lo*
approfondire deepen
7651 *vb*
appropriazione appropriation
8343 *le*
araldo herald
9044 *il*
aratro plow
9183 *il*
arbitrio will
7694 *il*
arbusto shrub
9655 *il*
arcangelo archangel
9296 *il*
archeologia archeology
7735 *le*
archeologo archaeologist|archaeologian
8512 *il*
archiviare file
7695 *vb*
ardere burn|blaze
7898 *vb*
ardito bold
8396 *adj*
arduo arduous|uphill
7681 *adj*
argano winch|capstan
9607 *il*
argenteo silvery
8817 *adj*
argine embankment|bank
9826 *il*
argomentazione argumentation
9461 *le*
ariano Aryan; Aryan
8710 *adj; il*
arido arid
9224 *adj*
aringa herring
9076 *la*
aristocratico aristocratic; aristocrat
8985 *adj; il*
armeria armory
7534 *la*
armistizio armistice
9491 *il*
arpa harp
9083 *la*
arpione harpoon
9724 *il*
arrampicata climbing|scramble
9122 *le*
arrangiare arrange
9433 *vb*
arredatore interior decorator
9871 *il*
arricchire enrich
8848 *vb*
arringa harangue
8712 *le*
arrossire blush|color
7555 *vb*
arrostire roast
9726 *vb*
arsenico arsenic; arsenical
9410 *il; adj*
artefatto artifact; artificial
8679 *il; adj*
artefice maker
9048 *il*
artigiano artisan|workman
9339 *il*
ascella armpit|lath
7635 *le*

ascendente ascending; influence
9077 *adj; il/la*
ascensione ascension|mounting
8057 *la*
asfissia asphyxiation
9610 *le*
aspirare aspire|suck
7568 *vb*
aspirazione suction|aspiration
8284 *le*
asportare remove
9646 *vb*
aspro sour|harsh
9187 *adj*
assalitore assailant
8974 *il*
assaporare savor
8088 *vb*
assegnazione assignment|allocation
9572 *la*
assenzio absinthe
9492 *il*
assessore assessor
8528 *gli*
assetato thirsty
8393 *adj*
assicuratore insurer
9911 *il*
assoldare engage
7693 *vb*
assordare deafen
8885 *vb*
assunto recruit
8228 *il*
astemio abstemious; teetotaler
9730 *adj; il*
astrologia astrology
8790 *la*
astronomia astronomy
8861 *le*
ateo atheist; atheistic
8017 *il; adj*
atrocità atrocity
7722 *le*
attaccabrighe wrangler
8860 *gli*
attaccamento attachment|adhesion
8915 *il*
attendente orderly
9715 *il*
attendibile reliable
7792 *adj*
attentato attempt
7561 *il*
attesa waiting|expectation
9104 *la*
attestare attest|vouch
9618 *vb*
attitudine attitude
8770 *le*
attivamente actively
9706 *adv*
attizzatoio poker
9807 *il*
attracco docking|mooring
7590 *il*
attribuire attribute|award
9845 *vb*
attributo attribute
8048 *gli*
attuare carry out
9505 *vb*
auricolare earphone; auricular
8733 *il; adj*
ausiliario auxiliary|subsidiary
8946 *adj*
auspicio omen
9576 *il*
austriaco Austrian; Austrian
8198 *adj; il*
autenticità authenticity|genuine
9864 *la*
autobiografia autobiography
8543 *le*
autocontrollo restraint
8035 *il*
automobilistico automotive
9513 *adj*
autonomia autonomy
8049 *la*
autonomo autonomous
9349 *adj*

autoradio car radio
7758 *le*
autostoppista hitch-hiker
9897 *il/la*
autrice authoress
8270 *le*
autunnale autumnal
9368 *adj*
avanzamento progress|promotion
8551 *il*
avarizia avarice
9079 *la*
avaro stingy; miser
8311 *adj; il*
aviatore aviator
8611 *il*
avocado avocado
8926 *gli*
avvento coming
7716 *il*
avventuriero adventurer
9880 *il*
avversione aversion|dislike
9982 *le*
avversità adversity|ill
8780 *le*
avvincere compelling|fascinating
9405 *adj*
avvistamento sighting
8042 *il*
azoto nitrogen
7798 *il*
azzeccare hit|guess
7906 *vb*

B

babbuino baboon
8485 *il*
bacheca showcase
9430 *la*
bagnino lifeguard
9040 *il*
Balcani Balkans
9269 *i*
balestra crossbow
9156 *la*
balistico ballistic
8052 *adj*
ballata ballad
7964 *la*
balordo stupid
8771 *adj*
balsamo balm|conditioner
7947 *il*
balzare jump|skip
7512 *vb*
bambinaia nanny
7688 *la*
bambinone baby
8502 *il*
bambolotto doll
9635 *il*
banalità banality|triviality
9587 *la*
bancarella stall|stand
9580 *la*
banchina quay|wharf
7952 *la*
bandierina pennant
8118 *la*
baratro chasm
8309 *il*
barattare trade|barter
10025 *vb*
baratto barter
8289 *il*
barbarie barbarism
9719 *la*
barbiturico barbiturate; barbituric
9762 *il; adj*
barboncino poodle
8530 *il*
barchetta small boat
8979 *la*
barlume glimmer|flicker
8689 *il*
barricare barricade
7718 *vb*
barricata barricade
8125 *la*
basco Basque; Basque

9551 *adj; il*
basilare basic
8918 *adj*
batosta blow
8507 *la*
battezzare baptize|Christen
7611 *vb*
bava slime
7847 *la*
bavarese Bavarian; Bavarian
9584 *adj; il/la*
bazooka bazooka
7691 *la*
beatitudine bliss
8453 *la*
beduino Bedouin; Bedouin
8785 *adj; il*
beffa mockery|hoax
9884 *la*
beffare mock|make fun of
8688 *vb*
beige beige
7699 *il*
belga Belgian; Belgian
7916 *adj; il/la*
bellico war-; warlike
9506 *pfx; adj*
bemolle flat
7831 *lo*
beneficiario beneficiary
9021 *il*
benestante well-off
8638 *adj*
benevolo benevolent|benign
7883 *adj*
bengala Bengal light
8651 *il*
benigno benign|genial
8250 *adj*
berciare jangle
9415 *vb*
berlina sedan|limousine
9019 *la*
bernoccolo bump
7838 *il*
bestemmia blasphemy|curse
7950 *la*
bestemmiare blaspheme
9126 *vb*
bettola tavern
8276 *la*
bevitore drinker
9395 *il*
biberon bottle
7902 *il*
biblico biblical
9007 *adj*
bicarbonato bicarbonate
9777 *il*
bidello janitor
8835 *il*
bile bile
9204 *la*
biopsia biopsy
8541 *la*
birbante rascal
8275 *il*
birichino mischievous; cheeky youngster
8331 *adj; il*
birreria brasserie
9772 *la*
bisnonna great grandmother
9071 *la*
bisognoso needy
8162 *adj*
bivio fork
7901 *il*
blasfemo blasphemous
7720 *adj*
bobina coil|reel
8046 *la*
boccale mug
8572 *il*
boccetta small bottle
9327 *la*
boccia bowl
9160 *la*
bocciolo bud
9681 *il*
bolide fireball|meteor
9232 *il*

bollente boiling
7771 *adj*
bollitore kettle|heater
8869 *il*
bolscevico Bolshevik; Bolshevik
7823 *adj; il*
bombola cylinder
7940 *la*
bonificare reclaim
7572 *vb*
borghesia bourgeoisie
8881 *la*
borgo village|borough
9876 *il*
borraccia water bottle
9094 *la*
borsellino purse
9684 *il*
boscaglia bush|brush
9814 *la*
boschetto grove
9698 *il*
bossolo box
8326 *il*
botanico botanist; botanic
8783 *il; adj*
botteghino box office
9898 *il*
bozza draft
7719 *la*
bozzolo cocoon
9533 *il*
bracciale bracelet
8184 *il*
bracciante laborer|worker
9757 *il/la*
brace embers
8227 *la*
brama craving|desire
7520 *la*
branca branch
9406 *la*
branchia gill
9144 *la*
bravata stunt
8367 *la*
bravura cleverness
7565 *la*
bretella suspender|strap
9086 *la*
brevemente briefly
8268 *adv*
brevettare patent
9565 *vb*
brevetto patent
7645 *il*
briccone rascal; rascally; miscreant
9885 *il; adv; adj*
briefing briefing
9150 *il*
brioche muffin
9621 *il*
brocca pitcher
8398 *la*
broker broker
9289 *il*
bronchite bronchitis
9197 *la*
brontolone growler
9672 *il*
bruciapelo point-blank
8957 *adj*
bruciatura burn|scorch
8105 *la*
bruscamente short|brusquely
7661 *adv*
buccia peel|husk
8949 *la*
buffonata farce|tomfoolery
8522 *la*
bulgaro Bulgarian; Bulgarian
9975 *adj; il*
bulldog bulldog
7697 *il*
bulldozer bulldozer
7734 *i*
bungalow bungalow
7669 *i*
buonumore good mood
9276 *il*
burattino puppet
7748 *il*

burlare make fun of
7650 *vb*
burlone joker
9381 *il*
bustarella bribe
9241 *la*
bustina sachet
8678 *la*

C

caffettiera coffeepot
9082 *la*
cagnetto doggy
9014 *il*
calabrone hornet
8874 *il*
calamaro squid
8361 *il*
calamità calamity|misfortune
8914 *le*
calamitare magnetize
7625 *vb*
calcare limestone; emphasize
10012 *il; vb*
calce lime
9366 *la*
calciare kick
9380 *vb*
calciatore soccer player
7866 *il*
calcolatore computer; calculating
8478 *il; adj*
caldamente warmly
9060 *adv*
calderone cauldron
9915 *il*
califfo caliph
8599 *il*
callo callus
8610 *il*
calmante calming; sedative
8628 *adj; il*
calunnia slander|libel
8337 *la*
calzamaglia tights
8070 *la*
camaleonte chameleon
9862 *il*
cambiale draft|bill
8399 *la*
camelia camellia
9760 *la*
cameratismo camaraderie
9890 *il*
camomilla chamomile
9233 *la*
campagnolo hillbilly
9699 *il*
cancellazione cancellation
9910 *la*
candelina taper
7577 *la*
candore candor|whiteness
9540 *il*
canino canine
8935 *adj*
cannonata cannon shot
9272 *la*
cantastorie ballad singer
9839 *i*
canzoncina ditty
8141 *la*
capannone shed
8372 *il*
caparra deposit
7920 *la*
capitalista capitalist
8040 *il/la*
capitolare capitulate; capitular
7595 *vb; adj*
capogiro dizziness
9605 *il*
caporeparto shopwalker
9804 *il*
capostazione stationmaster
9552 *il*
capote hood
7706 *la*
capovolgere invert|reverse
9630 *vb*
cappellaio hatter

8434 *il*
capriccioso capricious|whimsical
9270 *adj*
captare pick up
9134 *vb*
caramello caramel
8670 *il*
carboidrato carbohydrate
7875 *il*
carburatore carburetor|carburetter
7913 *il*
carceriere jailer|warder
8910 *il*
cardiologo cardiologist
9447 *il*
carezza caress
7709 *la*
caricamento loading
8753 *il*
carie caries
7587 *la*
carillon carillon
8216 *il*
carisma charisma
8961 *il*
caritatevole charitable
9824 *adj*
carnagione complexion
7626 *la*
carnefice executioner
8476 *il*
carpentiere carpenter
9363 *il*
carponi on all fours
10024 *adv*
carreggiata track
8676 *la*
carriola wheelbarrow
8425 *la*
carrozzina pram
8421 *la*
cartellone poster|program
7836 *il*
casata house
8460 *la*
casato stock|family

9348 *il*
cassapanca chest
9928 *la*
castagna chestnut
9124 *la*
castità chastity
8573 *la*
casto chaste
8202 *adj*
catacomba catacomb
9570 *la*
catalizzatore catalyst
9988 *il*
catastrofico catastrophic
9991 *adj*
catechismo catechism
7775 *il*
catrame tar
8148 *il*
cattedra chair
7505 *la*
cavallino pony; horsy
8414 *il; adj*
cavalluccio hobbyhorse
8827 *il*
cecità blindness
8420 *la*
cedimento subsidence
9748 *il*
celare conceal|be hidden
8390 *vb*
celestiale celestial
7985 *adj*
celibe single; bachelor
9930 *adj; lo*
cencio rag
9831 *il*
centralinista operator
8544 *il/la*
centrifugo centrifugal
9644 *adj*
cerbiatto fawn
9609 *il*
cerchia circle|ring
8751 *la*
ceretta waxing

8892 *la*
cero candle
8197 *il*
chalet chalet
8739 *lo*
chemioterapia chemotherapy
8177 *la*
cherosene kerosene
8619 *il*
chiatta barge
7782 *la*
chierichetto server
8233 *il*
chimera chimera
7943 *la*
ciabatta slipper
9396 *la*
cialda waffle
9833 *la*
ciancia babble
9963 *la*
cicca chewing gum
7740 *la*
cicerone guide
8459 *il*
cifrario code
9484 *il*
cigolare creak|grate
9545 *vb*
cilecca misfire
8631 *la*
ciliegia cherry
7522 *la*
cimelio relic
9602 *il*
cinematografo cinema
9516 *il*
cinguettio chirping|twittering
9115 *il*
cinismo cynicism
8684 *il*
cinquantina about fifty
8933 *la*
ciocca lock
8263 *la*
ciononostante nevertheless; in spite of this
7946 *adv; phr*
cipria powder
8505 *la*
circoncidere circumcise
8669 *vb*
circonferenza circumference
9959 *la*
circostante surrounding
9275 *adj*
citofono intercom
8150 *il*
ciuffo tuft
8353 *il*
civico civic
8901 *adj*
civilizzare civilize
8802 *vb*
civilizzazione civilization
8062 *la*
clamore clamor|outcry
8563 *il*
clarinetto clarinet
9931 *il*
classificato classified
9749 *adj*
claustrofobia claustrophobia
9955 *la*
clavicola clavicle
9808 *la*
clero clergy
8754 *il*
clic click
9541 *i*
cliché cliche
8774 *i*
clip clip
9111 *le*
clistere enema
9639 *il*
clitoride clitoris
8677 *la*
cloche joystick
8924 *la*
cloro chlorine
8856 *il*
coalizione coalition|bloc

7929 *la*
cocca nock
8025 *la*
coccinella ladybug
9171 *la*
coccio earthenware|shard
9435 *il*
cocomero watermelon
9426 *il*
codardia cowardice
8990 *la*
coerente consistent
7507 *adj*
cognizione cognition|acquaintance
8859 *la*
coincidere coincide
8110 *vb*
coke coke
9881 *il*
collaudare test
9028 *vb*
collezionare collect
8578 *vb*
collocamento placement|placing
7715 *il*
colmare fill|bridge
9266 *vb*
colombiano Columbian
7523 *adj*
colon colon
7545 *lo*
coloniale colonial
7829 *adj*
colorito colorful; color
7600 *adj; il*
colpetto tap|flick
8308 *il*
coltellata stab
8858 *la*
coltura culture
10006 *la*
combaciare match|join
7994 *vb*
combattivo combative
9569 *adj*
combustione combustion

7752 *la*
comfort comfort
8066 *il*
comicità comicality
9103 *la*
commemorare commemorate
9651 *vb*
commemorazione commemoration
9286 *la*
commestibile edible
9049 *adj*
commiato leave-taking
9173 *il*
commilitone fellow soldier
9660 *il*
commodoro commodore
7995 *il*
comodamente comfortably|easily
9203 *adv*
compassionevole compassionate
8161 *adj*
compatibile compatible
8590 *adj*
comperare buy
9123 *vb*
competente competent
7967 *adj*
competitivo competitive
9542 *adj*
compiacere please|satisfy
7570 *vb*
compimento fulfillment|completion
8206 *il*
complessità complexity
8618 *la*
completamento completion
8934 *il*
compressione compression
9842 *la*
compresso bowsprit
8571 *lo*
comunemente commonly
8811 *adv*
concilio council
8868 *il*
condiscendente condescending

9738 *adj*
condizionatore conditioner
8175 *il*
condottiero leader
9151 *il*
confederazione confederation|union
8470 *la*
confessionale confessional; confessional
7760 *adj; il*
confessore confessor
7676 *il*
confezionare pack|manufacture
9033 *vb*
conficcare stick|drive
9168 *vb*
configurazione configuration|layout
9633 *la*
confisca confiscation
9504 *la*
confiscare confiscate|disendow
7571 *vb*
confrontare compare
8804 *vb*
congelamento freezing|frostbite
8446 *il*
congelatore freezer
7619 *il*
congetturare conjecture
9944 *vb*
congiunto joined; kinsman
9282 *adj; il*
coniugale conjugal|marital
7772 *adj*
coniuge spouse|consort
9559 *il*
conquista conquest
7508 *la*
conquistatore conqueror
7596 *il*
consacrare consecrate|devote
8079 *vb*
consecutivo consecutive|running
9454 *adj*
conservatore conservator; Tory
8001 *il; adj*
conservatorio conservatory; conservative

8840 *il; adj*
considerevole considerable|sizable
7558 *adj*
consistenza consistency|texture
8977 *la*
consorzio consortium
9061 *il*
consultazione consultation|counsel
9711 *la*
consulto consultation
7764 *il*
contagiare infect
8082 *vb*
contagio contagion
8065 *il*
contaminazione contamination
8378 *la*
contatore counter|meter
7551 *il*
contemplare contemplate
8930 *vb*
contemporaneo contemporary
8871 *adj*
contestare challenge|contest
9020 *vb*
continentale continental
8538 *adj*
contingente contingent
9374 *adj*
contorto twisted
7864 *adj*
contrabbandiere smuggler
8122 *il*
contrabbasso contrabass
9535 *il*
contraddire contradict
9675 *vb*
contrariamente contrary to; in spite of
7966 *adv; prp*
contrastante conflicting
9561 *adj*
contrastare counteract
8387 *vb*
contrattare negotiate
8036 *vb*
contrazione contraction

8577 *la*
controspionaggio counterintelligence
8513 *il*
controverso controversial
9191 *adj*
convalescenza convalescence
8980 *la*
convenevole fitting
9612 *adj*
convenienza convenience|advantage
9832 *la*
conversare converse
7671 *vb*
conversione conversion
7700 *la*
convertire convert
8310 *vb*
convincente convincing
9005 *adj*
convivenza cohabitation
9051 *la*
cooperativo cooperative
9106 *adj*
coordinato coordinate
9326 *adj*
coordinatore coordinator
9360 *il*
coraggiosamente courageously|gamely
8828 *adv*
corallino coral
8999 *adj*
corallo coral
9073 *il*
corazzato armored
8316 *adj*
cordialmente cordially
9080 *adv*
coreografia choreography
8335 *la*
cornetto cornet
9844 *il*
cornicione cornice|eaves
8295 *il*
corporatura build
8767 *la*
corporeo bodily
7871 *adj*
corredo kit|equipment
9771 *il*
correttezza correctness
9045 *la*
corridore runner
7751 *il*
corsetto corset
9027 *il*
corteggiamento courtship|lovemaking
9087 *il*
corteggiare court
9841 *vb*
cortigiano courtier
7927 *il*
cosacco Cossack
7708 *il*
costanza constancy
9936 *la*
costituzionale constitutional
9324 *adj*
cottimo piece rate system
9623 *il*
cottura burning
8240 *la*
covare hatch|sit
9840 *vb*
cozzare clash|butt
9052 *vb*
cranico cranial
9065 *adj*
crasso crass
8109 *adj*
creditore creditor
7778 *il*
crema cream
8375 *la*
crematorio crematory
8374 *il*
cremazione cremation
9350 *la*
creta clay
7532 *la*
criceto hamster
8055 *il*
criniera mane

9502 *la*

criterio criterion|principle

8363 *il*

crocchetta croquette

9328 *la*

crocevia crossroads

9815 *le*

crocifiggere crucify

8539 *vb*

crocifissione crucifixion

8409 *la*

croissant croissant

8882 *i*

cromo chrome

9000 *il*

cronico chronic

9114 *adj*

cronometrare time|minute

7808 *vb*

crostaceo crustacean; shellfish

9571 *adj; il*

croupier croupier

9315 *i*

cuccetta bunk|couchette

8706 *la*

cucchiaino teaspoon

8139 *il*

curatore curator

9933 *il*

curiosità curiosity

7546 *la*

custodire keep|guard

9927 *vb*

D

danneggiato damaged

8164 *adj*

dannoso harmful|detrimental

8897 *adj*

dapprima at first

7609 *adv*

dardo dart

9444 *il*

davanzale sill

8267 *il*

decaffeinare decaffeinate

7544 *vb*

decappottabile convertible

7744 *adj*

decompressione decompression

9313 *la*

decretare decree|enact

9264 *vb*

dedito dedicated

8896 *adj*

deduzione deduction

8844 *la*

deficit deficit|deficiency

8037 *il*

deforme deformed|crooked

8111 *adj*

degenerare degenerate

7579 *vb*

degradante degrading

9256 *adj*

degradare degrade

8807 *vb*

demoniaco demoniac|fiendish

9803 *adj*

densità density|thickness

8672 *la*

denso dense|full

7633 *adj*

dentale dental

9413 *adj*

dentino denticle

8800 *il*

deplorevole regrettable|deplorable

8728 *adj*

deportare deport

8534 *vb*

deridere mock|deride

8687 *vb*

derivato derivative; offshoot

8132 *adj; il*

desiderabile desirable

9441 *adj*

desideroso eager|desirous

9707 *adj*

designare designate|appoint

8314 *vb*

desistere desist
9819 *vb*
desolazione desolation
8907 *la*
destare arouse|kindle
9566 *vb*
destinatario recipient|addressee
8330 *il*
destrezza dexterity
8776 *la*
destriero steed
7855 *il*
detector detector
8462 *il*
deterrente deterrent
9172 *adj*
detersivo detergent; detergent
8457 *adj; il*
detonare detonate
8463 *vb*
dettagliato detailed
7791 *adj*
devastazione devastation
8867 *la*
diabetico diabetic; diabetic
8439 *adj; il*
diacono deacon
8169 *il*
diadema diadem
8341 *il*
diaframma diaphragm|baffle
8251 *il*
diagnosticare diagnose
8442 *vb*
diagnostico diagnostic
9744 *adj*
diagramma diagram
8214 *il*
diavoletto imp
9208 *il*
dichiarato declared|avowed
8401 *adj*
difatti in fact
9968 *adv*
diffamazione defamation|libel
8324 *la*
diffida warning
9741 *la*
diffidente suspicious|distrustful
9449 *adj*
diffuso widespread
7773 *adj*
digestione digestion
7924 *la*
digitare type in
7539 *vb*
dignitoso decent
7620 *adj*
dimensionale dimensional
9992 *adj*
diminuendo diminuendo
9676 *lo*
diminutivo diminutive
9147 *adj*
diminuzione decrease|reduction
9372 *la*
dinamico dynamic
7721 *adj*
diocesi diocese|see
8755 *la*
diplomazia diplomacy
7607 *la*
direttivo directive|executive
8222 *adj*
dirigibile airship; dirigible
8997 *il; adj*
dirottamento hijacking|diversion
8380 *il*
dirottatore hijacker
9479 *il*
dirupo cliff
8912 *il*
disabile disabled
7813 *adj*
disapprovazione disapproval|disapprobation
9351 *la*
disappunto disappointment
9952 *il*
disarmato unarmed
7965 *adj*
disastroso disastrous|shattering
8370 *adj*

Word	Translation	No.	Part of speech
discretamente	discreetly	9035	*adv*
discreto	discreet	9088	*adj*
discriminazione	discrimination	8448	*la*
disdire	cancel|unsay	8630	*vb*
disegnatore	designer|draftsman	9307	*il*
disertare	desert|bolt	8604	*vb*
disfunzione	dysfunction	9543	*la*
disinfettare	disinfect	8095	*vb*
disinvolto	casual	8853	*adj*
disordinato	messy|disorderly	9615	*adj*
disorientare	disorient|confuse	7957	*vb*
dispaccio	dispatch	8720	*il*
disperare	despair	10020	*vb*
display	display	9382	*il*
disprezzare	despise|look down on	7897	*vb*
disputa	dispute|argument	9843	*la*
dissenso	dissent|disagreement	8786	*il*
dissenteria	dysentery	9394	*la*
distaccato	detached	7934	*adj*
distogliere	divert|distract	8277	*vb*
distorsione	distortion	7861	*la*
distruttivo	destructive	7737	*adj*
distruttore	destroyer	8294	*il*
disturbato	disturbed	8904	*adj*
disumano	inhuman	9369	*adj*
divergenza	divergence|difference	7887	*la*
diversità	diversity	8894	*le*
dizione	diction	9525	*la*
docente	professor	7923	*il/la*
docile	docile|tame	7794	*adj*
documentare	document	7956	*vb*
dodicesimo	twelfth|twelfth	8440	*adj*
doge	doge	9555	*il*
dolciume	sweets; sweet	8833	*il; adj*
dolente	sore|sorrowful	7899	*adj*
doloso	malicious	8627	*adj*
domare	tame	7826	*vb*
domatore	tamer	9616	*il*
dominatore	ruler	9178	*il*
dondolare	swing|rock	9901	*vb*
donnaccia	slut	9331	*la*
donnola	weasel	9302	*la*
donzella	damsel	8916	*la*
dopobarba	aftershave; aftershave	9078	*adj; il*
doppiamente	doubly	7977	*adv*
dormiglione	sleepyhead	8252	*il*

dosaggio dosage
9474 *il*
dotto learned; scholar
8492 *adj; il*
droghiere grocer
9227 *il*
druido Druid
9636 *il*
ducato duchy|ducat
8050 *il*
duetto duet
8207 *il*
duo duo
7736 *il*
duomo cathedral
8416 *il*
duplicato duplicate
9271 *il*
duplice dual|duplex
9099 *adj*
duraturo lasting|enduring
9116 *adj*
durezza hardness|toughness
9714 *la*

E

eccessivamente excessively|over
8546 *adv*
eccezionalmente exceptionally
9583 *adv*
ecografia echography
7816 *le*
economista economist
9994 *il/la*
edicola newsstand
9495 *le*
edile building; aedile
7935 *adj; il*
edilizio building
7881 *adj*
editoriale editorial; leader
7729 *adj; lo*
educativo educational
7756 *adj*
effettivo actual; strength
8497 *adj; il*
egizio Egyptian
9420 *adj*
egocentrico egocentric; egotist
7585 *adj; il*
eguale compeer
9210 *il*
eiaculazione ejaculation
9886 *la*
elaborato elaborate; script
9986 *adj; il*
elaborazione processing
9752 *la*
eletto elect
8056 *adj*
elettrizzante electrifying
8849 *adj*
elettrocardiogramm a electrocardiogram
9863 *il*
elettrodomestico household appliance
8745 *il*
elettrone electron
8256 *il*
elevato high|elevated
8940 *adj*
elogio praise
8189 *il*
eloquente eloquent|articulate
7962 *adj*
eludere circumvent|bypass
9042 *vb*
emanare issue|emanate
8063 *vb*
emarginare marginalize
9498 *vb*
emiliano emilian
7926 *adj*
eminente eminent
9157 *adj*
emiro emir
8249 *il*
emissario emissary
9332 *il*
emittente issuer; issuing
8107 *la; adj*

empatia empathy
8168 *le*
empio impious
8653 *adj*
encomio praise
9935 *il*
energico energetic
9799 *adj*
ennesimo umpteenth
7890 *adj*
epatite hepatitis
7993 *le*
epica epic
7835 *le*
epicentro epicenter|focus
9763 *lo*
epico epic
9319 *adj*
epilessia epilepsy
7872 *la*
epilettico epileptic
9739 *adj*
epilogo epilogue
9768 *il*
equamente equally
9882 *adv*
équipe team
9751 *le*
eretico heretic
9004 *adj*
ergersi rise
9257 *vb*
erotismo eroticism
10019 *il*
erroneamente wrongly
9688 *adv*
esagerazione exaggeration|aggrandizement
7860 *le*
esaltare exalt|celebrate
8851 *vb*
esaudire fulfill|grant
8474 *vb*
esaurito spent
8566 *adj*
eschimese Eskimo; Eskimo
9894 *adj; il/la*
esclusione exclusion
9990 *la*
escursione excursion|hike
7723 *le*
esecutore performer
9425 *il*
esibire show|show off
8602 *vb*
esibizionista exhibitionist
7636 *il/la*
esile slender|thin
9664 *adj*
esiliato exile
8071 *il*
esonerare exempt|exonerate
9386 *vb*
espandere expand|enlarge
7807 *vb*
espediente expedient|device
9823 *il*
espiare atone|pay
9329 *vb*
espiazione atonement
9174 *la*
esplicitamente roundly
9242 *adv*
esplicito explicit
9135 *adj*
espressamente expressly
7686 *adv*
establishment establishment
8815 *gli*
esteriore external|exterior
9634 *adj*
estetico aesthetic
7564 *adj*
estinguere extinguish
8964 *vb*
estradizione extradition
8145 *le*
estremista extremist
7997 *il/la*
esultanza exultation
8760 *la*
eterosessuale heterosexual
8816 *adj*

euforia euphoria
8163 *le*
eugenetico eugenic
9648 *adj*
eutanasia euthanasia
9317 *la*
evenienza eventuality
8185 *la*
eventualità eventuality|possibility
7770 *le*
eventualmente in case
9346 *adv*
evocare evoke
8744 *vb*
evolutivo evolutive
9947 *adj*
evoluto advanced
8044 *adj*
evolvere evolve
9284 *vb*
expo exhibition
9647 *le*

F

fabbricante manufacturer
8582 *il/la*
fabbricazione manufacture
9524 *la*
facilitare facilitate
9092 *vb*
fagiano pheasant
8951 *il*
faglia fault
9641 *la*
fagotto bassoon
7554 *il*
faida feud
9767 *la*
falce sickle
8444 *la*
falco hawk
7846 *il*
falcone falcon
8657 *il*
falena moth
9626 *la*
famigerato notorious
7738 *adj*
familiarità familiarity
9373 *la*
fandonia humbug
8981 *la*
fantasticare daydream
8825 *vb*
fante knave|infantryman
9084 *il*
fantoccio puppet
8503 *il*
farmaceutico pharmaceutical
8810 *adj*
fasciatura bandage|dressing
8830 *la*
fascio beam|bundle
7594 *il*
faticare labor|work hard
7614 *vb*
fauna fauna
7930 *la*
fausto auspicious|fortunate
9950 *adj*
fava bean
8149 *la*
favoreggiamento abetment
8796 *il*
fazione faction
8596 *la*
fedelmente faithfully
7712 *adv*
felino feline
7987 *adj*
femminista feminist
8973 *il/la*
fendere cleave|slit
7541 *vb*
fermaglio clip
9216 *il*
fermezza firmness
8659 *la*
fertilità fertility
9047 *la*
fertilizzare fertilize

8963 *vb*
fervido fervent
8404 *adj*
fervore fervor|zeal
9288 *il*
festino party
9529 *il*
fettina chip; rudeness
9620 *la; la*
feudo feud|fief
8467 *il*
fiaba fairy tale
7785 *la*
fiaccare sap|weaken
8028 *vb*
fibbia buckle
8917 *la*
fiduciario trustee; fiduciary
8465 *il; adj*
fiducioso confident
7856 *adj*
fifa funk
8130 *la*
figliastra stepdaughter
9852 *la*
figlioccio godson
8664 *il*
figuraccia poor figure
8781 *le*
figurina figurine
8344 *la*
filantropo philanthropist
9485 *il*
filastrocca doggerel
9421 *la*
filettare thread
7692 *vb*
filiale branch; filial
7504 *la; adj*
filone vein
9538 *il*
finanziatore financier
9154 *il*
finezza fineness|finesse
9298 *la*
finimondo pandemonium
9209 *il*
fionda sling
8237 *la*
fioraio florist
9392 *il*
fiorellino floret
8195 *il*
fisarmonica accordion
9419 *la*
fissato fixed|set
8568 *adj*
flagello scourge|plague
7601 *il*
flashback flashback
8131 *i*
fluire flow; flow
9246 *il; vb*
fluttuare fluctuate|float
9774 *vb*
fobia phobia
8313 *la*
focaccia cake
9023 *la*
focolare hearth; astronomer
9262 *il; il*
fondale backdrop|depth
7963 *il*
fondamentalista fundamentalist
9754 *il*
fondina holster
8417 *la*
forense forensic
8791 *adj*
forestale forest
8364 *adj*
forgiare forge|tilt
9075 *vb*
formicaio anthill
8519 *il*
formicolio tingling|pins and needles
9985 *il*
formulare formulate|express
8854 *vb*
fornace furnace
7567 *la*
fornaio baker

7680 *il*
fornello stove
8359 *il*
fornicazione fornication
9165 *la*
fortino blockhouse
8499 *il*
forziere coffer
9342 *il*
foschia mist
9907 *la*
fosco dark|gloomy
8210 *adj*
fotocopia photocopy
9031 *la*
fotocopiatrice photocopier
9860 *la*
fotogramma still
8200 *il*
foulard scarf
9137 *il*
frastuono uproar
7543 *il*
fraterno fraternal|sisterly
9376 *adj*
freccetta dart
8535 *la*
freddezza coldness|cold shoulder
9679 *la*
frenesia frenzy
9418 *la*
freschezza freshness
9942 *la*
frigido frigid
9251 *adj*
frizzante crisp
8511 *adj*
fronteggiare face|cope
7894 *vb*
frullatore mixer
9362 *il*
fruscio rustling|swish
8026 *il*
fruttare yield|fruit
9686 *vb*
fuga escape|get-away
8938 *la*
fugace fleeting|fugacious
9979 *adj*
fuggiasco fugitive|escapee
8798 *il*
fulcro fulcrum
9155 *il*
fuliggine soot
8838 *la*
fulminare fulminate
7932 *vb*
fumante smoking
7888 *adj*
funzionale functional
8562 *adj*
funzionamento operation|working
7657 *il*
fuorché except
9788 *prp*
furibondo furious|wild
8906 *adj*
furtivo furtive|slinky
9097 *adj*
fusibile fuse; fusible
8580 *il; adj*
fusto stem|drum
7789 *il*
futile futile|trivial
8983 *adj*

G

galante gallant
7969 *adj*
galantuomo gentleman
8842 *il*
galattico galactic
9865 *adj*
galeotto convict
9055 *il*
galleggiante floating; float
7502 *adj; il*
gallese Welsh; Welsh
9678 *adj; il*
galletto cockerel
9293 *il*

garbo politeness
8318 *il*
garofano carnation
8899 *il*
garzone boy
7904 *il*
gastrico gastric
9878 *adj*
gazza magpie
9918 *la*
gazzella gazelle
9217 *la*
gazzetta gazette
8900 *la*
gelsomino jasmine
9465 *il*
gemma gem|bud
8778 *la*
generico generic
8346 *adj*
generosamente generously
8722 *adv*
genesi genesis
8297 *la*
gengiva gum
9494 *la*
genovese Genoese
9133 *adj*
genuino genuine|authentic
9659 *adj*
geometria geometry
7900 *la*
gerarchia hierarchy
8451 *la*
germano German
9961 *adj*
germoglio bud|sprout
8096 *il*
geroglifico hieroglyph; hieroglyphic
7933 *il; adj*
gestore manager
7763 *il*
gesuita Jesuit
8805 *il*
gettone token
8876 *il*
ghiacciaio glacier
8803 *il*
ghiacciolo icicle
8971 *il*
ghiaia gravel
9056 *la*
ghianda acorn
8574 *la*
ghiandola gland
7602 *la*
ghigno fleer
9309 *il*
giaccone short coat
9214 *il*
giaguaro jaguar
9723 *il*
ginnasta gymnast
8537 *il/la*
giogo yoke
9059 *il*
gioielliere jeweler
8322 *il*
gioioso joyful
9179 *adj*
gioire rejoice
9225 *vb*
giornaliero daily; day-to-day
8768 *adj; il*
giostra carousel|joust
9598 *la*
giovare profit
9503 *vb*
gironzolare roam|wander about
8491 *vb*
girovagare wander|wander about
9539 *vb*
giugulare jugular vein
9599 *la*
giurisprudenza law
8339 *la*
glaciale glacial
7991 *adj*
gladiatore gladiator
8456 *il*
glassa icing
9549 *la*

globulare globular
8126 *adj*
gnocco dumpling
9161 *lo*
gnomo gnome|elf
8890 *lo*
gocciolare drip
8348 *vb*
goffo clumsy; hobbledehoy
7968 *adj; il*
gommone rubber dinghy
7814 *il*
gonfiore swelling|distension
9230 *il*
gotico Gothic
8113 *adj*
grafica graphics
7815 *la*
grammatica grammar
7976 *la*
grammofono gramophone
8073 *il*
grandine hailstorm
8488 *la*
gratifica bonus
9600 *la*
gratificare gratify
8650 *vb*
grattare scratch|scrape
8735 *vb*
gravitare gravitate
7702 *vb*
grizzly grizzly
9166 *i*
groppa back
7788 *la*
gruccia crutch
10003 *la*
grugnire grunt
8635 *vb*
gruzzolo hoard
8400 *il*
guadare wade
8911 *vb*
guaire yelp
9456 *vb*
guantone mitt
7865 *il*
guardiamarina midshipman
8570 *il*
guardone Peeping Tom
7986 *il*
guaritore healer
7992 *il*
gustare enjoy|taste
7961 *vb*
gustoso tasty|savory
7895 *adj*

I

iarda yard
8285 *la*
iato hiatus
8021 *lo*
ibernazione hibernation
9619 *la*
ibrido hybrid
8174 *adj*
icona icon
8014 *la*
idealista idealist
7769 *il/la*
idem idem; ditto; ideally
8085 *prn; il; adv*
identikit identikit
8461 *gli*
ideologia ideology
7878 *la*
idoneo suitable
7741 *adj*
idrante hydrant
8707 *il*
iena hyena
7598 *la*
ignaro unaware
9759 *adj*
illegittimo illegitimate
9781 *adj*
illeso unharmed|uninjured
9371 *adj*
illimitato unlimited|unrestricted

8435 *adj*
illudere deceive|delude oneself
8187 *vb*
illustrazione illustration
9887 *la*
imbarcazione boat
7604 *le*
imbattibile unbeatable
8024 *adj*
imbottito padded
8703 *adj*
imitatore imitator
9953 *il*
immigrare immigrate
8452 *vb*
immondo unclean|filthy
8685 *adj*
immutabile immutable
9200 *adj*
impacchettare pack|package
9720 *vb*
impadronirsi seize|master
9185 *vb*
imparziale impartial
8209 *adj*
impasto dough
8601 *lo*
impavido fearless
9337 *adj*
impazienza impatience
7556 *le*
impenetrabile impenetrable
7549 *adj*
imperativo imperative
8958 *adj*
imperfetto imperfect
9195 *adj*
imperialismo imperialism
9475 *il*
impeto impetus|fit
7825 *il*
impetuoso impetuous|dashing
8493 *adj*
impiantare implant|establish
9325 *vb*
impicciare meddle
8329 *vb*
impiccio mess|hindrance
7658 *il*
impigliare entangle
9523 *vb*
implacabile implacable
8069 *adj*
implicazione implication
7869 *le*
importazione import
8415 *le*
importunare bother|importune
9575 *vb*
impossibilità impossibility
9649 *la*
impostare set up|set out
9900 *vb*
impotenza impotence|impuissance
8886 *le*
imprecare curse|swear
8525 *vb*
imprimere give|impress
8637 *vb*
improvvisazione improvisation|ad-lib
8300 *la*
impudente impudent; jackanapes
9193 *adj; il/la*
impudenza impudence|nerve
9677 *le*
impugnatura handle|grip
9412 *la*
impuro impure
9522 *adj*
inaccessibile inaccessible
8970 *adj*
inammissibile inadmissible
8320 *adj*
inarrestabile unrestrainable
7937 *adj*
inaugurare inaugurate
9912 *vb*
incalzante pressing
8517 *adj*
incarcerare imprison
8814 *vb*
incarnazione incarnation

9499 *le*
incendiario arsonist; incendiary
9765 *il; adj*
inceneritore incinerator
9702 *il*
inceppare clog|obstruct
9468 *vb*
incesto incest
9091 *il*
incline prone|inclined
7753 *adj*
incombere impend
8471 *vb*
incompetenza incompetence
7812 *le*
incompleto incomplete
9039 *adj*
inconcepibile inconceivable
7793 *adj*
inconfutabile irrefutable
9902 *adj*
inconsapevole unaware|oblivious
9442 *adj*
incontrollabile uncontrollable
7747 *adj*
incoraggiante cheering
8594 *adj*
incoronazione coronation
7727 *le*
incorreggibile incorrigible
9775 *adj*
incrementare increase
8039 *vb*
incrociatore cruiser
8433 *il*
incurabile incurable
8643 *adj*
incuriosire excite curiosity
9848 *vb*
indaffarato busy
8905 *adj*
indebito undue
8629 *adj*
indebolire weaken|impair
8334 *vb*
indecenza indecency

9997 *la*
indeciso undecided
7656 *adj*
indennità bonus
8221 *le*
indennizzare indemnify
9712 *vb*
indescrivibile indescribable
9238 *adj*
indeterminato indeterminate
8740 *adj*
indice index|rate
7907 *i*
indietreggiare back|retreat
7958 *vb*
indigestione indigestion
8950 *la*
indignazione indignation|warmth
9809 *le*
indire call|announce
9354 *vb*
indiscreto indiscreet|prying
8135 *adj*
indole nature
7973 *il*
indomani next day
7647 *il*
indugiare linger|delay
9654 *vb*
indugio delay
8902 *il*
indulgente indulgent|charitable
7713 *adj*
indulgenza indulgence|pardon
8265 *le*
indumento garment
8287 *il*
inesistente non-existent
8087 *adj*
inesperto inexperienced|inexpert
8991 *adj*
infamare defame
9650 *vb*
infamia infamy
7552 *le*
infatuazione infatuation

9219 *la*
infedeltà infidelity|disloyalty
8418 *le*
infelicità unhappiness
7557 *le*
inferiorità inferiority
10001 *le*
infermità infirmity
7777 *le*
infermo infirm
9849 *adj*
infiammabile flammable|irascible
8713 *adj*
infiltrarsi infiltrate
9229 *vb*
infiltrazione infiltration
9742 *le*
infilzare stick
9223 *vb*
infinità infinity
8134 *le*
inflessibile inflexible|adamant
9190 *adj*
infliggere inflict
8668 *vb*
influenza influence|influenza
7998 *la*
informale informal
8032 *adj*
infortunarsi get injured
9158 *vb*
infortunio accident
8043 *il*
infrastruttura infrastructure
8846 *le*
infuori out
7948 *adv*
ingannevole misleading|tricky
9464 *adj*
ingelosire make jealous
8718 *vb*
ingenuità naivety|ingenuousness
9367 *le*
inghiottire swallow|gulp
8005 *vb*
ingiunzione injunction
9198 *le*
ingordo greedy
9074 *adj*
ingorgo jam
8142 *il*
ingranaggio gear|cog
8022 *il*
ingrandimento magnification|aggrandizemen
t
8560 *il*
ingrandire enlarge|expand
8306 *vb*
ingrossare swell|enlarge
8501 *vb*
inguine groin
8371 *il*
inimmaginabile unimaginable
8373 *adj*
innato innate|inborn
9450 *adj*
innaturale unnatural
7673 *adj*
innegabile undeniable
8702 *adj*
innescare trigger
9010 *vb*
innesco trigger
9062 *il*
innovativo innovative
9544 *adj*
inoffensivo harmless
8428 *adj*
inondare flood|overflow
9851 *vb*
inondazione flood|flooding
7755 *le*
inosservato unnoticed|unobserved
7608 *adj*
input input; input
9070 *gli; vb*
inquietare worry
8108 *vb*
inquieto restless|worried
8553 *adj*
inquietudine restlessness
9567 *le*

inquisizione inquisition
7683 *la*
insanguinare bathe in blood
8224 *vb*
insaziabile insatiable
8626 *adj*
insegna signboard|banner
9277 *le*
insensato senseless
7914 *adj*
insetticida insecticide
8354 *lo*
insicurezza insecurity
9090 *la*
insicuro insecure
7582 *adj*
insinuazione insinuation|implication
8839 *le*
insistenza insistence
8782 *la*
insostenibile unsustainable
8932 *adj*
instabilità instability
9578 *le*
installazione installation
9530 *la*
insubordinazione insubordination
8349 *la*
insuccesso failure
9452 *il*
insufficiente insufficient|inadequate
9303 *adj*
insufficienza insufficiency|lack
8526 *la*
intasare block|choke
9972 *vb*
integrante integral
9780 *adj*
integrare integrate
9869 *vb*
intenzionale intentional
8621 *adj*
intenzionato intentional
9729 *adj*
interagire interact
10014 *vb*
interazione interaction
8532 *la*
interfono intercom
7588 *gli*
interminabile endless
8984 *adj*
internato internee
8009 *il*
interrogativo questioning; interrogative
8555 *il; adj*
interstellare interstellar
9240 *adj*
interurbano interurban
8338 *adj*
intestare head
7795 *vb*
intoccabile untouchable; untouchable
8391 *adj; il/la*
intolleranza intolerance
9377 *la*
intonare intone|tone
8524 *vb*
intossicazione intoxication
9136 *le*
intraprendente enterprising
9308 *adj*
intrigo intrigue
7832 *il*
introvabile not to be found
9773 *adj*
inumare bury
9722 *vb*
invadente intrusive; intruder
7803 *adj; il/la*
invecchiamento aging
9353 *il*
inverosimile unlikely|tall
8749 *adj*
invitante inviting
9267 *adj*
invocare invoke|call upon
8394 *vb*
involontario involuntary|unintentional
9939 *adj*
involtino roulade
7757 *il*

iodio iodine
9378 *lo*
ipermercato hypermarket
8254 *il*
ipnotizzare hypnotize
9058 *vb*
ipotetico hypothetical|presumed
9969 *adj*
ippopotamo hippopotamus
8072 *il*
iraniano Iranian
9170 *adj*
irascibile irascible|cantankerous
7960 *adj*
irraggiungibile unattainable
8506 *adj*
irreparabile irreparable
9391 *adj*
irrequieto restless
9827 *adj*
irreversibile irreversible
8482 *adj*
irriconoscibile unrecognizable
9321 *adj*
irrigazione irrigation
9306 *la*
irrispettoso disrespectful
9792 *adj*
irritabile irritable|edgy
8384 *adj*
irritazione irritation|annoyance
9379 *le*
irrompere burst
7563 *vb*
islamico Islamic; Islam
7592 *adj; il*
isolante insulating; insulator
9164 *adj; il*
issare hoist
9043 *vb*
istantaneamente instantly
9285 *adv*
isterismo hysteria
9527 *gli*
istituire establish|charter
8386 *vb*
istruttivo instructive
9291 *adj*

J

jogging jogging
7703 *lo*
judo judo
9787 *il*
juke-box jukebox
8293 *il*

L

lacrimogeno lachrymatory
8736 *adj*
laghetto pond
7623 *il*
lampadario chandelier
7613 *il*
lampante glaring
10018 *adj*
lampione lamp
8432 *il*
lampone raspberry
9148 *il*
lanciafiamme flame thrower
8218 *il*
lanciatore thrower
7662 *il*
lappone Lapp; Laplander
9755 *adj; il*
lare lares
9069 *il*
larghezza width|span
8708 *la*
larva larva
8121 *la*
lasso period; weary
7857 *il; adj*
lastricare pave
7970 *vb*
latitante absconding; abscond
8793 *adj; il*
latitudine latitude
8328 *la*

lattaio milkman
8286 *il*
lavapiatti dishwasher
9113 *il/la*
lavastoviglie dishwasher
9534 *la*
lavata wash
8137 *la*
lavorativo working
9622 *adj*
lavorazione processing
8133 *la*
lealmente loyally
9589 *adv*
lebbra leprosy
8523 *la*
lebbroso leper; leprous
8158 *il; adj*
leccapiedi toady|flunky
8097 *il/la*
lega alloy
8076 *la*
legalità legality
9108 *la*
legittimare legitimize|justify
9512 *vb*
lentiggine freckle
9791 *la*
lenza line
9501 *la*
letargo hibernation
8624 *il*
letizia joy
8795 *la*
letterale literal
9008 *adj*
leva lever|draft
9847 *la*
libellula dragonfly
8051 *la*
lievemente slightly|lightly
9747 *adv*
lignaggio lineage|kin
9853 *il*
limbo limbo
8888 *il*
limitazione limitation|restraint
8724 *la*
limpido clear|limpid
8119 *adj*
lineamento feature|outline
8616 *il*
lineare linear|straightforward
9643 *adj*
linfa sap
8325 *la*
lingotto ingot
8245 *il*
liquirizia licorice
8640 *la*
lirico lyrical|operatic
8466 *adj*
localizzazione location
8681 *la*
lodevole commendable
9287 *adj*
loggia invulnerable
9656 *adj*
londinese Londoner; London's
9509 *il/la; adj*
longitudine longitude
9184 *la*
loquace talkative|voluble
8709 *adj*
lordo gross|filthy
9956 *adj*
losco shady|sinister
8029 *adj*
lozione lotion
7903 *la*
luccicante shimmering
9521 *adj*
lucciola firefly
8701 *la*
lucente shiny|lucent
7524 *adj*
lucidità lucidity
8181 *la*
lugubre dismal|lugubrious
9486 *adj*
lungi far
9595 *adv*

lusinga flattery
8642 *la*
lussuoso luxurious
7870 *adj*
lustrascarpe shoeshine|bootblack
9825 *i*
lustrino spangle
9507 *il*

M

macabro macabre
8015 *adj*
Macché! Not at all!
7655 *int*
macedonia fruit salad
8877 *la*
macellare slaughter
8763 *vb*
macelleria butcher's shop
7621 *la*
maestoso majestic|stately
8799 *adj*
maestria mastery
10011 *la*
maga sorceress
7640 *la*
maggiolino cockchafer
9248 *il*
magnesio magnesium
8662 *il*
magnete magnet
9954 *il*
magno great
8923 *adj*
maiuscola capital
7896 *la*
malanno illness
9793 *il*
maldestro clumsy|maladroit
7550 *adj*
malessere malaise|illness
8756 *il*
malfunzionamento malfunction
8112 *il*
malizia malice
9888 *la*
malocchio evil eye
7840 *il*
malta mortar
9508 *le*
maltempo bad weather
8013 *il*
maltese Maltese
9411 *adj*
malto propulsion
8588 *il*
maltrattamento maltreatment|misuse
9964 *il*
maltrattare abuse|mishandle
7628 *vb*
malumore bad mood
9117 *il*
mammut mammoth
7999 *i*
mandibola jaw|mandible
7536 *la*
mandorla almond
7653 *la*
mangime fodder
7925 *il*
manichino dummy
7618 *il*
manipolazione handling|falsification
7535 *la*
manna manna
8213 *la*
mannaia cleaver|ax
8660 *la*
manodopera labor|manpower
7889 *la*
manopola knob|handle
9440 *la*
manovale laborer|hand
9758 *il*
manovella crank
9770 *la*
manovrare maneuver|handle
8081 *vb*
mansione job|duty
7584 *la*
manto mantle

8205 *il*
manufatto artefact; manufactured

8381 *il; adj*
marca brand|mark

9932 *la*
marchiare mark|stamp

8219 *vb*
marmaglia rabble|riffraff

8342 *la*
martirio martyrdom|torture

9383 *il*
mascara mascara

9604 *il*
mascherata masquerade

9050 *la*
mascherina radiator grill

8945 *la*
masochista masochist

8966 *il/la*
masso boulder

8408 *il*
massone mason

9163 *il*
mastino mastiff

8646 *il*
maternità maternity|parenthood

7527 *la*
matricola freshman|number

7949 *la*
mecenate patron

9384 *il/la*
medesimo same

8982 *adj*
mediante through

7503 *prp*
mediatore mediator|broker

7951 *il*
medicare medicate

9573 *vb*
meditare meditate|brood

7810 *vb*
megafono megaphone

7867 *il*
megera shrew|harridan

8319 *la*
melanzana eggplant

9472 *la*
melassa molasses

9838 *la*
melodrammatico melodramatic

8936 *adj*
memoriale memorial

8060 *il*
menare lead

7990 *vb*
mendicare beg

9581 *vb*
menomare impair|maim

9022 *vb*
mensola shelf

9790 *la*
menzione mention

9336 *la*
mercantile merchant; merchantman

8011 *adj; il*
mercanzia merchandise

9072 *la*
mercatino flea market

9820 *il*
meritevole worthy|deserving

9236 *adj*
merlo blackbird|merlon

8154 *il*
mero mere

7834 *adj*
metabolismo metabolism

7780 *il*
metamorfosi metamorphosis

7617 *la*
meteorologico weather

9032 *adj*
meticcio mestizo

9855 *il*
metropoli metropolis

8045 *le*
microbo microbe

7682 *il*
militante militant

9355 *adj*
milza spleen

9713 *la*
mimo mime

9557 *il*
minaccioso threatening|ugly
7644 *adj*
minatore miner
7797 *il*
minerario mining
9764 *adj*
miope myopic; myope
9794 *adj; il/la*
miraggio mirage
9683 *il*
miscuglio mixture|blend
8230 *il*
missionario missionary; missionary
7739 *adj; il*
modellino model
8929 *il*
moderare moderate
7679 *vb*
moderazione moderation
9304 *la*
modestamente lowly
9938 *adv*
molestare harass|annoy
8180 *vb*
molestatore molester; molesting
9067 *il; adj*
molesto troublesome
9727 *adj*
mollusco shellfish|clam
9436 *il*
molotov molotov cocktail
9438 *il*
molteplice multiple|manifold
8614 *adj*
moltiplicare multiply
9514 *vb*
moltitudine multitude|crowd
8600 *la*
momentaneamente at the moment
9518 *adv*
monaca nun
9836 *la*
monarca monarch
9192 *il*
monarchia monarchy
8508 *la*
mondano worldly
9800 *adj*
mongolfiera hot-air balloon
9260 *la*
Mongolia Mongolia
7989 *la*
monotono monotonous|monotone
9258 *adj*
montacarichi elevator
9340 *il*
montatore fixer
9782 *il*
moralista moralist; moralistic
9976 *il/la; adj*
morbillo measles
8194 *il*
morboso morbid|unhealthy
8775 *adj*
moribondo dying; dying man
7911 *adj; il*
mormone mormon
9250 *adj*
mormorio murmur|hum
8865 *il*
mortadella mortadella
9358 *la*
mortaio mortar
7765 *il*
mortalità mortality
8920 *la*
mortorio funeral
9796 *adj*
moscerino gnat
9680 *il*
moscio soft
8880 *adj*
motivare motivate
7811 *vb*
motociclista motorcyclist
7634 *il/la*
motorizzazione motorization
8821 *la*
mousse mousse
8671 *la*
mozzafiato breathtaking

8160 *adj*

multinazionale multinational

7591 *adj*

muratore bricklayer

7684 *il*

muscoloso muscular|muscled

7886 *adj*

mutevole changing|changeable

10008 *adj*

mutilare mutilate

8278 *vb*

mutilazione mutilation

8921 *la*

N

nafta naphtha

8648 *la*

napalm napalm

7537 *il*

napoletano Neapolitan; Neapolitan

7678 *adj; il*

narcisista narcissist

9872 *il/la*

narrativo narrative

8007 *adj*

nasale nasal

8536 *adj*

nascente rising

9564 *adj*

natica buttock

7876 *la*

naufragio shipwreck|sinking

8837 *il*

nazionalità nationality

8823 *la*

negazione denial

8101 *la*

negligente negligent|careless

9668 *adj*

negoziato negotiation

7509 *il*

negoziatore negotiator

7759 *il*

nervosismo nervousness|jitters

8123 *il*

nettare nectar; clean

8504 *il; vb*

neurale neural

8682 *adj*

neutralizzare neutralize|counter

8667 *vb*

neutrone neutron

8165 *il*

nevrotico neurotic

9206 *adj*

nientemeno no less than

9414 *con*

ninfomane nymphomaniac

8665 *adj*

nitrato nitrate

8581 *il*

nitrire neigh

8447 *vb*

nitro nitre

9231 *il*

nocca knuckle

8843 *la*

noialtri we

8002 *prn*

nonnino grandpa

9132 *il*

nord-est northeast

8143 *il*

nordovest northwest

9692 *il*

nostromo boatswain

8018 *il*

notevolmente considerably

8509 *adv*

notificare notify

9957 *vb*

novecento nine hundred

7593 *num*

novello new|early

8260 *adj*

nullo null|insignificant

8622 *adj*

nume numen

7511 *il*

nuocere harm

7616 *vb*

nuotatore swimmer
9215 *il*
nutrice nurse
7612 *la*
nutriente nutritious|feeding
9311 *adj*
nutrimento nourishment|food
8518 *il*
nylon nylon
9801 *il*

O

oasi oasis
7804 *le*
obiettare object
8612 *vb*
obsoleto obsolete
9422 *adj*
occasionale occasional|casual
7862 *adj*
occasionalmente occasionally|by chance
8962 *adv*
occultamento concealment|occultation
7641 *il*
occulto occult|hidden
7882 *adj*
ode ode
9398 *le*
olfatto smell
8038 *il*
olimpico Olympic
8889 *adj*
oltraggioso offensive
8395 *adj*
oltremare overseas
9012 *adv*
omero humerus
8450 *il*
onta shame|offense
9732 *le*
opossum opossum
7799 *gli*
opportunista opportunist
9896 *il/la*
oppresso oppressed
8873 *il*
opprimente overwhelming|oppressive
8351 *adj*
opprimere oppress|bully
8392 *vb*
opuscolo brochure
8542 *il*
orbitale orbital
9850 *adj*
orca grampus
8054 *la*
orchidea orchid
8008 *la*
orda horde
9483 *la*
organizzatore organizer; organizing
8226 *gli; adj*
origliare eavesdrop
10022 *vb*
ormeggiare moor
9295 *vb*
orologeria watchmaking
8232 *le*
oroscopo horoscope
8641 *il*
orrido horrid|dreadful
9835 *adj*
orsetto bear cub
7519 *il*
ortica nettle
9817 *la*
ortodosso orthodox
7698 *adj*
orzo barley
8654 *il*
oscenità obscenity|filthiness
8757 *le*
ospitale hospitable
9926 *adj*
osseo bone|bony
9854 *adj*
ossessivo obsessive
8965 *adj*
ostacolare hinder|hamper
7632 *vb*
oste host|publican

8486 *il*
ostello hostel
9924 *il*
ostetrico obstetrician; obstetric
9143 *il; adj*
ostia host
7880 *la*
ostruzione obstruction
9471 *le*
ottimismo optimism
7707 *lo*
ottocento eight hundred
9294 *num*
ottuso obtuse; dolt
7743 *adj; il*
ovaia ovary
9873 *le*
ovile fold|pen
8288 *il*

P

pacifista pacifist
9478 *il/la*
paesano villager; village
8903 *il; adj*
paghetta pocket money
9244 *la*
pagnotta loaf
7790 *la*
paladino paladin
9297 *il*
palese obvious|evident
8666 *adj*
palestinese Palestinian; Palestinian
7704 *adj; il/la*
paletta scoop
8280 *la*
paletto stake|pole
8606 *il*
pallavolo volleyball
9987 *la*
palmare palmar
8382 *adj*
palombaro diver
7908 *il*
pancione paunch
8772 *il*
pancreas pancreas
8438 *lo*
panetteria relic
9601 *la*
papavero poppy
9743 *il*
papera gosling
8302 *la*
papero gander
9393 *il*
parabola parabola
8613 *la*
paragonabile comparable
8041 *adj*
paragonare compare|confront
7630 *vb*
pareggiare equalize|balance
7781 *vb*
parentela relationship|kinship
7921 *la*
parità equality|parity
8515 *la*
parodia parody|send-up
8067 *la*
parzialmente partly
7573 *adv*
passante passing; passer-by
7859 *adj; il/la*
passe-partout skeleton key
7982 *il*
passivo passive; liabilities
7730 *adj; il*
pastello pastel; pastel
8857 *adj; il*
pasticcino pastry
8078 *il*
paterno paternal
8059 *adj*
patibolo scaffold
7912 *il*
patologia pathology
7610 *la*
patriottico patriotic
8661 *adj*

patrizio patrician; patrician
7819 *adj; il*
patrono patron|patron saint
9585 *il*
patteggiare negotiate
8809 *vb*
pavone peacock
7652 *il*
pece pitch
9895 *la*
pedaggio toll
8953 *il*
pedalare pedal
9590 *vb*
pedana footboard
9923 *la*
pediatra pediatrician|paediatrist
9989 *il/la*
pedina pawn|piece
9017 *la*
pedone pedestrian|pawn
7863 *il*
pelare skin|fleece
8766 *vb*
pellegrinaggio pilgrimage
7514 *il*
pendio slope|hillside
9177 *il*
pendolare pendular
9112 *adj*
penicillina penicillin
8094 *la*
penisola peninsula
8700 *la*
pennarello pen
9874 *il*
pennuto fledged
9489 *adj*
pensatore thinker
9105 *il*
pensionamento retirement
8397 *il*
pentimento repentance
7599 *il*
pepita nugget
9837 *la*
per lo più mostly
8514 *adv*
percossa blow
9131 *la*
percussione percussion
9305 *la*
perdutamente hopelessly
9432 *adv*
perenne perennial|perpetual
9560 *adj*
perfezionare perfect|refine
9149 *vb*
perforare pierce|drill
8887 *vb*
periferico peripheral
9993 *adj*
periscopio periscope
7548 *il*
perlustrare search|scour
8291 *vb*
perlustrazione patrol
8556 *la*
permaloso touchy|sensitive
8879 *adj*
perpetuo perpetual
8261 *adj*
perplesso puzzled|perplexed
8183 *adj*
persecuzione persecution
7972 *la*
perseveranza perseverance
8104 *la*
persico perch
7685 *il*
perspicace perspicacious|discerning
7849 *adj*
persuadere persuade|convince
8737 *vb*
persuasione persuasion
7845 *la*
pertinente relevant
8607 *adj*
peschereccio fishing; fishing boat
8719 *adj; il*
pesco peach
8264 *il*

Word	Rank	Meaning	Type
peseta	7830	peseta	*la*
pesticida	8116	pesticide	*il*
pestilenza	8242	pestilence	*la*
petrolifero	7538	oil well	*lo*
pettorale	9746	pectoral	*adj*
piastra	8298	plate	*la*
piastrina	9515	platelet	*la*
piattino	9316	saucer	*il*
piedino	8603	toothsie	*il*
piedistallo	8068	pedestal	*il*
pignolo	9301	finicky; fastidious person	*adj; il*
pigrizia	9437	laziness|idleness	*la*
pilone	9806	pylon	*il*
piombare	8317	fall	*vb*
pioniere	7732	pioneer	*il*
piovra	8694	octopus	*la*
pipa	9100	pipe	*la*
piranha	9169	piranha	*i*
pirateria	7569	piracy	*la*
piroscafo	9592	steamer	*il*
pistacchio	9689	pistachio	*il*
pitone	8441	python	*il*
pittoresco	8711	picturesque|colorful	*adj*
pizzicare	8193	pinch|pluck	*vb*
pizzicato	9904	pizzicato	*lo*
placare	8283	appease|calm	*vb*
placca	7629	plate	*la*
plancia	8699	bridge	*la*
planetario	7922	planetary; planetarium	*adj; il*
platea	8004	audience	*la*
plurale	8469	plural; plural	*adj; il*
Plutone	9140	Pluto	*lo*
pluviale	9861	pluvial; waterspout	*adj; il*
podio	8410	podium|platform	*il*
poggiare	8115	rest|lean	*vb*
polemico	9701	polemical|controversial	*adj*
poligono	8077	polygon	*il*
pollame	9245	poultry	*il*
polmonare	8241	pulmonary	*adj*
poltiglia	7690	mush	*la*
pomata	8436	ointment|pomade	*la*
pomiciare	9637	neck	*vb*
pompelmo	9497	grapefruit	*il*
pomposo	9119	pompous	*adj*
popolarità	7553	popularity	*la*
poppa	8376	stern	*la*

poppante suckling
8794 *il/la*
porcospino porcupine|urchin
8585 *il*
poro pore
9213 *il*
portacenere ashtray
7710 *il*
portamento bearing|deportment
8587 *il*
portinaio porter|concierge
9830 *il*
portoricano Puerto Rican; Puerto Rican
8244 *adj; il*
portuale roustabout
9696 *lo*
posacenere ashtray
7631 *i*
posizionare position
9459 *vb*
possedimento possession
9568 *il*
potabile drinking|potable
8257 *adj*
potassio potassium
8423 *il*
potenzialità potentiality
8357 *le*
pozzanghera puddle
8732 *la*
precipitoso hasty|precipitous
9934 *adj*
predecessore predecessor
8483 *il*
predicare preach
7728 *vb*
predire predict
7581 *vb*
predone marauder
9945 *il*
preferenza preference
7854 *la*
preferibile preferable
9611 *adj*
preferibilmente preferably
8153 *adv*

prefettura prefecture
7824 *la*
pregio quality|merit
9905 *il*
prematrimoniale premarital|prematrimonial
7705 *adj*
premeditare premeditate
7513 *vb*
premeditazione premeditation|wilfulness
9913 *la*
premettere premise
10004 *vb*
premiato prize; prizewinner
9281 *adj; il*
premier premier
8947 *il*
premonizione premonition
9002 *la*
prerogativa prerogative|privelege
9995 *la*
prescrivere prescribe
7938 *vb*
prescrizione prescription
9167 *la*
presentabile presentable
8089 *adj*
presidio garrison|defense
9038 *il*
presiedere preside
8852 *vb*
pressa press
8106 *la*
pressappoco about
10021 *adv*
prestigioso prestigious
8053 *adj*
prevalere prevail|overbear
9026 *vb*
preventivo quote; preventive
7603 *il; adj*
prevenzione prevention|prophylaxis
9481 *la*
prezzemolo parsley
9829 *il*
primaverile vernal
9370 *adj*

primordiale primordial
7586 *adj*

privilegiato privileged
9037 *adj*

problematico problematic
8589 *adj*

procione raccoon|procyon
8006 *il*

proclama proclamation
8385 *lo*

proclamare proclaim|declare
8449 *vb*

procreare procreate
8956 *vb*

prodigo prodigal|lavish
8481 *adj*

profano profane; layman
9399 *adj; il*

profilo profile
9239 *il*

profumato scented|fragrant
7885 *adj*

progenie progeny
8617 *la*

progettazione design
8919 *la*

progettista designer
9152 *il/la*

prognosi prognosis
9162 *la*

programmatore programmer
9068 *il*

progressista progressive
9652 *il/la*

proibito prohibited
7848 *adj*

proibizionismo prohibition
8994 *il*

proiettare project|screen
8190 *vb*

prole offspring|children
7774 *la*

proletariato proletariat
8236 *il*

promotore promoter; promotive
9693 *il; adj*

propriamente properly
8705 *adv*

proroga extension
7850 *la*

prosa prose
9558 *la*

prosciugare drain
8199 *vb*

prosperare thrive|prosper
9159 *vb*

prospero prosperous|bonanza
8547 *adj*

prossimamente soon|in a short time
8909 *adv*

prossimità proximity|closeness
9265 *la*

protestante Protestant; Protestant
7884 *adj; il/la*

protesto protest
8475 *il*

protone proton
8819 *il*

provento income
9102 *il*

provetto proficient
9205 *adj*

provocante provocative
8862 *adj*

provocatorio provocative
9397 *adj*

psicanalisi psychoanalysis
9627 *la*

psicanalista psychoanalyst
9127 *il/la*

psichico psychic|mental
8247 *adj*

psicologicamente psychologically
7724 *adv*

pube pubis
9640 *il*

pubertà puberty
8895 *la*

pulcino chick
8092 *il*

pulsazione pulsation|throbbing
8479 *la*

pungente pungent; nippy
8806 *adj; il*
puntualità punctuality
9093 *la*
purificare purify|cleanse
9249 *vb*
purificazione purification|purifying
7945 *la*

Q

qualifica qualification
9941 *la*
qualora if
8765 *con*
quantico quantum
9628 *adj*
quartetto quartet
8188 *il*
quattromila four thousand
9510 *num*
questionario questionnaire
9553 *il*
questura police force
7517 *la*
quietare quiet|calm
8822 *vb*
quindicesimo fifteenth
9731 *num*
quintale quintal
9226 *il*
quoziente quotient
8529 *il*

R

racchetta racket
8299 *la*
raccordo junction
9673 *il*
racimolare glean
9766 *vb*
raddrizzare straighten|right
9416 *vb*
radiare expel
9300 *vb*
radioattività radioactivity
8797 *la*
radiofonico radio
10023 *adj*
radiografia radiography|radiograph
8155 *la*
radioso radiant
8558 *adj*
raffineria refinery
8636 *la*
raffreddamento cooling
7745 *il*
raggirare circumvent|deceive
9404 *vb*
raggiungibile attainable
7978 *adj*
rallegrare cheer|brighten
9006 *vb*
rallentatore slow motion
8172 *il*
rally rally
9347 *il*
rammollire soften
8152 *vb*
rapidità speed|rapidity
9657 *la*
rappresaglia retaliation
9036 *la*
rappresentanza representation
8437 *la*
rasare shave|mow
9446 *vb*
rassegnare resign oneself
8272 *vb*
rassegnazione resignation
9937 *la*
rastrello rake
8831 *il*
rattristare sadden
9222 *vb*
razziale racial
7637 *adj*
realismo realism
8406 *il*
recapitare deliver
9661 *vb*

Word	Rank	Translation	Part of speech
recapito	8561	delivery	*il*
recessione	9243	recession	*la*
recipiente	8634	container	*il*
reciso	9054	flat	*adj*
reclusione	7649	imprisonment	*la*
recupero	8683	recovery	*il*
redditizio	9202	profitable	*adj*
regolatore	8931	regulator	*il*
relatività	9974	relativity	*la*
relitto	7526	wreck|wreckage	*il*
remare	7726	row	*vb*
remata	8099	row	*la*
rena	7754	sand	*la*
rendita	7796	income	*la*
renna	8262	reindeer	*la*
repellente	8841	repellent|repulsive	*adj*
reperto	8047	find	*il*
replicare	9145	replicate|reply	*vb*
represso	9674	repressed	*adj*
reprimere	8808	repress|suppress	*vb*
requiem	9694	requiem	*il*
residenziale	8586	residential	*adj*
residuo	7516	residue; residual	*il; adj*
respiratore	9548	respirator	*il*
respiratorio	9870	respiratory	*adj*
restituzione	8548	return|rebate	*la*
restringere	9403	restrict|narrow	*vb*
retaggio	8729	heritage|survival	*il*
retroguardia	8608	rearguard	*la*
rettile	7529	reptile	*il*
rettilineo	9554	straight; straight	*adj; il*
rettitudine	9908	rectitude	*la*
reumatismo	9182	rheumatism	*il*
revocare	9812	revoke|reverse	*vb*
riabilitare	9234	rehabilitate	*vb*
riaccompagnare	9176	take back	*vb*
riacquistare	9816	regain|buy back	*vb*
rialzo	8727	rise	*il*
riassumere	8836	summarize|reassume	*vb*
riassunto	7873	summary|brief	*il*
ribasso	9703	fall|decline	*il*
ribollire	10002	boil|boil again	*vb*
ricadere	8203	fall|fall back	*vb*
ricambiare	7837	return|reciprocate	*vb*
ricapitolare	8872	recap|summarize	*vb*
ricattatore	9588	blackmailer	*il*

ricatto blackmail
7959 *il*

ricavo proceeds
9921 *il*

ricettatore fence
7654 *il*

riciclare recycle
8730 *vb*

ricognitore scout
9344 *il*

ricompensa reward|award
9546 *la*

riconciliazione reconciliation
7627 *la*

riconquistare recapture
8151 *vb*

riconsiderare reconsider
7809 *vb*

ricorrente recurrent
7606 *adj*

ricucire sew up
9153 *vb*

rielezione re-election
9361 *la*

rifilare trim|foist
9786 *vb*

rigenerazione regeneration
8490 *la*

rigo line|staff
9273 *il*

rigorosamente rigorously
9805 *adv*

riluttanza reluctance
9387 *la*

rimando return
8955 *il*

rimanente remaining; leftovers
8656 *adj; il*

rimbalzare bounce|bounce back
7575 *vb*

rimedio remedy|help
8103 *il*

rimorchiatore tug
9528 *il*

rimproverare reproach|blame
9631 *vb*

rimprovero reproach|rebuke
7578 *il*

Rinascimento Renaissance
9130 *il*

rincorrere run after
9016 *vb*

rinforzare strengthen|reinforce
9323 *vb*

rinfrescante refreshing
8691 *adj*

rinfrescare refresh|cool
8215 *vb*

ringhiare growl
8345 *vb*

ringhio snarl
9603 *il*

rinnovamento renovation|regeneration
9877 *il*

rinnovo renewal
8721 *il*

rinomato renowned
9493 *adj*

rinviare postpone|refer
8922 *vb*

riordinare rearrange|tidy
8516 *vb*

ripasso revision
9685 *il*

ripensamento afterthought
9745 *il*

ripercussione repercussion
7725 *la*

ripetizione repetition|private lesson
7988 *la*

ripiano shelf|terrace
9237 *il*

ripiegare fall back|fold up
7917 *vb*

ripieno filling; stuffed
7984 *il; adj*

riporre put
8605 *vb*

risaia paddy field
9458 *la*

risaltare stand out|show up
9778 *vb*

riscontrare find|verify
9408 *vb*
riscrivere rewrite
8010 *vb*
risentito resentful
9889 *adj*
risoluto resolute
8429 *adj*
rispedire send back
8281 *vb*
rispettoso respectful
7580 *adj*
risplendere shine|sparkle
8652 *vb*
risposare remarry
8332 *vb*
ristoro refreshment
9279 *il*
ristrutturazione renovation
7533 *la*
risucchiare suck
9001 *vb*
risuonare ring
8686 *vb*
ritaglio cut-out|clipping
8090 *il*
ritoccare retouch
8533 *vb*
ritornello refrain
8217 *il*
rivelatore detector
9345 *il*
rivendicare claim
8777 *vb*
rivestimento coating|jacket
8743 *il*
rivestito clad
8147 *adj*
rivoltare turn over
7983 *vb*
rivoltella revolver
8255 *la*
rizzare raise
8891 *vb*
rocca fortress
8591 *la*
roccaforte stronghold
9903 *la*
roccioso rocky
8734 *adj*
roditore rodent
8424 *adj*
rognoso mangy
8761 *adj*
rollare roll
10015 *vb*
rompicapo puzzle
9118 *il*
rondine swallow
8575 *la*
ronzare hum|whir
9098 *vb*
ruffiano pander
8554 *il*
rullare roll
8510 *vb*
rumba rumba
9671 *la*
rumeno Romanian
8942 *adj*
runa rune
9642 *la*
rupe cliff
9024 *la*
rurale rural
9756 *adj*
russare snore
8321 *vb*
rutto burp|retch
8746 *il*

S

sabotare sabotage
8170 *vb*
saccheggiare plunder|loot
9322 *vb*
saccheggio plunder|sack
8928 *il*
sacerdotessa priestess
9582 *la*
sacrilegio sacrilege

7821 *il*
saga saga
7905 *la*
saldamente securely|tight
9335 *adv*
salice willow
9960 *la*
salina saltern
8704 *la*
salmo psalm
9967 *il*
salvagente life buoy|life jacket
7766 *il*
salvaguardare safeguard
8655 *vb*
samaritano Samaritan
8186 *il*
sanatorio sanatorium
8832 *il*
sanguinario bloodthirsty|slaughterous
8455 *adj*
sanguinoso bloody
8913 *adj*
santino holy picture
7701 *il*
sapientone wise guy|know-all
7742 *il*
sapienza wisdom
7822 *la*
saponetta soap
8645 *la*
saporito tasty|savory
8473 *adj*
sarcastico sarcastic|derisive
8649 *adj*
sarcofago sarcophagus
9563 *il*
sarta seamstress
9129 *la*
sartoria tailoring
8986 *la*
sassofono saxophone
8146 *il*
sassone Saxon; Saxon
8495 *adj; il*
satira satire|lampoon

10013 *la*
savana savannah
9856 *la*
sazio full|sated
9917 *adj*
sbadato careless; scatterbrain
9181 *adj; lo*
sbalorditivo amazing
7560 *adj*
sbandare slide|disperse
9057 *vb*
sbando drift
9663 *lo*
sbarramento barrier
9946 *lo*
sbavare drool|smudge
9733 *vb*
sbocciare bloom|open
9235 *vb*
sbruffone boaster
8027 *lo*
scacchiera chessboard
9431 *la*
scagionare exonerate
9614 *vb*
scaglia scale
9962 *la*
scalpore sensation
8333 *lo*
scampare escape
7733 *vb*
scansafatiche loafer|shirker
8943 *il/la*
scapolare scapulary
8064 *lo*
scarabocchiare doodle|scribble
8403 *vb*
scaraventare hurl
9920 *vb*
scarpone boot
8564 *lo*
scarto waste
8138 *lo*
scassinatore burglar
9330 *lo*
scatolone carton

7939 *lo*
scavalcare climb over
8531 *vb*
sceneggiare dramatize
8355 *vb*
scenetta sketch
10007 *la*
scenografo set designer
9003 *lo*
schedare file|record
8952 *vb*
schiacciata smash
9457 *la*
schiaffeggiare slap
9263 *vb*
schiamazzo noise|cackle
9943 *lo*
schiappa duffer
7776 *la*
schieramento array
9785 *lo*
schierare deploy|line up
7510 *vb*
schivare dodge|avoid
8993 *vb*
schivo shy|reserved
8714 *adj*
schizofrenico schizophrenic
8750 *adj*
scià shah
8365 *lo*
sciabola saber
9212 *la*
sciacquone flushing device
8239 *lo*
sciagura disaster
8620 *la*
sciame swarm
8870 *lo*
sciolto loose|dissolved
7528 *adj*
scivoloso slippery
8356 *adj*
scocciare bother|be fed up
7915 *vb*
scocciatura nuisance

8279 *la*
scollatura neckline
9779 *la*
scolo drain
8114 *lo*
scolpire sculpt|carve
9658 *vb*
scombussolare upset|mess up
9922 *vb*
scomodare disturb|be inconvenient
8336 *vb*
sconcertante disconcerting
7844 *adj*
sconfinare trespass
9662 *vb*
sconsiderato inconsiderate|thoughtless
7909 *adj*
scontato discounted
8696 *adj*
scontento discontent; displeased
7768 *lo; adj*
scontroso grumpy|surly
8824 *adj*
scopa broom
9445 *la*
scoraggiare discourage|be discouraged
8639 *vb*
scorbutico scorbutic
9996 *adj*
scoria slag|waste
8632 *la*
scorza rind|peel
9606 *la*
scottante pressing
9892 *adj*
scremare skim
9591 *vb*
scricchiolio crunch|creaking
8675 *lo*
scrigno casket
7767 *lo*
scrivano scribe|clerk
9448 *lo*
scroto scrotum
8464 *lo*
sculacciare spank

	8156	*vb*
scultore		sculptor
	8129	*lo*
sdegno		indignation|disdain
	9488	*lo*
sdolcinato		sloppy
	8747	*adj*
sdraio		deckchair
	8083	*le*
seccare		dry|bother
	7714	*vb*
secchione		nerd
	7981	*il*
secondare		comply
	8801	*vb*
secondino		jailer|warder
	8368	*il*
sedano		celery
	9984	*il*
sedicesimo		sixteenth|sixteenth
	8282	*adj*
seduttore		seducer
	7762	*il*
seduzione		seduction|allurement
	7639	*la*
segatura		sawdust
	9180	*la*
seggio		seat
	8647	*il*
seggiolino		seat
	8369	*il*
segheria		sawmill
	7659	*la*
selvaggina		game
	9511	*la*
senile		senile
	9978	*adj*
sensualità		sensuality
	9463	*la*
separatista		separatist
	9736	*il/la*
sepolcro		tomb|sepulcher
	8496	*il*
seppia		cuttlefish
	9473	*la*
serbare		keep|remain

	9388	*vb*
serenata		serenade
	9669	*la*
serietà		seriousness|reliability
	8615	*la*
serrata		lockout
	8579	*la*
sesamo		sesame
	7892	*il*
setacciare		sift|search
	9089	*vb*
setaccio		sieve
	9617	*il*
sfasciare		smash up
	9708	*vb*
sferrare		launch
	9857	*vb*
sfidante		challenger; challenging
	7531	*il/la; adj*
sfiducia		distrust
	9697	*la*
sfinge		sphinx
	9532	*la*
sfogare		vent
	8229	*vb*
sfrattare		evict
	9700	*vb*
sfratto		evicted
	8179	*lo*
sfrontato		cheeky
	9519	*adj*
sfumatura		shade|nuance
	8347	*la*
sgabuzzino		storage room
	7853	*lo*
sgarbato		rude|impolite
	8274	*adj*
sgobbare		slog|work hard
	9029	*vb*
sgomberare		clear
	7597	*vb*
siamese		Siamese; Siamese
	8789	*adj; il/la*
sibilo		hiss|hissing
	9443	*il*
siccità		drought

8084 *la*
siepe hedge
7955 *la*
silenziatore silencer
8091 *il*
sillabare syllabify
9828 *vb*
silo silo
9875 *il*
simboleggiare symbolize|epitomize
9343 *vb*
simbolico symbolic|token
7566 *adj*
simbolismo symbolism
9973 *il*
simmetria symmetry
9906 *la*
simulare simulate|mimic
8405 *vb*
simulatore simulator
9253 *il*
simultaneamente concurrently
8377 *adv*
sincronizzare synchronize|time
8967 *vb*
sincronizzazione synchronization|timing
9858 *la*
singhiozzare sob
7910 *vb*
sinonimo synonymous; synonym
8098 *adj; il*
sintesi synthesis
7971 *la*
sintetico synthetic
9125 *adj*
sintonizzare tune
8673 *vb*
situare place|situate
8117 *vb*
slam slam
9891 *lo*
slogare dislocate|sprain
9046 *vb*
sloggiare dislodge
8422 *vb*
smaltire dispose of
9462 *vb*
smanceria affectation
9725 *la*
smantellare dismantle
9359 *vb*
smascherare unmask
8358 *vb*
smistamento sorting
9357 *lo*
smorfia grimace
8411 *la*
smuovere move|shift
9467 *vb*
soave sweet
8304 *adj*
soccorritore rescuer
8000 *il*
socializzare socialize
9423 *vb*
socievole sociable
7801 *adj*
sociologia sociology
9789 *la*
sodio sodium
8593 *il*
sofà sofa
8340 *il*
soffocante suffocating|stifling
9221 *adj*
soggezione awe
8592 *la*
soldatino toy soldier
8238 *il*
solfare sulphurise
9667 *vb*
sollevato relieved
8445 *i*
soma pack|burden
7562 *la*
sommerso black
9333 *adj*
somministrare administer|give
9428 *vb*
sommozzatore diver|scuba diver
9141 *il*
sonnambulo sleepwalker

8758 *il*
sopportabile bearable
9278 *adj*
sopprimere abolish
7833 *vb*
soprannominare nickname
8100 *vb*
sopravvalutare overestimate|overvalue
7891 *vb*
sorcio mouse
8829 *il*
sordomuto deaf and dumb; deaf mute
9893 *adj; il*
sorellastra stepsister
8061 *la*
sorgente source; rising
8692 *la; adj*
sorpassare overtake|surpass
9292 *vb*
sorvolare fly over
8875 *vb*
sostanziale substantial
9429 *adj*
sostare stop|pause
9064 *vb*
sostentamento sustenance|maintenance
7677 *il*
sostituzione replacement
7827 *la*
sotterfugio subterfuge
9879 *il*
sotterrare bury
8315 *vb*
sottomettere submit|subdue
9247 *vb*
sottomissione submission|subjection
8323 *la*
sottosegretario undersecretary
8468 *il*
sottostante below; underlying
9624 *adv; adj*
sottoveste petticoat
8998 *la*
sottufficiale non-comissioned officer
9338 *il/la*
sovranità sovereignty
8978 *la*
sovversivo subversive
8565 *adj*
spaccatura split
7638 *la*
spalancare open wide
9259 *vb*
spalare shovel
9958 *vb*
spargimento scatter
8182 *lo*
sparpagliare scatter
7576 *vb*
spartire share
8927 *vb*
spartito score
9310 *lo*
sparviere hawk
9365 *lo*
spasmo spasm
9451 *lo*
spassoso amusing|entertaining
9613 *adj*
spastico spastic; spastic
8454 *adj; lo*
spazzaneve snowplow
9629 *gli*
specializzare specialize
7559 *vb*
specificamente particularly
9980 *adv*
specificare specify|state
9687 *vb*
speculazione speculation|flutter
8305 *la*
spensierato carefree|light-hearted
9608 *adj*
spergiuro perjury
9318 *lo*
speronare ram
8826 *vb*
spessore thickness
8034 *lo*
spettrale spectral|phantom
8884 *adj*
spezzatino stew

8715 *lo*
spiaccicare mash
9916 *vb*
spiccare stand out|issue
9966 *vb*
spicciare hurry up
8937 *vb*
spiedo spit
8792 *lo*
spifferare blurt out|blab
9596 *vb*
spilorcio stingy; miser
8407 *adj; lo*
spinale spinal
8494 *adj*
spremere squeeze|squeeze out
8352 *vb*
sprofondare collapse
10005 *vb*
sprovvisto devoid
8019 *adj*
spruzzare spray|sprinkle
8738 *vb*
spumante sparkling; sparkling wine
9030 *adj; lo*
spunto cue
8016 *lo*
squarciare rip|slash
8748 *vb*
squaw squaw
7852 *le*
squilibrio imbalance
9482 *lo*
squillare ring
7779 *vb*
sradicare eradicate|root up
9120 *vb*
staffetta relay
8992 *la*
stampante printer
8893 *la*
stampato printed; printout
8301 *adj; lo*
stampella crutch
8327 *la*
stanare drive out
9965 *vb*
stanzetta room
8557 *la*
stanzino closet
9632 *lo*
starnutire sneeze
8020 *vb*
starnuto sneeze
9107 *lo*
statico static
9562 *adj*
statuetta statuette
7646 *la*
statuto statute
8458 *lo*
stellina starlet
8625 *la*
stendardo standard
9665 *lo*
sterminare exterminate
8259 *vb*
stesura drawing up
7786 *la*
steward steward
9063 *gli*
stilare draw up|draft
7879 *vb*
stilista stylist
8818 *il/la*
stimolare stimulate|spur
8764 *vb*
stipulare stipulate
8787 *vb*
stirare iron|stretch
7506 *vb*
stock stock
9261 *lo*
stormo flock
8120 *lo*
stracciare tear|shred
9625 *vb*
straccione ragamuffin
8500 *lo*
strangolamento strangling
8976 *lo*
strangolatore choker

9417 *lo*
strapazzare scramble|mistreat
8266 *vb*
strappato torn
7666 *adj*
stratagemma stratagem|trick
9320 *lo*
strategico strategic
8220 *adj*
straziante heartbreaking|harrowing
8383 *adj*
strepitoso resounding
7674 *adj*
stridio screech
7931 *lo*
strillo scream|squeal
7542 *lo*
striscio scratch
9517 *lo*
strizzare wring|squeeze
9427 *vb*
strofa stanza
8127 *la*
strofinare rub
8412 *vb*
strozzare throttle|choke
10000 *vb*
strozzino usurer
8389 *lo*
strumentale instrumental
8058 *adj*
strutturale structural
8379 *adj*
struzzo ostrich
9798 *lo*
stucco stucco
9018 *lo*
stuzzicadenti toothpick
9268 *lo*
subacqueo underwater
9283 *adj*
subbuglio confusion
8773 *il*
subdolo sneaky; seismic
9556 *adj; adj*
successone wow

8698 *il*
sud-ovest southwest
9704 *il*
sudato sweaty
8360 *adj*
sudiciume dirt|filth
8140 *la*
suggestione suggestion
9402 *la*
suicida suicide; suicidal
8752 *la; adj*
summit summit
7750 *il*
suola sole
9769 *la*
suonatore player
8157 *il*
supernova supernova
8253 *la*
superstizioso superstitious
8426 *adj*
superstrada highway|freeway
7583 *la*
supplementare additional|supplementary
9400 *adj*
supplemento supplement|extra charge
9434 *il*
suppliziare torment
8969 *vb*
supremazia supremacy
7936 *la*
surrogato surrogate; ersatz
8178 *il; adj*
suscettibile susceptible|liable
7711 *adj*
suscitare arouse|elicit
8995 *vb*
sussurro whisper|murmur
8941 *il*
sutura suture
8674 *la*
svaligiare rob
8996 *vb*
svariato varied
7696 *adj*
svendita sale